CRIMINAL PROCEDI

Second edition

Other titles available from Law Society Publishing:

CLSA Duty Solicitors' Handbook (3rd edn)
Andrew Keogh

Criminal Defence (3rd edn)
Roger Ede and Anthony Edwards

Criminal Justice and Immigration Act 2008
Angela Burns and Nikki Walsh

Drinking and Driving Offences (2nd edn)
Jonathan Black

Road Traffic Offences Handbook
Kenneth Carr, Frank Lockhart and Patrick Musters

All books from Law Society Publishing can be ordered through good bookshops or direct from our distributors, Prolog, by telephone 0870 850 1422 or email **lawsociety@prolog.uk.com**. Please confirm the price before ordering.

Alternatively please visit our online bookshop at **www.lawsociety.org.uk/bookshop**.

CRIMINAL PROCEDURE RULES

A Guide to the Key Changes

SECOND EDITION

Edited by Andrew Keogh

The Law Society

ISBN-13: 978-1-85328-783-1

Published in 2009 by the Law Society
113 Chancery Lane, London WC2A 1PL

Typeset by Columns Design Ltd, Reading
Printed by TJ International Ltd, Padstow, Cornwall

The paper used for the text pages of this book is FSC certified. FSC (the Forest Stewardship Council) is an international network to promote responsible management of the world's forests.

FSC
Mixed Sources
Product group from well-managed
forests and other controlled sources

Cert no. SGS-COC-2482
www.fsc.org
© 1996 Forest Stewardship Council

CONTENTS

PREFACE

In just three years, the Criminal Procedure Rules have gone from being a document that most thought would have little impact upon the criminal courts, to being an essential litigation framework that criminal practitioners ignore at their peril. Amendments to the rules in later years now provide a cradle-to-grave pathway for practitioners to follow, and codify the rules that were previously set out in hundreds of different documents.

An emphasis on bringing cases more quickly through the system, along with costs sanctions for non-compliance with the rules, mean that practitioners cannot afford to ignore the revolution taking place in the criminal courts.

The courts have embraced the Criminal Procedure Rules and this book seeks to not only set out the rules, but explain the legislative and case law developments that give them their teeth. All key rulings, including cases such as R v. *Musone* and R *(Kelly)* v *Warley Justices* are explained in full, along with an essential guide on how to make sense of this new brave world of case management.

This second edition also incorporates Law Society guidance on solicitors' duties under the Criminal Procedure Rules, the Adult Criminal Case Management Framework and practice guidance on trials involving youths, fraud and terrorism.

Andrew Keogh

1 September 2008

COMMENTARY

THE CRIMINAL PROCEDURE RULES EXPLAINED

Introduction

Prior to the introduction of the Criminal Procedure Rules in 2005, finding the rules that applied to any particular aspect of criminal litigation was time-consuming and frustrating. There was inconsistency in language, timescales and general approach, with most rules being observed in the breach. Local practices and widespread ignorance of many rules helped contribute to a general perception among many that the criminal justice system was not operating in as efficient a manner as it could.

While people had been commentating for many years about the inefficiencies inherent in the criminal justice system, it took a wide-ranging report by Lord Justice Auld before matters would be considered by the legislature. Auld was stinging in his criticism of the system, and observed that:

> Fairness, efficiency and effectiveness of the criminal justice system demand that its procedures should be simple, accessible and, so far as practicable, the same for every level and type of criminal jurisdiction. There are many features of criminal procedure that are common to summary proceedings and those on indictment, yet at present they are separately provided for in each jurisdiction and in a multiplicity of instruments and, often, in quite different language. Such a mix of different provisions providing for common procedural needs is an impediment to understanding by courts, legal practitioners, parties and others of the workings of the courts, and thus to the accessibility of the law.

Auld reported in September 2001, and it was to be almost four years later before the consolidated rule book he envisaged took effect. The intervening period was not wasted, however, as judges and practitioners were able to watch the effect the Civil Procedure Rules, implemented in 1999, were having on the civil courts.

If we reflect for a moment on Auld's report, on first reading it might be thought that the rules were merely intended to be a convenient consolidation of legislation that was spread far and wide. Although that was one aim, admirable enough in itself, the real objective was to provide judges with a robust framework for the efficient management of cases.

Rules 1 and 3 of the Criminal Procedure Rules, dealing with the overriding objective and case management powers of the court, were taken directly from the

Civil Procedure Rules; by 2005 one could see that the revolution that had taken place in the civil courts might well be replicated in the criminal justice system.

The overriding objective provides:

1.1   The overriding objective

(1) The overriding objective of this new code is that criminal cases be dealt with justly.

(2) Dealing with a criminal case justly includes –

    (a) acquitting the innocent and convicting the guilty;

    (b) dealing with the prosecution and the defence fairly;

    (c) recognising the rights of a defendant, particularly those under Article 6 of the European Convention on Human Rights;

    (d) respecting the interests of witnesses, victims and jurors and keeping them informed of the progress of the case;

    (e) dealing with the case efficiently and expeditiously;

    (f) ensuring that appropriate information is available to the court when bail and sentence are considered; and

    (g) dealing with the case in ways that take into account –

        (i) the gravity of the offence alleged,

        (ii) the complexity of what is in issue,

        (iii) the severity of the consequences for the defendant and others affected, and

        (iv) the needs of other cases.

Practitioners, however, had their own ideas of how (and if) the rules should work in practice. For the first time a battle would be played out in the courts between the lawyers, who had built for themselves a convenient practitioner-led domain, and the modernising judges, who had recognised the failings of the system. For the first time, judges were being forced to recognise not only the obvious self-interest of the lawyers, but also the interests of witnesses and the taxpayer.

To understand the changes brought about by the rules, we need to examine some of the cases that have shaped the law over the last few years.

The warning shot

Counsel in *R v Gleeson* [2003] EWCA Crim 3357 drew a short straw at the Court of Appeal when it came to the choice of judge: none other than Lord Justice Auld. In *Gleeson*, counsel spotted that the charge preferred was the wrong one in law, and kept his powder dry until half time before submitting that there was no case to answer. In response to the argument the trial judge permitted the prosecution to amend the indictment in order to save the case. Gleeson's argument, that the jury should be discharged as the case would have been run differently had the charge featured on the indictment in the first instance, was rejected, and Gleeson was convicted. On appeal, counsel's arguments were given short shrift, which in itself is not worthy of comment, save that Auld went much further in making these comments:

[Counsel] frankly acknowledged that he could have notified the prosecution and the judge of the "Nock" point at a much earlier stage, and that he had not done so because he would have lost the tactical advantage for which he had hoped from leaving it to the latest possible moment, that is at the close of the prosecution case. Implicit in that acknowledgement was his expectation that it would be more difficult for the prosecution to secure amendment of the indictment to cover the position at that stage than it would have been if it had been dealt with at the outset of the trial.

Just as a defendant should not be penalised for errors of his legal representatives in the conduct of his defence if he is unfairly prejudiced by them, so also should a prosecution not be frustrated by errors of the prosecutor, unless such errors have irremediably rendered a fair trial for the defendant impossible. For defence advocates to seek to take advantage of such errors by deliberately delaying identification of an issue of fact or law in the case until the last possible moment is, in our view, no longer acceptable, given the legislative and procedural changes to our criminal justice process in recent years. Indeed, we consider it to be contrary to the requirement on an accused in section 5(6) of the 1996 Act, in particular paragraph (b), to indicate "the matters on which he takes issue with the prosecution", and to their professional duty to the court – and not in the legitimate interests of the defendant.

To the extent that the prosecution may legitimately wish to fill possible holes in its case once issues have been identified by the defence statement, it is understandable why as a matter of tactics a defendant might prefer to keep his case close to his chest. But that is not a valid reason for preventing a full and fair hearing on the issues canvassed at the trial. A criminal trial is not a game under which a guilty defendant should be provided with a sporting chance. It is a search for truth in accordance with the twin principles that the prosecution must prove its case and that a defendant is not obliged to inculpate himself, the object being to convict the guilty and acquit the innocent. Requiring a defendant to indicate in advance what he disputes about the prosecution case offends neither of those principles.

A particularly interesting feature of *Gleeson*, which was to be revisited in academic commentary to be discussed later, was the ruling that such conduct breached a lawyer's professional duty to the court. So, for the first time, such tactics were dismissed not merely as a "nice try that failed", but with a severe reprimand. While to date there have been no publicised disciplinary proceedings flowing from breaches of the Criminal Procedure Rules, some of the later amendments to the rules allow for wasted costs orders to be made.

Practitioners need to be aware, however, that they ignore the rules – and in particular, breach them – at their peril.

Charting the case law

In *R (Robinson) v Sutton Coldfield Justices* [2006] EWHC 307 (Admin), heard shortly after the rules took effect, the court was faced with a challenge to a decision to admit evidence of bad character, notwithstanding the prosecution's breach of the rules in serving the applications later than they ought to have done. The court ruled:

Mr Bishop [counsel for the appellant] submits that it is crucial that at this early stage in the life of the Code a culture of non-compliance should not be permitted to take root. That is a proposition with which, for my part, I wholeheartedly agree. He further submits that the necessity of strict compliance is particularly apposite in proceedings in the Magistrates' Court where the large volume of routine cases may encourage a lax approach to the requirements of the Code, and that, for reasons of public policy, the court should only exercise its discretion to extend time under rule 35(8) in exceptional circumstances, where it has been provided with sufficiently good reasons as to why the prosecution could not comply with the mandatory time limit.

The first point to be made is that time limits must be observed. The objective of the Criminal Procedure Rules "to deal with all cases efficiently and expeditiously" depends upon adherence to the timetable set out in the rules. Secondly, Parliament has given the court a discretionary power to shorten a time limit or to extend it even after it has expired: rule 35(8). In the exercise of that discretion the court will take account of all the relevant considerations, including the furtherance of the over-riding objective. I am not persuaded that the discretion should be fettered in the manner for which the claimant contends, namely that the time should only be extended in exceptional circumstances.

In this case there were two principal material considerations: first the reason for the failure to comply with the rules. As to that a party seeking an extension must plainly explain the reasons for its failure. Secondly, there was the question of whether the claimant's position was prejudiced by the failure.

R (*Crown Prosecution Service*) v *City of London Magistrates' Court* (2006) *The Times*, 17 April also dealt with a failure to serve a notice in time. This case was slightly more complex in that there was also an argument about which rules applied to service of evidence during committal proceedings. The court, applying the overriding objective, held that no court would have ruled against the prosecution on the grounds of breach of time limit. This case is good authority for the proposition that the rules are not to be seen as creating a procedural straitjacket, as that in itself may collapse the overriding objective of achieving justice in a case.

In *Malcolm v Director of Public Prosecutions* (2007) *The Times*, 4 April, the court was faced with a case in which the defence had commented during a closing speech that a mandatory warning required under section 7(7) of the Road Traffic Act 1988 had not been given. The prosecution was allowed to reopen its case in order to adduce further evidence. It is worthy of note that the prosecution in reality did not need to do this: a warning under section 7(7) is not a legal requirement for proving the case, but an argument for the defence to exclude the specimen. Either way, the court once again had the opportunity to consider the Criminal Procedure Rules.

In dismissing the appeal the court held:

> In my judgment, Miss Calder's submissions, which emphasised the obligation of the prosecution to prove its case in its entirety before closing its case, and certainly before end of the final speech for the defence, had an anachronistic, and obsolete, ring. Criminal trials are no longer to be treated as a game, in which each move is final and any omission by the prosecution leads to its failure. It is the duty of the defence to make its defence and the issues it raises clear to the prosecution and to the court at an early stage.

It is worth pausing here to reflect on what the court said. Many defence lawyers were taken aback by the notion of a legal duty for them to make the prosecution prove its case and to expose prosecution weaknesses. The idea that the defence could sit back and "make the prosecution prove it" had an "anachronistic and obsolete ring". However, be in no doubt that this was clearly the intention of the court as it went on to say:

That duty is implicit in rule 3.3 of the Criminal Procedure Rules, which requires the parties actively to assist the exercise by the court of its case management powers, the exercise of which requires early identification of the real issues. Even in a relatively straightforward trial such as the present, in the magistrates' court (where there is not yet any requirement of a defence statement or a pre-trial review), it is the duty of the defence to make the real issues clear *at the latest* before the prosecution closes its case. In *R v Pydar Justices ex parte Foster* [1995] 160 JP 87 at 90B Curtis J. commented on the submission that a defending advocate was entitled to "keep his powder dry". He said: Without any doubt whatsoever, it is the duty of a defending advocate properly to lay the ground for a submission, either by cross examination or, if appropriate, by calling evidence.

To take the section 7(7) point in the final speech was a classic and improper defence ambush of the prosecution. In *Cook v DPP* 2000 WL 33116475, the Divisional Court considered *Jolly*. Schiemann LJ said, at [33]:

"It seems to me that if at the close of the prosecution case the defence is of the view that the evidence called on behalf of the prosecution does not disclose a prima facie case, then the defence should, in general, make that submission at the end of the prosecution case. If that submission succeeds, then the prosecution can apply to recall someone. That application may be granted or may be rejected, depending on the facts of the case, essentially on the question whether any prejudice to the defendant would be caused. But what seems to me quite indefensible is the submission by Mr Ley that the defence can, by reserving the submission until after the close of the defence case, put itself in a stronger position than it would have been had it made the submission earlier on. That seems to me to encourage a totally wrong approach to the administration of justice."

Barrister James Richardson responded to the judgment in the following way:

Nobody would suggest that the defence should be able to take advantage of the prosecution having been misled or of a simple mistake by a competent prosecutor; but indulgence of the incompetent prosecutor merely serves to encourage a culture of non-compliance and of declining standards.

If the senior judiciary want to know why their ire is provoked by cases such as the instant one, they may care to reflect on the possibility that it is precisely because of their unwillingness to insist on compliance with the rules of criminal practice. With the emergence of a culture of non-compliance, there will inevitably be a further diminution in the standards of legal practice – why learn the rules, if their observance is a matter of secondary importance?

In *R v Clarke and McDaid* (2008) *The Times*, 7 February, HL, the highest court in the land was charged with considering the effect of the overriding objective in a case where the indictment had not been signed. The same point arose in the earlier case of *R v Draz* (better known by reference to the conjoined case of *R v Ashton* [2007] 1 WLR 181): the court had upheld the conviction, and in doing so turned a large number of earlier authorities on their head. The court in *Ashton* commented that the new approach (to procedural non-compliance) was in line with the Criminal Procedure Rules.

Few were prepared for the judgment in *Clarke and McDaid* which held that:

...the effect of the sea-change which [earlier cases] wrought has been exaggerated and they do not warrant a wholesale jettisoning of all rules affecting procedure irrespective of their legal effect.

James Richardson writing in *Criminal Law Week* observed:

> This unanimous decision should achieve landmark status for the blow it strikes at the case management culture, inspired by the "overriding objective" of the Criminal Procedure Rules 2005... that has threatened to engulf criminal practice in this jurisdiction. This culture dictates that cases should be "managed" (not "tried") by the court so as to further the "overriding objective" (which, in practice, appears to have much more to do with convicting those against whom there is any evidence of guilt than with acquitting those who may be innocent); and this is an objective which all parties, including the defendant, are expected to pursue. Mere rules of procedure were not to be allowed to get in the way. The consequences were, first, that the system of criminal justice was becoming progressively more inquisitorial (indeed an adversarial system is fundamentally incompatible with a rule that obliges the defence to conduct their case with a view to furthering the overriding objective) and, secondly, standards were on a seemingly inexorable downward path. Why should practitioners bother to learn the rules, if the courts routinely indulge breaches? Indeed, why would the brightest young talent want to practise criminal law at all, if becoming truly learned in the law is going to do them and their cause no good?

> This new approach was exemplified in Ashton, ante, and in a series of subsequent decisions of the High Court and the Court of Appeal, in which Ashton – now a busted flush – has been relied on in order to justify indulgence of some procedural irregularity.

> More generally, their Lordships' judgments demonstrate a refreshing attitude towards the role of the courts and the responsibilities of the prosecution: regret was expressed that convictions should have to be quashed on what might seem to be a technicality, but Lord Bingham pointed out, in justification, that "the duty of the court is to apply the law, which is sometimes technical, and it may be thought that if the state exercises its coercive power to put a citizen on trial for serious crime a certain degree of formality is not out of place", and, as Lord Brown pointed out, "the problem is easily enough avoided and will only occur if the Crown is at fault." Such sentiments are too seldom expressed in the criminal courts of this country today.

R (Kelly) v Warley Justices [2007] EWHC 1836 (Admin) was a further landmark case in limiting the extent of case management powers (see the Law Society's Practice Note in Section H), but as we will see, amendments to the rules swiftly followed in this regard.

It would appear then that the true measure of the rules has yet to be felt, certainly as far as procedural non-compliance is concerned, and an intellectual battle rages between the Court of Appeal and House of Lords in relation to how far the overriding objective can be used in place of specific statutory authority.

Academic commentary

Surprisingly, aside from commentary specifically on case law, little has been written in relation to the potential conflict between the Criminal Procedure Rules, on the one hand, and the conduct rules of the legal profession, on the other.

Professor Ed Cape wrote a major piece in *Legal Ethics*, Volume 9, which is highly recommended reading. Cape writes:

> It has been argued here that the government, and elements of the judiciary, are engaged in a concerted campaign to transform the criminal justice process, away

from one founded upon fair trial rights towards one where those rights are subjugated to the demands of economy and efficiency. Since, in an adversarial system, defence lawyers have an obligation to act as zealous advocates on behalf of their clients, and thus are likely to inhibit managerialist objectives, attempts have been made to co-opt defence lawyers into facilitating this transformation through a combination of signing them up to explicit system objectives, adverse judicial decisions and comments, and negating the impact of legal advice. As defence lawyers have sought to give effect to the adversarial rights of their clients, so they have been subjected to increasing influence and control by the state and by the judiciary…

If the ethical foundation of the defence lawyer's role is a constitutional responsibility for maintaining fundamental guarantees central to the justice system, then the professional conduct rules should provide a clear ethical framework for performing this role. This means that lawyers' professional bodies must understand and articulate the concerns about the transformation in the criminal justice process currently being wrought, and confront and challenge the changes that threaten those guarantees. Professional conduct rules explicitly and unambiguously founded upon fair trial rights, and which do not avoid the most difficult issues, should then follow.

Conclusion

Superficially, one could hardly have any objection to the intention of those who frame the rules. The overriding objective is in itself a noble one, but it takes no regard of the wider picture and does not recognise the dangers that might arise when procedural rules are cast aside. The adversarial system is weakened before any assessment can be made of the consequences of a system that is not adversarial, but not inquisitorial in the true sense either.

The changes have taken place with barely a whimper heard from the profession, and one must step back, pause and be grateful for the fearless advocates in *Clarke and McDaid* who dared challenge the hitherto done deal and persuaded their Lordships that the pace of change needed slowing. Practitioners would do well to take advantage of the temporary lull: it may not last long as changes in the Supreme Court could easily restore the *Ashton* mentality before too long.

It is regrettable that the Law Society has not yet made an effort at all to try and reconcile, or even debate, the points raised by Cape, but instead has issued a Practice Note that does nothing to challenge the ethical and jurisprudential basis of the sea-change that is indeed taking place in the criminal justice system.

RULE AMENDMENTS

[The following notes reproduce the Explanatory Note to the Criminal Procedure (Amendment) Rules 2008, SI 2008/2076 (L.9), and are Crown copyright.]

October 2008

[The latest amendment of the Criminal Procedure Rules came into force in October 2008:]

- a new **Part 7** (Starting a prosecution in a magistrates' court) in substitution for the existing Part 7 (Commencing proceedings in a magistrates' court). The new Part 7 rules revise and simplify the present rules. They apply as described in rule 3, to criminal cases in magistrates' courts started by one of three specified actions, on or after 6 October 2008. In other cases, the rules replaced by those rules apply.
- a new **Part 63** (Appeal to the Crown Court) in substitution for existing Part 63 (Appeal to the Crown Court). The new Part 63 rules revise and simplify the present rules so that they correspond broadly with the other appeal rules which have recently been revised and simplified. Omissions and modifications ensure that the new Part 63 rules are appropriate to the particular rights of appeal and the jurisdiction involved.
- new rules in **Part 2** (Understanding and applying the Rules) make transitional provision and explain when the new rules in Part 7 and Part 63 will apply.

In addition the following amendments are made:

- **Part 2** (Understanding and applying the Rules) is amended to include a new rule about representatives and "supporting adults" to clarify, in one place, which representatives can act in criminal proceedings.
- **Part 4** (Service of documents) is amended to clarify the operation of Criminal Procedure Rule 4.4 (Service by leaving or posting a document) and to avoid confusion in respect of service on a company registered in Scotland or in Northern Ireland.
- **Part 37** (Summary trial) is amended to include three rules transferred from the existing Part 7 (Commencing proceedings in magistrates' courts), on its revision and simplification. First, existing rule 7.4 (Duty of court officer receiving statutory declaration under section 14(1) of the Magistrates' Courts Act 1980) becomes new rule 37.11; second, existing rule 7.5 (Notice of order under section 25 of the Road Traffic Offenders Act 1988) becomes new rule 37.10; finally, existing rule 7.9 (Magistrates' court officer to have copies of documents sent to accused under section 12(1) of the Magistrates' Courts Act 1980) becomes new rule 37.9.
- **Part 44** (Sentencing children and young persons) is amended to omit reference to "local education authority" which is now redundant as there is also a reference to "local authority" in the rule (44.1(2)(d)). That reference is sufficient to include local education authorities.
- **Part 55** (Road traffic penalties) is amended to include existing rule 7.6 (Statutory declaration under sections 72 and 73 of the Road Traffic Offenders Act 1988), which has been transferred, with minor revision, on the revision and simplification of existing Part 7.
- **Part 65** (Appeal to the Court of Appeal: general rules) is amended to reflect recent legislation and to enhance the notes. First, rule 65.5(1) (Renewing an application refused by a judge or the Registrar) is amended to take account of the amendment to section 31C of the Criminal Appeal Act 1968 by the Criminal Justice and Immigration Act 2008 (removing the right of appeal to the

Court of Appeal from a procedural direction given by a single judge). Second, the notes to rules are amended:

(i)   to include reference in the note to rule 65.1, to the powers of a single judge under Serious Crime Act 2007 (Appeals under section 24) Order 2008; and

(ii)   to cite comprehensively in the note to rule 65.5, primary and secondary legislation relating to the right to renew an application to a judge or to the Court of Appeal. Rule 65.11 is amended to correct a typographical error.

- **Part 66** (Appeal to the Court of Appeal against ruling at preparatory hearing) is amended to reflect the amendment to section 31 of the Criminal Appeal Act 1968 effected by section 47 of, and paragraph 11 of Schedule 8 to, the Criminal Justice and Immigration Act 2008.
- **Part 68** (Appeal to the Court of Appeal about conviction or sentence) is amended to make provision for rights of appeal to the Court of Appeal:

  (i)   against wasted costs orders and third party costs orders, and

  (ii)   against a serious crime prevention order where a case is certified fit for appeal.

- **Part 78** (Costs orders against the parties) is amended because the new Part 63 rules remove the three-day time limit for giving notice to abandon an appeal to the Crown Court. The associated costs rule in Part 78 is amended to remove reference to that time limit and to allow the exercise of judicial discretion as to costs where such an appeal is abandoned.

[The notes on previous changes to the Criminal Procedure Rules are reproduced from the Ministry of Justice's website at *www.justice.gov.uk*, issued 18 August 2008, and are Crown copyright.]

April 2008

The fifth amendment of the Criminal Procedure Rules came into force in April 2008. This introduced new rules about case management, anti-social behaviour orders and serious crime prevention orders. To complete the committee's comprehensive revision and simplification of the procedure rules for the Court of Appeal, there are new rules about appeals from that court to the House of Lords. All of these changes came into force on 7 April 2008.

The rules about proceedings under the Proceeds of Crime Act 2002, which were amended to take account of provisions in the Serious Crime Act 2007, came into effect from 1 April 2008.

October 2007

The fourth amendment of the Criminal Procedure Rules 2005 came into force on 1 October 2007. This introduced new rules for appeals to the Court of Appeal and about applications to change a guilty plea.

March 2007

The third amendment came into force on 2 April 2007 and introduced new rules about service of documents (Part 4), the indictment (Part 14) and witness summonses, warrants and orders (Part 28). Amendments were made to the rules about bail (Part 19) and about restrictions on cross-examination by a defendant in person (Part 31).

October 2006

The second amendment came into force on 6 November 2006 and introduced the first rules about expert evidence (Part 33) and rules about evidence of a complainant's previous sexual behaviour (Part 36). Revised rules about service of documents (Part 4), starting proceedings in the magistrates' courts (Part 7), disclosure (Part 24) and special measures directions (Part 29) were also made.

March 2006

The first amendment came into force on 3 April 2006 and introduced a new part on preparatory hearings in serious fraud and other complex or lengthy hearings in the Crown Court (Part 15), and a new part about warrants (Part 18).

The Criminal Procedure Rules 2005 came into force on 4 April 2005.

LEGISLATION AND GUIDANCE

Section A

CRIMINAL PROCEDURE RULES 2005 (SI 2005/384) AS AMENDED

PART 1 THE OVERRIDING OBJECTIVE

1.1 The overriding objective

(1) The overriding objective of this new code is that criminal cases be dealt with justly.

(2) Dealing with a criminal case justly includes –

    (a)   acquitting the innocent and convicting the guilty;

    (b)   dealing with the prosecution and the defence fairly;

    (c)   recognising the rights of a defendant, particularly those under Article 6 of the European Convention on Human Rights;

    (d)   respecting the interests of witnesses, victims and jurors and keeping them informed of the progress of the case;

    (e)   dealing with the case efficiently and expeditiously;

    (f)   ensuring that appropriate information is available to the court when bail and sentence are considered; and

    (g)   dealing with the case in ways that take into account –

        (i)   the gravity of the offence alleged,

        (ii)   the complexity of what is in issue,

        (iii)   the severity of the consequences for the defendant and others affected, and

        (iv)   the needs of other cases.

1.2 The duty of the participants in a criminal case

(1) Each participant, in the conduct of each case, must –

    (a)   prepare and conduct the case in accordance with the overriding objective;

    (b)   comply with these Rules, practice directions and directions made by the court; and

    (c)   at once inform the court and all parties of any significant failure (whether or not that participant is responsible for that failure) to take any procedural step required by these Rules, any practice direction or any direction of the court. A failure is significant if it might hinder the court in furthering the overriding objective.

(2) Anyone involved in any way with a criminal case is a participant in its conduct for the purposes of this rule.

1.3 The application by the court of the overriding objective

The court must further the overriding objective in particular when –

(a)   exercising any power given to it by legislation (including these Rules);
(b)   applying any practice direction; or
(c)   interpreting any rule or practice direction.

PART 2   UNDERSTANDING AND APPLYING THE RULES

2.1   When the Rules apply

(1) In general, the Criminal Procedure Rules apply –

(a)   in all criminal cases in magistrates' courts and in the Crown Court; and
(b)   in all cases in the criminal division of the Court of Appeal.

(2) If a rule applies only in one or two of those courts, the rule makes that clear.
(3) The Rules apply on and after 4 th April, 2005, but do not affect any right or duty existing under the rules of court revoked by the coming into force of these Rules.
(4) The rules in Part 33 apply in all cases in which the defendant is charged on or after 6th November 2006 and in other cases if the court so orders.
(5) The rules in Part 14 apply in cases in which one of the events listed in sub-paragraphs (a) to (d) of rule 14.1(1) takes place on or after 2nd April 2007. In other cases the rules of court replaced by those rules apply.
(6) The rules in Part 28 apply in cases in which an application under rule 28.3 is made on or after 2nd April 2007. In other cases the rules replaced by those rules apply.
(7) The rules in Parts 65, 66, 67, 68, 69 and 70 apply where an appeal, application or reference, to which one of those Parts applies, is made on or after 1st October 2007. In other cases the rules replaced by those rules apply.
(8) The rules in Parts 57–62 apply in proceedings to which one of those Parts applies that begin on or after 1st April 2008. In such proceedings beginning before that date the rules in those Parts apply as if –

(a)   the amendments made to them by The Criminal Procedure (Amendment No. 3) Rules 2007 had not been made; and
(b)   references to the Director of the Assets Recovery Agency or to that Agency were references to the Serious Organised Crime Agency.

(9) The rules in Part 50 apply in cases in which the defendant is charged on or after 7th April 2008 and in other cases if the court so orders. Otherwise, the rules replaced by those rules apply.
(10) The rules in Part 74 apply where an appeal, application or reference, to which Part 74 applies, is made on or after 7th April 2008. In other cases the rules replaced by those rules apply.
(11) The rules in Part 7 apply in cases in which on or after 6th October 2008 –

(a)   a prosecutor serves an information on the court officer or presents it to a magistrates' court;
(b)   a public prosecutor issues a written charge; or
(c)   a person who is in custody is charged with an offence.

In other cases the rules replaced by those rules apply.

(12) The rules in Part 63 apply in cases in which the decision that is the subject of the appeal, or reference, to which that Part applies is made on or after 6th October 2008. In other cases the rules replaced by those rules apply.

[*Note. The rules replaced by the first Criminal Procedure Rules (The Criminal Procedure Rules 2005) were revoked when those Rules came into force by provisions of the Courts Act 2003, The Courts Act 2003 (Consequential Amendments) Order 2004 and The Courts Act 2003 (Commencement No. 6 and Savings) Order 2004. The first Criminal Procedure Rules reproduced the substance of all the rules they replaced.*]

2.2   Definitions

(1)   In these Rules, unless the context makes it clear that something different is meant:

"business day" means any day except Saturday, Sunday, Christmas Day, Boxing Day, Good Friday, Easter Monday or a bank holiday;

"court" means a tribunal with jurisdiction over criminal cases. It includes a judge, recorder, District Judge (Magistrates' Courts), lay justice and, when exercising their judicial powers, the Registrar of Criminal Appeals, a justices' clerk or assistant clerk;

"court officer" means the appropriate member of the staff of a court;

"live link" means an arrangement by which a person can see and hear, and be seen and heard by, the court when that person is not in court;

"Practice Direction" means the Lord Chief Justice's Consolidated Criminal Practice Direction, as amended; and

"public interest ruling" means a ruling about whether it is in the public interest to disclose prosecution material under sections 3(6), 7A(8) or 8(5) of the Criminal Procedure and Investigations Act 1996.

(2)   Definitions of some other expressions are in the rules in which they apply.

2.3   References to Acts of Parliament and to Statutory Instruments

In these Rules, where a rule refers to an Act of Parliament or to subordinate legislation by title and year, subsequent references to that Act or to that legislation in the rule are shortened: so, for example, after a reference to the Criminal Procedure and Investigations Act 1996 that Act is called "the 1996 Act"; and after a reference to the Criminal Procedure and Investigations Act 1996 (Defence Disclosure Time Limits) Regulations 1997 those Regulations are called "the 1997 Regulations".

2.4   The glossary

The glossary at the end of the Rules is a guide to the meaning of certain legal expressions used in them.

2.5   Representatives

(1)   Under these Rules, unless the context makes it clear that something different is meant, anything that a party may or must do may be done –

(a)   by a legal representative on that party's behalf;

(b)   by a person with the corporation's written authority, where that party is a corporation;

(c)   with the help of a parent, guardian or other suitable supporting adult where that party is a defendant –

(i)   who is under 18, or

(ii)   whose understanding of what the case involves is limited.

(2)   Anyone with a prosecutor's authority to do so may, on that prosecutor's behalf –

(a)   serve on the magistrates' court officer, or present to a magistrates' court, an information under section 1 of the Magistrates' Courts Act 1980; or

(b)   issue a written charge and requisition under section 29 of the Criminal Justice Act 2003.

[Note. See also section 122 of the Magistrates' Courts Act 1980. A party's legal representative must be entitled to act as such under section 27 or 28 of the Courts and Legal Services Act 1990.

Section 33(6) of the Criminal Justice Act 1925, section 46 of the Magistrates' Courts Act 1980 and Schedule 3 to that Act provide for the representation of a corporation.

Part 7 contains rules about starting a prosecution.]

PART 3   CASE MANAGEMENT

3.1   The scope of this Part

This Part applies to the management of each case in a magistrates' court and in the Crown Court (including an appeal to the Crown Court) until the conclusion of that case.

Rules that apply to procedure in the Court of Appeal are in Parts 65 to 73 of these Rules.

3.2   The duty of the court

(1) The court must further the overriding objective by actively managing the case.
(2) Active case management includes –

    (a)   the early identification of the real issues;
    (b)   the early identification of the needs of witnesses;
    (c)   achieving certainty as to what must be done, by whom, and when, in particular by the early setting of a timetable for the progress of the case;
    (d)   monitoring the progress of the case and compliance with directions;
    (e)   ensuring that evidence, whether disputed or not, is presented in the shortest and clearest way;
    (f)   discouraging delay, dealing with as many aspects of the case as possible on the same occasion, and avoiding unnecessary hearings;
    (g)   encouraging the participants to co-operate in the progression of the case; and
    (h)   making use of technology.

(3) The court must actively manage the case by giving any direction appropriate to the needs of that case as early as possible.

3.3   The duty of the parties

Each party must –

    (a)   actively assist the court in fulfilling its duty under rule 3.2, without or if necessary with a direction; and
    (b)   apply for a direction if needed to further the overriding objective.

3.4   Case progression officers and their duties

(1) At the beginning of the case each party must, unless the court otherwise directs –

    (a)   nominate an individual responsible for progressing that case; and
    (b)   tell other parties and the court who he is and how to contact him.

(2) In fulfilling its duty under rule 3.2, the court must where appropriate –

    (a)   nominate a court officer responsible for progressing the case; and
    (b)   make sure the parties know who he is and how to contact him.

(3) In this Part a person nominated under this rule is called a case progression officer.
(4) A case progression officer must –

    (a)   monitor compliance with directions;
    (b)   make sure that the court is kept informed of events that may affect the progress of that case;
    (c)   make sure that he can be contacted promptly about the case during ordinary business hours;
    (d)   act promptly and reasonably in response to communications about the case; and

(e)   if he will be unavailable, appoint a substitute to fulfil his duties and inform the other case progression officers.

3.5   The court's case management powers

(1) In fulfilling its duty under rule 3.2 the court may give any direction and take any step actively to manage a case unless that direction or step would be inconsistent with legislation, including these Rules.

(2) In particular, the court may –

(a)   nominate a judge, magistrate, justices' clerk or assistant to a justices' clerk to manage the case;

(b)   give a direction on its own initiative or on application by a party;

(c)   ask or allow a party to propose a direction;

(d)   for the purpose of giving directions, receive applications and representations by letter, by telephone or by any other means of electronic communication, and conduct a hearing by such means;

(e)   give a direction without a hearing;

(f)   fix, postpone, bring forward, extend or cancel a hearing;

(g)   shorten or extend (even after it has expired) a time limit fixed by a direction;

(h)   require that issues in the case should be determined separately, and decide in what order they will be determined; and

(i)   specify the consequences of failing to comply with a direction.

(3) A magistrates' court may give a direction that will apply in the Crown Court if the case is to continue there.

(4) The Crown Court may give a direction that will apply in a magistrates' court if the case is to continue there.

(5) Any power to give a direction under this Part includes a power to vary or revoke that direction.

(6) If a party fails to comply with a rule or a direction, the court may –

(a)   fix, postpone, bring forward, extend, cancel or adjourn a hearing;

(b)   exercise its powers to make a costs order; and

(c)   impose such other sanction as may be appropriate.

[Depending upon the nature of a case and the stage that it has reached, its progress may be affected by other Criminal Procedure Rules and by other legislation. The note at the end of this Part lists other rules and legislation that may apply.

See also rule 3.10.

The court may make a costs order under –

(a)   *section 19 of the Prosecution of Offences Act 1985, where the court decides that one party to criminal proceedings has incurred costs as a result of an unnecessary or improper act or omission by, or on behalf of, another party;*

(b)   *section 19A of that Act, where the court decides that a party has incurred costs as a result of an improper, unreasonable or negligent act or omission on the part of a legal representative;*

(c)   *section 19B of that Act, where the court decides that there has been serious misconduct by a person who is not a party.*

Under some other legislation, including Parts 24, 34 and 35 of these Rules, if a party fails to comply with a rule or a direction then in some circumstances –

(a)   *the court may refuse to allow that party to introduce evidence;*

(b)   *evidence that that party wants to introduce may not be admissible;*

(c)   *the court may draw adverse inferences from the late introduction of an issue or evidence.*

See also –

section 81(1) of the Police and Criminal Evidence Act 1984 and section 20(3) of the Criminal Procedure and Investigations Act 1996 (advance disclosure of expert evidence);

section 11(5) of the Criminal Procedure and Investigations Act 1996 (faults in disclosure by accused);

section 132(5) of the Criminal Justice Act 2003 (failure to give notice of hearsay evidence).]

3.6   Application to vary a direction

(1) A party may apply to vary a direction if –

    (a)   the court gave it without a hearing;

    (b)   the court gave it at a hearing in his absence; or

    (c)   circumstances have changed.

(2) A party who applies to vary a direction must –

    (a)   apply as soon as practicable after he becomes aware of the grounds for doing so; and

    (b)   give as much notice to the other parties as the nature and urgency of his application permits.

3.7   Agreement to vary a time limit fixed by a direction

(1) The parties may agree to vary a time limit fixed by a direction, but only if –

    (a)   the variation will not –

        (i)   affect the date of any hearing that has been fixed, or

        (ii)   significantly affect the progress of the case in any other way;

    (b)   the court has not prohibited variation by agreement; and

    (c)   the court's case progression officer is promptly informed.

(2) The court's case progression officer must refer the agreement to the court if he doubts the condition in paragraph (1)(a) is satisfied.

3.8   Case preparation and progression

(1) At every hearing, if a case cannot be concluded there and then the court must give directions so that it can be concluded at the next hearing or as soon as possible after that.

(2) At every hearing the court must, where relevant –

    (a)   if the defendant is absent, decide whether to proceed nonetheless;

    (b)   take the defendant's plea (unless already done) or if no plea can be taken then find out whether the defendant is likely to plead guilty or not guilty;

    (c)   set, follow or revise a timetable for the progress of the case, which may include a timetable for any hearing including the trial or (in the Crown Court) the appeal;

    (d)   in giving directions, ensure continuity in relation to the court and to the parties' representatives where that is appropriate and practicable; and

    (e)   where a direction has not been complied with, find out why, identify who was responsible, and take appropriate action.

(3) In order to prepare for a trial in the Crown Court, the court must conduct a plea and case management hearing unless the circumstances make that unnecessary.

3.9   Readiness for trial or appeal

(1) This rule applies to a party's preparation for trial or (in the Crown Court) appeal, and in this rule and rule 3.10 trial includes any hearing at which evidence will be introduced.

(2) In fulfilling his duty under rule 3.3, each party must –

(a) comply with directions given by the court;
(b) take every reasonable step to make sure his witnesses will attend when they are needed;
(c) make appropriate arrangements to present any written or other material; and
(d) promptly inform the court and the other parties of anything that may –

  (i) affect the date or duration of the trial or appeal, or
  (ii) significantly affect the progress of the case in any other way.

(3) The court may require a party to give a certificate of readiness.

3.10 Conduct of a trial or an appeal

In order to manage a trial or (in the Crown Court) an appeal –

(a) the court must establish, with the active assistance of the parties, what disputed issues they intend to explore; and
(b) the court may require a party to identify –

  (i) which witnesses that party wants to give oral evidence,
  (ii) the order in which that party wants those witnesses to give their evidence,
  (iii) whether that party requires an order compelling the attendance of a witness,
  (iv) what arrangements are desirable to facilitate the giving of evidence by a witness,
  (v) what arrangements are desirable to facilitate the participation of any other person, including the defendant,
  (vi) what written evidence that party intends to introduce,
  (vii) what other material, if any, that person intends to make available to the court in the presentation of the case,
  (viii) whether that party intends to raise any point of law that could affect the conduct of the trial or appeal, and
  (ix) what timetable that party proposes and expects to follow.

[*Note. See also rule 3.5.*]

3.11 Case management forms and records

(1) The case management forms set out in the Practice Direction must be used, and where there is no form then no specific formality is required.
(2) The court must make available to the parties a record of directions given.

[*Case management may be affected by the following other rules and legislation:*

Criminal Procedure Rules
Parts 10.4 and 27.2: reminders of right to object to written evidence being read at trial
Part 12.2: time for first appearance of accused sent for trial
Part 13: dismissal of charges sent or transferred to the Crown Court
Part 14: the indictment
Part 15: preparatory hearings in serious fraud and other complex or lengthy cases
Parts 21 – 26: the rules that deal with disclosure
Parts 27 – 36: the rules that deal with evidence
Part 37: summary trial
Part 38: trial of children and young persons
Part 39: trial on indictment

Regulations
Prosecution of Offences (Custody Time Limits) Regulations 1987
Criminal Justice Act 1987 (Notice of Transfer) Regulations 1988

Criminal Justice Act 1991 (Notice of Transfer) Regulations 1992
Criminal Procedure and Investigations Act 1996 (Defence Disclosure Time Limits) Regulations
1997
Crime and Disorder Act 1998 (Service of Prosecution Evidence) Regulations 2005

Provisions of Acts of Parliament
Sections 5, 10 and 18, Magistrates' Courts Act 1980: powers to adjourn hearings
Sections 128 and 129, Magistrates' Courts Act 1980: remand in custody by magistrates' courts
Part 1, Criminal Procedure and Investigations Act 1996: disclosure
Schedule 2, Criminal Procedure and Investigations Act 1996: use of witness statements at trial
Section 2, Administration of Justice (Miscellaneous Provisions) Act 1933: procedural conditions
for trial in the Crown Court
Section 6, Magistrates' Courts Act 1980: committal for trial
Section 4, Criminal Justice Act 1987; section 53, Criminal Justice Act 1991; section 51 and (so far
as it is in force) section 51A, Crime and Disorder Act 1998: other procedures by which a case
reaches the Crown Court
Section 7, Criminal Justice Act 1987; Parts III and IV, Criminal Procedure and Investigations Act
1996: pre-trial and preparatory hearings in the Crown Court
Section 9, Criminal Justice Act 1967: proof by written witness statement]

PART 4   SERVICE OF DOCUMENTS

4.1   When this Part applies

The rules in this Part apply to the service of every document in a case to which these Rules apply, subject to any special rules in other legislation (including other Parts of these Rules) or in the Practice Direction.

4.2   Methods of service

A document may be served by any of the methods described in rules 4.3 to 4.6 (subject to rule 4.7), or in rule 4.8.

4.3   Service by handing over a document

(1) A document may be served on –

    (a)   an individual by handing it to him or her;
    (b)   a corporation by handing it to a person holding a senior position in that corporation;
    (c)   an individual or corporation who is legally represented in the case by handing it to that representative;
    (d)   the prosecution by handing it to the prosecutor or to the prosecution representative;
    (e)   the court officer by handing it to a court officer with authority to accept it at the relevant court office; and
    (f)   the Registrar of Criminal Appeals by handing it to a court officer with authority to accept it at the Criminal Appeal Office.

(2) If an individual is 17 or under, a copy of a document served under paragraph (1)(a) must be handed to his or her parent, or another appropriate adult, unless no such person is readily available.

[*Note. Certain legislation treats a body that is not a corporation as if it were one for the purposes of rules about service of documents. See for example section 143 of the Adoption and Children Act 2002.*]

4.4   Service by leaving or posting a document

(1) A document may be served by leaving it at the appropriate address for service under this rule or by sending it to that address by first class post or by the equivalent of first class post.

(2) The address for service under this rule on –

    (a)   an individual is an address where it is reasonably believed that he or she will receive it;

    (b)   a corporation is its principal office, and if there is no readily identifiable principal office then any place where it carries on its activities or business;

    (c)   an individual or corporation who is legally represented in the case is that representative's office;

    (d)   the prosecution is the prosecutor's office;

    (e)   the court officer is the relevant court office; and

    (f)   the Registrar of Criminal Appeals is the Criminal Appeal Office, Royal Courts of Justice, Strand, London WC2A 2LL.

[*Note. In addition to service in England and Wales for which these rules provide, service outside England and Wales may be allowed under other legislation. See –*

    (a)   *section 39 of the Criminal Law Act 1977 (service of summons, etc. in Scotland and Northern Ireland);*

    (b)   *section 725(3) of the Companies Act 1985 and section 1139 of the Companies Act 2006 (service of copy summons, etc. on company's registered office in Scotland and Northern Ireland);*

    (c)   *sections 3, 4, 4A and 4B of the Crime (International Co-operation) Act 2003 (service of summons, etc. outside the United Kingdom) and rules 32.1 and 32.2; and*

    (d)   *section 695(1) and (2) of the Companies Act 1985 and section 1139(2) of the Companies Act 2006 (service on overseas company).*]

4.5   Service through a document exchange

A document may be served by document exchange (DX) where –

    (a)   the writing paper of the person to be served gives a DX box number; and

    (b)   that person has not refused to accept service by DX.

4.6   Service by fax, e-mail or other electronic means

(1) A document may be served by fax, e-mail or other electronic means where –

    (a)   the person to be served has given a fax, e-mail or other electronic address; and

    (b)   that person has not refused to accept service by that means.

(2) Where a document is served under this rule the person serving it need not provide a paper copy as well.

4.7   Documents that must be served only by handing them over, leaving or posting them

(1) The documents listed in this rule may be served –

    (a)   on an individual only under rule 4.3(1)(a) or rule 4.4(1) and (2)(a); and

    (b)   on a corporation only under rule 4.3(1)(b) or rule 4.4(1) and (2)(b).

(2) Those documents are –

    (a)   a summons, requisition or witness summons;

    (b)   notice of an order under section 25 of the Road Traffic Offenders Act 1988;

    (c)   a notice of registration under section 71(6) of that Act;

(d)   a notice of discontinuance under section 23(4) of the Prosecution of Offences Act 1985;

(e)   notice under rule 37.3(1) of the date, time and place to which the trial of an information has been adjourned, where it was adjourned in the defendant's absence;

(f)   a notice of fine or forfeited recognizance required by rule 52.1(1);

(g)   notice under section 86 of the Magistrates' Courts Act 1980 of a revised date to attend a means inquiry;

(h)   notice of a hearing to review the postponement of the issue of a warrant of commitment under section 77(6) of the Magistrates' Courts Act 1980;

(i)   a copy of the minute of a magistrates' court order required by rule 52.7(1);

(j)   an invitation to make observations or attend a hearing under rule 53.1(2) on the review of a compensation order under section 133 of the Powers of Criminal Courts (Sentencing) Act 2000;

(k)   any notice or document served under Part 19.

4.8   Service by person in custody

(1)   A person in custody may serve a document by handing it to the custodian addressed to the person to be served.

(2)   The custodian must –

(a)   endorse it with the time and date of receipt;

(b)   record its receipt; and

(c)   forward it promptly to the addressee.

4.9   Service by another method

(1)   The court may allow service of a document by a method other than those described in rules 4.3 to 4.6 and in rule 4.8.

(2)   An order allowing service by another method must specify –

(a)   the method to be used; and

(b)   the date on which the document will be served.

4.10   Date of service

(1)   A document served under rule 4.3 or rule 4.8 is served on the day it is handed over.

(2)   Unless something different is shown, a document served on a person by any other method is served –

(a)   in the case of a document left at an address, on the next business day after the day on which it was left;

(b)   in the case of a document sent by first class post or by the equivalent of first class post, on the second business day after the day on which it was posted or despatched;

(c)   in the case of a document served by document exchange, on the second business day after the day on which it was left at the addressee's DX or at a correspondent DX;

(d)   in the case of a document transmitted by fax, e-mail or other electronic means, on the next business day after it was transmitted; and

(e)   in any case, on the day on which the addressee responds to it if that is earlier.

(3)   Unless something different is shown, a document produced by a court computer system is to be taken as having been sent by first class post or by the equivalent of first class post to the addressee on the business day after the day on which it was produced.

(4)   In this Part "business day" means any day except Saturday, Sunday, Christmas Day, Boxing Day, Good Friday, Easter Monday or a bank holiday.

(5) Where a document is served on or by the court officer, "business day" does not include a day on which the court office is closed.

4.11   Proof of service

The person who serves a document may prove that by signing a certificate explaining how and when it was served.

4.12   Court's power to give directions about service

(1) The court may specify the time as well as the date by which a document must be –

    (a)   served under rule 4.3 or rule 4.8; or

    (b)   transmitted by fax, e-mail or other electronic means if it is served under rule 4.6.

(2) The court may treat a document as served if the addressee responds to it even if it was not served in accordance with the rules in this Part.

PART 5   FORMS

5.1   Forms

The forms set out in the Practice Direction shall be used as appropriate in connection with the rules to which they apply.

5.2   Magistrates' court forms in Welsh

(1) Subject to the provisions of this rule, the Welsh language forms set out in the Practice Direction or forms to the like effect may be used in connection with proceedings in magistrates' courts in Wales.

(2) Both a Welsh form and an English form may be used in the same document.

(3) When only a Welsh form set out in the Practice Direction accompanying this rule, or only the corresponding English form, is used in connection with proceedings in magistrates' courts in Wales, there shall be added the following words in Welsh and English:

"Darperir y ddogfen hon yn Gymraeg / Saesneg os bydd arnoch ei heisiau. Dylech wneud cais yn ddi-oed i (Glerc Llys yr Ynadon) (rhodder yma'r cyfeiriad) [...]

This document will be provided in Welsh / English if you require it. You should apply immediately to (the Justices' Clerk to the Magistrates' Court) (address) [...]

If a person other than a justices' clerk is responsible for sending or giving the document, insert that person's name."

(4) The justices' clerk or other person responsible for the service of a form bearing the additional words set out in paragraph (3) above shall, if any person upon whom the form is served so requests, provide him with the corresponding English or Welsh form.

(5) In this rule any reference to serving a document shall include the sending, giving or other delivery of it.

(6) In the case of a discrepancy between an English and Welsh text the English text shall prevail.

[*Formerly rules 2 to 6 of, and Schedule 2 to, the Magistrates' Courts (Welsh Forms) Rules 1986*).]

5.3   Signature of magistrates' court forms by justices' clerk

(1) Subject to paragraph (2) below, where any form prescribed by these Rules contains provision for signature by a justice of the peace only, the form shall have effect as if it contained provision in the alternative for signature by the justices' clerk.

(2)   This rule shall not apply to any form of information, complaint, statutory declaration or warrant, other than a warrant of commitment or of distress.

(3)   In this rule where a signature is required on a form or warrant other than an arrest, remand or commitment warrant, an electronic signature incorporated into the document will satisfy this requirement.

[*Formerly rule 109 of the Magistrates' Court Rules 1981.*]

PART 6   COURT RECORDS

6.1   Magistrates' court register

(1)   A magistrates' court officer shall keep a register in which there shall be entered –

    (a)   a minute or memorandum of every adjudication of the court; and

    (b)   a minute or memorandum of every other proceeding or thing required by these Rules or any other enactment to be so entered.

(2)   The register may be stored in electronic form on the court computer system and entries in the register shall include, where relevant, the following particulars –

    (a)   the name of the informant, complainant or applicant;

    (b)   the name and date of birth (if known) of the defendant or respondent;

    (c)   the nature of offence, matter of complaint or details of the application;

    (d)   the date of offence or matter of complaint;

    (e)   the plea or consent to order; and

    (f)   the minute of adjudication.

(3)   Particulars of any entry relating to a decision about bail or the reasons for any such decisions or the particulars of any certificate granted under section 5(6A) of the Bail Act 1976 may be made in a book separate from that in which the entry recording the decision itself is made, but any such separate book shall be regarded as forming part of the register.

(4)   Where, by virtue of section 128(3A) of the Magistrates' Courts Act 1980 , an accused gives his consent to the hearing and determination in his absence of any application for his remand on an adjournment of the case under sections 5, 10(1) or 18(4) of that Act, the court shall cause the consent of the accused, and the date on which it was notified to the court, to be entered in the register.

(5)   Where any consent mentioned in paragraph (4) is withdrawn, the court shall cause the withdrawal of the consent and the date on which it was notified to the court to be entered in the register.

(6)   On the summary trial of an information the accused's plea shall be entered in the register.

(7)   Where a court tries any person summarily in any case in which he may be tried summarily only with his consent, the court shall cause his consent to be entered in the register and, if the consent is signified by a person representing him in his absence, the court shall cause that fact also to be entered in the register.

(8)   Where a person is charged before a magistrates' court with an offence triable either way the court shall cause the entry in the register to show whether he was present when the proceedings for determining the mode of trial were conducted and, if they were conducted in his absence, whether they were so conducted by virtue of section 18(3) of the 1980 Act (disorderly conduct on his part) or by virtue of section 23(1) of that Act (consent signified by person representing him).

(9)   In any case to which section 22 of the 1980 Act (certain offences triable either way to be tried summarily if value involved is small) applies, the court shall cause its decision as to the value involved or, as the case may be, the fact that it is unable to reach such a decision to be entered in the register.

(10) Where a court has power under section 53(3) of the 1980 Act to make an order with the

consent of the defendant without hearing evidence, the court shall cause any consent of the defendant to the making of the order to be entered in the register.

(11) In the case of conviction or dismissal, the register shall clearly show the nature of the offence of which the accused is convicted or, as the case may be, the nature of the offence charged in the information that is dismissed.

(12) An entry of a conviction in the register shall state the date of the offence.

(13) Where a court is required under section 130(3) of the Powers of Criminal Courts (Sentencing) Act 2000 to give reasons for not making a compensation order the court shall cause the reasons given to be entered in the register.

(14) Where a court passes a custodial sentence, the court shall cause a statement of whether it obtained and considered a pre-sentence report before passing sentence to be entered in the register.

(15) Every register shall be open to inspection during reasonable hours by any justice of the peace, or any person authorised in that behalf by a justice of the peace or the Lord Chancellor.

(16) A record of summary conviction or order made on complaint required for an appeal or other legal purpose may be in the form of certified extract from the court register.

(17) Such part of the register as relates to proceedings in a youth court may be recorded separately and stored in electronic form on the court computer system.

[*Formerly rules 16 and 66 of the Magistrates' Court Rules 1981, and rule 25 of the Magistrates' Courts (Children and Young Persons) Rules 1992.*]

6.2 Registration of endorsement of licence under section 57 of the Road Traffic Offenders Act 1988

A magistrates' court officer or justices' clerk who, as a fixed penalty clerk within the meaning of section 69(4) of the Road Traffic Offenders Act 1988, endorses a driving licence under section 57(3) or (4) of that Act (endorsement of licences without hearing) shall register the particulars of the endorsement in a book separate from the register kept under rule 6.1 but any such book shall be regarded as forming part of the register.

[*Formerly rule 66A of the Magistrates' Courts Rules 1981.*]

6.3 Registration of certificate issued under section 70 of the Road Traffic Offenders Act 1988

A magistrates' court officer shall register receipt of a registration certificate issued under section 70 of the Road Traffic Offenders Act 1988 (sum payable in default of fixed penalty to be enforced as a fine) in a book separate from the register kept under rule 6.1 but any such book shall be regarded as forming part of the register.

[*Formerly rule 66B of the Magistrates' Courts Rules 1981.*]

6.4 Proof of proceedings in magistrates' courts

The register of a magistrates' court, or an extract from the register certified by the magistrates' court officer as a true extract, shall be admissible in any legal proceedings as evidence of the proceedings of the court entered in the register.

[*Formerly rule 68 of the Magistrates' Courts Rules 1981. As to the requirement to keep a register, see rule 6.1.*]

PART 7   STARTING A PROSECUTION IN A MAGISTRATES' COURTS

7.1 When this Part applies

(1) This Part applies in a magistrates' court where –

(a)   a prosecutor wants the court to issue a summons or warrant under section 1 of the Magistrates' Courts Act 1980;

(b)   a public prosecutor –

  (i)   wants the court to issue a warrant under section 1 of the Magistrates' Courts Act 1980, or

  (ii)   issues a written charge and requisition under section 29 of the Criminal Justice Act 2003; or

(c)   a person who is in custody is charged with an offence.

(2) In this Part, "public prosecutor" means one of those public prosecutors listed in section 29 of the Criminal Justice Act 2003.

[*Note. Under section 1 of the Magistrates' Courts Act 1980, on receiving a formal statement (described in that section as an "information") alleging that someone has committed an offence, the court may issue –*

(a)   *a summons requiring that person to attend court; or*

(b)   *a warrant for that person's arrest, if –*

  (i)   *the alleged offence must or may be tried in the Crown Court,*

  (ii)   *the alleged offence is punishable with imprisonment, or*

  (iii) *the person's address cannot be established sufficiently clearly to serve a summons or requisition.*

The powers of the court to which this Part applies may be exercised by a single justice of the peace.

Under section 29 of the Criminal Justice Act 2003, a public prosecutor listed in that section may issue a written charge alleging that someone has committed an offence, and a requisition requiring that person to attend court. Section 30 of that Act contains other provisions about written charges and requisitions.

A person detained under a power of arrest may be charged if the custody officer decides that there is sufficient evidence to do so. See sections 37 and 38 of the Police and Criminal Evidence Act 1984.]

7.2   Information and written charge

(1) A prosecutor who wants the court to issue a summons must –

(a)   serve an information in writing on the court officer; or

(b)   unless other legislation prohibits this, present an information orally to the court, with a written record of the allegation that it contains.

(2) A prosecutor who wants the court to issue a warrant must –

(a)   serve on the court officer –

  (i)   an information in writing, or

  (ii)   a copy of a written charge that has been issued; or

(b)   present to the court either of those documents.

(3) A public prosecutor who issues a written charge must notify the court officer immediately.

(4) A single document may contain –

(a)   more than one information; or

(b)   more than one written charge.

(5) Where an offence can be tried only in a magistrates' court, then unless other legislation otherwise provides –

(a)   a prosecutor must serve an information on the court officer or present it to the court; or

(b)   a public prosecutor must issue a written charge,

not more than 6 months after the offence alleged.

(6)   Where an offence can be tried in the Crown Court then –

    (a)   a prosecutor must serve an information on the court officer or present it to the court; or

    (b)   a public prosecutor must issue a written charge,

within any time limit that applies to that offence.

[*Note. In some legislation, including the Magistrates' Courts Act 1980, serving an information on the court officer or presenting it to the court is described as "laying" that information.*

The time limits for serving or presenting an information and for issuing a written charge are prescribed by section 127 of the Magistrates' Courts Act 1980 and section 30(5) of the Criminal Justice Act 2003.

Part 2 contains rules allowing someone with a prosecutor's authority, on that prosecutor's behalf, to –

    (a)   serve on the court officer or present to the court an information; or

    (b)   issue a written charge and requisition.

See Part 3 for the court's general powers of case management, including power to consider applications and give directions for (among other things) the amendment of an information or charge and for separate trials.

The Practice Direction sets out forms of information for use in connection with this rule.]

7.3   Allegation of offence in information or charge

(1)   An allegation of an offence in an information or charge must contain –

    (a)   a statement of the offence that –

        (i)   describes the offence in ordinary language, and

        (ii)   identifies any legislation that creates it; and

    (b)   such particulars of the conduct constituting the commission of the offence as to make clear what the prosecutor alleges against the defendant.

(2)   More than one incident of the commission of the offence may be included in the allegation if those incidents taken together amount to a course of conduct having regard to the time, place or purpose of commission.

7.4   Summons, warrant and requisition

(1)   The court may issue or withdraw a summons or warrant –

    (a)   without giving the parties an opportunity to make representations; and

    (b)   at a hearing in public or in private; or

    (c)   without a hearing.

(2)   A summons, warrant or requisition may be issued in respect of more than one offence.

(3)   A summons or requisition must –

    (a)   contain notice of when and where the defendant is required to attend the court;

    (b)   specify each offence in respect of which it is issued; and

    (c)   identify the person under whose authority it is issued.

(4)   A summons may be contained in the same document as an information.

(5)   A requisition may be contained in the same document as a written charge.

(6)   Where the court issues a summons –

    (a)   the prosecutor must –

        (i)   serve it on the defendant, and

    (ii)   notify the court officer; or

(b)   the court officer must –

    (i)   serve it on the defendant, and
    (ii)   notify the prosecutor.

(7) Where a public prosecutor issues a requisition that prosecutor must –

    (a)   serve on the defendant –

    (i)   the requisition, and
    (ii)   the written charge; and

    (b)   serve a copy of each on the court officer.

(8) Unless it would be inconsistent with other legislation, a replacement summons or requisition may be issued without a fresh information or written charge where the one replaced –

    (a)   was served by leaving or posting it under rule 4.7 (documents that must be served only by handing them over, leaving or posting them); but
    (b)   is shown not to have been received by the addressee.

(9) A summons or requisition issued to a defendant under 18 may require that defendant's parent or guardian to attend the court with the defendant, or a separate summons or requisition may be issued for that purpose.

[*Note. Part 18 contains other rules about warrants.*

Section 47 of the Magistrates' Courts Act 1980 and section 30(5) of the Criminal Justice Act 2003 make special provision about time limits under other legislation for the issue and service of a summons or requisition, where service by post is not successful.

Section 34A of the Children and Young Persons Act 1933 allows, and in some cases requires, the court to summon the parent or guardian of a defendant under 18.]

PART 8   OBJECTING TO THE DISCONTINUANCE OF PROCEEDINGS IN A MAGISTRATES' COURT

8.1   Time for objecting

The period within which an accused person may give notice under section 23(7) of the Prosecution of Offences Act 1985 that he wants proceedings against him to continue is 35 days from the date when the proceedings were discontinued under that section.

[*Formerly rule 3 of the Magistrates' Courts (Discontinuance of Proceedings) Rules 1986. For the equivalent procedure in the Crown Court see section 23A of the 1985 Act.*]

8.2   Form of notice

Notice under section 23(3), (4) or (7) of the Prosecution of Offences Act 1985 shall be given in writing and shall contain sufficient particulars to identify the particular offence to which it relates.

[*This rule derives in part from rule 4 of the Magistrates' Courts (Discontinuance of Proceedings) Rules 1986.*]

8.3   Duty of Director of Public Prosecutions

On giving notice under section 23(3) or (4) of the Prosecution of Offences Act 1985 the Director of Public Prosecutions shall inform any person who is detaining the accused person for the offence in relation to which the notice is given that he has given such notice and of the effect of the notice.

[Formerly rule 5 of the Magistrates' Courts (Discontinuance of Proceedings) Rules 1986.]

8.4   Duty of magistrates' court

On being given notice under section 23(3) of the Prosecution of Offences Act 1985 in relation to an offence for which the accused person has been granted bail by a court, a magistrates' court officer shall inform –

(a)   any sureties of the accused; and

(b)   any persons responsible for securing the accused's compliance with any conditions of bail

that he has been given such notice and of the effect of the notice.

[Formerly rule 6 of the Magistrates' Courts (Discontinuance of Proceedings) Rules 1986.]

PART 9   PRE-TRIAL HEARINGS IN MAGISTRATES' COURTS

[There are currently no rules in this Part.]

PART 10   COMMITTAL FOR TRIAL

10.1   Restrictions on reports of committal proceedings

(1)   Except in a case where evidence is, with the consent of the accused, to be tendered in his absence under section 4(4)(b) of the Magistrates' Courts Act 1980 (absence caused by ill health), a magistrates' court acting as examining justices shall before admitting any evidence explain to the accused the restrictions on reports of committal proceedings imposed by section 8 of that Act and inform him of his right to apply to the court for an order removing those restrictions.

(2)   Where a magistrates' court has made an order under section 8(2) of the 1980 Act removing restrictions on the reports of committal proceedings, such order shall be entered in the register.

(3)   Where the court adjourns any such proceedings to another day, the court shall, at the beginning of any adjourned hearing, state that the order has been made.

[Formerly rule 5 of the Magistrates' Courts Rules 1981. On the coming into force of Schedule 3 to the Criminal Justice Act 2003 committal for trial will be abolished and cases triable either way will be sent to the Crown Court under sections 51 and 51A of the Crime and Disorder Act 1998 in the same way as cases triable only on indictment.]

10.2   Committal for trial without consideration of the evidence

(1)   This rule applies to committal proceedings where the accused has a solicitor acting for him in the case and where the court has been informed that all the evidence falls within section 5A(2) of the Magistrates' Courts Act 1980.

(2)   A magistrates' court inquiring into an offence in committal proceedings to which this rule applies shall cause the charge to be written down, if this has not already been done, and read to the accused and shall then ascertain whether he wishes to submit that there is insufficient evidence to put him on trial by jury for the offence with which he is charged.

(3)   If the court is satisfied that the accused or, as the case may be, each of the accused does not wish to make such a submission as is referred to in paragraph (2) it shall, after receiving any written evidence falling within section 5A(3) of the 1980 Act, determine whether or not to commit the accused for trial without consideration of the evidence, and where it determines not to so commit the accused it shall proceed in accordance with rule 10.3.

[Formerly rule 6 of the Magistrates' Courts Rules 1981. On the coming into force of Schedule 3 to the Criminal Justice Act 2003, committal for trial will be abolished and cases triable either way will be sent to the Crown Court under sections 51 and 51A of the Crime and Disorder Act 1998 in the same way as cases triable only on indictment.]

10.3   Consideration of evidence at committal proceedings

(1)   This rule does not apply to committal proceedings where under section 6(2) of the Magistrates' Courts Act of 1980 a magistrates' court commits a person for trial without consideration of the evidence.

(2)   A magistrates' court inquiring into an offence as examining justices, having ascertained –

(a)   that the accused has no legal representative acting for him in the case; or

(b)   that the accused's legal representative has requested the court to consider a submission that there is insufficient evidence to put the accused on trial by jury for the offence with which he is charged, as the case may be,

shall permit the prosecutor to make an opening address to the court, if he so wishes, before any evidence is tendered.

(3)   After such opening address, if any, the court shall cause evidence to be tendered in accordance with sections 5B(4), 5C(4), 5D(5) and 5E(3) of the 1980 Act, that is to say by being read out aloud, except where the court otherwise directs or to the extent that it directs that an oral account be given of any of the evidence.

(4)   The court may view any exhibits produced before the court and may take possession of them.

(5)   After the evidence has been tendered the court shall hear any submission which the accused may wish to make as to whether there is sufficient evidence to put him on trial by jury for any indictable offence.

(6)   The court shall permit the prosecutor to make a submission –

(a)   in reply to any submission made by the accused in pursuance of paragraph (5); or

(b)   where the accused has not made any such submission but the court is nevertheless minded not to commit him for trial.

(7)   After hearing any submission made in pursuance of paragraph (5) or (6) the court shall, unless it decides not to commit the accused for trial, cause the charge to be written down, if this has not already been done, and, if the accused is not represented by counsel or a solicitor, shall read the charge to him and explain it in ordinary language.

[Formerly rule 7 of the Magistrates' Courts Rules 1981. On the coming into force of Schedule 3 to the Criminal Justice Act 2003 committal for trial will be abolished and cases triable either way will be sent to the Crown Court under sections 51 and 51A of the Crime and Disorder Act 1998 in the same way as cases triable only on indictment.]

10.4   Court's reminder to a defendant of right to object to evidence being read at trial without further proof

A magistrates' court which commits a person for trial shall forthwith remind him of his right to object, by written notification to the prosecutor and the Crown Court within 14 days of being committed unless that court in its discretion permits such an objection to be made outside that period, to a statement or deposition being read as evidence at the trial without oral evidence being given by the person who made the statement or deposition, and without the opportunity to cross-examine that person.

[Formerly rule 8 of the Magistrates' Courts Rules 1981. As to the duty on the prosecution to notify the defendant of this right, see rule 27.2. On the coming into force of Schedule 3 to the Criminal Justice Act 2003 committal for trial will be abolished and cases triable either way will be sent to

the Crown Court under sections 51 and 51A of the Crime and Disorder Act 1998 in the same way as cases triable only on indictment.]

10.5   Material to be sent to court of trial

(1) As soon as practicable after the committal of any person for trial, and in any case within 4 days from the date of his committal (not counting Saturdays, Sundays, Good Friday, Christmas Day or Bank Holidays), the magistrates' court officer shall, subject to the provisions of section 7 of the Prosecution of Offences Act 1985 (which relates to the sending of documents and things to the Director of Public Prosecutions), send to the Crown Court officer –

(a)   the information, if it is in writing;

(b)   (i)   the evidence tendered in accordance with section 5A of the Magistrates' Courts Act 1980 and, where any of that evidence consists of a copy of a deposition or documentary exhibit which is in the possession of the court, any such deposition or documentary exhibit, and

(ii)   a certificate to the effect that that evidence was so tendered;

(c)   any notification by the prosecutor under section 5D(2) of the 1980 Act regarding the admissibility of a statement under section 23 or 24 of the Criminal Justice Act 1988 (first hand hearsay; business documents);

(d)   a copy of the record made in pursuance of section 5 of the Bail Act 1976 relating to the grant or withholding of bail in respect of the accused on the occasion of the committal;

(e)   any recognizance entered into by any person as surety for the accused together with a statement of any enlargement thereof under section 129(4) of the 1980 Act;

(f)   a list of the exhibits produced in evidence before the justices or treated as so produced;

(g)   such of the exhibits referred to in paragraph (1)(f) as have been retained by the justices;

(h)   the names and addresses of any interpreters engaged for the defendant for the purposes of the committal proceedings, together with any telephone numbers at which they can be readily contacted, and details of the languages or dialects in connection with which they have been so engaged;

(i)   if the committal was under section 6(2) of the 1980 Act (committal for trial without consideration of the evidence), a statement to that effect;

(j)   if the magistrates' court has made an order under section 8(2) of the 1980 Act (removal of restrictions on reports of committal proceedings), a statement to that effect;

(k)   the certificate of the examining justices as to the costs of the prosecution under the Costs in Criminal Cases (General) Regulations 1986;

(l)   if any person under the age of 18 is concerned in the committal proceedings, a statement whether the magistrates' court has given a direction under section 39 of the Children and Young Persons Act 1933 (prohibition of publication of certain matter in newspapers);

(m)   a copy of any representation order previously made in the case;

(n)   a copy of any application for a representation order previously made in the case which has been refused; and

(o)   any documents relating to an appeal by the prosecution against the granting of bail.

(2) The period of 4 days specified in paragraph (1) may be extended in relation to any committal for so long as the Crown Court officer directs, having regard to the length of any document mentioned in that paragraph or any other relevant circumstances.

[Formerly rule 11 of the Magistrates' Courts Rules 1981. On the coming into force of Schedule 3 to the Criminal Justice Act 2003 committal for trial will be abolished and cases triable either way will be sent to the Crown Court under sections 51 and 51A of the Crime and Disorder Act 1998 in the same way as cases triable only on indictment.]

PART 11   TRANSFER FOR TRIAL OF SERIOUS FRAUD CASES OR CASES INVOLVING CHILDREN

11.1   Interpretation of this Part

(1) In this Part:

   "notice of transfer" means a notice referred to in section 4(1) of the Criminal Justice Act 1987 or section 53(1) of the Criminal Justice Act 1991.

(2) Where this Part requires a document to be given or sent, or a notice to be communicated in writing, it may, with the consent of the addressee, be sent by electronic communication.

(3) Electronic communication means a communication transmitted (whether from one person to another, from one device to another or from a person to a device or vice versa) –

   (a)   by means of an electronic communications network (within the meaning of the Communications Act 2003; or

   (b)   by other means but while in an electronic form.

[Formerly rule 2 of the Magistrates' Courts (Notice of Transfer) Rules 1988 and rule 2 of the Magistrates' Courts (Notice of Transfer) (Children's Evidence) Rules 1992. See also sections 4 and 5 of the Criminal Justice Act 1987 and section 53 of, and Schedule 6 to, the Criminal Justice Act 1991. On the coming into force of Schedule 3 to the Criminal Justice Act 2003 those provisions will be replaced with sections 51B and 51C of the Crime and Disorder Act 1998, which are to similar effect. For the duties of the prosecuting authority see the Criminal Justice Act 1987 (Notice of Transfer) Regulations 1988 and the Criminal Justice Act 1991 (Notice of Transfer) Regulations 1992.]

11.2   Transfer on bail

(1) Where a person in respect of whom notice of transfer has been given –

   (a)   is granted bail under section 5(3) or (7A) of the Criminal Justice Act 1987 by the magistrates' court to which notice of transfer was given; or

   (b)   is granted bail under paragraph 2(1) or (7) of Schedule 6 to the Criminal Justice Act 1991 by the magistrates' court to which notice of transfer was given,

   the magistrates' court officer shall give notice thereof in writing to the governor of the prison or remand centre to which the said person would have been committed by that court if he had been committed in custody for trial.

(2) Where notice of transfer is given under section 4(1) of the 1987 Act in respect of a corporation the magistrates' court officer shall give notice thereof to the governor of the prison to which would be committed a male over 21 committed by that court in custody for trial.

[Formerly rule 3 of the Magistrates' Courts (Notice of Transfer) Rules 1988 and rule 3 of the Magistrates' Courts (Notice of Transfer) (Children's Evidence) Rules 1992. For bail generally, see Part 19.]

11.3   Notice where person removed to hospital

Where a transfer direction has been given by the Secretary of State under section 47 or 48 of the Mental Health Act 1983 in respect of a person remanded in custody by a magistrates' court and, before the direction ceases to have effect, notice of transfer is given in respect of that person, the magistrates' court officer shall give notice thereof in writing –

(a)   to the governor of the prison to which that person would have been committed by that court if he had been committed in custody for trial; and

(b)   to the managers of the hospital where he is detained.

[*Formerly rule 4 of the Magistrates' Courts (Notice of Transfer) Rules 1988 and rule 4 of the Magistrates' Courts (Notice of Transfer) (Children's Evidence) Rules 1992.*]

11.4   Variation of arrangements for bail

(1) A person who intends to make an application to a magistrates' court under section 3(8) of the Bail Act 1976 as that subsection has effect under section 3(8A) of that Act shall give notice thereof in writing to the magistrates' court officer, and to the designated authority or the defendant, as the case may be, and to any sureties concerned.

(2) Where, on an application referred to in paragraph (1), a magistrates' court varies or imposes any conditions of bail, the magistrates' court officer shall send to the Crown Court officer a copy of the record made in pursuance of section 5 of the 1976 Act relating to such variation or imposition of conditions.

[*Formerly rule 5 of the Magistrates' Courts (Notice of Transfer) Rules 1988.*]

11.5   Documents etc to be sent to Crown Court

As soon as practicable after a magistrates' court to which notice of transfer has been given has discharged the functions reserved to it under section 4(1) of the Criminal Justice Act 1987 or section 53(3) of the Criminal Justice Act 1991, the magistrates' court officer shall send to the Crown Court officer –

(a)   a list of the names, addresses and occupations of the witnesses;

(b)   a copy of the record made in pursuance of section 5 of the Bail Act 1976 relating to the grant of withholding of bail in respect of the accused;

(c)   any recognizance entered into by any person as surety for the accused together with a statement of any enlargement thereof;

(d)   a copy of any representation order previously made in the case; and

(e)   a copy of any application for a representation order previously made in the case which has been refused.

[*Formerly rule 7 of the Magistrates' Courts (Notice of Transfer) Rules 1988 and rule 6 of the Magistrates' Courts (Notice of Transfer) (Children's Evidence) Rules 1992.*]

PART 12   SENDING FOR TRIAL

12.1   Documents to be sent to the Crown Court

(1) As soon as practicable after any person is sent for trial (pursuant to section 51 of the Crime and Disorder Act 1998, and in any event within 4 days from the date on which he is sent (not counting Saturdays, Sundays, Good Friday, Christmas Day or Bank Holidays), the magistrates' court officer shall, subject to section 7 of the Prosecution of Offences Act 1985 (which relates to the sending of documents and things to the Director of Public Prosecutions), send to the Crown Court officer –

(a)   the information, if it is in writing;

(b)   the notice required by section 51(7) of the 1998 Act;

(c)   a copy of the record made in pursuance of section 5 of the Bail Act 1976 relating to the granting or withholding of bail in respect of the accused on the occasion of the sending;

(d)   any recognizance entered into by any person as surety for the accused together with any enlargement thereof under section 129(4) of the Magistrates' Courts Act 1980;

(e)   the names and addresses of any interpreters engaged for the defendant for the purposes of the appearance in the magistrates' court, together with any telephone numbers at which they can be readily contacted, and details of the languages or dialects in connection with which they have been so engaged;

(f)   if any person under the age of 18 is concerned in the proceedings, a statement whether the magistrates' court has given a direction under section 39 of the Children and Young Persons Act 1933 (prohibition of publication of certain matter in newspapers);

(g)   a copy of any representation order previously made in the case;

(h)   a copy of any application for a representation order previously made in the case which has been refused; and

(i)   any documents relating to an appeal by the prosecution against the granting of bail.

(2) The period of 4 days specified in paragraph (1) may be extended in relation to any sending for trial for so long as the Crown Court officer directs, having regard to any relevant circumstances.

[Formerly rule 11A of the Magistrates' Courts Rules 1981. See also section 51 of the Crime and Disorder Act 1998. On the coming into force of Schedule 3 to the Criminal Justice Act 2003 section 51 of the 1998 Act will apply to either way as well as indictable only offences, and section 51A will extend the section 51 procedure to children and young persons. For the procedure governing the service of evidence by the prosecution where an accused is sent for trial, see the Crime and Disorder Act 1998 (Service of Prosecution Evidence) Regulations 2000.]

12.2   Time for first appearance of accused sent for trial

A Crown Court officer to whom notice has been given under section 51(7) of the Crime and Disorder Act 1998, shall list the first Crown Court appearance of the person to whom the notice relates in accordance with any directions given by the magistrates' court.

[Formerly rule 24ZA of the Crown Court Rules 1982. The provisions of that rule regarding the listing of the first appearance within set periods of time no longer apply.]

PART 13   DISMISSAL OF CHARGES TRANSFERRED OR SENT TO THE CROWN COURT

13.1   Interpretation of this Part

In this Part:

"notice of transfer" means a notice referred to in section 4(1) of the Criminal Justice Act 1987 or section 53(1) of the Criminal Justice Act 1991; and

"the prosecution" means the authority by or on behalf of whom notice of transfer was given under the 1987 or 1991 Acts, or the authority by or on behalf of whom documents were served under paragraph 1 of Schedule 3 to the Crime and Disorder Act 1998.

[Formerly rule 1 of the Criminal Justice Act 1987 (Dismissal of Transferred Charges) Rules 1988, rule 1 of the Criminal Justice Act 1991 (Dismissal of Transferred Charges) Rules 1992 and rule 1 of the Crime and Disorder Act 1998 (Dismissal of Charges Sent) Rules 1998. See also section 6 of the Criminal Justice Act 1987, section 53 of, and Schedule 6 to, the Criminal Justice Act 1991 and sections 51 and 52 of, and Schedule 3 to, the Crime and Disorder Act 1998.]

13.2   Written notice of oral application for dismissal

(1) Where notice of transfer has been given under the Criminal Justice Act 1987 or the Criminal Justice Act 1991, or a person has been sent for trial under the Crime and Disorder Act 1998, and the person concerned proposes to apply orally –

  (a)   under section 6(1) of the 1987 Act;

  (b)   under paragraph 5(1) of Schedule 6 to the 1991 Act; or

  (c)   under paragraph 2(1) of Schedule 3 to the 1998 Act

for any charge in the case to be dismissed, he shall give notice of his intention in writing to the Crown Court officer at the place specified by the notice of transfer under the 1987 or 1991 Acts or the notice given under section 51(7) of the 1998 Act as the proposed place of trial. Notice of intention to make an application under the 1987 or 1991 Acts shall be in the form set out in the Practice Direction.

(2) Notice of intention to make an application shall be given –

  (a)   in the case of an application to dismiss charges transferred under the 1987 Act, not later than 28 days after the day on which notice of transfer was given;

  (b)   in the case of an application to dismiss charges transferred under the 1991 Act, not later than 14 days after the day on which notice of transfer was given; and

  (c)   in the case of an application to dismiss charges sent under the 1998 Act, not later than 14 days after the day on which the documents were served under paragraph 1 of Schedule 3 to that Act,

and a copy of the notice shall be given at the same time to the prosecution and to any person to whom the notice of transfer relates or with whom the applicant for dismissal is jointly charged.

(3) The time for giving notice may be extended, either before or after it expires, by the Crown Court, on an application made in accordance with paragraph (4).

(4) An application for an extension of time for giving notice shall be made in writing to the Crown Court officer, and a copy thereof shall be given at the same time to the prosecution and to any other person to whom the notice of transfer relates or with whom the applicant for dismissal is jointly charged. Such an application made in proceedings under the 1987 or 1991 Acts shall be in the form set out in the Practice Direction.

(5) The Crown Court officer shall give notice in the form set out in the Practice Direction of the judge's decision on an application under paragraph (3) –

  (a)   to the applicant for dismissal;

  (b)   to the prosecution; and

  (c)   to any other person to whom the notice of transfer relates or with whom the applicant for dismissal is jointly charged.

(6) A notice of intention to make an application under section 6(1) of the 1987 Act, paragraph 5(1) of Schedule 6 to the 1991 Act or paragraph 2(1) of Schedule 3 to the 1998 Act shall be accompanied by a copy of any material on which the applicant relies and shall –

  (a)   specify the charge or charges to which it relates;

  (b)   state whether the leave of the judge is sought under section 6(3) of the 1987 Act, paragraph 5(4) of Schedule 6 to the 1991 Act or paragraph 2(4) of Schedule 3 to the 1998 Act to adduce oral evidence on the application, indicating what witnesses it is proposed to call at the hearing; and

  (c)   in the case of a transfer under the 1991 Act, confirm in relation to each such witness that he is not a child to whom paragraph 5(5) of Schedule 6 to that Act applies.

(7) Where leave is sought from the judge for oral evidence to be given on an application,

notice of his decision, indicating what witnesses are to be called if leave is granted, shall be given in writing by the Crown Court officer to the applicant for dismissal, the prosecution and to any other person to whom the notice of transfer relates or with whom the applicant for dismissal is jointly charged. Notice of a decision in proceedings under the 1987 or 1991 Acts shall be in the form set out in the Practice Direction.

(8)   Where an application for dismissal under section 6(1) of the 1987 Act, paragraph 5(1) of Schedule 6 to the 1991 Act or paragraph 2(1) of Schedule 3 to the 1998 Act is to be made orally, the Crown Court officer shall list the application for hearing before a judge of the Crown Court and the prosecution shall be given the opportunity to be represented at the hearing.

[Formerly rule 2 of the Criminal Justice Act 1987 (Dismissal of Transferred Charges) Rules 1988, rule 2 of the Criminal Justice Act 1991 (Dismissal of Transferred Charges) Rules 1992 and rule 2 of the Crime and Disorder Act 1998 (Dismissal of Charges Sent) Rules 1998.]

13.3   Written application for dismissal

(1)   Application may be made for dismissal under section 6(1) of the Criminal Justice Act 1987, paragraph 5(1) of Schedule 6 to the Criminal Justice Act 1991 or paragraph 2(1) of Schedule 3 to the Crime and Disorder Act 1998 without an oral hearing. Such an application shall be in writing, and in proceedings under the 1987 or 1991 Acts shall be in the form set out in the Practice Direction.

(2)   The application shall be sent to the Crown Court officer and shall be accompanied by a copy of any statement or other document, and identify any article, on which the applicant for dismissal relies.

(3)   A copy of the application and of any accompanying documents shall be given at the same time to the prosecution and to any other person to whom the notice of transfer relates or with whom the applicant for dismissal is jointly charged.

(4)   A written application for dismissal shall be made –

    (a)   not later than 28 days after the day on which notice of transfer was given under the 1987 Act;

    (b)   not later than 14 days after the day on which notice of transfer was given under the 1991 Act; or

    (c)   not later than 14 days after the day on which documents required by paragraph 1 of Schedule 3 to the 1998 Act were served

unless the time for making the application is extended, either before or after it expires, by the Crown Court; and rule 13.2(4) and (5) shall apply for the purposes of this paragraph as if references therein to giving notice of intention to make an oral application were references to making a written application under this rule.

[Formerly rule 3 of the Criminal Justice Act 1987 (Dismissal of Transferred Charges) Rules 1988, rule 3 of the Criminal Justice Act 1991 (Dismissal of Transferred Charges) Rules 1992 and rule 3 of the Crime and Disorder Act 1998 (Dismissal of Charges Sent) Rules 1998.]

13.4   Prosecution reply

(1)   Not later than seven days from the date of service of notice of intention to apply orally for the dismissal of any charge contained in a notice of transfer or based on documents served under paragraph 1 of Schedule 3 to the Crime and Disorder Act 1998, the prosecution may apply to the Crown Court under section 6(3) of the Criminal Justice Act 1987, paragraph 5(4) of Schedule 6 to the Criminal Justice Act 1991 or paragraph 2(4) of Schedule 3 to the 1998 Act for leave to adduce oral evidence at the hearing of the application, indicating what witnesses it is proposed to call.

(2)   Not later than seven days from the date of receiving a copy of an application for dismissal under rule 13.3, the prosecution may apply to the Crown Court for an oral hearing of the application.

(3) An application under paragraph (1) or (2) shall be served on the Crown Court officer in writing and, in the case of an application under paragraph (2), shall state whether the leave of the judge is sought to adduce oral evidence and, if so, shall indicate what witnesses it is proposed to call. Where leave is sought to adduce oral evidence under paragraph 5(4) of Schedule 6 to the 1991 Act, the application should confirm in relation to each such witness that he is not a child to whom paragraph 5(5) of that Schedule applies. Such an application in proceedings under the 1987 or 1991 Acts shall be in the form set out in the Practice Direction.

(4) Notice of the judge's determination upon an application under paragraph (1) or (2), indicating what witnesses (if any) are to be called shall be served in writing by the Crown Court officer on the prosecution, on the applicant for dismissal and on any other party to whom the notice of transfer relates or with whom the applicant for dismissal is jointly charged. Such a notice in proceedings under the 1987 or 1991 Acts shall be in the form set out in the Practice Direction.

(5) Where, having received the material specified in rule 13.2 or, as the case may be, rule 13.3, the prosecution proposes to adduce in reply thereto any written comments or any further evidence, the prosecution shall serve any such comments, copies of the statements or other documents outlining the evidence of any proposed witnesses, copies of any further documents and, in the case of an application to dismiss charges transferred under the 1991 Act, copies of any video recordings which it is proposed to tender in evidence, on the Crown Court officer not later than 14 days from the date of receiving the said material, and shall at the same time serve copies thereof on the applicant for dismissal and any other person to whom the notice of transfer relates or with whom the applicant is jointly charged. In the case of a defendant acting in person, copies of video recordings need not be served but shall be made available for viewing by him.

(6) The time for –

(a)   making an application under paragraph (1) or (2) above; or

(b)   serving any material on the Crown Court officer under paragraph (5) above

may be extended, either before or after it expires, by the Crown Court, on an application made in accordance with paragraph (7) below.

(7) An application for an extension of time under paragraph (6) above shall be made in writing and shall be served on the Crown Court officer, and a copy thereof shall be served at the same time on to the applicant for dismissal and on any other person to whom the notice of transfer relates or with whom the applicant for dismissal is jointly charged. Such an application in proceedings under the 1987 or 1991 Acts shall be in the form set out in the Practice Direction.

[Formerly rule 4 of the Criminal Justice Act 1987 (Dismissal of Transferred Charges) Rules 1988, rule 4 of the Criminal Justice Act 1991 (Dismissal of Transferred Charges) Rules 1992 and rule 4 of the Crime and Disorder Act 1998 (Dismissal of Charges Sent) Rules 1998.]

13.5   Determination of applications for dismissal – procedural matters

(1) A judge may grant leave for a witness to give oral evidence on an application for dismissal notwithstanding that notice of intention to call the witness has not been given in accordance with the foregoing provisions of this Part.

(2) Where an application for dismissal is determined otherwise than at an oral hearing, the Crown Court officer shall as soon as practicable, send to all the parties to the case written notice of the outcome of the application. Such a notice in proceedings under the 1987 and 1991 Acts shall be in the form set out in the Practice Direction.

[Formerly rule 5 of the Criminal Justice Act 1987 (Dismissal of Transferred Charges) Rules 1988, rule 5 of the Criminal Justice Act 1991 (Dismissal of Transferred Charges) Rules 1992 and rule 5 of the Crime and Disorder Act 1998 (Dismissal of Charges Sent) Rules 1998.]

13.6   [Revoked]

PART 14   THE INDICTMENT

[Note. The rules in this Part derive from rules formerly in the Indictment Rules 1971 and the Indictments (Procedure) Rules 1971. See also sections 3, 4 and 5 of the Indictments Act 1915 and section 2 of the Administration of Justice (Miscellaneous Provisions) Act 1933.]

14.1   Signature and service of indictment

(1)   The prosecutor must serve a draft indictment on the Crown Court officer not more than 28 days after –

    (a)   service on the defendant and on the Crown Court officer of copies of the documents containing the evidence on which the charge or charges are based, in a case where the defendant is sent for trial;

    (b)   a High Court judge gives permission to serve a draft indictment;

    (c)   the Court of Appeal orders a retrial; or

    (d)   the committal or transfer of the defendant for trial.

(2)   The Crown Court may extend the time limit, even after it has expired.

(3)   Unless the Crown Court otherwise directs, the court officer must –

    (a)   sign and date the draft, which then becomes an indictment; and

    (b)   serve a copy of the indictment on all parties.

[Note. Serving a draft indictment was described as "preferring a bill of indictment" in the rules from which these rules derive.

See Part 3 for the court's general powers of case management, including power to consider applications and give directions for (among other things) the amendment of an indictment and for separate trials under section 5 of the Indictments Act 1915.

A magistrates' court may send a defendant for trial in the Crown Court under section 51 or 51A of the Crime and Disorder Act 1998. Under section 51D of that Act the magistrates' court must notify the Crown Court of the offence or offences for which the defendant is sent for trial. Paragraph 1 of Schedule 3 to that Act, and the Crime and Disorder Act 1998 (Service of Prosecution Evidence) Regulations 2005, deal with the service of prosecution evidence in a case sent for trial.

The procedure for applying for the permission of a High Court judge to serve a draft indictment is in rules 6 to 10 of the Indictments (Procedure) Rules 1971. See also direction IV.35 of the Practice Direction.

The Court of Appeal may order a retrial under section 8 of the Criminal Appeal Act 1968 (on a defendant's appeal against conviction) or under section 77 of the Criminal Justice Act 2003 (on a prosecutor's application for the retrial of a serious offence after acquittal). Section 8 of the 1968 Act, and rules 41.14 and 41.15, require the arraignment of a defendant within 2 months.

When it comes into force, Schedule 3 to the Criminal Justice Act 2003 will abolish committal for trial under section 6 of the Magistrates' Courts Act 1980, and transfer for trial under section 4 of the Criminal Justice Act 1987) (serious fraud cases) or under section 53 of the Criminal Justice Act 1991 (certain cases involving children).]

14.2   Form and content of indictment

(1)   An indictment must be in one of the forms set out in the Practice Direction and must contain, in a paragraph called a "count" –

    (a)   a statement of the offence charged that –

        (i)   describes the offence in ordinary language, and

        (ii)   identifies any legislation that creates it; and

(b)   such particulars of the conduct constituting the commission of the offence as to make clear what the prosecutor alleges against the defendant.

(2)   More than one incident of the commission of the offence may be included in a count if those incidents taken together amount to a course of conduct having regard to the time, place or purpose of commission.

(3)   An indictment may contain more than one count if all the offences charged –

(a)   are founded on the same facts; or
(b)   form or are a part of a series of offences of the same or a similar character.

(4)   The counts must be numbered consecutively.

(5)   An indictment may contain –

(a)   any count charging substantially the same offence as one –

(i)   specified in the notice of the offence or offences for which the defendant was sent for trial,
(ii)   on which the defendant was committed for trial, or
(iii) specified in the notice of transfer given by the prosecutor; and

(b)   any other count based on the prosecution evidence already served which the Crown Court may try.

[Note. In certain circumstances the Crown Court may try a defendant for an offence other than one sent, committed or transferred for trial: see section 2(2) of the Administration of Justice (Miscellaneous Provisions) Act 1933 (indictable offences founded on the prosecution evidence on which the sending, committal or transfer was based) and section 40 of the Criminal Justice Act 1988 (specified summary offences founded on that evidence).]

PART 15   PREPARATORY HEARINGS IN CASES OF SERIOUS FRAUD AND OTHER COMPLEX, SERIOUS OR LENGTHY CASES IN THE CROWN COURT

15.1   Application for a preparatory hearing

(1)   A party who wants the court to order a preparatory hearing under section 7(2) of the Criminal Justice Act 1987 or under section 29(4) of the Criminal Procedure and Investigations Act 1996 must –

(a)   apply in the form set out in the Practice Direction;
(b)   include a short explanation of the reasons for applying; and
(c)   serve the application on the court officer and all other parties.

(2)   A prosecutor who wants the court to order that –

(a)   the trial will be conducted without a jury under section 43 or section 44 of the Criminal Justice Act 2003; or
(b)   the trial of some of the counts included in the indictment will be conducted without a jury under section 17 of the Domestic Violence, Crime and Victims Act 2004,

must apply under this rule for a preparatory hearing, whether or not the defendant has applied for one.

[Note. The rules in this Part derive in part from rules formerly in the Criminal Justice Act 1987 (Preparatory Hearings) Rules 1997 and the Criminal Procedure and Investigations Act 1996 (Preparatory Hearings) Rules 1997. See also sections 7 to 9A of the Criminal Justice Act 1987 (cases of serious or complex fraud) and sections 29 to 32 of the Criminal Procedure and Investigations Act 1996 (other complex, serious or lengthy cases).

For the provisions governing applications for the trial to be conducted without a jury, see sections 43 to 48 of the Criminal Justice Act 2003 (trials without a jury in serious or complex fraud cases or where there is a danger of jury tampering). For the rules governing an appeal under section 47 of that Act, see rule 65.11 (appeal against order following discharge of jury because of jury tampering).]

15.2   Time for applying for a preparatory hearing

(1)   A party who applies under rule 15.1 must do so not more than 28 days after –

    (a)   the committal of the defendant;

    (b)   the consent to the preferment of a bill of indictment in relation to the case;

    (c)   the service of a notice of transfer; or

    (d)   where a person is sent for trial, the service of copies of the documents containing the evidence on which the charge or charges are based.

(2)   A prosecutor who applies under rule 15.1 because he wants the court to order a trial without a jury under section 44 of the Criminal Justice Act 2003 (jury tampering) must do so as soon as reasonably practicable where the reasons do not arise until after that time limit has expired.

(3)   The court may extend the time limit, even after it has expired.

[Note. A notice of transfer may be served under section 4 of the Criminal Justice Act 1987 (serious or complex fraud cases), or under section 53 of the Criminal Justice Act 1991 (certain cases involving children).

A person is sent for trial under section 51 of the Crime and Disorder Act 1998 (indictable-only offences sent for trial) or (so far as it is in force) under section 51A of the Crime and Disorder Act 1998 (certain cases involving children). As to the service of prosecution evidence in such a case, see paragraph 1 of Schedule 3 to the 1998 Act and the Crime and Disorder Act 1998 (Service of Prosecution Evidence) Regulations 2005.]

15.3   Representations concerning an application

(1)   A party who wants to make written representations concerning an application made under rule 15.1 must –

    (a)   do so within 7 days of receiving a copy of that application; and

    (b)   serve those representations on the court officer and all other parties.

(2)   A defendant who wants to oppose an application for an order that the trial will be conducted without a jury under section 43 or section 44 of the Criminal Justice Act 2003 must serve written representations under this rule, including a short explanation of the reasons for opposing that application.

[Note. The grounds on which a judge may allow or refuse an application for an order that the trial will be conducted without a jury under section 43 or 44 of the Criminal Justice Act 2003 Act are set out in those sections of that Act.]

15.4   Determination of an application

(1)   Where an application has been made under rule 15.1(2), the court must hold a preparatory hearing.

(2)   Other applications made under rule 15.1 should normally be determined without a hearing.

(3)   The court officer must serve on the parties in the case, in the form set out in the Practice Direction –

    (a)   notice of the determination of an application made under rule 15.1; and

    (b)   an order for a preparatory hearing made by the court of its own initiative, including one that the court is required to make.

[*Note. Section 45 of the Criminal Justice Act 2003 provides that an application by the prosecution for an order that the trial will be conducted without a jury must be determined at a preparatory hearing and the parties to the preparatory hearing must be given an opportunity to make representations with respect to that application.*]

15.5   Orders for disclosure by prosecution or defence

(1)   Any disclosure order under section 9 of the Criminal Justice Act 1987, or section 31 of the Criminal Procedure and Investigations Act 1996, must identify any documents that are required to be prepared and served by the prosecutor under that order.

(2)   A disclosure order under either of those sections does not require a defendant to disclose who will give evidence, except to the extent that disclosure is required –

   (a)   by section 6A(2) of the 1996 Act (disclosure of alibi); or
   (b)   by Part 24 of these Rules (disclosure of expert evidence).

(3)   The court officer must serve notice of the order, in the relevant form set out in the Practice Direction, on the parties.

[*Note. Under section 9(4) of the Criminal Justice Act 1987 or section 31(4) of the Criminal Procedure and Investigations Act 1996, the judge can require the prosecution to set out its case in a written statement, to arrange its evidence in a form that will be easiest for the jury to understand, to prepare a list of agreed facts, and to amend the case statement as directed by the judge following representations from the defence.*

Under section 9(5) of the 1987 Act or section 31(6), (7) and (9) of the 1996 Act, the judge can require the defence to give notice of any objection to the prosecution case statement, to give notice stating the extent of agreement with the prosecution as to documents and other matters and the reason for any disagreement.]

15.6   [Revoked]

PART 16   RESTRICTIONS ON REPORTING AND PUBLIC ACCESS

16.1   Application for a reporting direction under section 46(6) of the Youth Justice and Criminal Evidence Act 1999

(1)   An application for a reporting direction made by a party to any criminal proceedings, in relation to a witness in those proceedings, must be made in the form set out in the Practice Direction or orally under rule 16.3.

(2)   If an application for a reporting direction is made in writing, the applicant shall send that application to the court officer and copies shall be sent at the same time to every other party to those proceedings.

[*Formerly rule 2 of the Magistrates' Courts (Reports Relating to Adult Witnesses) Rules 2004 and rule 2 of the Crown Court (Reports Relating to Adult Witnesses) Rules 2004. Section 46 of the Youth Justice and Criminal Evidence Act 1999 applies to adult witnesses the quality of whose evidence, or whose Cupertino, is likely to be diminished if their identity is made public. For reporting restrictions generally see direction I.3 in the Practice Direction.*]

16.2   Opposing an application for a reporting direction under section 46(6) of the Youth Justice and Criminal Evidence Act 1999

(1)   If an application for a reporting direction is made in writing, any party to the proceedings who wishes to oppose that application must notify the applicant and the court officer in writing of his opposition and give reasons for it.

(2)   A person opposing an application must state in the written notification whether he disputes that the –

(a)   witness is eligible for protection under section 46 of the Youth Justice and Criminal Evidence Act 1999; or

(b)   granting of protection would be likely to improve the quality of the evidence given by the witness or the level of co-operation given by the witness to any party to the proceedings in connection with that party's preparation of its case.

(3)   The notification under paragraph (1) must be given within five business days of the date the application was served on him unless an extension of time is granted under rule 16.6.

[Formerly rule 3 of the Magistrates' Courts (Reports Relating to Adult Witnesses) Rules 2004 and rule 3 of the Crown Court (Reports Relating to Adult Witnesses) Rules 2004.]

16.3   Urgent action on an application under section 46(6) of the Youth Justice and Criminal Evidence Act 1999

(1)   The court may give a reporting direction under section 46 of the Youth Justice and Criminal Evidence Act 1999 in relation to a witness in those proceedings, notwithstanding that the five business days specified in rule 16.2(3) have not expired if –

(a)   an application is made to it for the purposes of this rule; and
(b)   it is satisfied that, due to exceptional circumstances, it is appropriate to do so.

(2)   Any party to the proceedings may make the application under paragraph (1) whether or not an application has already been made under rule 16.1.
(3)   An application under paragraph (1) may be made orally or in writing.
(4)   If an application is made orally, the court may hear and take into account representations made to it by any person who in the court's view has a legitimate interest in the application before it.
(5)   The application must specify the exceptional circumstances on which the applicant relies.

[Formerly rule 4 of the Magistrates' Courts (Reports Relating to Adult Witnesses) Rules 2004 and rule 4 of the Crown Court (Reports Relating to Adult Witnesses) Rules 2004.]

16.4   Excepting direction under section 46(9) of the Youth Justice and Criminal Evidence Act 1999

(1)   An application for an excepting direction under section 46(9) of the Youth Justice and Criminal Evidence Act 1999 (a direction dispensing with restrictions imposed by a reporting direction) may be made by –

(a)   any party to those proceedings; or
(b)   any person who, although not a party to the proceedings, is directly affected by a reporting direction given in relation to a witness in those proceedings.

(2)   If an application for an excepting direction is made, the applicant must state why –

(a)   the effect of a reporting direction imposed places a substantial and unreasonable restriction on the reporting of the proceedings; and
(b)   it is in the public interest to remove or relax those restrictions.

(3)   An application for an excepting direction may be made in writing, pursuant to paragraph (4), at any time after the commencement of the proceedings in the court or orally at a hearing of an application for a reporting direction.
(4)   If the application for an excepting direction is made in writing it must be in the form set out in the Practice Direction and the applicant shall send that application to the court officer and copies shall be sent at the same time to every party to those proceedings.
(5)   Any person served with a copy of an application for an excepting direction who wishes to oppose it, must notify the applicant and the court officer in writing of his opposition and give reasons for it.

(6) The notification under paragraph (5) must be given within five business days of the date the application was served on him unless an extension of time is granted under rule 16.6.

[Formerly rule 5 of the Magistrates' Courts (Reports Relating to Adult Witnesses) Rules 2004 and rule 5 of the Crown Court (Reports Relating to Adult Witnesses) Rules 2004.]

16.5   Variation or revocation of a reporting or excepting direction under section 46 of the Youth Justice and Criminal Evidence Act 1999

(1) An application for the court to –

(a)   revoke a reporting direction; or

(b)   vary or revoke an excepting direction,

may be made to the court at any time after the commencement of the proceedings in the court.

(2) An application under paragraph (1) may be made by a party to the proceedings in which the direction was issued, or by a person who, although not a party to those proceedings, is in the opinion of the court directly affected by the direction.

(3) An application under paragraph (1) must be made in writing and the applicant shall send that application to the officer of the court in which the proceedings commenced, and at the same time copies of the application shall be sent to every party or, as the case may be, every party to the proceedings.

(4) The applicant must set out in his application the reasons why he seeks to have the direction varied or, as the case may be, revoked.

(5) Any person served with a copy of an application who wishes to oppose it, must notify the applicant and the court officer in writing of his opposition and give reasons for it.

(6) The notification under paragraph (5) must be given within five business days of the date the application was served on him unless an extension of time is granted under rule 16.6.

[Formerly rule 6 of the Magistrates' Courts (Reports Relating to Adult Witnesses) Rules 2004 and rule 6 of the Crown Court (Reports Relating to Adult Witnesses) Rules 2004.]

16.6   Application for an extension of time in proceedings under section 46 of the Youth Justice and Criminal Evidence Act 1999

(1) An application may be made in writing to extend the period of time for notification under rule 16.2(3), rule 16.4(6) or rule 16.5(6) before that period has expired.

(2) An application must be accompanied by a statement setting out the reasons why the applicant is unable to give notification within that period.

(3) An application must be sent to the court officer and a copy of the application must be sent at the same time to the applicant.

[Formerly rule 7 of the Magistrates' Courts (Reports Relating to Adult Witnesses) Rules 2004 and rule 7 of the Crown Court (Reports Relating to Adult Witnesses) Rules 2004.]

16.7   Decision of the court on an application under section 46 of the Youth Justice and Criminal Evidence Act 1999

(1) The court may –

(a)   determine any application made under rules 16.1 and rules 16.3 to 16.6 without a hearing; or

(b)   direct a hearing of any application.

(2) The court officer shall notify all the parties of the court's decision as soon as reasonably practicable.

(3) If a hearing of an application is to take place, the court officer shall notify each party to the proceedings of the time and place of the hearing.

(4) A court may hear and take into account representations made to it by any person who in the court's view has a legitimate interest in the application before it.

[*Formerly rule 8 of the Magistrates' Courts (Reports Relating to Adult Witnesses) Rules 2004 and rule 8 of the Crown Court (Reports Relating to Adult Witnesses) Rules 2004.*]

16.8   Proceedings sent or transferred to the Crown Court with direction under section 46 of the Youth Justice and Criminal Evidence Act 1999 in force

Where proceedings in which reporting directions or excepting directions have been ordered are sent or transferred from a magistrates' court to the Crown Court, the magistrates' court officer shall forward copies of all relevant directions to the Crown Court officer at the place to which the proceedings are sent or transferred.

[*Formerly rule 9 of the Magistrates' Courts (Reports Relating to Adult Witnesses) Rules 2004.*]

16.9   Hearings in camera and applications under section 46 of the Youth Justice and Criminal Evidence Act 1999

If in any proceedings, a prosecutor or defendant has served notice under rule 16.10 of his intention to apply for an order that all or part of a trial be held in camera, any application under this Part relating to a witness in those proceedings need not identify the witness by name and date of birth.

[*Formerly rule 9 of the Crown Court (Reports Relating to Adult Witnesses) Rules 2004.*]

16.10   Application to hold a Crown Court trial in camera

(1) Where a prosecutor or a defendant intends to apply for an order that all or part of a trial be held in camera for reasons of national security or for the protection of the identity of a witness or any other person, he shall not less than 7 days before the date on which the trial is expected to begin serve a notice in writing to that effect on the Crown Court officer and the prosecutor or the defendant as the case may be.

(2) On receiving such notice, the court officer shall forthwith cause a copy thereof to be displayed in a prominent place within the precincts of the Court.

(3) An application by a prosecutor or a defendant who has served such a notice for an order that all or part of a trial be heard in camera shall, unless the Court orders otherwise, be made in camera, after the defendant has been arraigned but before the jury has been sworn and, if such an order is made, the trial shall be adjourned until whichever of the following shall be appropriate –

   (a)   24 hours after the making of the order, where no application for leave to appeal from the order is made; or

   (b)   after the determination of an application for leave to appeal, where the application is dismissed; or

   (c)   after the determination of the appeal, where leave to appeal is granted.

[*Formerly rule 24A of the Crown Court Rules 1982. As to the procedure for appealing against an order, see rule 67.2.*]

16.11   Crown Court hearings in chambers

(1) The criminal jurisdiction of the Crown Court specified in the following paragraph may be exercised by a judge of the Crown Court sitting in chambers.

(2) The said jurisdiction is –

   (a)   hearing applications for bail;

   (b)   issuing a summons or warrant;

(c)   hearing any application relating to procedural matters preliminary or inciden-
         tal to criminal proceedings in the Crown Court, including applications relating
         to legal aid;

(d)   jurisdiction under rules 12.2 (listing first appearance of accused sent for trial),
         28.3 (application for witness summons), 63.2(5) (extending time for appeal
         against decision of magistrates' court), and 64.7 (application to state case for
         consideration of High Court);

(e)   hearing an application under section 41(2) of the Youth Justice and Criminal
         Evidence Act 1999 (evidence of complainant's previous sexual history);

(f)   hearing applications under section 22(3) of the Prosecution of Offences Act
         1985 (extension or further extension of custody time limit imposed by regula-
         tions made under section 22(1) of that Act);

(g)   hearing an appeal brought by an accused under section 22(7) of the 1985 Act
         against a decision of a magistrates' court to extend, or further extend, such a
         time limit, or brought by the prosecution under section 22(8) of the same Act
         against a decision of a magistrates' court to refuse to extend, or further extend,
         such a time limit;

(h)   hearing appeals under section 1 of the Bail (Amendment) Act 1993 (against
         grant of bail by magistrates' court); and

(i)   hearing appeals under section 16 of the Criminal Justice Act 2003 (against
         condition of bail imposed by magistrates' court).

[*Formerly rule 27 of the Crown Court Rules 1982. As to hearing restraint and receivership
proceedings under the Proceeds of Crime Act 2002 in chambers see rule 61.4.*]

PART 17   EXTRADITION

17.1   Refusal to make an order of committal

(1) Where a magistrates' court refuses to make an order of committal in relation to a person
     in respect of the offence or, as the case may be, any of the offences to which the authority
     to proceed relates and the state, country or colony seeking the surrender of that person
     immediately informs the court that it intends to make an application to the court to state
     a case for the opinion of the High Court, if the magistrates' court makes an order in
     accordance with section 10(2) of the Extradition Act 1989 releasing that person on bail,
     the court officer shall forthwith send a copy of that order to the Administrative Court
     Office.

(2) Where a magistrates' court refuses to make an order of committal in relation to a person
     in respect of the offence or, as the case may be, any of the offences to which the authority
     to proceed relates and the state, country or colony seeking his surrender wishes to apply
     to the court to state a case for the opinion of the High Court under section 10(1) of the
     1989 Act, such application must be made to the magistrates' court within the period of
     21 days following the day on which the court refuses to make the order of committal
     unless the court grants a longer period within which the application is to be made.

(3) Such an application shall be made in writing and shall identify the question or questions
     of law on which the opinion of the High Court is sought.

(4) Within 21 days after receipt of an application to state a case under section 10(1) of the
     1989 Act, the magistrates' court officer shall send a draft case to the solicitor for the
     state, country or colony and to the person whose surrender is sought or his solicitor and
     shall allow each party 21 days within which to make representations thereon; within 21
     days after the latest day on which such representations may be made the court of
     committal shall, after considering any such representations and making such adjust-
     ments, if any, to the draft case as it thinks fit, state and sign the case which the court
     officer shall forthwith send to the solicitor for the state, country or colony.

[Formerly rule 4 of the Magistrates' Courts (Extradition) Rules 1989. This rule has effect only in proceedings where the request for extradition was received by the relevant authority in the United Kingdom on or before 31st December 2003.]

17.2   Notice of waiver

(1) A notice given under section 14 of, or paragraph 9 of Schedule 1 to, the Extradition Act 1989 (notice of waiver under the simplified procedure) shall be in the form set out in the Practice Direction or a form to the like effect.
(2) Such a notice shall be signed in the presence of the Senior District Judge (Chief Magistrate) or another District Judge (Magistrates' Courts) designated by him for the purposes of the Act, a justice of the peace or a justices' clerk.
(3) Any such notice given by a person in custody shall be delivered to the Governor of the prison in whose custody he is.
(4) If a person on bail gives such notice he shall deliver it to, or send it by post in a registered letter or by recorded delivery service addressed to, the Under Secretary of State, Home Office, London SW1H 9AT.

[Formerly rule 5 of the Magistrates' Courts (Extradition) Rules 1989. This rule has effect only in proceedings where the request for extradition was received by the relevant authority in the United Kingdom on or before 31st December 2003.]

17.3   Notice of consent

(1) A person arrested in pursuance of a warrant under section 8 of or paragraph 5 of Schedule 1 to the Extradition Act 1989 may at any time consent to his return; and where such consent is given in accordance with the following provisions of this rule, the Senior District Judge (Chief Magistrate) or another District Judge (Magistrates' Courts) designated by him for the purposes of the Act may order the committal for return of that person in accordance with section 14(2) of that Act or, as the case may be, paragraph 9(2) of Schedule 1 to the Act.
(2) A notice of consent for the purposes of this rule shall be given in the form set out in the Practice Direction and shall be signed in the presence of the Senior District Judge (Chief Magistrate) or another District Judge (Magistrates' Courts) designated by him for the purposes of the 1989 Act.

[Formerly rule 6 of the Magistrates' Courts (Extradition) Rules 1989. This rule has effect only in proceedings where the request for extradition was received by the relevant authority in the United Kingdom on or before 31st December 2003.]

17.4   Notice of consent (parties to 1995 Convention)

(1) This rule applies as between the United Kingdom and states other than the Republic of Ireland that are parties to the Convention drawn up on the basis of Article 31 of the Treaty on European Union on Simplified Extradition Procedures between the Member States of the European Union, in relation to which section 14A of the Extradition Act 1989 applies by virtue of section 34A and Schedule 1A of that Act.
(2) Notice of consent for the purposes of section 14A(3) of the 1989 Act shall be given in the form set out in the Practice Direction and shall be signed in the presence of the Senior District Judge (Chief Magistrate) or another District Judge (Magistrates' Courts) designated by him for the purposes of that Act.
(3) A Senior District Judge (Chief Magistrate) or another District Judge (Magistrates' Courts) designated by him for the purposes of the Act may order the committal for return of a person if he gives consent under section 14A of the 1989 Act in accordance with paragraph (2) above before he is committed under section 9 of that Act.

[Formerly rule 7 of the Magistrates' Courts (Extradition) Rules 1989. This rule has effect only in proceedings where the request for extradition was received by the relevant authority in the United Kingdom on or before 31st December 2003.]

17.5   Consent to early removal to Republic of Ireland

(1)   A notice given under section 3(1)(a) of the Backing of Warrants (Republic of Ireland) Act 1965 (consent to surrender earlier than is otherwise permitted) shall be signed in the presence of a justice of the peace or a justices' clerk.

(2)   Any such notice given by a person in custody shall be delivered to the Governor of the prison in whose custody he is.

(3)   If a person on bail gives such notice, he shall deliver it to, or send it by post in a registered letter or by recorded delivery service addressed to, the police officer in charge of the police station specified in his recognizance.

(4)   Any such notice shall be attached to the warrant ordering the surrender of that person.

[Formerly rule 2 of the Magistrates' Courts (Backing of Warrants) Rules 1965. This rule has effect only in proceedings where the request for extradition was received by the relevant authority in the United Kingdom on or before 31st December 2003.]

17.6   Bail pending removal to Republic of Ireland

(1)   The person taking the recognizance of a person remanded on bail under section 2(1) or 4(3) of the Backing of Warrants (Republic of Ireland) Act 1965 shall furnish a copy of the recognizance to the police officer in charge of the police station specified in the recognizance.

(2)   The court officer for a magistrates' court which ordered a person to be surrendered and remanded him on bail shall deliver to, or send by post in a registered letter or by recorded delivery service addressed to, the police officer in charge of the police station specified in the recognizance the warrant ordering the person to be surrendered.

(3)   The court officer for a magistrates' court which refused to order a person to be delivered under section 2 of the 1965 Act but made an order in accordance with section 2A(2) of that Act releasing that person on bail, upon the chief officer of police immediately informing the court that he intended to make an application to the court to state a case for the opinion of the High Court, shall forthwith send a copy of that order to the Administrative Court Office.

[Formerly rule 3 of the Magistrates' Courts (Backing of Warrants) Rules 1965. This rule has effect only in proceedings where the request for extradition was received by the relevant authority in the United Kingdom on or before 31st December 2003.]

17.7   Delivery of warrant issued in Republic of Ireland

(1)   The court officer for a magistrates' court which ordered a person to be surrendered under section 2(1) of the Backing of Warrants (Republic of Ireland) Act 1965 shall deliver to, or send by post in a registered letter or by recorded delivery service addressed to –

(a)   if he is remanded in custody under section 5(1)(a) of the 1965 Act, the prison Governor to whose custody he is committed;

(b)   if he is remanded on bail under section 5(1)(b) of the 1965 Act, the police officer in charge of the police station specified in the recognizance; or

(c)   if he is committed to the custody of a constable pending the taking from him of a recognizance under section 5(1) of the 1965 Act, the police officer in charge of the police station specified in the warrant of commitment,

the warrant of arrest issued by a judicial authority in the Republic of Ireland and endorsed in accordance with section 1 of the 1965 Act.

(2)   The Governor or police officer to whom the said warrant of arrest is delivered or sent shall arrange for it to be given to the member of the police force of the Republic into whose custody the person is delivered when the person is so delivered.

[Formerly rule 4 of the Magistrates' Courts (Backing of Warrants) Rules 1965. This rule has effect only in proceedings where the request for extradition was received by the relevant authority in the United Kingdom on or before 31st December 2003.]

17.8   Verification of warrant etc. issued in Republic of Ireland

(1)   A document purporting to be a warrant issued by a judicial authority in the Republic of Ireland shall, for the purposes of section 7(a) of the Backing of Warrants (Republic of Ireland) Act 1965, be verified by a certificate purporting to be signed by a judicial authority, a clerk of a court or a member of the police force of the Republic and certifying that the document is a warrant and is issued by a judge or justice of a court or a peace commissioner.

(2)   A document purporting to be a copy of a summons issued by a judicial authority in the Republic shall, for the purposes of section 7(a) of the 1965 Act, be verified by a certificate purporting to be signed by a judicial authority, a clerk of a court or a member of the police force of the Republic and certifying that the document is a true copy of such a summons.

(3)   A deposition purporting to have been made in the Republic, or affidavit or written statement purporting to have been sworn therein, shall, for the purposes of section 7(c) of the 1965 Act, be verified by a certificate purporting to be signed by the person before whom it was sworn and certifying that it was so sworn.

[Formerly rule 5 of the Magistrates' Courts (Backing of Warrants) Rules 1965. This rule has effect only in proceedings where the request for extradition was received by the relevant authority in the United Kingdom on or before 31st December 2003.]

17.9   Application to state a case where court declines to order removal to Republic of Ireland

(1)   Where a magistrates' court refuses to make an order in relation to a person under section 2 of the Backing of Warrants (Republic of Ireland) Act 1965, any application to the court under section 2A(1) of that Act to state a case for the opinion of the High Court on any question of law arising in the proceedings must be made to the court by the chief officer of police within the period of 21 days following the day on which the order was refused, unless the court grants a longer period within which the application is to be made.

(2)   Such an application shall be made in writing and shall identify the question or questions of law on which the opinion of the High Court is sought.

[Formerly rule 5A of the Magistrates' Courts (Backing of Warrants) Rules 1965. This rule has effect only in proceedings where the request for extradition was received by the relevant authority in the United Kingdom on or before 31st December 2003.]

17.10   Draft case where court declines to order removal to Republic of Ireland

Within 21 days after receipt of an application to state a case under section 2A(1) of the Backing of Warrants (Republic of Ireland) Act 1965, the magistrates' court officer shall send a draft case to the applicant or his solicitor and to the person to whom the warrant relates or his solicitor and shall allow each party 21 days within which to make representations thereon; within 21 days after the latest day on which such representations may be made the court shall, after considering such representations and making such adjustments, if any, to the draft case as it thinks fit, state and sign the case which the court officer shall forthwith send to the applicant or his solicitor.

[Formerly rule 5B of the Magistrates' Courts (Backing of Warrants) Rules 1965. This rule has effect only in proceedings where the request for extradition was received by the relevant authority in the United Kingdom on or before 31st December 2003.]

17.11   Forms for proceedings for removal to Republic of Ireland

Where a requirement is imposed by the Backing of Warrants (Republic of Ireland) Act 1965 for the use of a form, and an appropriate form is contained in the Practice Direction, that form shall be used.

[*Formerly rule 1 of the Magistrates' Courts (Backing of Warrants) Rules 1965. This rule has effect only in proceedings where the request for extradition was received by the relevant authority in the United Kingdom on or before 31st December 2003.*]

PART 18   WARRANTS

18.1   Scope of this Part and interpretation

(1)   This Part applies to any warrant issued by a justice of the peace.

(2)   Where a rule applies to some of those warrants and not others, it says so.

(3)   In this Part, the "relevant person" is the person against whom the warrant is issued.

[*Note. For the rules governing the issue and execution of a search warrant, see sections 15 and 16 of the Police and Criminal Evidence Act 1984. For those governing warrants of distress (warrants to enforce payments of fines etc.), see rule 52.8.*]

18.2   Warrants must be signed

Every warrant under the Magistrates' Courts Act 1980 must be signed by the justice issuing it, unless rule 5.3 permits the justices' clerk to sign it.

18.3   Warrants issued when the court office is closed

(1)   If a warrant is issued when the court office is closed, the applicant must –

(a)   serve on the court officer any information on which that warrant is issued; and

(b)   do so within 72 hours of that warrant being issued.

(2)   In this rule, the court office is the office for the local justice area in which the justice is acting when he issues the warrant.

18.4   Commitment to custody must be by warrant

(1)   A justice of the peace must issue a warrant of commitment when committing a person to –

(a)   a prison;

(b)   a young offender institution;

(c)   a remand centre;

(d)   detention at a police station under section 128(7) of the Magistrates' Courts 1980 Act; or

(e)   customs detention under section 152 of the Criminal Justice Act 1988.

18.5   Terms of a warrant of arrest

A warrant of arrest must require the persons to whom it is directed to arrest the relevant person.

18.6   Terms of a warrant of commitment or detention: general rules

(1)   A warrant of commitment or detention must require –

(a)   the persons to whom it is directed to –

(i)   arrest the relevant person, if he is at large,

(ii)   take him to the prison or place specified in the warrant, and

        (iii)   deliver him with the warrant to the governor or keeper of that prison or place; and

    (b)   the governor or keeper to keep the relevant person in custody at that prison or place –

        (i)   for as long as the warrant requires, or
        (ii)   until he is delivered, in accordance with the law, to the court or other proper place or person.

(2) Where the justice issuing a warrant of commitment or detention is aware that the relevant person is already detained in a prison or other place of detention, the warrant must be delivered to the governor or keeper of that prison or place.

[*Note. Rule 18.6(1) does not apply to a warrant committing a person to customs detention under section 152 of the Criminal Justice Act 1988; see rule 18.7(2). Where rule 18.12 applies (place of detention), the relevant person may be taken to a prison or other place which is not specified in the warrant.*]

18.7   Terms of a warrant committing a person to customs detention

(1) A warrant committing a person to customs detention under section 152 of the 1988 Act must –

    (a)   be directed to the officers of Her Majesty's Revenue and Customs; and
    (b)   require those officers to keep the person committed in their custody, unless in the meantime he be otherwise delivered, in accordance with the law, to the court or other proper place or person, for a period (not exceeding 192 hours) specified in the warrant.

(2) Rules 18.6(1), 18.10 and 18.12 do not apply where this rule applies.

18.8   Form of warrant where male aged 15 or 16 is committed

(1) This rule applies where a male aged 15 or 16 years is remanded or committed to –

    (a)   local authority accommodation, with a requirement that he be placed and kept in secure accommodation;
    (b)   a remand centre; or
    (c)   a prison.

(2) The court must include in the warrant of commitment a statement of any declaration that is required in connection with that remand or committal.

[*Note. Section 23(4) of the Children and Young Persons Act 1969, as modified by section 98 of the Crime and Disorder Act 1998, allows a magistrates' court to remand or commit a boy, aged 15 or 16, to local authority secure accommodation, a remand centre or a prison in order to protect the public from serious harm. Section 23(4) of the 1969 Act requires the court to declare that the boy is one to whom section 23(5) of that Act, as modified by section 98(3) of the 1998 Act, applies (e.g. violent or sexual offence, history of absconding etc.).*]

18.9   Information to be included in a warrant

A warrant of arrest, commitment or detention must contain the following information –

    (a)   the name or a description of the relevant person; and
    (b)   either –

        (i)   a statement of the offence with which the relevant person is charged,
        (ii)   a statement of the offence of which the person to be committed or detained was convicted; or
        (iii)   any other ground on which the warrant is issued.

18.10   Persons who may execute a warrant

A warrant of arrest, commitment or detention may be executed by –

(a)   the persons to whom it is directed; or

(b)   by any of the following persons, whether or not it was directed to them –

   (i)   a constable for any police area in England and Wales, acting in his own police area, and

   (ii)   any person authorised under section 125A (civilian enforcement officers) or section 125B (approved enforcement agencies) of the Magistrates' Courts Act 1980.

[Note: This rule does not apply to a warrant committing a person to customs detention under section 152 of the Criminal Justice Act 1988; see rule 18.7(2).]

18.11   Making an arrest under a warrant

(1)   The person executing a warrant of arrest, commitment or detention must, when arresting the relevant person –

(a)   either –

   (i)   show the warrant (if he has it with him) to the relevant person, or

   (ii)   tell the relevant person where the warrant is and what arrangements can be made to let that person inspect it;

(b)   explain, in ordinary language, the charge and the reason for the arrest; and

(c)   (unless he is a constable in uniform) show documentary proof of his identity.

(2)   If the person executing the warrant is one of the persons referred to in rule 18.10(b)(ii) (civilian enforcement officers or approved enforcement agencies), he must also show the relevant person a written statement under section 125A(4) or section 125B(4) of the Magistrates' Courts Act 1980, as appropriate.

18.12   Place of detention

(1)   This rule applies to any warrant of commitment or detention.

(2)   The person executing the warrant is required to take the relevant person to the prison or place of detention specified in the warrant.

(3)   But where it is not immediately practicable to do so, or where there is some other good reason, the relevant person may be taken to any prison or place where he may be lawfully detained until such time when he can be taken to the prison or place specified in the warrant.

(4)   If (and for as long as) the relevant person is detained in a place other than the one specified in the warrant, the warrant will have effect as if it specified the place where he is in fact being detained.

(5)   The court must be kept informed of the prison or place where the relevant person is in fact being detained.

(6)   The governor or keeper of the prison or place, to which the relevant person is delivered, must give a receipt on delivery.

[Note. This rule does not apply to a warrant committing a person to customs detention under section 152 of the Criminal Justice Act 1988; see rule 18.7(2).]

18.13   Duration of detention where bail is granted subject to pre-release conditions

(1)   This rule applies where a magistrates' court –

(a)   grants bail to a person subject to conditions which must be met prior to release on bail; and

(b)   commits that person to custody until those conditions are satisfied.

(2)   The warrant of commitment must require the governor or keeper of the prison or place of detention to bring the relevant person to court either before or at the end of a period of 8 clear days from the date the warrant was issued, unless section 128(3A) or section 128A of the Magistrates' Courts Act 1980 applies to permit a longer period.

18.14   Validity of warrants that contain errors

A warrant of commitment or detention will not be invalidated on the ground that it contains an error, provided that the warrant –

  (a)   is issued in relation to a valid –

     (i)   conviction, or
     (ii)   order requiring the relevant person to do, or to abstain from doing, something; and

  (b)   it states that it is issued in relation to that conviction or order.

[*Note. Section 123 of the Magistrates' Courts Act 1980 applies in relation to any error in a warrant of arrest that is issued for the purpose of securing a person's attendance at court.*]

18.15   Circumstances in which a warrant will cease to have effect

(1)   A warrant issued under any of the provisions listed in paragraph (2) will cease to have effect when –

  (a)   the sum in respect of which the warrant is issued (together with the costs and charges of commitment, if any) is paid to the person who is executing the warrant;

  (b)   that sum is offered to, but refused by, the person who is executing the warrant; or

  (c)   a receipt for that sum given by –

     (i)   the court officer for the court which issued the warrant, or
     (ii)   the charging or billing authority,

     is produced to the person who is executing the warrant.

(2)   Those provisions are –

  (a)   section 76 (warrant to enforce fines and other sums);
  (b)   section 83(1) and (2) (warrant to secure attendance of offender for purposes of section 82);
  (c)   section 86(4) (warrant to arrest offender following failure to appear on day fixed for means inquiry);
  (d)   section 136 (committal to custody overnight at police station),

  of the Magistrates' Courts Act 1980.

(3)   No person may execute, or continue to execute, a warrant that ceases to have effect under this rule.

18.16   Warrant endorsed for bail (record to be kept)

A person executing a warrant of arrest that is endorsed for bail under section 117 of the Magistrates' Courts Act 1980 must –

  (a)   make a record stating –

     (i)   the name of the person arrested,
     (ii)   the charge and the reason for the arrest,
     (iii)   the fact that the person is to be released on bail,
     (iv)   the date, time and place at which the person is required to appear before the court, and
     (v)   any other details which he considers to be relevant; and

(b)   after making the record –

    (i)   sign the record,

    (ii)   invite the person arrested to sign the record and, if they refuse, make a note of that refusal on the record,

    (iii)   make a copy of the record and give it to the person arrested, and

    (iv)   send the original record to the court officer for the court which issued the warrant.

PART 19   BAIL IN MAGISTRATES' COURTS AND THE CROWN COURT

19.1   Application to a magistrates' court to vary conditions of police bail

(1) An application under section 43B(1) of the Magistrates' Courts Act of 1980 or section 47(1E) of the Police and Criminal Evidence Act 1984 shall –

(a)   be made in writing;

(b)   contain a statement of the grounds upon which it is made;

(c)   where the applicant has been bailed following charge, specify the offence with which he was charged and, in any other case, specify the offence under investigation;

(d)   specify, or be accompanied by a copy of the note of, the reasons given by the custody officer for imposing or varying the conditions of bail; and

(e)   specify the name and address of any surety provided by the applicant before his release on bail to secure his surrender to custody.

(2) Any such application shall be sent to the court officer for –

(a)   the magistrates' court appointed by the custody officer as the court before which the applicant has a duty to appear; or

(b)   if no such court has been appointed, a magistrates' court acting for the local justice area in which the police station at which the applicant was granted bail or at which the conditions of his bail were varied, as the case may be, is situated.

(3) The court officer to whom an application is sent under paragraph (2) above shall serve notice in writing of the date, time and place fixed for the hearing of the application on –

(a)   the applicant;

(b)   the prosecutor or, if the applicant has not been charged, the chief officer of police or other investigator, together with a copy of the application; and

(c)   any surety in connection with bail in criminal proceedings granted to, or the conditions of which were varied by a custody officer in relation to, the applicant.

(4) The time fixed for the hearing shall be not later than 72 hours after receipt of the application. In reckoning for the purposes of this paragraph any period of 72 hours, no account shall be taken of Christmas Day, Boxing Day, Good Friday, any bank holiday, or any Saturday or Sunday.

(5) [Revoked]

(6) If the magistrates' court hearing an application under section 43B(1) of the 1980 Act or section 47(1E) of the 1984 Act discharges or enlarges any recognizance entered into by any surety or increases or reduces the amount in which that person is bound, the court officer shall forthwith give notice thereof to the applicant and to any such surety.

(7) In this rule, "the applicant" means the person making an application under section 43B(1) of the 1980 Act or section 47(1E) of the 1984 Act.

[*Note. This rule derives in part from rule 84A of the Magistrates' Courts Rules 1981. See also section 43B of the Magistrates' Courts Act 1980 and section 47 of the Police and Criminal Evidence Act 1984.*]

19.2   Application to a magistrates' court to reconsider grant of police bail

(1) The appropriate court for the purposes of section 5B of the Bail Act 1976 in relation to the decision of a constable to grant bail shall be –

  (a)   the magistrates' court appointed by the custody officer as the court before which the person to whom bail was granted has a duty to appear; or

  (b)   if no such court has been appointed, a magistrates' court acting for the local justice area in which the police station at which bail was granted is situated.

(2) An application under section 5B(1) of the 1976 Act shall –

  (a)   be made in writing;

  (b)   contain a statement of the grounds on which it is made;

  (c)   specify the offence which the proceedings in which bail was granted were connected with, or for;

  (d)   specify the decision to be reconsidered (including any conditions of bail which have been imposed and why they have been imposed);

  (e)   specify the name and address of any surety provided by the person to whom the application relates to secure his surrender to custody; and

  (f)   contain notice of the powers available to the court under section 5B of the 1976 Act.

(3) The court officer to whom an application is sent under paragraph (2) above shall serve notice in writing of the date, time and place fixed for the hearing of the application on –

  (a)   the prosecutor who made the application;

  (b)   the person to whom bail was granted, together with a copy of the application; and

  (c)   any surety specified in the application.

(4) The time fixed for the hearing shall be not later than 72 hours after receipt of the application. In reckoning for the purpose of this paragraph any period of 72 hours, no account shall be taken of Christmas Day, Good Friday, any bank holiday or any Sunday.

(5) [Revoked]

(6) At the hearing of an application under section 5B of the 1976 Act the court shall consider any representations made by the person affected (whether in writing or orally) before taking any decision under that section with respect to him; and, where the person affected does not appear before the court, the court shall not take such a decision unless it is proved to the satisfaction of the court, on oath or in the manner set out by rule 4.2(1), that the notice required to be given under paragraph (3) of this rule was served on him before the hearing.

(7) Where the court proceeds in the absence of the person affected in accordance with paragraph (6) –

  (a)   if the decision of the court is to vary the conditions of bail or impose conditions in respect of bail which has been granted unconditionally, the court officer shall notify the person affected;

  (b)   if the decision of the court is to withhold bail, the order of the court under section 5B(5)(b) of the 1976 Act (surrender to custody) shall be signed by the justice issuing it or state his name and be authenticated by the signature of the clerk of the court.

(8) [Revoked]

[*This rule derives in part from rule 93B of the Magistrates' Courts Rules 1981. See also section 5B of the Bail Act 1976.*]

19.3   Notice of change of time for appearance before magistrates' court

Where –

(a)   a person has been granted bail under the Police and Criminal Evidence Act 1984 subject to a duty to appear before a magistrates' court and the court before which he is to appear appoints a later time at which he is to appear; or

(b)   a magistrates' court further remands a person on bail under section 129 of the Magistrates' Courts Act 1980 in his absence,

it shall give him and his sureties, if any, notice thereof.

[*Formerly rule 91 of the Magistrates' Courts Rules 1981.*]

19.4   Directions by a magistrates' court as to security, etc

Where a magistrates' court, under section 3(5) or (6) of the Bail Act 1976, imposes any requirement to be complied with before a person's release on bail, the court may give directions as to the manner in which and the person or persons before whom the requirement may be complied with.

[*Formerly rule 85 of the Magistrates' Courts Rules 1981. See also section 3 of the Bail Act 1976. As to the estreatment of recognizances in magistrates' courts on failure to surrender see section 120 of the Magistrates' Courts Act 1980. For the procedure where a defendant fails to surrender, see also direction I.13 in the Practice Direction.*]

19.5   Requirements to be complied with before release on bail granted by a magistrates' court

(1) Where a magistrates' court has fixed the amount in which a person (including any surety) is to be bound by a recognizance, the recognizance may be entered into –

(a)   in the case of a surety where the accused is in a prison or other place of detention, before the governor or keeper of the prison or place as well as before the persons mentioned in section 8(4)(a) of the Bail Act 1976;

(b)   in any other case, before a justice of the peace, a justices' clerk, a magistrates' court officer, a police officer who either is of the rank of inspector or above or is in charge of a police station or, if the person to be bound is in a prison or other place of detention, before the governor or keeper of the prison or place; or

(c)   where a person other than a police officer is authorised under section 125A or 125B of the Magistrates' Courts Act 1980 to execute a warrant of arrest providing for a recognizance to be entered into by the person arrested (but not by any other person), before the person executing the warrant.

(2) The court officer for a magistrates' court which has fixed the amount in which a person (including any surety) is to be bound by a recognizance or, under section 3(5), (6) or (6A) of the 1976 Act imposed any requirement to be complied with before a person's release on bail or any condition of bail shall issue a certificate showing the amount and conditions, if any, of the recognizance, or as the case may be, containing a statement of the requirement or condition of bail; and a person authorised to take the recognizance or do anything in relation to the compliance with such requirement or condition of bail shall not be required to take or do it without production of such a certificate as aforesaid.

(3) If any person proposed as a surety for a person committed to custody by a magistrates' court produces to the governor or keeper of the prison or other place of detention in which the person so committed is detained a certificate to the effect that he is acceptable as a surety, signed by any of the justices composing the court or the clerk of the court and signed in the margin by the person proposed as surety, the governor or keeper shall take the recognizance of the person so proposed.

(4) Where the recognizance of any person committed to custody by a magistrates' court or of any surety of such a person is taken by any person other than the court which committed the first-mentioned person to custody, the person taking the recognizance shall send it to the court officer for that court:

Provided that, in the case of a surety, if the person committed has been committed to the Crown Court for trial or under any of the enactments mentioned in rule 43.1(1), the person taking the recognizance shall send it to the Crown Court officer.

[Formerly rule 86 of the Magistrates' Courts Rules 1981.]

19.6   Notice to governor of prison, etc, where release from custody is ordered by a magistrates' court

Where a magistrates' court has, with a view to the release on bail of a person in custody, fixed the amount in which he or any surety of such a person shall be bound or, under section 3(5), (6) or (6A) of the Bail Act 1976, imposed any requirement to be complied with before his release or any condition of bail –

(a)   the magistrates' court officer shall give notice thereof to the governor or keeper of the prison or place where that person is detained by sending him such a certificate as is mentioned in rule 19.5(2); and

(b)   any person authorised to take the recognizance of a surety or do anything in relation to the compliance with such requirement shall, on taking or doing it, send notice thereof by post to the said governor or keeper and, in the case of a recognizance of a surety, shall give a copy of the notice to the surety.

[Formerly rule 87 of the Magistrates' Courts Rules 1981.]

19.7   Release when notice received by governor of prison that recognizances have been taken or requirements complied with

Where a magistrates' court has, with a view to the release on bail of a person in custody, fixed the amount in which he or any surety of such a person shall be bound or, under section 3(5) or (6) of the Bail Act 1976, imposed any requirement to be complied with before his release and given notice thereof in accordance with this Part to the governor or keeper of the prison or place where that person is detained, the governor or keeper shall, when satisfied that the recognizances of all sureties required have been taken and that all such requirements have been complied with, and unless he is in custody for some other cause, release him.

[Formerly rule 88 of the Magistrates' Courts Rules 1981.]

19.8   Notice from a magistrates' court of enlargement of recognizances

(1) If a magistrates' court before which any person is bound by a recognizance to appear enlarges the recognizance to a later time under section 129 of the Magistrates' Courts Act 1980 in his absence, it shall give him and his sureties, if any, notice thereof.

(2) If a magistrates' court, under section 129(4) of the 1980 Act, enlarges the recognizance of a surety for a person committed for trial on bail, it shall give the surety notice thereof.

[Formerly rule 84 of the Magistrates' Courts Rules 1981. See also section 129 of the Magistrates' Courts Act 1980.]

19.9   Further remand of minors by a youth court

Where a child or young person has been remanded, and the period of remand is extended in his absence in accordance with section 48 of the Children and Young Persons Act 1933, notice shall be given to him and his sureties (if any) of the date at which he will be required to appear before the court.

[Formerly rule 12 of the Magistrates' Courts (Children and Young Persons) Rules 1992.]

19.10   Notes of argument in magistrates' court bail hearings

Where a magistrates' court hears full argument as to bail, the clerk of the court shall take a note of that argument.

[Formerly rule 90A of the Magistrates' Courts Rules 1981.]

19.11   Bail records to be entered in register of magistrates' court

Any record required by section 5 of the Bail Act 1976 to be made by a magistrates' court (together with any note of reasons required by section 5(4) to be included and the particulars set out in any certificate granted under section 5(6A)) shall be made by way of an entry in the register.

[Formerly rule 90 of the Magistrates' Courts Rules 1981. See also section 5 of the Bail Act 1976. As to the general requirement to keep a register, see rule 6.1.]

19.12   Notification of bail decision by magistrate after arrest while on bail

Where a person who has been released on bail and is under a duty to surrender into the custody of a court is brought under section 7(4)(a) of the Bail Act 1976 before a justice of the peace, the justice shall cause a copy of the record made in pursuance of section 5 of that Act relating to his decision under section 7(5) of that Act in respect of that person to be sent to the court officer for that court:

Provided that this rule shall not apply where the court is a magistrates' court acting for the same local justice area as that for which the justice acts.

[Formerly rule 92 of the Magistrates' Courts Rules 1981. See also section 7 of the Bail Act 1976.]

19.13   Transfer of remand hearings

(1) Where a magistrates' court, under section 130(1) of the Magistrates' Courts Act 1980, orders that an accused who has been remanded in custody be brought up for any subsequent remands before an alternate magistrates' court, the court officer for the first-mentioned court shall, as soon as practicable after the making of the order and in any case within 2 days thereafter (not counting Sundays, Good Friday, Christmas Day or bank holidays), send to the court officer for the alternate court –

   (a)   a statement indicating the offence or offences charged;
   (b)   a copy of the record made by the first-mentioned court in pursuance of section 5 of the Bail Act 1976 relating to the withholding of bail in respect of the accused when he was last remanded in custody;
   (c)   a copy of any representation order previously made in the same case;
   (d)   a copy of any application for a representation order;
   (e)   if the first-mentioned court has made an order under section 8(2) of the 1980 Act (removal of restrictions on reports of committal proceedings), a statement to that effect.
   (f)   a statement indicating whether or not the accused has a solicitor acting for him in the case and has consented to the hearing and determination in his absence of any application for his remand on an adjournment of the case under sections 5, 10(1) and 18(4) of the 1980 Act together with a statement indicating whether or not that consent has been withdrawn;
   (g)   a statement indicating the occasions, if any, on which the accused has been remanded under section 128(3A) of the 1980 Act without being brought before the first-mentioned court; and
   (h)   if the first-mentioned court remands the accused under section 128A of the 1980 Act on the occasion upon which it makes the order under section 130(1) of that Act, a statement indicating the date set under section 128A(2) of that Act.

(2) Where the first-mentioned court is satisfied as mentioned in section 128(3A) of the 1980 Act, paragraph (1) shall have effect as if for the words "an accused who has been

remanded in custody be brought up for any subsequent remands before" there were substituted the words "applications for any subsequent remands of the accused be made to".

(3)   The court officer for an alternate magistrates' court before which an accused who has been remanded in custody is brought up for any subsequent remands in pursuance of an order made as aforesaid shall, as soon as practicable after the order ceases to be in force and in any case within 2 days thereafter (not counting Sundays, Good Friday, Christmas Day or bank holidays), send to the court officer for the magistrates' court which made the order –

(a)   a copy of the record made by the alternate court in pursuance of section 5 of the 1976 Act relating to the grant or withholding of bail in respect of the accused when he was last remanded in custody or on bail;

(b)   a copy of any representation order made by the alternate court;

(c)   a copy of any application for a representation order made to the alternate court;

(d)   if the alternate court has made an order under section 8(2) of the 1980 Act (removal of restrictions on reports of committal proceedings), a statement to that effect;

(e)   a statement indicating whether or not the accused has a solicitor acting for him in the case and has consented to the hearing and determination in his absence of any application for his remand on an adjournment of the case under sections 5, 10(1) and 18(4) of the 1980 Act together with a statement indicating whether or not that consent has been withdrawn; and

(f)   a statement indicating the occasions, if any, on which the accused has been remanded by the alternate court under section 128(3A) of the 1980 Act without being brought before that court.

(4)   Where the alternate court is satisfied as mentioned in section 128(3A) of the 1980 Act paragraph (2) above shall have effect as if for the words "an accused who has been remanded in custody is brought up for any subsequent remands" there shall be substituted the words "applications for the further remand of the accused are to be made".

[*Formerly rule 25 of the Magistrates' Court Rules 1981.*]

19.14   Notice of further remand in certain cases

Where a transfer direction has been given by the Secretary of State under section 47 of the Mental Health Act 1983 in respect of a person remanded in custody by a magistrates' court and the direction has not ceased to have effect, the court officer shall give notice in writing to the managers of the hospital where he is detained of any further remand under section 128 of the Magistrates' Courts Act 1980.

[*Formerly rule 26 of the Magistrates' Courts Rules 1981.*]

19.15   Cessation of transfer direction

Where a magistrates' court directs, under section 52(5) of the Mental Health Act 1983, that a transfer direction given by the Secretary of State under section 48 of that Act in respect of a person remanded in custody by a magistrates' court shall cease to have effect, the court officer shall give notice in writing of the court's direction to the managers of the hospital specified in the Secretary of State's direction and, where the period of remand has not expired or the person has been committed to the Crown Court for trial or to be otherwise dealt with, to the Governor of the prison to which persons of the sex of that person are committed by the court if remanded in custody or committed in custody for trial.

[*Formerly rule 110 of the Magistrates' Courts Rules 1981. As to the requirement to give notice to the prison governor and hospital authorities when a defendant subject to a transfer direction is transferred, committed or sent to the Crown Court for trial, see rules 11.3 and 19.20.*]

19.16   Lodging an appeal against a grant of bail by a magistrates' court

(1)   Where the prosecution wishes to exercise the right of appeal, under section 1 of the Bail (Amendment) Act 1993, to a judge of the Crown Court against a decision to grant bail, the oral notice of appeal must be given to the justices' clerk and to the person concerned, at the conclusion of the proceedings in which such bail was granted and before the release of the person concerned.

(2)   When oral notice of appeal is given, the justices' clerk shall announce in open court the time at which such notice was given.

(3)   A record of the prosecution's decision to appeal and the time the oral notice of appeal was given shall be made in the register and shall contain the particulars set out.

(4)   Where an oral notice of appeal has been given the court shall remand the person concerned in custody by a warrant of commitment.

(5)   On receipt of the written notice of appeal required by section 1(5) of the 1993 Act, the court shall remand the person concerned in custody by a warrant of commitment, until the appeal is determined or otherwise disposed of.

(6)   A record of the receipt of the written notice of appeal shall be made in the same manner as that of the oral notice of appeal under paragraph (3).

(7)   If, having given oral notice of appeal, the prosecution fails to serve a written notice of appeal within the two hour period referred to in section 1(5) of the 1993 Act the justices' clerk shall, as soon as practicable, by way of written notice (served by a court officer) to the persons in whose custody the person concerned is, direct the release of the person concerned on bail as granted by the magistrates' court and subject to any conditions which it imposed.

(8)   If the prosecution serves notice of abandonment of appeal on a court officer, the justices' clerk shall, forthwith, by way of written notice (served by the court officer) to the governor of the prison where the person concerned is being held, or the person responsible for any other establishment where such a person is being held, direct his release on bail as granted by the magistrates' court and subject to any conditions which it imposed.

(9)   A court officer shall record the prosecution's failure to serve a written notice of appeal, or its service of a notice of abandonment.

(10) Where a written notice of appeal has been served on a magistrates' court officer, he shall provide as soon as practicable to a Crown Court officer a copy of that written notice, together with –

    (a)   the notes of argument made by the court officer for the court under rule 19.10; and

    (b)   a note of the date, or dates, when the person concerned is next due to appear in the magistrates' court, whether he is released on bail or remanded in custody by the Crown Court.

(11) References in this rule to "the person concerned" are references to such a person within the meaning of section 1 of the 1993 Act.

[Formerly rule 93A of the Magistrates' Courts Rules 1981.]

19.17   Crown Court procedure on appeal against grant of bail by a magistrates' court

(1)   This rule shall apply where the prosecution appeals under section 1 of the Bail (Amendment) Act 1993 against a decision of a magistrates' court granting bail and in this rule, "the person concerned" has the same meaning as in that Act.

(2)   The written notice of appeal required by section 1(5) of the 1993 Act shall be in the form set out in the Practice Direction and shall be served on –

    (a)   the magistrates' court officer; and

    (b)   the person concerned.

(3) The Crown Court officer shall enter the appeal and give notice of the time and place of the hearing to –

    (a)   the prosecution;

    (b)   the person concerned or his legal representative; and

    (c)   the magistrates' court officer.

(4) The person concerned shall not be entitled to be present at the hearing of the appeal unless he is acting in person or, in any other case of an exceptional nature, a judge of the Crown Court is of the opinion that the interests of justice require him to be present and gives him leave to be so.

(5) Where a person concerned has not been able to instruct a solicitor to represent him at the appeal, he may give notice to the Crown Court requesting that the Official Solicitor shall represent him at the appeal, and the court may, if it thinks fit, assign the Official Solicitor to act for the person concerned accordingly.

(6) At any time after the service of written notice of appeal under paragraph (2), the prosecution may abandon the appeal by giving notice in writing in the form set out in the Practice Direction.

(7) The notice of abandonment required by the preceding paragraph shall be served on –

    (a)   the person concerned or his legal representative;

    (b)   the magistrates' court officer; and

    (c)   the Crown Court officer.

(8) Any record required by section 5 of the Bail Act 1976 (together with any note of reasons required by subsection (4) of that section to be included) shall be made by way of an entry in the file relating to the case in question and the record shall include the following particulars, namely –

    (a)   the effect of the decision;

    (b)   a statement of any condition imposed in respect of bail, indicating whether it is to be complied with before or after release on bail; and

    (c)   where bail is withheld, a statement of the relevant exception to the right to bail (as provided in Schedule 1 to the 1976 Act) on which the decision is based.

(9) The Crown Court officer shall, as soon as practicable after the hearing of the appeal, give notice of the decision and of the matters required by the preceding paragraph to be recorded to –

    (a)   the person concerned or his legal representative;

    (b)   the prosecution;

    (c)   the police;

    (d)   the magistrates' court officer; and

    (e)   the governor of the prison or person responsible for the establishment where the person concerned is being held.

(10) Where the judge hearing the appeal grants bail to the person concerned, the provisions of rule 19.18(9) (informing the Court of any earlier application for bail) and rule 19.22 (conditions attached to bail granted by the Crown Court) shall apply as if that person had applied to the Crown Court for bail.

(11) The notices required by paragraphs (3), (5), (7) and (9) of this rule may be served under rule 4.6 (service by fax, e-mail or other electronic means) and the notice required by paragraph (3) may be given by telephone.

[*This rule derives in part from rule 11A of the Crown Court Rules 1982.*]

19.18   Applications to Crown Court relating to bail

(1) This rule applies where an application to the Crown Court relating to bail is made otherwise than during the hearing of proceedings in the Crown Court.

(2) Subject to paragraph (7) below, notice in writing of intention to make such an

application to the Crown Court shall, at least 24 hours before it is made, be given to the prosecutor and if the prosecution is being carried on by the Crown Prosecution Service, to the appropriate Crown Prosecutor or, if the application is to be made by the prosecutor or a constable under section 3(8) of the Bail Act 1976, to the person to whom bail was granted.

(3) On receiving notice under paragraph (2), the prosecutor or appropriate Crown Public Prosecutor or, as the case may be, the person to whom bail was granted shall –

  (a)   notify the Crown Court officer and the applicant that he wishes to be represented at the hearing of the application;

  (b)   notify the Crown Court officer and the applicant that he does not oppose the application; or

  (c)   give to the Crown Court officer, for the consideration of the Crown Court, a written statement of his reasons for opposing the application, at the same time sending a copy of the statement to the applicant.

(4) A notice under paragraph (2) shall be in the form set out in the Practice Direction or a form to the like effect, and the applicant shall give a copy of the notice to the Crown Court officer.

(5) Except in the case of an application made by the prosecutor or a constable under section 3(8) of the 1976 Act, the applicant shall not be entitled to be present on the hearing of his application unless the Crown Court gives him leave to be present.

(6) Where a person who is in custody or has been released on bail desires to make an application relating to bail and has not been able to instruct a solicitor to apply on his behalf under the preceding paragraphs of this rule, he may give notice in writing to the Crown Court of his desire to make an application relating to bail, requesting that the Official Solicitor shall act for him in the application, and the Court may, if it thinks fit, assign the Official Solicitor to act for the applicant accordingly.

(7) Where the Official Solicitor has been so assigned the Crown Court may, if it thinks fit, dispense with the requirements of paragraph (2) and deal with the application in a summary manner.

(8) Any record required by section 5 of the 1976 Act (together with any note of reasons required by section 5(4) to be included) shall be made by way of an entry in the file relating to the case in question and the record shall include the following particulars, namely –

  (a)   the effect of the decision;

  (b)   a statement of any condition imposed in respect of bail, indicating whether it is to be complied with before or after release on bail;

  (c)   where conditions of bail are varied, a statement of the conditions as varied; and

  (d)   where bail is withheld, a statement of the relevant exception to the right to bail (as provided in Schedule 1 to the 1976 Act) on which the decision is based.

(9) Every person who makes an application to the Crown Court relating to bail shall inform the Court of any earlier application to the High Court or the Crown Court relating to bail in the course of the same proceedings.

[*Formerly rule 19 and paragraph (1) of rule 20 of the Crown Court Rules 1982. As to applications for bail before committal for trial see also direction V.53, and for bail during trial see also direction III.25, in the Practice Direction.*]

19.19   Notice to governor of prison of committal on bail

(1) Where the accused is committed or sent for trial on bail, a magistrates' court officer shall give notice thereof in writing to the governor of the prison to which persons of the sex of the person committed or sent are committed or sent by that court if committed or sent in custody for trial and also, if the person committed or sent is under 21, to the governor of the remand centre to which he would have been committed or sent if the court had refused him bail.

(2)   Where a corporation is committed or sent for trial, a magistrates' court officer shall give notice thereof to the governor of the prison to which would be committed or sent a man committed or sent by that court in custody for trial.

[Formerly rule 9 of the Magistrates' Courts Rules 1981. For the equivalent provision where a defendant is transferred for trial, see rule 11.2. On the coming into force of Schedule 3 to the Criminal Justice Act 2003 committal for trial will be abolished and cases triable either way will be sent to the Crown Court under sections 51 and 51A of the Crime and Disorder Act 1998 in the same way as cases triable only on indictment.]

19.20   Notices on committal of person subject to transfer direction

Where a transfer direction has been given by the Secretary of State under section 48 of the Mental Health Act 1983 in respect of a person remanded in custody by a magistrates' court and, before the direction ceases to have effect, that person is committed or sent for trial, a magistrates' court officer shall give notice –

(a)   to the governor of the prison to which persons of the sex of that person are committed or sent by that court if committed or sent in custody for trial; and

(b)   to the managers of the hospital where he is detained.

[Formerly rule 10 of the Magistrates' Courts Rules 1981. For the equivalent provision where a defendant is transferred for trial see rule 11.3. On the coming into force of Schedule 3 to the Criminal Justice Act 2003 committal for trial will be abolished and cases triable either way will be sent to the Crown Court under sections 51 and 51A of the Crime and Disorder Act 1998 in the same way as cases triable only on indictment.]

19.21   Variation of arrangements for bail on committal to Crown Court

Where a magistrates' court has committed or sent a person on bail to the Crown Court for trial or under any of the enactments mentioned in rule 43.1(1) and subsequently varies any conditions of the bail or imposes any conditions in respect of the bail, the magistrates' court officer shall send to the Crown Court officer a copy of the record made in pursuance of section 5 of the Bail Act 1976 relating to such variation or imposition of conditions.

[Formerly rule 93 of the Magistrates' Courts Rules 1981. See also section 5 of the Bail Act 1976. For the equivalent provision where a defendant is transferred to the Crown Court, see rule 11.4. On the coming into force of Schedule 3 to the Criminal Justice Act 2003 committal for trial will be abolished and cases triable either way will be sent to the Crown Court under sections 51 and 51A of the Crime and Disorder Act 1998 in the same way as cases triable only on indictment.]

19.22   Conditions attached to bail granted by the Crown Court

(1)   Where the Crown Court grants bail, the recognizance of any surety required as a condition of bail may be entered into before an officer of the Crown Court or, where the person who has been granted bail is in a prison or other place of detention, before the governor or keeper of the prison or place as well as before the persons specified in section 8(4) of the Bail Act 1976.

(2)   Where the Crown Court under section 3(5) or (6) of the 1976 Act imposes a requirement to be complied with before a person's release on bail, the Court may give directions as to the manner in which and the person or persons before whom the requirement may be complied with.

(3)   A person who, in pursuance of an order made by the Crown Court for the grant of bail, proposes to enter into a recognizance or give security must, unless the Crown Court otherwise directs, give notice to the prosecutor at least 24 hours before he enters into the recognizance or gives security as aforesaid.

(4)   Where, in pursuance of an order of the Crown Court, a recognizance is entered into or any requirement imposed under section 3(5) or (6) of the 1976 Act is complied with (being a requirement to be complied with before a person's release on bail) before any

person, it shall be his duty to cause the recognizance or, as the case may be, a statement of the requirement to be transmitted forthwith to the court officer; and a copy of the recognizance or statement shall at the same time be sent to the governor or keeper of the prison or other place of detention in which the person named in the order is detained, unless the recognizance was entered into or the requirement was complied with before such governor or keeper.

(5) Where, in pursuance of section 3(5) of the 1976 Act, security has been given in respect of a person granted bail with a duty to surrender to the custody of the Crown Court and either –

(a)   that person surrenders to the custody of the Court; or
(b)   that person having failed to surrender to the custody of the Court, the Court decides not to order the forfeiture of the security,

the court officer shall as soon as practicable give notice of the surrender to custody or, as the case may be, of the decision not to forfeit the security to the person before whom the security was given.

[*Formerly paragraphs (2), (3), (5), (6) and (7) of rule 20 of the Crown Court Rules 1982.*]

19.23   Estreat of recognizances in respect of person bailed to appear before the Crown Court

(1) Where a recognizance has been entered into in respect of a person granted bail to appear before the Crown Court and it appears to the Court that a default has been made in performing the conditions of the recognizance, other than by failing to appear before the Court in accordance with any such condition, the Court may order the recognizance to be estreated.

(2) Where the Crown Court is to consider making an order under paragraph (1) for a recognizance to be estreated, the court officer shall give notice to that effect to the person by whom the recognizance was entered into indicating the time and place at which the matter will be considered; and no such order shall be made before the expiry of 7 days after the notice required by this paragraph has been given.

[*Formerly rule 21 of the Crown Court Rules 1982. As to forfeiture of recognizances on failure to surrender, see rule 19.24.*]

19.24   Forfeiture of recognizances in respect of person bailed to appear before the Crown Court

(1) Where a recognizance is conditioned for the appearance of an accused before the Crown Court and the accused fails to appear in accordance with the condition, the Court shall declare the recognizance to be forfeited.

(2) Where the Crown Court declares a recognizance to be forfeited under paragraph (1), the court officer shall issue a summons to the person by whom the recognizance was entered into requiring him to appear before the Court at a time and place specified in the summons to show cause why the Court should not order the recognizance to be estreated.

(3) At the time specified in the summons the Court may proceed in the absence of the person by whom the recognizance was entered into if it is satisfied that he has been served with the summons.

[*Formerly rule 21A of the Crown Court Rules 1982. As to the estreat of recognizances on failure to comply with conditions of bail, see rule 19.23. For the procedure where a defendant fails to surrender see also direction I.13 in the Practice Direction.*]

PART 20   CUSTODY TIME LIMITS

20.1   Appeal to the Crown Court against a decision of a magistrates' court in respect of a custody time limit

(1) This rule applies –

(a)   to any appeal brought by an accused, under section 22(7) of the Prosecution of Offences Act 1985, against a decision of a magistrates' court to extend, or further extend, a custody time limit imposed by regulations made under section 22(1) of the 1985 Act; and

(b)   to any appeal brought by the prosecution, under section 22(8) of the 1985 Act, against a decision of a magistrates' court to refuse to extend, or further extend, such a time limit.

(2)   An appeal to which this rule applies shall be commenced by the appellant's giving notice in writing of appeal –

(a)   to the court officer for the magistrates' court which took the decision;

(b)   if the appeal is brought by the accused, to the prosecutor and, if the prosecution is to be carried on by the Crown Prosecution Service, to the appropriate Crown Prosecutor;

(c)   if the appeal is brought by the prosecution, to the accused; and

(d)   to the Crown Court officer.

(3)   The notice of an appeal to which this rule applies shall state the date on which the custody time limit applicable to the case is due to expire and, if the appeal is brought by the accused under section 22(7) of the 1985 Act, the date on which the custody time limit would have expired had the court decided not to extend or further extend that time limit.

(4)   On receiving notice of an appeal to which this rule applies, the Crown Court officer shall enter the appeal and give notice of the time and place of the hearing to –

(a)   the appellant;

(b)   the other party to the appeal; and

(c)   the court officer for the magistrates' court which took the decision.

(5)   Without prejudice to the power of the Crown Court to give leave for an appeal to be abandoned, an appellant may abandon an appeal to which this rule applies by giving notice in writing to any person to whom notice of the appeal was required to be given by paragraph (2) of this rule not later than the third day preceding the day fixed for the hearing of the appeal:

Provided that, for the purpose of determining whether notice was properly given in accordance with this paragraph, there shall be disregarded any Saturday and Sunday and any day which is specified to be a bank holiday in England and Wales under section 1(1) of the Banking and Financial Dealings Act 1971.

[*Formerly rule 27A of the Crown Court Rules 1982. See also section 22 of the Prosecution of Offences Act 1985, and for the procedure for applying for an extension of a custody time limit see the Prosecution of Offences (Custody Time Limits) Regulations 1987.*]

PART 21   ADVANCE INFORMATION

21.1   Scope of procedure for furnishing advance information

This Part applies in respect of proceedings against any person ("the accused") for an offence triable either way.

[*Formerly rule 2 of the Magistrates' Courts (Advance Information) Rules 1985.*]

21.2   Notice to accused regarding advance information

As soon as practicable after a person has been charged with an offence in proceedings in respect of which this Part applies or a summons has been served on a person in connection with such an offence, the prosecutor shall provide him with a notice in writing explaining the effect of rule 21.3 and setting out the address at which a request under that section may be made.

[Formerly rule 3 of the Magistrates' Courts (Advance Information) Rules 1985.]

21.3   Request for advance information

(1)   If, in any proceedings in respect of which this Part applies, either before the magistrates' court considers whether the offence appears to be more suitable for summary trial or trial on indictment or, where the accused has not attained the age of 18 years when he appears or is brought before a magistrates' court, before he is asked whether he pleads guilty or not guilty, the accused or a person representing the accused requests the prosecutor to furnish him with advance information, the prosecutor shall, subject to rule 21.4, furnish him as soon as practicable with either –

  (a)   a copy of those parts of every written statement which contain information as to the facts and matters of which the prosecutor proposes to adduce evidence in the proceedings; or

  (b)   a summary of the facts and matters of which the prosecutor proposes to adduce evidence in the proceedings.

(2)   In paragraph (1) above, "written statement" means a statement made by a person on whose evidence the prosecutor proposes to rely in the proceedings and, where such a person has made more than one written statement one of which contains information as to all the facts and matters in relation to which the prosecutor proposes to rely on the evidence of that person, only that statement is a written statement for purposes of paragraph (1) above.

(3)   Where in any part of a written statement or in a summary furnished under paragraph (1) above reference is made to a document on which the prosecutor proposes to rely, the prosecutor shall, subject to rule 21.4, when furnishing the part of the written statement or the summary, also furnish either a copy of the document or such information as may be necessary to enable the person making the request under paragraph (1) above to inspect the document or a copy thereof.

[Formerly rule 4 of the Magistrates' Courts (Advance Information) Rules 1985.]

21.4   Refusal of request for advance information

(1)   If the prosecutor is of the opinion that the disclosure of any particular fact or matter in compliance with the requirements imposed by rule 21.3 might lead to any person on whose evidence he proposes to rely in the proceedings being intimidated, to an attempt to intimidate him being made or otherwise to the course of justice being interfered with, he shall not be obliged to comply with those requirements in relation to that fact or matter.

(2)   Where, in accordance with paragraph (1) above, the prosecutor considers that he is not obliged to comply with the requirements imposed by rule 21.3 in relation to any particular fact or matter, he shall give notice in writing to the person who made the request under that section to the effect that certain advance information is being withheld by virtue of that paragraph.

[Formerly rule 5 of the Magistrates' Courts (Advance Information) Rules 1985.]

21.5   Duty of court regarding advance information

(1)   Subject to paragraph (2), where an accused appears or is brought before a magistrates' court in proceedings in respect of which this Part applies, the court shall, before it considers whether the offence appears to be more suitable for summary trial or trial on

indictment, satisfy itself that the accused is aware of the requirements which may be imposed on the prosecutor under rule 21.3.

(2) Where the accused has not attained the age of 18 years when he appears or is brought before a magistrates' court in proceedings in respect of which this rule applies, the court shall, before the accused is asked whether he pleads guilty or not guilty, satisfy itself that the accused is aware of the requirements which may be imposed on the prosecutor under rule 21.3.

[Formerly rule 6 of the Magistrates' Courts (Advance Information) Rules 1985.]

21.6   Adjournment pending furnishing of advance information

(1) If, in any proceedings in respect of which this Part applies, the court is satisfied that, a request under rule 21.3 having been made to the prosecutor by or on behalf of the accused, a requirement imposed on the prosecutor by that section has not been complied with, the court shall adjourn the proceedings pending compliance with the requirement unless the court is satisfied that the conduct of the case for the accused will not be substantially prejudiced by non-compliance with the requirement.

(2) Where, in the circumstances set out in paragraph (1) above, the court decides not to adjourn the proceedings, a record of that decision and of the reasons why the court was satisfied that the conduct of the case for the accused would not be substantially prejudiced by non-compliance with the requirement shall be entered in the register kept under rule 6.1.

[Formerly rule 7 of the Magistrates' Courts (Advance Information) Rules 1985.]

PART 22   DISCLOSURE BY THE PROSECUTION

[There are currently no rules in this Part. As to the duty of the prosecution to make initial disclosure see sections 3 and 4 of the Criminal Procedure and Investigations Act 1996. As to the continuing duty of disclosure see section 7A of the same Act.]

PART 23   DISCLOSURE BY THE DEFENCE

[There are currently no rules in this Part. As to the duty of the accused to make disclosure see sections 5 to 6E of the Criminal Procedure and Investigations Act 1996, and as to timing see the Criminal Procedure and Investigations Act 1996 (Defence Disclosure Time Limits) Regulations 1997.]

PART 24   DISCLOSURE OF EXPERT EVIDENCE

24.1   Requirement to disclose expert evidence

(1) Following –

(a)   a plea of not guilty by any person to an alleged offence in respect of which a magistrates' court proceeds to summary trial;

(b)   the committal for trial of any person;

(c)   the transfer to the Crown Court of any proceedings for the trial of a person by virtue of a notice of transfer given under section 4 of the Criminal Justice Act 1987;

(d)   the transfer to the Crown Court of any proceedings for the trial of a person by virtue of a notice of transfer served on a magistrates' court under section 53 of the Criminal Justice Act 1991;

(e)   the sending of any person for trial under section 51 of the Crime and Disorder Act 1998;

(f)   the preferring of a bill of indictment charging a person with an offence under the authority of section 2(2)(b) of the Administration of Justice (Miscellaneous Provisions) Act 1933; or

(g)   the making of an order for the retrial of any person,

if any party to the proceedings proposes to adduce expert evidence (whether of fact or opinion) in the proceedings (otherwise than in relation to sentence) he shall as soon as practicable, unless in relation to the evidence in question he has already done so or the evidence is the subject of an application for leave to adduce such evidence in accordance with section 41 of the Youth Justice and Criminal Evidence Act 1999 –

    (i)   furnish the other party or parties and the court with a statement in writing of any finding or opinion which he proposes to adduce by way of such evidence, and notify the expert of this disclosure, and

    (ii)   where a request in writing is made to him in that behalf by any other party, provide that party also with a copy of (or if it appears to the party proposing to adduce the evidence to be more practicable, a reasonable opportunity to examine) the record of any observation, test, calculation or other procedure on which such finding or opinion is based and any document or other thing or substance in respect of which any such procedure has been carried out.

(2)   A party may by notice in writing waive his right to be furnished with any of the matters mentioned in paragraph (1) and, in particular, may agree that the statement mentioned in paragraph (1)(a) may be furnished to him orally and not in writing.

(3)   In paragraph (1), "document" means anything in which information of any description is recorded.

[Formerly rule 3 of the Magistrates' Courts (Advance Notice of Expert Evidence) Rules 1997 and rule 3 of the Crown Court (Advance Notice of Expert Evidence) Rules 1987. For the equivalent requirement in Crown Court proceedings under Part 2 of the Proceeds of Crime Act 2002 see rule 57.9. Part 33 contains rules about the duties of an expert and the content of an expert's report.]

24.2   Withholding evidence

(1)   If a party has reasonable grounds for believing that the disclosure of any evidence in compliance with the requirements imposed by rule 24.1 might lead to the intimidation, or attempted intimidation, of any person on whose evidence he intends to rely in the proceedings, or otherwise to the course of justice being interfered with, he shall not be obliged to comply with those requirements in relation to that evidence.

(2)   Where, in accordance with paragraph (1), a party considers that he is not obliged to comply with the requirements imposed by rule 24.1 with regard to any evidence in relation to any other party, he shall give notice in writing to that party to the effect that the evidence is being withheld and the grounds for doing so.

[Formerly rule 4 of the Magistrates' Courts (Advance Notice of Expert Evidence) Rules 1997 and rule 4 of the Crown Court (Advance Notice of Expert Evidence) Rules 1987. For the equivalent exception in Crown Court proceedings under Part 2 of the Proceeds of Crime Act 2002 see rule 57.10.]

24.3   Effect of failure to disclose

A party who seeks to adduce expert evidence in any proceedings and who fails to comply with rule 24.1 shall not adduce that evidence in those proceedings without the leave of the court.

[Formerly rule 5 of the Magistrates' Courts (Advance Notice of Expert Evidence) Rules 1997 and rule 5 of the Crown Court (Advance Notice of Expert Evidence) Rules 1987.]

PART 25   APPLICATIONS FOR PUBLIC INTEREST IMMUNITY AND SPECIFIC DISCLOSURE

25.1   Public interest: application by prosecutor

(1)   This rule applies to the making of an application by the prosecutor under section 3(6), 7A(8) or 8(5) of the Criminal Procedure and Investigations Act 1996.

(2)   Notice of such an application shall be served on the court officer and shall specify the nature of the material to which the application relates.

(3)   Subject to paragraphs (4) and (5) below, a copy of the notice of application shall be served on the accused by the prosecutor.

(4)   Where the prosecutor has reason to believe that to reveal to the accused the nature of the material to which the application relates would have the effect of disclosing that which the prosecutor contends should not in the public interest be disclosed, paragraph (3) above shall not apply but the prosecutor shall notify the accused that an application to which this rule applies has been made.

(5)   Where the prosecutor has reason to believe that to reveal to the accused the fact that an application is being made would have the effect of disclosing that which the prosecutor contends should not in the public interest be disclosed, paragraph (3) above shall not apply.

(6)   Where an application is made in the Crown Court to which paragraph (5) above applies, notice of the application may be served on the trial judge or, if the application is made before the start of the trial, on the judge, if any, who has been designated to conduct the trial instead of on the court officer.

[*Formerly rule 2 of the Magistrates' Courts (Criminal Procedure and Investigations Act 1996) (Disclosure) Rules 1997 and rule 2 of the Crown Court (Criminal Procedure and Investigations Act 1996) (Disclosure) Rules 1997.*]

25.2   Public interest: hearing of application by prosecutor

(1)   This rule applies to the hearing of an application by the prosecutor under section 3(6), 7A(8) or 8(5) of the Criminal Procedure and Investigations Act 1996.

(2)   Where notice of such an application is served on the Crown Court officer, the officer shall on receiving it refer it –

(a)   if the trial has started, to the trial judge; or

(b)   if the application is received before the start of the trial either –

(i)   to the judge who has been designated to conduct the trial, or

(ii)   if no judge has been designated for that purpose, to such judge as may be designated for the purposes of hearing the application.

(3)   Where such an application is made and a copy of the notice of application has been served on the accused in accordance with rule 25.1(3), then subject to paragraphs (4) and (5) below –

(a)   the court officer shall on receiving notice of the application give notice to –

(i)   the prosecutor,

(ii)   the accused, and

(iii)   any person claiming to have an interest in the material to which the application relates who has applied under section 16(b) of the 1996 Act to be heard by the court,

of the date and time when and the place where the hearing will take place and, unless the court orders otherwise, such notice shall be given in writing;

(b)   the hearing shall be inter partes; and

(c)   the prosecutor and the accused shall be entitled to make representations to the court.

(4)   Where the prosecutor applies to the court for leave to make representations in the absence of the accused, the court may for that purpose sit in the absence of the accused and any legal representative of his.

(5)   Subject to rule 25.5(4) (interested party entitled to make representations), where a copy of the notice of application has not been served on the accused in accordance with rule 25.1(3) –

(a)   the hearing shall be ex parte;

(b)   only the prosecutor shall be entitled to make representations to the court;

(c)   the accused shall not be given notice as specified in paragraph (3)(a)(ii) of this rule; and

(d)   where notice of the application has been served in the Crown Court in pursuance of rule 25.1(6), the judge on whom it is served shall take such steps as he considers appropriate to ensure that notice is given as required by paragraph (3)(a)(i) and (iii) of this rule.

[*Formerly rule 3 of the Magistrates' Courts (Criminal Procedure and Investigations Act 1996) (Disclosure) Rules 1997 and rule 3 of the Crown Court (Criminal Procedure and Investigations Act 1996) (Disclosure) Rules 1997.*]

25.3   Public interest: non-disclosure order

(1)   This rule applies to an order under section 3(6), 7A(8) or 8(5) of the Criminal Procedure and Investigations Act 1996.

(2)   On making an order to which this rule applies, the court shall state its reasons for doing so. Where such an order is made in the Crown Court, a record shall be made of the statement of the court's reasons.

(3)   In a case where such an order is made following –

(a)   an application to which rule 25.1(4) (nature of material not to be revealed) applies; or

(b)   an application notice of which has been served on the accused in accordance with rule 25.1(3) but the accused has not appeared or been represented at the hearing of that application,

the court officer shall notify the accused that an order has been made. No notification shall be given in a case where an order is made following an application to which rule 25.1(5) (fact of application not to be revealed) applies.

[*Formerly rule 4 of the Magistrates' Courts (Criminal Procedure and Investigations Act 1996) (Disclosure) Rules 1997 and rule 4 of the Crown Court (Criminal Procedure and Investigations Act 1996) (Disclosure) Rules 1997.*]

25.4   Review of non-disclosure order: application by accused

(1)   This rule applies to an application by the accused under section 14(2) or section 15(4) of the Criminal Procedure and Investigations Act 1996.

(2)   Such an application shall be made by notice in writing to the court officer for the court that made the order under section 3(6), 7A(8) or 8(5) of the 1996 Act and shall specify the reason why the accused believes the court should review the question whether it is still not in the public interest to disclose the material affected by the order.

(3)   A copy of the notice referred to in paragraph (2) shall be served on the prosecutor at the same time as it is sent to the court officer.

(4)   Where such an application is made in a magistrates' court, the court officer shall take such steps as he thinks fit to ensure that the court has before it any document or other material which was available to the court which made the order mentioned in section 14(2) of the 1996 Act.

(5)   Where such an application is made in the Crown Court, the court officer shall refer it –

(a)   if the trial has started, to the trial judge; or

(b)   if the application is received before the start of the trial either –

  (i)   to the judge who has been designated to conduct the trial, or

  (ii)   if no judge has been designated for that purpose, to the judge who made the order to which the application relates.

(6) The judge to whom such an application has been referred under paragraph (5) shall consider whether the application may be determined without a hearing and, subject to paragraph (7), may so determine it if he thinks fit.

(7) No application to which this rule applies shall be determined by the Crown Court without a hearing if it appears to the judge that there are grounds on which the court might conclude that it is in the public interest to disclose material to any extent.

(8) Where a magistrates' court considers that there are no grounds on which it might conclude that it is in the public interest to disclose material to any extent it may determine an application to which this rule applies without hearing representations from the accused, the prosecutor or any person claiming to have an interest in the material to which the application relates.

(9) Subject to paragraphs (10) and (11) of this rule and to rule 25.5(4) (interested party entitled to make representations), the hearing of an application to which this rule applies shall be inter partes and the accused and the prosecutor shall be entitled to make representations to the court.

(10) Where after hearing the accused's representations the prosecutor applies to the court for leave to make representations in the absence of the accused, the court may for that purpose sit in the absence of the accused and any legal representative of his.

(11) Subject to rule 25.5(4), where the order to which the application relates was made following an application of which the accused was not notified under rule 25.1(3) or (4), the hearing shall be ex parte and only the prosecutor shall be entitled to make representations to the court.

(12) The court officer shall give notice in writing to –

(a)   the prosecutor;

(b)   except where a hearing takes place in accordance with paragraph (11), the accused; and

(c)   any person claiming to have an interest in the material to which the application relates who has applied under section 16(b) of the 1996 Act to be heard by the court,

of the date and time when and the place where the hearing of an application to which this rule applies will take place and of any order which is made by the court following its determination of the application.

(13) Where such an application is determined without a hearing in pursuance of paragraph (6), the court officer shall give notice in writing in accordance with paragraph (12) of any order which is made by the judge following his determination of the application.

[*Formerly rule 5 of the Magistrates' Courts (Criminal Procedure and Investigations Act 1996) (Disclosure) Rules 1997 and rule 5 of the Crown Court (Criminal Procedure and Investigations Act 1996) (Disclosure) Rules 1997.*]

25.5   Public interest applications: interested persons

(1) Where the prosecutor has reason to believe that a person who was involved (whether alone or with others and whether directly or indirectly) in the prosecutor's attention being brought to any material to which an application under section 3(6), 7A(8), 8(5), 14(2) or 15(4) of the Criminal Procedure and Investigations Act 1996 relates may claim to have an interest in that material, the prosecutor shall –

(a)   in the case of an application under section 3(6), 7A(8) or 8(5) of the 1996 Act, at the same time as notice of the application is served under rule 25.1(2) or (6); or

(b)   in the case of an application under section 14(2) or 15(4) of the 1996 Act, when he receives a copy of the notice referred to in rule 25.4(2),

give notice in writing to –

(i)   the person concerned of the application, and
(ii)   the court officer or, as the case may require, the judge of his belief and the grounds for it.

(2)   An application under section 16(b) of the 1996 Act shall be made by notice in writing to the court officer or, as the case may require, the judge as soon as is reasonably practicable after receipt of notice under paragraph (1)(i) above or, if no such notice is received, after the person concerned becomes aware of the application referred to in that sub-paragraph and shall specify the nature of the applicant's interest in the material and his involvement in bringing the material to the prosecutor's attention.

(3)   A copy of the notice referred to in paragraph (2) shall be served on the prosecutor at the same time as it is sent to the court officer or the judge as the case may require.

(4)   At the hearing of an application under section 3(6), 7A(8), 8(5), 14(2) or 15(4) of the 1996 Act a person who has made an application under section 16(b) in accordance with paragraph (2) of this rule shall be entitled to make representations to the court.

[*Formerly rule 6 of the Magistrates' Courts (Criminal Procedure and Investigations Act 1996) (Disclosure) Rules 1997 and rule 6 of the Crown Court (Criminal Procedure and Investigations Act 1996) (Disclosure) Rules 1997.*]

25.6   Disclosure: application by accused and order of court

(1)   This rule applies to an application by the accused under section 8(2) of the Criminal Procedure and Investigations Act 1996.

(2)   Such an application shall be made by notice in writing to the court officer and shall specify –

(a)   the material to which the application relates;
(b)   that the material has not been disclosed to the accused;
(c)   the reason why the material might be expected to assist the applicant's defence as disclosed by the defence statement given under section 5 or 6 of the 1996 Act; and
(d)   the date of service of a copy of the notice on the prosecutor in accordance with paragraph (3).

(3)   A copy of the notice referred to in paragraph (2) shall be served on the prosecutor at the same time as it is sent to the court officer.

(4)   Where such an application is made in the Crown Court, the court officer shall refer it –

(a)   if the trial has started, to the trial judge, or
(b)   if the application is received before the start of the trial –

(i)   to the judge who has been designated to conduct the trial, or
(ii)   if no judge has been designated for that purpose, to such judge as may be designated for the purposes of determining the application.

(5)   A prosecutor receiving notice under paragraph (3) of an application to which this rule applies shall give notice in writing to the court officer within 14 days of service of the notice that –

(a)   he wishes to make representations to the court concerning the material to which the application relates; or
(b)   if he does not so wish, that he is willing to disclose that material,

and a notice under paragraph 5(a) shall specify the substance of the representations he wishes to make.

(6) A court may determine an application to which this rule applies without hearing representations from the applicant or the prosecutor unless –

    (a)   the prosecutor has given notice under paragraph (5)(a) and the court considers that the representations should be made at a hearing; or

    (b)   the court considers it necessary to hear representations from the applicant or the prosecutor in the interests of justice for the purposes of determining the application.

(7) Subject to paragraph (8), where a hearing is held in pursuance of this rule –

    (a)   the court officer shall give notice in writing to the prosecutor and the applicant of the date and time when and the place where the hearing will take place;

    (b)   the hearing shall be inter partes; and

    (c)   the prosecutor and the applicant shall be entitled to make representations to the court.

(8) Where the prosecutor applies to the court for leave to make representations in the absence of the accused, the court may for that purpose sit in the absence of the accused and any legal representative of his.

(9) A copy of any order under section 8(2) of the 1996 Act shall be served on the prosecutor and the applicant.

[Formerly rule 7 of the Magistrates' Courts (Criminal Procedure and Investigations Act 1996) (Disclosure) Rules 1997 and rule 7 of the Crown Court (Criminal Procedure and Investigations Act 1996) (Disclosure) Rules 1997.]

25.7   Disclosure: application for extension of time limit and order of the court

(1) This rule applies to an application under regulation 3(2) of the Criminal Procedure and Investigations Act 1996 (Defence Disclosure Time Limits) Regulations 1997, including that regulation as applied by regulation 4(2).

(2) An application to which this rule applies shall be made by notice in writing to the court officer and shall, in addition to the matters referred to in regulation 3(3)(a) to (c) of the 1997 Regulations, specify the date of service of a copy of the notice on the prosecutor in accordance with paragraph (3) of this rule.

(3) A copy of the notice referred to in paragraph (2) of this rule shall be served on the prosecutor at the same time as it is sent to the court officer.

(4) The prosecutor may make representations to the court concerning the application and if he wishes to do so he shall do so in writing within 14 days of service of a notice under paragraph (3) of this rule.

(5) On receipt of representations under paragraph (4) above, or on the expiration of the period specified in that paragraph if no such representations are received within that period, the court shall consider the application and may, if it wishes, do so at a hearing.

(6) Where a hearing is held in pursuance of this rule –

    (a)   the court officer shall give notice in writing to the prosecutor and the applicant of the date and time when and the place where the hearing will take place;

    (b)   the hearing shall be inter partes; and

    (c)   the prosecutor and the applicant shall be entitled to make representations to the court.

(7) A copy of any order under regulation 3(1) or 4(1) of the 1997 Regulations shall be served on the prosecutor and the applicant.

[Formerly rule 8 of the Magistrates' Courts (Criminal Procedure and Investigations Act 1996) (Disclosure) Rules 1997 and rule 8 of the Crown Court (Criminal Procedure and Investigations Act 1996) (Disclosure) Rules 1997.]

25.8   Public interest and disclosure applications: general

(1) Any hearing held under this Part may be adjourned from time to time.

(2) Any hearing referred to in paragraph (1) other than one held under rule 25.7 may be held in private.

(3) Where a Crown Court hearing, or any part thereof, is held in private under paragraph (2), the court may specify conditions subject to which the record of its statement of reasons made in pursuance of rule 25.3(2) is to be kept.

(4) Where an application or order to which any provision of this rule applies is made after the start of a trial in the Crown Court, the trial judge may direct that any provision of this rule requiring notice of the application or order to be given to any person shall not have effect and may give such direction as to the giving of notice in relation to that application or order as he thinks fit.

[Formerly rule 9 of the Magistrates' Courts (Criminal Procedure and Investigations Act 1996) (Disclosure) Rules 1997 and rule 9 of the Crown Court (Criminal Procedure and Investigations Act 1996) (Disclosure) Rules 1997.]

PART 26   CONFIDENTIAL MATERIAL

26.1   Application for permission to use or disclose object or information

(1) This rule applies to an application under section 17(4) of the Criminal Procedure and Investigations Act 1996.

(2) Such an application shall be made by notice in writing to the court officer for the court which conducted or is conducting the proceedings for whose purposes the applicant was given, or allowed to inspect, the object to which the application relates.

(3) The notice of application shall –

(a)   specify the object which the applicant seeks to use or disclose and the proceedings for whose purposes he was given, or allowed to inspect, it;

(b)   where the applicant seeks to use or disclose any information recorded in the object specified in pursuance of paragraph (3)(a), specify that information;

(c)   specify the reason why the applicant seeks permission to use or disclose the object specified in pursuance of paragraph (3)(a) or any information specified in pursuance of paragraph (3)(b);

(d)   describe any proceedings in connection with which the applicant seeks to use or disclose the object or information referred to in paragraph (3)(c); and

(e)   specify the name and address of any person to whom the applicant seeks to disclose the object or information referred to in paragraph (3)(c).

(4) Where the court officer receives an application to which this rule applies, the court officer or the clerk of the magistrates' court shall fix a date and time for the hearing of the application.

(5) The court officer shall give the applicant and the prosecutor at least 28 days' notice of the date fixed in pursuance of paragraph (4) and shall at the same time send to the prosecutor a copy of the notice given to him in pursuance of paragraph (2).

(6) Where the prosecutor has reason to believe that a person may claim to have an interest in the object specified in a notice of application in pursuance of paragraph (3)(a), or in any information so specified in pursuance of paragraph (3)(b), he shall, as soon as reasonably practicable after receipt of a copy of that notice under paragraph (5), send a copy of the notice to that person and inform him of the date fixed in pursuance of paragraph (4).

[Formerly rule 2 of the Magistrates' Courts (Criminal Procedure and Investigations Act 1996) (Confidentiality) Rules 1997 and rule 2 of the Crown Court (Criminal Procedure and Investigations Act 1996) (Confidentiality) Rules 1997.]

26.2   Prosecutor or interested party wishing to be heard

(1) This rule applies to an application under section 17(6)(b) of the Criminal Procedure and Investigations Act 1996.

(2) An application to which this rule applies shall be made by notice in writing to the court officer of the court referred to in rule 26.1(2) not less than 7 days before the date fixed in pursuance of rule 26.1(4).

(3) The applicant shall at the same time send to the person whose application under section 17(4) of the 1996 Act is concerned a copy of the notice given in pursuance of paragraph (2).

[Formerly rule 3 of the Magistrates' Courts (Criminal Procedure and Investigations Act 1996) (Confidentiality) Rules 1997 and rule 3 of the Crown Court (Criminal Procedure and Investigations Act 1996) (Confidentiality) Rules 1997.]

26.3   Decision on application for use or disclosure

(1) Where no application to which rule 26.2 applies is made in accordance with paragraph (2) of that rule, the court shall consider whether the application under section 17(4) of the Criminal Procedure and Investigations Act 1996 may be determined without hearing representations from the accused, the prosecutor or any person claiming to have an interest in the object or information to which the application relates, and may so determine it if the court thinks fit.

(2) Where an application to which rule 26.1 applies is determined without hearing any such representations the court officer shall give notice in writing to the person who made the application and to the prosecutor of any order made under section 17(4) of the 1996 Act or, as the case may be, that no such order has been made.

[Formerly rule 4 of the Magistrates' Courts (Criminal Procedure and Investigations Act 1996) (Confidentiality) Rules 1997 and rule 4 of the Crown Court (Criminal Procedure and Investigations Act 1996) (Confidentiality) Rules 1997.]

26.4   Unauthorised use or disclosure

(1) This rule applies to proceedings to deal with a contempt of court under section 18 of the Criminal Procedure and Investigations Act 1996.

(2) In such proceedings before a magistrates' court the Magistrates' Courts Act 1980 shall have effect subject to the modifications contained in paragraphs (3) to (7) (being provisions equivalent to those in Schedule 3 to the Contempt of Court Act 1981 subject to modifications which the Lord Chancellor considered appropriate after consultation with the rule committee for magistrates' courts).

(3) Where proceedings to which this rule applies are taken of the court's own motion the provisions of the 1980 Act listed in paragraph (4) shall apply as if a complaint had been made against the person against whom the proceedings are taken and subject to the modifications specified in paragraphs (5) and (6).

(4) The provisions referred to in paragraph (3) are –

  (a)   section 51 (issue of summons);
  (b)   section 53(1) and (2) (procedure on hearing);
  (c)   section 54 (adjournment);
  (d)   section 55 (non-appearance of defendant);
  (e)   section 97(1) (summons to witness);
  (f)   section 101 (onus of proving exceptions etc);
  (g)   section 121(1) and (3)(a) (constitution and place of sitting of court); and
  (h)   section 123 (defect in process).

(5) In –

  (a)   section 55(1) for the words "the complainant appears but the defendant does not" there shall be substituted the words "the defendant does not appear"; and
  (b)   section 55(2) the words "if the complaint has been substantiated on oath, and" shall be omitted.

(6) In section 123(1) and (2) the words "adduced on behalf of the prosecutor or complainant" shall be omitted.

(7) Where proceedings to which this rule applies are taken by way of complaint for an order –

    (a)   section 127 of the 1980 Act (limitation of time) shall not apply to the complaint;

    (b)   the complaint may be made by the prosecutor or by any other person claiming to have an interest in the object, or in any information recorded in an object, the use or disclosure of which is alleged to contravene section 17 of the 1996 Act; and

    (c)   the complaint shall be made to the magistrates' court officer for the magistrates' court which conducted or is conducting the proceedings for whose purposes the object mentioned in paragraph (7)(b) was given or inspected.

(8) An application to the Crown Court for an order of committal or for the imposition of a fine in proceedings to which this rule applies may be made by the prosecutor or by any other person claiming to have an interest in the object, or in any information recorded in an object, the use or disclosure of which is alleged to contravene section 17 of the 1996 Act. Such an application shall be made in accordance with paragraphs (9) to (20).

(9) An application such as is referred to in paragraph (8) shall be made by notice in writing to the court officer at the same place as that in which the Crown Court sat or is sitting to conduct the proceedings for whose purposes the object mentioned in paragraph (2) was given or inspected.

(10) The notice referred to in paragraph (9) shall set out the name and a description of the applicant, the name, description and address of the person sought to be committed or fined and the grounds on which his committal or the imposition of a fine is sought and shall be supported by an affidavit verifying the facts.

(11) Subject to paragraph (12), the notice referred to in paragraph (9), accompanied by a copy of the affidavit in support of the application, shall be served personally on the person sought to be committed or fined.

(12) The court may dispense with service of the notice under this rule if it is of the opinion that it is necessary to do so in order to protect the applicant or for another purpose identified by the court.

(13) Nothing in the foregoing provisions of this rule shall be taken as affecting the power of the Crown Court to make an order of committal or impose a fine of its own motion against a person guilty of a contempt under section 18 of the 1996 Act.

(14) Subject to paragraph (15), proceedings to which this rule applies shall be heard in open court.

(15) Proceedings to which this rule applies may be heard in private where –

    (a)   the object, the use or disclosure of which is alleged to contravene section 17 of the 1996 Act, is; or

    (b)   the information, the use or disclosure of which is alleged to contravene that section, is recorded in,

an object which is, or forms part of, material in respect of which an application was made under section 3(6), 7A(8) or 8(5) of the 1996 Act, whether or not the court made an order that the material be not disclosed:

Provided that where the court hears the proceedings in private it shall nevertheless, if it commits any person to custody or imposes a fine on him in pursuance of section 18(3) of the 1996 Act, state in open court the name of that person, the period specified in the order of committal or, as the case may be, the amount of the fine imposed, or both such period and such amount where both are ordered.

(16) Except with the leave of the court hearing an application for an order of committal or for the imposition of a fine no grounds shall be relied upon at the hearing except the grounds set out in the notice referred to in paragraph (9).

(17) If on the hearing of the application the person sought to be committed or fined expresses a wish to give oral evidence on his own behalf, he shall be entitled to do so.

(18) The court by whom an order of committal is made may by order direct that the execution of the order of committal shall be suspended for such period or on such terms or conditions as it may specify.

(19) Where execution of an order of committal is suspended by an order under paragraph (18), the applicant for the order of committal must, unless the court otherwise directs, serve on the person against whom it was made a notice informing him of the making and terms of the order under that paragraph.

(20) The court may, on the application of any person committed to custody for a contempt under section 18 of the 1996 Act, discharge him.

[Formerly rule 5 of the Magistrates' Courts (Criminal Procedure and Investigations Act 1996) (Confidentiality) Rules 1997 and rule 5 of the Crown Court (Criminal Procedure and Investigations Act 1996) (Confidentiality) Rules 1997.]

26.5   Forfeiture of object used or disclosed without authority

(1) Where the Crown Court finds a person guilty of contempt under section 18 of the Criminal Procedure and Investigations Act 1996 and proposes to make an order under section 18(4) or (7), the court may adjourn the proceedings.

(2) Where the court adjourns the proceedings under paragraph (1), the court officer shall give notice to the person found guilty and to the prosecutor –

    (a) that the court proposes to make such an order and that, if an application is made in accordance with paragraph (5), it will before doing so hear any representations made by the person found guilty, or by any person in respect of whom the prosecutor gives notice to the court under paragraph (3); and

    (b) of the time and date of the adjourned hearing.

(3) Where the prosecutor has reason to believe that a person may claim to have an interest in the object which has been used or disclosed in contravention of section 17 of the 1996 Act he shall, on receipt of notice under paragraph (2), give notice of that person's name and address to the court office for the court which made the finding of guilt.

(4) Where the court officer receives a notice under paragraph (3), he shall, within 7 days of the finding of guilt, notify the person specified in that notice –

    (a) that the court has made a finding of guilt under section 18 of the 1996 Act, that it proposes to make an order under section 18(4) or, as the case may be, 18(7) and that, if an application is made in accordance with paragraph (5), it will before doing so hear any representations made by him; and

    (b) of the time and date of the adjourned hearing.

(5) An application under section 18(6) of the 1996 Act shall be made by notice in writing to the court officer not less than 24 hours before the time set for the adjourned hearing.

[Formerly rule 6 of the Crown Court (Criminal Procedure and Investigations Act 1996) (Confidentiality) Rules 1997.]

PART 27   WITNESS STATEMENTS

27.1   Witness statements in magistrates' courts

(1) Written statements to be tendered in evidence in accordance with section 5B of the Magistrates' Courts Act 1980 or section 9 of the Criminal Justice Act 1967 shall be in the form set out in the Practice Direction.

(2) When a copy of any of the following evidence, namely –

    (a) evidence tendered in accordance with section 5A of the 1980 Act (committal for trial); or

     (b)   a written statement tendered in evidence under section 9 of the 1967 Act (proceedings other than committal for trial),

is given to or served on any party to the proceedings a copy of the evidence in question shall be given to the court officer as soon as practicable thereafter, and where a copy of any such statement as is referred to in sub-paragraph (b) is given or served by or on behalf of the prosecutor, the accused shall be given notice by or on behalf of the prosecutor of his right to object to the statement being tendered in evidence.

(3) Where –

     (a)   a statement or deposition to be tendered in evidence in accordance with section 5A of the 1980 Act; or

     (b)   a written statement to be tendered in evidence under section 9 of the 1967 Act,

refers to any document or object as an exhibit, that document or object shall wherever possible be identified by means of a label or other mark of identification signed by the maker of the statement or deposition, and before a magistrates' court treats any document or object referred to as an exhibit in such a statement or deposition as an exhibit produced and identified in court by the maker of the statement or deposition, the court shall be satisfied that the document or object is sufficiently described in the statement or deposition for it to be identified.

(4) If it appears to a magistrates' court that any part of any evidence tendered in accordance with section 5A of the 1980 Act or a written statement tendered in evidence under section 9 of the 1967 Act is inadmissible there shall be written against that part –

     (a)   in the case of any evidence tendered in accordance with section 5A of the 1980 Act, but subject to paragraph (5) of this rule, the words "Treated as inadmissible" together with the signature and name of the examining justice or, where there is more than one examining justice, the signature and name of one of the examining justices by whom the evidence is so treated;

     (b)   in the case of a written statement tendered in evidence under section 9 of the 1967 Act the words "Ruled inadmissible" together with the signature and name of one of the justices who ruled the statement to be inadmissible.

(5) Where the nature of the evidence referred to in paragraph (4)(a) is such that it is not possible to write on it, the words set out in that sub-paragraph shall instead be written on a label or other mark of identification which clearly identifies the part of the evidence to which the words relate and contains the signature and name of an examining justice in accordance with that sub-paragraph.

(6) Where, before a magistrates' court –

     (a)   a statement or deposition is tendered in evidence in accordance with section 5A of the 1980 Act; or

     (b)   a written statement is tendered in accordance with section 9 of the 1967 Act,

the name of the maker of the statement or deposition shall be read aloud unless the court otherwise directs.

(7) Where –

     (a)   under section 5B(4), 5C(4), 5D(5) or 5E(3) of the 1980 Act; or

     (b)   under section 9(6) of the 1967 Act,

in any proceedings before a magistrates' court any part of the evidence has to be read out aloud, or an account has to be given orally of so much of any evidence as is not read out aloud, the evidence shall be read or the account given by or on behalf of the party which has tendered the evidence.

(8) Statements and depositions tendered in evidence in accordance with section 5A of the

1980 Act before a magistrates' court acting as examining justices shall be authenticated by a certificate signed by one of the examining justices.

(9) Where, before a magistrates' court –

(a)   evidence is tendered as indicated in paragraph (2)(a) of this rule, retained by the court, and not sent to the Crown Court under rule 10.5; or

(b)   a written statement is tendered in evidence as indicated in paragraph (2)(b) of this rule and not sent to the Crown Court under rule 43.1 or 43.2,

all such evidence shall, subject to any direction of the court in respect of non-documentary exhibits falling within paragraph (9)(a), be preserved for a period of three years by the magistrates' court officer for the magistrates' court.

[*Formerly rule 70 of the Magistrates' Courts Rules 1981. See also section 9 of the Criminal Justice Act 1967 and section 5A of the Magistrates' Courts Act 1980. On the editing of witness statements, see also direction III.24 in the Practice Direction.*]

27.2   Right to object to evidence being read in Crown Court trial

(1) The prosecutor shall, when he serves on any other party a copy of the evidence to be tendered in committal proceedings, notify that party that if he is committed for trial he has the right to object, by written notification to the prosecutor and the Crown Court within 14 days of being so committed unless the court in its discretion permits such an objection to be made outside that period, to a statement or deposition being read as evidence at the trial without oral evidence being given by the person who made the statement or deposition and without the opportunity to cross-examine that person.

(2) The prosecutor shall, on notifying a party as indicated in paragraph (1), send a copy of such notification to the magistrates' court officer.

(3) Any objection under paragraph 1(3)(c) or paragraph 2(3)(c) of Schedule 2 to the Criminal Procedure and Investigations Act 1996 to the reading out at the trial of a statement or deposition without further evidence shall be made in writing to the prosecutor and the Crown Court within 14 days of the accused being committed for trial unless the court at its discretion permits such an objection to be made outside that period.

[*Formerly rule 4B of the Magistrates' Courts Rules 1981 and rule 22 of the Crown Court Rules 1982. On the coming into force of Schedule 3 to the Criminal Justice Act 2003 committal for trial will be abolished and cases will be sent for trial under sections 51 and 51A of the Crime and Disorder Act 1998.*]

PART 28   WITNESS SUMMONSES, WARRANTS AND ORDERS

[*Note. The rules in this Part derive in part from those formerly contained in rule 107 of the Magistrates' Courts Rules 1981 and rules 23, 23ZA, 23ZB and 23ZC of the Crown Court Rules 1982.*

A magistrates' court may require the attendance of a witness to give evidence or to produce in evidence a document or thing by a summons, or in some circumstances a warrant for the witness' arrest, under section 97 of the Magistrates' Courts Act 1980. The Crown Court may do so under sections 2, 2D, 3 and 4 of the Criminal Procedure (Attendance of Witnesses) Act 1965. Either court may order the production in evidence of a copy of an entry in a banker's book without the attendance of an officer of the bank, under sections 6 and 7 of the Bankers' Books Evidence Act 1879.

See Part 3 for the court's general powers to consider an application and to give directions.]

28.1   When this Part applies

(1) This Part applies in magistrates' courts and in the Crown Court where –

(a)   a party wants the court to issue a witness summons, warrant or order under –

  (i)   section 97 of the Magistrates' Courts Act 1980,
  (ii)   section 2 of the Criminal Procedure (Attendance of Witnesses) Act 1965, or
  (iii) section 7 of the Bankers' Books Evidence Act 1879;

(b)   the court considers the issue of such a summons, warrant or order on its own initiative as if a party had applied; or

(c)   one of those listed in rule 28.7 wants the court to withdraw such a summons, warrant or order.

(2) A reference to a "witness" in this Part is a reference to a person to whom such a summons, warrant or order is directed.

[*Note. See section 2D of the Criminal Procedure (Attendance of Witnesses) Act 1965 for the Crown Court's power to issue a witness summons on the court's own initiative.*]

28.2   Issue etc. of summons, warrant or order with or without a hearing

(1) The court may issue or withdraw a witness summons, warrant or order with or without a hearing.
(2) A hearing under this Part must be in private unless the court otherwise directs.

[*Note. If rule 28.5 applies, a person served with an application for a witness summons will have an opportunity to make representations about whether there should be a hearing of that application before the witness summons is issued.*]

28.3   Application for summons, warrant or order: general rules

(1) A party who wants the court to issue a witness summons, warrant or order must apply as soon as practicable after becoming aware of the grounds for doing so.
(2) The party applying must –

(a)   identify the proposed witness;
(b)   explain –

  (i)   what evidence the proposed witness can give or produce,
  (ii)   why it is likely to be material evidence, and
  (iii) why it would be in the interests of justice to issue a summons, order or warrant as appropriate.

(2) The application may be made orally unless –

(a)   rule 28.5 applies; or
(b)   the court otherwise directs.

[*Note. The court may issue a warrant for a witness' arrest if that witness fails to obey a witness summons directed to him: see section 97(3) of the Magistrates' Courts Act 1980 and section 4 of the Criminal Procedure (Attendance of Witnesses) Act 1965. Before a magistrates' court may issue a warrant under section 97(3) of the 1980 Act the witness must first be paid or offered a reasonable amount for costs and expenses.*]

28.4   Written application: form and service

(1) An application in writing under rule 28.3 must be in the form set out in the Practice Direction, containing the same declaration of truth as a witness statement.
(2) The party applying must serve the application –

(a)   in every case, on the court officer and as directed by the court; and
(b)   as required by rule 28.5, if that rule applies.

[*Note. Declarations of truth in witness statements are required by section 9 of the Criminal Justice Act 1967 and section 5B of the Magistrates' Courts Act 1980. Section 89 of the 1967 Act makes it an offence to make a written statement under section 9 of that Act which the person making it knows to be false or does not believe to be true.*]

28.5   Application for summons to produce a document, etc.: special rules

(1)   This rule applies to an application under rule 28.3 for a witness summons requiring the proposed witness –

(a)   to produce in evidence a document or thing; or
(b)   to give evidence about information apparently held in confidence,

that relates to another person.

(2)   The application must be in writing in the form required by rule 28.4.
(3)   The party applying must serve the application –

(a)   on the proposed witness, unless the court otherwise directs; and
(b)   on one or more of the following, if the court so directs –

(i)   a person to whom the proposed evidence relates,
(ii)   another party.

(4)   The court must not issue a witness summons where this rule applies unless –

(a)   everyone served with the application has had at least 14 days in which to make representations, including representations about whether there should be a hearing of the application before the summons is issued; and
(b)   the court is satisfied that it has been able to take adequate account of the duties and rights, including rights of confidentiality, of the proposed witness and of any person to whom the proposed evidence relates.

(5)   This rule does not apply to an application for an order to produce in evidence a copy of an entry in a banker's book.

[*Note. Under section 2A of the Criminal Procedure (Attendance of Witnesses) Act 1965 a witness summons to produce a document or thing issued by the Crown Court may require the witness to produce it for inspection by the applicant before producing it in evidence.*]

28.6   Application for summons to produce a document, etc.: court's assessment of relevance and confidentiality

(1)   This rule applies where a person served with an application for a witness summons requiring the proposed witness to produce in evidence a document or thing objects to its production on the ground that –

(a)   it is not likely to be material evidence; or
(b)   even if it is likely to be material evidence, the duties or rights, including rights of confidentiality, of the proposed witness or of any person to whom the document or thing relates outweigh the reasons for issuing a summons.

(2)   The court may require the proposed witness to make the document or thing available for the objection to be assessed.
(3)   The court may invite –

(a)   the proposed witness or any representative of the proposed witness; or
(b)   a person to whom the document or thing relates or any representative of such a person,

to help the court assess the objection.

28.7   Application to withdraw a summons, warrant or order

(1)   The court may withdraw a witness summons, warrant or order if one of the following applies for it to be withdrawn –

(a)   the party who applied for it, on the ground that it no longer is needed;

(b)   the witness, on the grounds that –

      (i)   he was not aware of any application for it, and

      (ii)   he cannot give or produce evidence likely to be material evidence, or

      (iii)   even if he can, his duties or rights, including rights of confidentiality, or those of any person to whom the evidence relates outweigh the reasons for the issue of the summons, warrant or order; or

(c)   any person to whom the proposed evidence relates, on the grounds that –

      (i)   he was not aware of any application for it, and

      (ii)   that evidence is not likely to be material evidence, or

      (iii)   even if it is, his duties or rights, including rights of confidentiality, or those of the witness outweigh the reasons for the issue of the summons, warrant or order.

(2) A person applying under the rule must –

(a)   apply in writing as soon as practicable after becoming aware of the grounds for doing so, explaining why he wants the summons, warrant or order to be withdrawn; and

(b)   serve the application on the court officer and as appropriate on –

      (i)   the witness,

      (ii)   the party who applied for the summons, warrant or order, and

      (iii)   any other person who he knows was served with the application for the summons, warrant or order.

(3) Rule 28.6 applies to an application under this rule that concerns a document or thing to be produced in evidence.

[*Note. See sections 2B, 2C and 2E of the Criminal Procedure (Attendance of Witnesses) Act 1965 for the Crown Court's powers to withdraw a witness summons, including the power to order costs.*]

28.8   Court's power to vary requirements under this Part

(1) The court may –

(a)   shorten or extend (even after it has expired) a time limit under this Part; and

(b)   where a rule or direction requires an application under this Part to be in writing, allow that application to be made orally instead.

(2) Someone who wants the court to allow an application to be made orally under paragraph (1)(b) of this rule must –

(a)   give as much notice as the urgency of his application permits to those on whom he would otherwise have served an application in writing; and

(b)   in doing so explain the reasons for the application and for wanting the court to consider it orally.

PART 29   SPECIAL MEASURES DIRECTIONS

29.1   Application for special measures directions

(1) An application by a party in criminal proceedings for a magistrates' court or the Crown Court to give a special measures direction under section 19 of the Youth Justice and Criminal Evidence Act 1999 must be made in writing in the form set out in the Practice Direction.

(2) If the application is for a special measures direction –

(a)   enabling a witness to give evidence by means of a live link, the information sought in Part B of that form must be provided;

(b)   providing for any examination of a witness to be conducted through an intermediary, the information sought in Part C of that form must be provided; or

(c)   enabling a video recording of an interview of a witness to be admitted as evidence in chief of the witness, the information sought in Part D of that form must be provided.

(3) The application under paragraph (1) above must be sent to the court officer and at the same time a copy thereof must be sent by the applicant to every other party to the proceedings.

(4) The court officer must receive the application –

(a)   in the case of an application to a youth court, within 28 days of the date on which the defendant first appears or is brought before the court in connection with the offence;

(b)   in the case of an application to a magistrates' court, within 14 days of the defendant indicating his intention to plead not guilty to any charge brought against him and in relation to which a special measures direction may be sought; and

(c)   in the case of an application to the Crown Court, within 28 days of

(i)   the committal of the defendant, or

(ii)   the consent to the preferment of a bill of indictment in relation to the case, or

(iii)   the service of a notice of transfer under section 53 of the Criminal Justice Act 1991, or

(iv)   where a person is sent for trial under section 51 of the Crime and Disorder Act 1998, the service of copies of the documents containing the evidence on which the charge or charges are based under paragraph 1 of Schedule 3 to that Act, or

(v)   the service of a Notice of Appeal from a decision of a youth court or a magistrates' court.

(5) A party to whom an application is sent in accordance with paragraph (3) may oppose the application for a special measures direction in respect of any, or any particular, measure available in relation to the witness, whether or not the question whether the witness is eligible for assistance by virtue of section 16 or 17 of the 1999 Act is in issue.

(6) A party who wishes to oppose the application must, within 14 days of the date the application was served on him, notify the applicant and the court officer, as the case may be, in writing of his opposition and give reasons for it.

(7) Paragraphs (5) and (6) do not apply in respect of an application for a special measures direction enabling a child witness in need of special protection to give evidence by means of a live link if the opposition is that the special measures direction is not likely to maximise the quality of the witness's evidence.

(8) In order to comply with paragraph (6) –

(a)   a party must in the written notification state whether he –

(i)   disputes that the witness is eligible for assistance by virtue of section 16 or 17 of the 1999 Act,

(ii)   disputes that any of the special measures available would be likely to improve the quality of evidence given by the witness or that such measures (or a combination of them) would be likely to maximise the quality of that evidence, and

(iii)   opposes the granting of a special measures direction; and

(b)   where the application relates to the admission of a video recording, a party who receives a recording must provide the information required by rule 29.7(7) below.

(9) Except where notice is received in accordance with paragraph (6), the court (including, in the case of an application to a magistrates' court, a single justice of the peace) may –

(a)   determine the application in favour of the applicant without a hearing; or
(b)   direct a hearing.

(10) Where a party to the proceedings notifies the court in accordance with paragraph (6) of his opposition to the application, the justices' clerk or the Crown Court must direct a hearing of the application.

(11) Where a hearing of the application is to take place in accordance with paragraph (9) or (10) above, the court officer shall notify each party to the proceedings of the time and place of the hearing.

(12) A party notified in accordance with paragraph (11) may be present at the hearing and be heard.

(13) The court officer must, within 3 days of the decision of the court in relation to an application under paragraph (1) being made, notify all the parties of the decision, and if the application was made for a direction enabling a video recording of an interview of a witness to be admitted as evidence in chief of that witness, the notification must state whether the whole or specified parts only of the video recording or recordings disclosed are to be admitted in evidence.

(14) In this Part:

"an intermediary" has the same meaning as in section 29 of the 1999 Act; and

"child witness in need of protection" shall be construed in accordance with section 21(1) of the 1999 Act.

[*Formerly rules 1 and 2 of the Magistrates' Courts (Special Measures Directions) Rules 2002 and rules 1 and 2 of the Crown Court (Special Measures Directions and Directions Prohibiting Cross-examination) Rules 2002. See also chapter I of Part II of the Youth Justice and Criminal Evidence Act 1999.*]

29.2   Application for an extension of time

(1) An application may be made in writing for the period of 14 days or, as the case may be, 28 days specified in rule 29.1(4) to be extended.

(2) The application may be made either before or after that period has expired.

(3) The application must be accompanied by a statement setting out the reasons why the applicant is or was unable to make the application within that period and a copy of the application and the statement must be sent to every other party to the proceedings.

(4) An application for an extension of time under this rule shall be determined by a single justice of the peace or a judge of the Crown Court without a hearing unless the justice or the judge otherwise directs.

(5) The court officer shall notify all the parties of the court's decision.

[*Formerly rule 3 of the Magistrates' Courts (Special Measures Directions) Rules 2002 and rule 3 of the Crown Court (Special Measures Directions and Directions Prohibiting Cross-examination) Rules 2002.*]

29.3   Late applications

(1) Notwithstanding the requirements of rule 29.1 –

(a)   an application may be made for a special measures direction orally at the trial; or
(b)   a magistrates' court or the Crown Court may of its own motion raise the issue whether a special measures direction should be given.

(2) Where an application is made in accordance with paragraph (1)(a) –

(a)   the applicant must state the reasons for the late application; and
(b)   the court must be satisfied that the applicant was unable to make the application in accordance with rule 29.1.

(3) The court shall determine before making a special measures direction –

  (a)   whether to allow other parties to the proceedings to make representations on the question;
  (b)   the time allowed for making such representations (if any); and
  (c)   whether the question should be determined following a hearing at which the parties to the proceedings may be heard.

(4) Paragraphs (2) and (3) do not apply in respect of an application made orally at the trial for a special measures direction –

  (a)   enabling a child witness in need of special protection to give evidence by means of a live link; or
  (b)   enabling a video recording of such a child to be admitted as evidence in chief of the witness,

if the opposition is that the special measures direction will not maximise the quality of the witness's evidence.

[Formerly rule 4 of the Magistrates' Courts (Special Measures Directions) Rules 2002 and rule 4 of the Crown Court (Special Measures Directions and Directions Prohibiting Cross-examination) Rules 2002. An application to make or vary a special measures direction also may be made in the time allowed under rule 36.6.]

29.4   Discharge or variation of a special measures direction

(1) An application to a magistrates' court or the Crown Court to discharge or vary a special measures direction under section 20(2) of the Youth Justice and Criminal Evidence Act 1999 must be in writing and each material change of circumstances which the applicant alleges has occurred since the direction was made must be set out.
(2) An application under paragraph (1) must be sent to the court officer as soon as reasonably practicable after the change of circumstances occurs.
(3) The applicant must also send copies of the application to each party to the proceedings at the same time as the application is sent to the court officer.
(4) A party to whom an application is sent in accordance with paragraph (3) may oppose the application on the ground that it discloses no material change of circumstances.
(5) Rule 29.1(6) to (13) shall apply to an application to discharge or vary a special measures direction as it applies to an application for a direction.

[Formerly rule 5 of the Magistrates' Courts (Special Measures Directions) Rules 2002 and rule 5 of the Crown Court (Special Measures Directions and Directions Prohibiting Cross-examination) Rules 2002.]

29.5   Renewal application following a material change of circumstances

(1) Where an application for a special measures direction has been refused by a magistrates' court or the Crown Court, the application may only be renewed ("renewal application") where there has been a material change of circumstances since the court refused the application.
(2) The applicant must –

  (a)   identify in the renewal application each material change of circumstances which is alleged to have occurred; and
  (b)   send the renewal application to the court officer as soon as reasonably practicable after the change occurs.

(3) The applicant must also send copies of the renewal application to each of the parties to the proceedings at the same time as the application is sent to the court officer.
(4) A party to whom the renewal application is sent in accordance with paragraph (3) above may oppose the application on the ground that it discloses no material change of circumstances.

(5) Rules 29.1(6) to (13), 29.6 and 29.7 apply to a renewal application as they apply to the application which was refused.

[Formerly rule 6 of the Magistrates' Courts (Special Measures Directions) Rules 2002 and rule 6 of the Crown Court (Special Measures Directions and Directions Prohibiting Cross-examination) Rules 2002.]

29.6   Application for special measures direction for witness to give evidence by means of a live television link

(1) Where the application for a special measures direction is made, in accordance with rule 29.1(2)(a), for a witness to give evidence by means of a live link, the following provisions of this rule shall also apply.

(2) A party who seeks to oppose an application for a child witness to give evidence by means of a live link must, in order to comply with rule 29.1(5), state why in his view the giving of a special measures direction would not be likely to maximise the quality of the witness's evidence.

(3) However, paragraph (2) does not apply in relation to a child witness in need of special protection.

(4) Where a special measures direction is made enabling a witness to give evidence by means of a live link, the witness shall be accompanied at the live link only by persons acceptable to the court.

(5) If the special measures directions combine provisions for a witness to give evidence by means of a live link with provision for the examination of the witness to be conducted through an intermediary, the witness shall be accompanied at the live link only by –

(a)   the intermediary; and
(b)   such other persons as may be acceptable to the court.

[Formerly rule 7 of the Magistrates' Courts (Special Measures Directions) Rules 2002 and rule 7 of the Crown Court (Special Measures Directions and Directions Prohibiting Cross-examination) Rules 2002. As to the provision of support for witnesses giving evidence by live television link see also direction III.29 in the Practice Direction.]

29.7   Video recording of testimony from witnesses

(1) Where an application is made to a magistrates' court or the Crown Court for a special measures direction enabling a video recording of an interview of a witness to be admitted as evidence in chief of the witness, the following provisions of this rule shall also apply.

(2) The application made in accordance with rule 29.1(1) must be accompanied by the video recording which it is proposed to tender in evidence and must include –

(a)   the name of the defendant and the offence to be charged;
(b)   the name and date of birth of the witness in respect of whom the application is made;
(c)   the date on which the video recording was made;
(d)   a statement as to whether, and if so at what point in the video recording, an oath was administered to, or a solemn declaration made by, the witness;
(e)   a statement that, in the opinion of the applicant, either –

(i)   the witness is available for cross-examination, or
(ii)   the witness is not available for cross-examination and the parties have agreed that there is no need for the witness to be so available;

(f)   a statement of the circumstances in which the video recording was made which complies with paragraph (4) of this rule; and
(g)   the date on which the video recording was disclosed to the other party or parties.

(3) Where it is proposed to tender part only of a video recording of an interview with the witness, the application must specify that part and be accompanied by a video recording of the entire interview, including those parts which it is not proposed to tender in evidence, and by a statement of the circumstances in which the video recording of the entire interview was made which complies with paragraph (4) of this rule.

(4) The statement of the circumstances in which the video recording was made referred to in paragraphs (2)(f) and (3) of this rule shall include the following information, except in so far as it is contained in the recording itself –

  (a) the times at which the recording commenced and finished, including details of interruptions;

  (b) the location at which the recording was made and the usual function of the premises;

  (c) in relation to each person present at any point during, or immediately before, the recording –

    (i) their name, age and occupation,
    (ii) the time for which each person was present, and
    (iii) the relationship, if any, of each person to the witness and to the defendant;

  (d) in relation to the equipment used for the recording –

    (i) a description of the equipment,
    (ii) the number of cameras used,
    (iii) whether the cameras were fixed or mobile,
    (iv) the number and location of the microphones,
    (v) the video format used; and
    (vi) whether it offered single or multiple recording facilities and, if so, which were used; and

  (e) the location of the mastertape if the video recording is a copy and details of when and by whom the copy was made.

(5) If the special measures directions enabling a video recording of an interview of a witness to be admitted as evidence in chief of the witness with provision for the examination of the witness to be conducted through an intermediary, the information to be provided under paragraph (4)(c) shall be the same as that for other persons present at the recording but with the addition of details of the declaration made by the intermediary under rule 29.9.

(6) If the special measures directions enabling a video recording of an interview of a witness to be admitted as evidence in chief of the witness with provision for the witness, in accordance with section 30 of the Youth Justice and Criminal Evidence Act 1999, to be provided with a device as an aid to communication during the video recording of the interview the information to be included under paragraph (4)(d) shall include also details of any such device used for the purposes of recording.

(7) A party who receives a recording under paragraph (2) must within 14 days of its receipt, notify the applicant and the court officer, in writing –

  (a) whether he objects to the admission under section 27 of the 1999 Act of any part of the video recording or recordings disclosed, giving his reasons why it would not be in the interests of justice for the recording or any part of it to be admitted;

  (b) whether he would agree to the admission of part of the video recording or recordings and, if so, which part or parts; and

  (c) whether he wishes to be represented at any hearing of the application.

(8) A party who seeks to oppose an application for a special measures direction enabling a video recording of an interview of a child witness to be admitted as evidence in chief of

the witness must, in order to comply with rule 29.1(6), state why in his view the giving of a special measures direction would not be likely to maximise the quality of the witness's evidence.

(9)   However, paragraph (8) does not apply if the witness is a child witness in need of special protection.

(10) Notwithstanding the provisions of rule 29.1 and this rule, any video recording which the defendant proposes to tender in evidence need not be sent to the prosecution until the close of the prosecution case at the trial.

(11) The court may determine an application by the defendant to tender in evidence a video recording even though the recording has not, in accordance with paragraph (10), been served upon the prosecution.

(12) Where a video recording which is the subject of a special measures direction is sent to the prosecution after the direction has been made, the prosecutor may apply to the court for the direction to be varied or discharged.

(13) An application under paragraph (12) may be made orally to the court.

(14) A prosecutor who makes an application under paragraph (12) must state –

(a)   why he objects to the admission under section 27 of the 1999 Act of any part of the video recording or recordings disclosed, giving his reasons why it would not be in the interests of justice for the recording or any part of it to be admitted; and

(b)   whether he would agree to the admission of part of the video recording or recordings and, if so, which part or parts.

(15) The court must, before determining the application –

(a)   direct a hearing of the application; and

(b)   allow all the parties to the proceedings to be present and be heard on the application.

(16) The court officer must notify all parties to the proceedings of the decision of the court as soon as may be reasonable after the decision is given.

(17) Any decision varying a special measures direction must state whether the whole or specified parts of the video recording or recordings subject to the application are to be admitted in evidence.

[*Formerly rule 8 of the Magistrates' Courts (Special Measures Directions) Rules 2002 and rule 8 of the Crown Court (Special Measures Directions and Directions Prohibiting Cross-examination) Rules 2002. As to the use of video-recorded evidence in chief see also direction IV.40 in the Practice Direction.*]

29.8   Expert evidence in connection with special measures directions

Any party to proceedings in a magistrates' court or the Crown Court who proposes to adduce expert evidence (whether of fact or opinion) in connection with an application or renewal application for, or for varying or discharging, a special measures direction must, not less than 14 days before the date set for the trial to begin –

(a)   furnish the other party or parties and the court with a statement in writing of any finding or opinion which he proposes to adduce by way of such evidence and notify the expert of this disclosure; and

(b)   where a request is made to him in that behalf by any other party to those proceedings, provide that party also with a copy of (or if it appears to the party proposing to adduce the evidence to be more practicable, a reasonable opportunity to examine) the record of any observation, test, calculation or other procedure on which such finding or opinion is based and any document or other thing or substance in respect of which any such procedure has been carried out.

[Formerly rule 9 of the Magistrates' Courts (Special Measures Directions) Rules 2002 and rule 9 of the Crown Court (Special Measures Directions and Directions Prohibiting Cross-examination) Rules 2002. Part 33 contains rules about the duties of an expert and the content of an expert's report.]

29.9   Intermediaries

The declaration required to be made by an intermediary in accordance with section 29(5) of the Youth Justice and Criminal Evidence Act 1999 shall be in the following form:

> "I solemnly, sincerely and truly declare that I will well and faithfully communicate questions and answers and make true explanation of all matters and things as shall be required of me according to the best of my skill and understanding."

[Formerly rule 9A of the Magistrates' Courts (Special Measures Directions) Rules 2002 and rule 9A of the Crown Court (Special Measures Directions and Directions Prohibiting Cross-examination) Rules 2002.]

PART 30   USE OF LIVE TELEVISION LINK OTHER THAN FOR VULNERABLE WITNESSES

30.1   Evidence by live television link in the Crown Court where witness is outside the United Kingdom

(1)   Any party may apply for leave under section 32(1) of the Criminal Justice Act 1988 for evidence to be given through a live television link by a witness who is outside the United Kingdom.

(2)   An application under paragraph (1), and any matter relating thereto which, by virtue of the following provisions of this rule, falls to be determined by the Crown Court, may be dealt with in chambers by any judge of the Crown Court.

(3)   An application under paragraph (1) shall be made by giving notice in writing, which shall be in the form set out in the Practice Direction.

(4)   An application under paragraph (1) shall be made within 28 days after the date of the committal of the defendant or, as the case may be, of the giving of a notice of transfer under section 4(1)(c) of the Criminal Justice Act 1987, or of the service of copies of the documents containing the evidence on which the charge or charges are based under paragraph 1 of Schedule 3 to the Crime and Disorder Act 1998, or of the preferring of a bill of indictment in relation to the case.

(5)   The period of 28 days in paragraph (4) may be extended by the Crown Court, either before or after it expires, on an application made in writing, specifying the grounds of the application. The court officer shall notify all the parties of the decision of the Crown Court.

(6)   The notice under paragraph (3) or any application under paragraph (5) shall be sent to the court officer and at the same time a copy thereof shall be sent by the applicant to every other party to the proceedings.

(7)   A party who receives a copy of a notice under paragraph (3) shall, within 28 days of the date of the notice, notify the applicant and the court officer, in writing –

    (a)   whether or not he opposes the application, giving his reasons for any such opposition; and

    (b)   whether or not he wishes to be represented at any hearing of the application.

(8)   After the expiry of the period referred to in paragraph (7), the Crown Court shall determine whether an application under paragraph (1) is to be dealt with –

    (a)   without a hearing; or

    (b)   at a hearing at which the applicant and such other party or parties as the court may direct may be represented;

(c)   and the court officer shall notify the applicant and, where necessary, the other party or parties, of the time and place of any such hearing.

(9) The court officer shall notify all the parties of the decision of the Crown Court in relation to an application under paragraph (1) and, where leave is granted, the notification shall state –

(a)   the country in which the witness will give evidence;
(b)   if known, the place where the witness will give evidence;
(c)   where the witness is to give evidence on behalf of the prosecutor, or where disclosure is required by section 5(7) of the Criminal Procedure and Investigations Act 1996 (alibi) or by rules under section 81 of the Police and Criminal Evidence Act 1984 (expert evidence), the name of the witness;
(d)   the location of the Crown Court at which the trial should take place; and
(e)   any conditions specified by the Crown Court in accordance with paragraph (10).

(10) The Crown Court dealing with an application under paragraph (1) may specify that as a condition of the grant of leave the witness should give the evidence in the presence of a specified person who is able and willing to answer under oath or affirmation any questions the trial judge may put as to the circumstances in which the evidence is given, including questions about any persons who are present when the evidence is given and any matters which may affect the giving of the evidence.

[*Formerly rule 23B of the Crown Court Rules 1982. For the corresponding rule in the Court of Appeal see rule 68.19.*]

PART 31   RESTRICTION ON CROSS-EXAMINATION BY A DEFENDANT ACTING IN PERSON

31.1   Restrictions on cross-examination of witness

(1) This rule and rules 31.2 and 31.3 apply where an accused is prevented from cross-examining a witness in person by virtue of section 34, 35 or 36 of the Youth Justice and Criminal Evidence Act 1999.

(2) The court shall explain to the accused as early in the proceedings as is reasonably practicable that he –

(a)   is prevented from cross-examining a witness in person; and
(b)   should arrange for a legal representative to act for him for the purpose of cross-examining the witness.

(3) The accused shall notify the court officer within 7 days of the court giving its explanation, or within such other period as the court may in any particular case allow, of the action, if any, he has taken.

(4) Where he has arranged for a legal representative to act for him, the notification shall include details of the name and address of the representative.

(5) The notification shall be in writing.

(6) The court officer shall notify all other parties to the proceedings of the name and address of the person, if any, appointed to act for the accused.

(7) Where the court gives its explanation under paragraph (2) to the accused either within 7 days of the day set for the commencement of any hearing at which a witness in respect of whom a prohibition under section 34, 35 or 36 of the 1999 Act applies may be cross-examined or after such a hearing has commenced, the period of 7 days shall be reduced in accordance with any directions issued by the court.

(8) Where at the end of the period of 7 days or such other period as the court has allowed, the court has received no notification from the accused it may grant the accused an extension of time, whether on its own motion or on the application of the accused.

(9) Before granting an extension of time, the court may hold a hearing at which all parties to the proceedings may attend and be heard.

(10) Any extension of time shall be of such period as the court considers appropriate in the circumstances of the case.

(11) The decision of the court as to whether to grant the accused an extension of time shall be notified to all parties to the proceedings by the court officer.

[*This rule derives in part from rule 24B of the Crown Court Rules 1982.*]

31.2 Appointment of legal representative

(1) Where the court decides, in accordance with section 38(4) of the Youth Justice and Criminal Evidence Act 1999, to appoint a qualified legal representative, the court officer shall notify all parties to the proceedings of the name and address of the representative.

(2) An appointment made by the court under section 38(4) of the 1999 Act shall, except to such extent as the court may in any particular case determine, terminate at the conclusion of the cross-examination of the witness or witnesses in respect of whom a prohibition under section 34, 35 or 36 of the 1999 Act applies.

[*This rule derives in part from rule 24C of the Crown Court Rules 1982.*]

31.3 Appointment arranged by the accused

(1) The accused may arrange for the qualified legal representative, appointed by the court under section 38(4) of the Youth Justice and Criminal Evidence Act 1999, to be appointed to act for him for the purpose of cross-examining any witness in respect of whom a prohibition under section 34, 35 or 36 of the 1999 Act applies.

(2) Where such an appointment is made –

    (a) both the accused and the qualified legal representative appointed shall notify the court of the appointment; and

    (b) the qualified legal representative shall, from the time of his appointment, act for the accused as though the arrangement had been made under section 38(2)(a) of the 1999 Act and shall cease to be the representative of the court under section 38(4).

(3) Where the court receives notification of the appointment either from the qualified legal representative or from the accused but not from both, the court shall investigate whether the appointment has been made, and if it concludes that the appointment has not been made, paragraph (2)(b) shall not apply.

(4) An accused may, notwithstanding an appointment by the court under section 38(4) of the 1999 Act, arrange for a legal representative to act for him for the purpose of cross-examining any witness in respect of whom a prohibition under section 34, 35 or 36 of the 1999 Act applies.

(5) Where the accused arranges for, or informs the court of his intention to arrange for, a legal representative to act for him, he shall notify the court, within such period as the court may allow, of the name and address of any person appointed to act for him.

(6) Where the court is notified within the time allowed that such an appointment has been made, any qualified legal representative appointed by the court in accordance with section 38(4) of the 1999 Act shall be discharged.

(7) The court officer shall, as soon as reasonably practicable after the court receives notification of an appointment under this rule or, where paragraph (3) applies, after the court is satisfied that the appointment has been made, notify all the parties to the proceedings –

    (a) that the appointment has been made;

    (b) where paragraph (4) applies, of the name and address of the person appointed; and

(c)   that the person appointed by the court under section 38(4) of the 1999 Act has been discharged or has ceased to act for the court.

[*This rule derives in part from rule 24D of the Crown Court Rules 1982.*]

31.4   Prohibition on cross-examination of witness

(1)   An application by the prosecutor for the court to give a direction under section 36 of the Youth Justice and Criminal Evidence Act 1999 in relation to any witness must be sent to the court officer and at the same time a copy thereof must be sent by the applicant to every other party to the proceedings.

(2)   In his application the prosecutor must state why, in his opinion –

(a)   the evidence given by the witness is likely to be diminished if cross-examination is undertaken by the accused in person;

(b)   the evidence would be improved if a direction were given under section 36(2) of the 1999 Act; and

(c)   it would not be contrary to the interests of justice to give such a direction.

(3)   On receipt of the application the court officer must refer it –

(a)   if the trial has started, to the court of trial; or

(b)   if the trial has not started when the application is received –

(i)   to the judge or court designated to conduct the trial, or

(ii)   if no judge or court has been designated for that purpose, to such judge or court designated for the purposes of hearing that application.

(4)   Where a copy of the application is received by a party to the proceedings more than 14 days before the date set for the trial to begin, that party may make observations in writing on the application to the court officer, but any such observations must be made within 14 days of the receipt of the application and be copied to the other parties to the proceedings.

(5)   A party to whom an application is sent in accordance with paragraph (1) who wishes to oppose the application must give his reasons for doing so to the court officer and the other parties to the proceedings.

(6)   Those reasons must be notified –

(a)   within 14 days of the date the application was served on him, if that date is more than 14 days before the date set for the trial to begin;

(b)   if the trial has begun, in accordance with any directions issued by the court; or

(c)   if neither paragraph (6)(a) nor (b) applies, before the date set for the trial to begin.

(7)   Where the application made in accordance with paragraph (1) is made before the date set for the trial to begin and –

(a)   is not contested by any party to the proceedings, the court may determine the application without a hearing;

(b)   is contested by a party to the proceedings, the court must direct a hearing of the application.

(8)   Where the application is made after the trial has begun –

(a)   the application may be made orally; and

(b)   the court may give such directions as it considers appropriate to deal with the application.

(9)   Where a hearing of the application is to take place, the court officer shall notify each party to the proceedings of the time and place of the hearing.

(10) A party notified in accordance with paragraph (9) may be present at the hearing and be heard.

(11) The court officer must, as soon as possible after the determination of an application

made in accordance with paragraph (1), give notice of the decision and the reasons for it to all the parties to the proceedings.

(12) A person making an oral application under paragraph (8)(a) must –

    (a)   give reasons why the application was not made before the trial commenced; and

    (b)   provide the court with the information set out in paragraph (2).

[*This rule derives in part from rule 24E of the Crown Court Rules 1982.*]

PART 32   INTERNATIONAL CO-COPERATION

32.1   Notice required to accompany process served outside the United Kingdom and translations

(1) The notice which by virtue of section 3(4)(b) of the Crime (International Co-operation) Act 2003 (general requirements for service of process) must accompany any process served outside the United Kingdom must give the information specified in paragraphs (2) and (4) below.

(2) The notice must –

    (a)   state that the person required by the process to appear as a party or attend as a witness can obtain information about his rights in connection therewith from the relevant authority; and

    (b)   give the particulars specified in paragraph (4) about that authority.

(3) The relevant authority where the process is served –

    (a)   at the request of the prosecuting authority, is that authority; or

    (b)   at the request of the defendant or the prosecutor in the case of a private prosecution, is the court by which the process is served.

(4) The particulars referred to in paragraph (2) are –

    (a)   the name and address of the relevant authority, together with its telephone and fax numbers and e-mail address; and

    (b)   the name of a person at the relevant authority who can provide the information referred to in paragraph (2)(a), together with his telephone and fax numbers and e-mail address.

(5) The justices' clerk or Crown Court officer must send, together with any process served outside the United Kingdom –

    (a)   any translation which is provided under section 3(3)(b) of the 2003 Act; and

    (b)   any translation of the information required to be given by this rule which is provided to him.

(6) In this rule "process" has the same meaning as in section 51(3) of the 2003 Act.

[*Formerly rule 3 of the Magistrates' Courts (Crime (International Co-operation)) Rules 2004 and rule 30 of the Crown Court Rules 1982.*]

32.2   Proof of service outside the United Kingdom

(1) A statement in a certificate given by or on behalf of the Secretary of State –

    (a)   that process has been served on any person under section 4(1) of the Crime (International Co-operation) Act 2003 (service of process otherwise than by post);

    (b)   of the manner in which service was effected; and

    (c)   of the date on which process was served;

shall be admissible as evidence of any facts so stated.

(2) In this rule "process" has the same meaning as in section 51(3) of the 2003 Act.

[Formerly rule 4 of the Magistrates' Courts (Crime (International Co-operation)) Rules 2004 and rule 31 of the Crown Court Rules 1982.]

32.3   Supply of copy of notice of request for assistance abroad

Where a request for assistance under section 7 of the Crime (International Co-operation) Act 2003 is made by a justice of the peace or a judge exercising the jurisdiction of the Crown Court and is sent in accordance with section 8(1) of the 2003 Act, the justices' clerk or the Crown Court officer shall send a copy of the letter of request to the Secretary of State as soon as practicable after the request has been made.

[Formerly rule 5 of the Magistrates' Courts (Crime (International Co-operation)) Rules 2004 and rule 32 of the Crown Court Rules 1982.]

32.4   Persons entitled to appear and take in proceedings before a nominated court and exclusion of public

A court nominated under section 15(1) of the Crime (International Co-operation) Act 2003 (nominating a court to receive evidence) may –

  (a)   determine who may appear or take part in the proceedings under Schedule 1 to the 2003 Act before the court and whether a party to the proceedings is entitled to be legally represented; and

  (b)   direct that the public be excluded from those proceedings if it thinks it necessary to do so in the interests of justice.

[Formerly rule 6 of the Magistrates' Courts (Crime (International Co-operation)) Rules 2004 and rule 32A of the Crown Court Rules 1982.]

32.5   Record of proceedings to receive evidence before a nominated court

(1)   Where a court is nominated under section 15(1) of the Crime (International Co-operation) Act 2003 the justices' clerk or Crown Court officer shall enter in an overseas record –

  (a)   details of the request in respect of which the notice under section 15(1) of the 2003 Act was given;

  (b)   the date on which, and place at which, the proceedings under Schedule 1 to the 2003 Act in respect of that request took place;

  (c)   the name of any witness who gave evidence at the proceedings in question;

  (d)   the name of any person who took part in the proceedings as a legal representative or an interpreter;

  (e)   whether a witness was required to give evidence on oath or (by virtue of section 5 of the Oaths Act 1978 after making a solemn affirmation; and

  (f)   whether the opportunity to cross-examine any witness was refused.

(2)   When the court gives the evidence received by it under paragraph 6(1) of Schedule 1 to the 2003 Act to the court or authority that made the request or to the territorial authority for forwarding to the court or authority that made the request, the justices' clerk or Crown Court officer shall send to the court, authority or territorial authority (as the case may be) a copy of an extract of so much of the overseas record as relates to the proceedings in respect of that request.

[Formerly rule 7 of the Magistrates' Courts (Crime (International Co-operation)) Rules 2004 and rule 32B of the Crown Court Rules 1982. As to the keeping of an overseas record, see rule 32.9.]

32.6   Interpreter for the purposes of proceedings involving a television or telephone link

(1)   This rule applies where a court is nominated under section 30(3) (hearing witnesses in

the UK through television links) or section 31(4) (hearing witnesses in the UK by telephone) of the Crime (International Co-operation) Act 2003.

(2)   Where it appears to the justices' clerk or the Crown Court officer that the witness to be heard in the proceedings under Part 1 or 2 of Schedule 2 to the 2003 Act ("the relevant proceedings") is likely to give evidence in a language other than English, he shall make arrangements for an interpreter to be present at the proceedings to translate what is said into English.

(3)   Where it appears to the justices' clerk or the Crown Court officer that the witness to be heard in the relevant proceedings is likely to give evidence in a language other than that in which the proceedings of the court referred to in section 30(1) or, as the case may be, 31(1) of the 2003 Act ("the external court") will be conducted, he shall make arrangements for an interpreter to be present at the relevant proceedings to translate what is said into the language in which the proceedings of the external court will be conducted.

(4)   Where the evidence in the relevant proceedings is either given in a language other than English or is not translated into English by an interpreter, the court shall adjourn the proceedings until such time as an interpreter can be present to provide a translation into English.

(5)   Where a court in Wales understands Welsh –

(a)   paragraph (2) does not apply where it appears to the justices' clerk or Crown Court officer that the witness in question is likely to give evidence in Welsh;

(b)   paragraph (4) does not apply where the evidence is given in Welsh; and

(c)   any translation which is provided pursuant to paragraph (2) or (4) may be into Welsh instead of English.

[*Formerly rule 8 of the Magistrates' Courts (Crime (International Co-operation)) Rules 2004 and rule 32C of the Crown Court Rules 1982.*]

32.7   Record of television link hearing before a nominated court

(1)   This rule applies where a court is nominated under section 30(3) of the Crime (International Co-operation) Act 2003.

(2)   The justices' clerk or Crown Court officer shall enter in an overseas record –

(a)   details of the request in respect of which the notice under section 30(3) of the 2003 Act was given;

(b)   the date on which, and place at which, the proceedings under Part 1 of Schedule 2 to that Act in respect of that request took place;

(c)   the technical conditions, such as the type of equipment used, under which the proceedings took place;

(d)   the name of the witness who gave evidence;

(e)   the name of any person who took part in the proceedings as a legal representative or an interpreter; and

(f)   the language in which the evidence was given.

(3)   As soon as practicable after the proceedings under Part 1 of Schedule 2 to the 2003 Act took place, the justices' clerk or Crown Court officer shall send to the external authority that made the request a copy of an extract of so much of the overseas record as relates to the proceedings in respect of that request.

[*Formerly rule 9 of the Magistrates' Courts (Crime (International Co-operation)) Rules 2004 and rule 32D of the Crown Court Rules 1982. As to the keeping of an overseas record, see rule 32.9.*]

32.8   Record of telephone link hearing before a nominated court

(1)   This rule applies where a court is nominated under section 31(4) of the Crime (International Co-operation) Act 2003.

(2)   The justices' clerk or Crown Court officer shall enter in an overseas record –

(a)   details of the request in respect of which the notice under section 31(4) of the 2003 Act was given;
(b)   the date, time and place at which the proceedings under Part 2 of Schedule 2 to the 2003 Act took place;
(c)   the name of the witness who gave evidence;
(d)   the name of any interpreter who acted at the proceedings; and
(e)   the language in which the evidence was given.

[*Formerly rule 10 of the Magistrates' Courts (Crime (International Co-operation)) Rules 2004 and rule 32E of the Crown Court Rules 1982. As to the keeping of an overseas record, see rule 32.9.*]

32.9   Overseas record

(1)   The overseas records of a magistrates' court shall be part of the register (within the meaning of section 150(1) of the Magistrates' Courts Act 1980 and shall be kept in a separate book.
(2)   The overseas records of any court shall not be open to inspection by any person except –

(a)   as authorised by the Secretary of State; or
(b)   with the leave of the court.

[*Formerly rule 11 of the Magistrates' Courts (Crime (International Co-operation)) Rules 2004 and rule 32F of the Crown Court Rules 1982. As to the keeping of a register by a magistrates' court, see rule 6.1.*]

PART 33   EXPERT EVIDENCE

[*Note. See rule 2.1(4) for the application of the rules in this Part. Part 24 contains rules about the disclosure of the substance of expert evidence. For the use of an expert report as evidence, see section 30 of the Criminal Justice Act 1988.*]

33.1   Reference to expert

A reference to an "expert" in this Part is a reference to a person who is required to give or prepare expert evidence for the purpose of criminal proceedings, including evidence required to determine fitness to plead or for the purpose of sentencing.

[*Note. Expert medical evidence may be required to determine fitness to plead under section 4 of the Criminal Procedure (Insanity) Act 1964. It may be required also under section 11 of the Powers of Criminal Courts (Sentencing) Act 2000, under Part III of the Mental Health Act 1983 or under Part 12 of the Criminal Justice Act 2003. Those Acts contain requirements about the qualification of medical experts.*]

33.2   Expert's duty to the court

(1)   An expert must help the court to achieve the overriding objective by giving objective, unbiased opinion on matters within his expertise.
(2)   This duty overrides any obligation to the person from whom he receives instructions or by whom he is paid.
(3)   This duty includes an obligation to inform all parties and the court if the expert's opinion changes from that contained in a report served as evidence or given in a statement under Part 24 or Part 29.

33.3   Content of expert's report

(1)   An expert's report must –

(a)   give details of the expert's qualifications, relevant experience and accreditation;
(b)   give details of any literature or other information which the expert has relied on in making the report;

(c)   contain a statement setting out the substance of all facts given to the expert which are material to the opinions expressed in the report or upon which those opinions are based;

(d)   make clear which of the facts stated in the report are within the expert's own knowledge;

(e)   say who carried out any examination, measurement, test or experiment which the expert has used for the report and –

    (i)   give the qualifications, relevant experience and accreditation of that person,

    (ii)   say whether or not the examination, measurement, test or experiment was carried out under the expert's supervision, and

    (iii)   summarise the findings on which the expert relies;

(f)   where there is a range of opinion on the matters dealt with in the report –

    (i)   summarise the range of opinion, and

    (ii)   give reasons for his own opinion;

(g)   if the expert is not able to give his opinion without qualification, state the qualification;

(h)   contain a summary of the conclusions reached;

(i)   contain a statement that the expert understands his duty to the court, and has complied and will continue to comply with that duty; and

(j)   contain the same declaration of truth as a witness statement.

(2) Only sub-paragraphs (i) and (j) of rule 33.3(1) apply to a summary by an expert of his conclusions served in advance of that expert's report.

[Note. Part 24 contains rules about the disclosure of the substance of expert evidence. Part 27 contains rules about witness statements. Declarations of truth in witness statements are required by section 9 of the Criminal Justice Act 1967 and section 5B of the Magistrates' Courts Act 1980. A party who accepts another party's expert's conclusions may admit them as facts under section 10 of the Criminal Justice Act 1967. Evidence of examinations etc. on which an expert relies may be admissible under section 127 of the Criminal Justice Act 2003.]

33.4   Expert to be informed of service of report

A party who serves on another party or on the court a report by an expert must, at once, inform that expert of that fact.

33.5   Pre-hearing discussion of expert evidence

(1) This rule applies where more than one party wants to introduce expert evidence.

(2) The court may direct the experts to –

    (a)   discuss the expert issues in the proceedings; and

    (b)   prepare a statement for the court of the matters on which they agree and disagree, giving their reasons.

(3) Except for that statement, the content of that discussion must not be referred to without the court's permission.

33.6   Failure to comply with directions

A party may not introduce expert evidence without the court's permission if the expert has not complied with a direction under rule 33.5.

[Note. At a pre-trial hearing a court may make binding rulings about the admissibility of evidence and about questions of law under section 7 of the Criminal Justice Act 1987; sections 31 and 40 of the Criminal Procedure and Investigations Act 1996; and section 45 of the Courts Act 2003.]

33.7   Court's power to direct that evidence is to be given by a single joint expert

(1)   Where more than one defendant wants to introduce expert evidence on an issue at trial, the court may direct that the evidence on that issue is to be given by one expert only.

(2)   Where the co-defendants cannot agree who should be the expert, the court may –

(a)   select the expert from a list prepared or identified by them; or

(b)   direct that the expert be selected in such other manner as the court may direct.

33.8   Instructions to a single joint expert

(1)   Where the court gives a direction under rule 33.7 for a single joint expert to be used, each of the co-defendants may give instructions to the expert.

(2)   When a co-defendant gives instructions to the expert he must, at the same time, send a copy of the instructions to the other co-defendant(s).

(3)   The court may give directions about –

(a)   the payment of the expert's fees and expenses; and

(b)   any examination, measurement, test or experiment which the expert wishes to carry out.

(4)   The court may, before an expert is instructed, limit the amount that can be paid by way of fees and expenses to the expert.

(5)   Unless the court otherwise directs, the instructing co-defendants are jointly and severally liable for the payment of the expert's fees and expenses.

PART 34   HEARSAY EVIDENCE

34.1   When this applies

This Part applies in a magistrates' court and in the Crown Court where a party wants to introduce evidence on one or more of the grounds set out in section 114(1)(d), section 116, section 117 and section 121 of the Criminal Justice Act 2003, and in this Part that evidence is called "hearsay evidence".

[*Section 114 of the 2003 Act provides that a statement not made in oral evidence in criminal proceedings is admissible as evidence of any matter stated only on certain conditions. This Part applies only to evidence that is admissible on one or more of the following grounds set out in the 2003 Act, namely where (a) it is in the interests of justice for it to be admissible (see section 114(1)(d)), (b) the witness is unavailable to attend (see section 116), (c) the evidence is contained in a business, or other, document (see section 117) or (d) the evidence is multiple hearsay (see section 121). The meaning of "statements" and "matter stated" is explained in section 115 of the 2003 Act. "Oral evidence" is defined in section 134(1) of that Act. For the introduction of hearsay evidence in the Court of Appeal, see rule 68.20.*]

34.2   Notice of hearsay evidence

The party who wants to introduce hearsay evidence must give notice in the form set out in the Practice Direction to the court officer and all other parties.

34.3   When the prosecutor must give notice of hearsay evidence

The prosecutor must give notice of hearsay evidence –

(a)   in a magistrates' court, at the same time as he complies or purports to comply with section 3 of the Criminal Procedure and Investigations Act 1996 (disclosure by prosecutor); or

(b)   in the Crown Court, not more than 14 days after –

(i)   the committal of the defendant, or

(ii)   the consent to the preferment of a bill of indictment in relation to the case, or

(iii)   the service of a notice of transfer under section 4 of the Criminal Justice Act 1987 (serious fraud cases) or under section 53 of the Criminal Justice Act 1991 (certain cases involving children), or

(iv)   where a person is sent for trial under section 51 of the Crime and Disorder Act 1998 (indictable-only offences sent for trial), the service of copies of the documents containing the evidence on which the charge or charges are based under paragraph 1 of Schedule 3 to the 1998 Act.

34.4   When a defendant must give notice of hearsay evidence

A defendant must give notice of hearsay evidence not more than 14 days after the prosecutor has complied with or purported to comply with section 3 of the Criminal Procedure and Investigations Act 1996 (disclosure by prosecutor).

34.5   Opposing the introduction of hearsay evidence

A party who receives a notice of hearsay evidence may oppose it by giving notice within 14 days in the form set out in the Practice Direction to the court officer and all other parties.

34.6   [Revoked]

34.7   Court's power to vary requirements under this Part

The court may –

(a)   dispense with the requirement to give notice of hearsay evidence;

(b)   allow notice to be given in a different form, or orally; or

(c)   shorten a time limit or extend it (even after it has expired).

34.8   Waiving the requirement to give a notice of hearsay evidence

A party entitled to receive a notice of hearsay evidence may waive his entitlement by so informing the court and the party who would have given the notice.

PART 35   EVIDENCE OF BAD CHARACTER

35.1   When this Part applies

This Part applies in a magistrates' court and in the Crown Court when a party wants to introduce evidence of bad character as defined in section 98 of the Criminal Justice Act 2003.

[For the introduction of evidence of bad character in the Court of Appeal see rule 68.21.]

35.2   Introducing evidence of non-defendant's bad character

A party who wants to introduce evidence of a non-defendant's bad character or who wants to cross-examine a witness with a view to eliciting that evidence, under section 100 of the Criminal Justice Act 2003 must apply in the form set out in the Practice Direction and the application must be received by the court officer and all other parties to the proceedings –

(a)   not more than 14 days after the prosecutor has –

    (i)   complied or purported to comply with section 3 of the Criminal Procedure and Investigations Act 1996 (initial disclosure by the prosecutor), or

    (ii)   disclosed the previous convictions of that non-defendant; or

(b)   as soon as reasonably practicable, where the application concerns a non-defendant who is to be invited to give (or has given) evidence for a defendant.

[*Formerly rule 72A(1) of the Magistrates' Courts Rules 1981 and rule 23E(1) of the Crown Court Rules 1982.*]

35.3   Opposing introduction of evidence of non-defendant's bad character

A party who receives a copy of an application under rule 35.2 may oppose that application by giving notice in writing to the court officer and all other parties to the proceedings not more than 14 days after receiving that application.

[*Formerly rule 72A(2) of the Magistrates' Courts Rules 1981 and rule 23E(2) of the Crown Court Rules 1982.*]

35.4   Prosecutor introducing evidence of defendant's bad character

(1) A prosecutor who wants to introduce evidence of a defendant's bad character or who wants to cross-examine a witness with a view to eliciting that evidence, under section 101 of the Criminal Justice Act 2003 must give notice in the form set out in the Practice Direction to the court officer and all other parties to the proceedings.

(2) Notice under paragraph (1) must be given –

    (a)   in a case to be tried in a magistrates' court, at the same time as the prosecutor complies or purports to comply with section 3 of the Criminal Procedure and Investigations Act 1996; and

    (b)   in a case to be tried in the Crown Court, not more than 14 days after –

        (i)   the committal of the defendant, or

        (ii)   the consent to the preferment of a bill of indictment in relation to the case, or

        (iii)   the service of notice of transfer under section 4(1) of the Criminal Justice Act 1987 (notices of transfer) or under section 53(1) of the Criminal Justice Act 1991 (notices of transfer in certain cases involving children), or

        (iv)   where a person is sent for trial under section 51 of the Crime and Disorder Act 1998 (sending cases to the Crown Court) the service of copies of the documents containing the evidence on which the charge or charges are based under paragraph 1 of Schedule 3 to that Act.

[*Formerly rule 72A(3) of the Magistrates' Courts Rules 1981 and rule 23E(3) of the Crown Court Rules 1982.*]

35.5   Co-defendant introducing evidence of defendant's bad character

A co-defendant who wants to introduce evidence of a defendant's bad character or who wants to cross-examine a witness with a view to eliciting that evidence under section 101 of the Criminal Justice Act 2003 must give notice in the form set out in the Practice Direction to the court officer and all other parties to the proceedings not more than 14 days after the prosecutor has complied or purported to comply with section 3 of the Criminal Procedure and Investigations Act 1996.

[*Formerly rule 72A(4) of the Magistrates' Courts Rules 1981 and rule 23E(4) of the Crown Court Rules 1982.*]

35.6   Defendant applying to exclude evidence of his own bad character

A defendant's application to exclude bad character evidence must be in the form set out in the Practice Direction and received by the court officer and all other parties to the proceedings not more than 14 days after receiving a notice given under rules 35.4 or 35.5.

[*Formerly rule 72A(5) of the Magistrates' Courts Rules 1981 and rule 23E(5) of the Crown Court Rules 1982.*]

35.7   [Revoked]

35.8   Court's power to vary requirements under this Part

The court may –

    (a)   allow a notice or application required under this rule to be given in a different form, or orally; or

    (b)   shorten a time-limit under this rule or extend it even after it has expired.

[*Formerly rule 72A(7) of the Magistrates' Courts Rules 1981 and rule 23E(7) of the Crown Court Rules 1982.*]

35.9   Defendant waiving right to receive notice

A defendant entitled to receive a notice under this Part may waive his entitlement by so informing the court and the party who would have given the notice.

[*Formerly rule 72A(6) of the Magistrates' Courts Rules 1981 and rule 23E(6) of the Crown Court Rules 1982.*]

PART 36   EVIDENCE ABOUT A COMPLAINANT'S SEXUAL BEHAVIOUR

[*Note. The rules in this Part derive in part from rule 23D of the Crown Court Rules 1982.*

Section 41 of the Youth Justice and Criminal Evidence Act 1999 prohibits evidence or cross-examination about the sexual behaviour of a complainant of a sexual offence, subject to exceptions.

See also:

■   *section 42 of the 1999 Act, which among other things defines "sexual behaviour" and "sexual offence";*

■   *section 43(4), which among other things, requires –*

    –   *an application under section 41 to be heard in private and in the absence of the complainant,*

    –   *the reasons for the court's decision on an application to be given in open court,*

    –   *the court to state in open court the extent to which evidence may be introduced or questions asked;*

■   *section 34, which prohibits cross-examination by a defendant in person of the complainant of a sexual offence.*]

36.1   When this Part applies

This Part applies in magistrates' courts and in the Crown Court where a defendant wants to –

    (a)   introduce evidence; or

    (b)   cross-examine a witness

about a complainant's sexual behaviour despite the prohibition in section 41 of the Youth Justice and Criminal Evidence Act 1999.

36.2   Application for permission to introduce evidence or cross-examine

The defendant must apply for permission to do so –

    (a)   in writing; and

    (b)   not more than 28 days after the prosecutor has complied or purported to comply with section 3 of the Criminal Procedure and Investigations Act 1996 (disclosure by prosecutor).

[*Note. See Part 3 for the court's general powers to consider an application with or without a hearing and to give directions.*

At a pre-trial hearing a court may make binding rulings about the admissibility of evidence and about questions of law under section 7 of the Criminal Justice Act 1987; sections 31 and 40 of the Criminal Procedure and Investigations Act 1996; and section 45 of the Courts Act 2003.]

36.3   Content of application

The application must –

(a)   identify the issue to which the defendant says the complainant's sexual behaviour is relevant;

(b)   give particulars of –

(i)   any evidence that the defendant wants to introduce, and

(ii)   any questions that the defendant wants to ask;

(c)   identify the exception to the prohibition in section 41 of the Youth Justice and Criminal Evidence Act 1999 on which the defendant relies; and

(d)   give the name and date of birth of any witness whose evidence about the complainant's sexual behaviour the defendant wants to introduce.

36.4   Service of application

The defendant must serve the application on the court officer and all other parties.

36.5   Reply to application

A party who wants to make representations about an application under rule 36.2 must –

(a)   do so in writing not more than 14 days after receiving it; and

(b)   serve those representations on the court officer and all other parties.

36.6   Application for special measures

If the court allows an application under rule 36.2 then –

(a)   a party may apply not more than 14 days later for a special measures direction or for the variation of an existing special measures direction; and

(b)   the court may shorten the time for opposing that application.

[*Note. Special measures to improve the quality of evidence given by certain witnesses may be directed by the court under section 19 of the Youth Justice and Criminal Evidence Act 1999 and varied under section 20. An application for a special measures direction may be made by a party under Part 29 or the court may make a direction on its own initiative. Rule 29.1(6) sets the usual time limit (14 days) for opposing a special measures application.*]

36.7   Court's power to vary requirements under this Part

The court may shorten or extend (even after it has expired) a time limit under this Part.

PART 37   SUMMARY TRIAL

37.1   Order of evidence and speeches: information

(1)   On the summary trial of an information, where the accused does not plead guilty, the prosecutor shall call the evidence for the prosecution, and before doing so may address the court.

(2)   At the conclusion of the evidence for the prosecution, the accused may address the court, whether or not he afterwards calls evidence.

(3) At the conclusion of the evidence, if any, for the defence, the prosecutor may call evidence to rebut that evidence.

(4) At the conclusion of the evidence for the defence and the evidence, if any, in rebuttal, the accused may address the court if he has not already done so.

(5) Either party may, with the leave of the court, address the court a second time, but where the court grants leave to one party it shall not refuse leave to the other.

(6) Where both parties address the court twice the prosecutor shall address the court for the second time before the accused does so.

[Formerly rule 13 of the Magistrates' Courts Rules 1981.]

37.2   Procedure on information where accused is not legally represented

(1) The court shall explain to an accused who is not legally represented the substance of the charge in simple language.

(2) If an accused who is not legally represented, instead of asking a witness in support of the charge questions by way of cross-examination, makes assertions, the court shall then put to the witness such questions as it thinks necessary on behalf of the accused and may for this purpose question the accused in order to bring out or clear up any point arising out of such assertions.

[Formerly rule 13A of the Magistrates' Courts Rules 1981.]

37.3   Adjournment of trial of information

(1) Where in the absence of the accused a magistrates' court adjourns the trial of an information, the court officer shall give to the accused notice in writing of the time and place at which the trial is to be resumed.

(2) [Revoked]

[This rule derives in part from rule 15 of the Magistrates' Court Rules 1981.]

37.4   Formal admissions

Where under section 10 of the Criminal Justice Act 1967 a fact is admitted orally in court by or on behalf of the prosecutor or defendant for the purposes of the summary trial of an offence the court shall cause the admission to be written down and signed by or on behalf of the party making the admission.

[Formerly rule 71 of the Magistrates' Courts Rules 1981.]

37.5   Notice of intention to cite previous convictions

Service on any person of a notice of intention to cite previous convictions under section 104 of the Magistrates' Courts Act 1980 or section 13 of the Road Traffic Offenders Act 1988 may be effected by delivering it to him or by sending it by post in a registered letter or by recorded delivery service, or by first class post addressed to him at his last known or usual place of abode.

[Formerly rule 72 of the Magistrates' Courts Rules 1981.]

37.6   Application to change a plea of guilty

(1) The defendant must apply as soon as practicable after becoming aware of the grounds for making an application to change a plea of guilty, and may only do so before the final disposal of the case, by sentence or otherwise.

(2) Unless the court otherwise directs, the application must be in writing and it must –

    (a)   set out the reasons why it would be unjust for the guilty plea to remain unchanged;

    (b)   indicate what, if any, evidence the defendant wishes to call;

(c)   identify any proposed witness; and
(d)   indicate whether legal professional privilege is waived, specifying any material name and date.

(3) The defendant must serve the written application on –

(a)   the court officer; and
(b)   the prosecutor.

37.7   Preservation of depositions where offence triable either way is dealt with summarily

The magistrates' court officer for the magistrates' court by which any person charged with an offence triable either way has been tried summarily shall preserve for a period of three years such depositions as have been taken.

[Formerly rule 22 of the Magistrates' Courts Rules 1981.]

37.8   Order of evidence and speeches: complaint

(1) On the hearing of a complaint, except where the court determines under section 53(3) of the Magistrates' Courts Act 1980 to make the order with the consent of the defendant without hearing evidence, the complainant shall call his evidence, and before doing so may address the court.
(2) At the conclusion of the evidence for the complainant the defendant may address the court, whether or not he afterwards calls evidence.
(3) At the conclusion of the evidence, if any, for the defence, the complainant may call evidence to rebut that evidence.
(4) At the conclusion of the evidence for the defence and the evidence, if any, in rebuttal, the defendant may address the court if he has not already done so.
(5) Either party may, with the leave of the court, address the court a second time, but where the court grants leave to one party it shall not refuse leave to the other.
(6) Where the defendant obtains leave to address the court for a second time his second address shall be made before the second address, if any, of the complainant.

[Formerly rule 14 of the Magistrates' Courts Rules 1981. For criminal proceedings commenced by complaint see rules 50.3 (variation or discharge of certain orders), 53.1 (review of compensation order) and 55.2 (removal of driving disqualification).]

37.9   Magistrates' court officer to have copies of documents sent to accused under section 12(1) of the Magistrates' Courts Act 1980

Where the prosecutor notifies a magistrates' court officer that the documents mentioned in section 12(1)(a) and 12(1)(b) of the Magistrates' Courts Act 1980 have been served upon the accused, the prosecutor shall send to the court officer a copy of the documents mentioned in section 12(1)(b).

[Note. Formerly rule 7.9 of these Rules, which derived from rule 73 of the Magistrates' Courts Rules 1981. Section 12 of the Magistrates' Courts Act 1980 applies where a summons has been issued requiring a person to appear before a magistrates' court, other than a youth court, to answer an information for a summary offence. The documents mentioned in section 12(1)(b) are: a notice stating the effect of section 12, and either a statement of the facts to be placed before the court if the accused pleads guilty by post, or copies of the statements of the prosecution witnesses.]

37.10   Notice of order under section 25 of the Road Traffic Offenders Act 1988

Where a magistrates' court makes an order under section 25 of the Road Traffic Offenders Act 1988 that an offender shall inform the court of his date of birth or sex or both and the offender is not present in court, the court officer shall serve notice in writing of the order on the offender.

[*Note: Formerly rule 7.5 of these Rules, which derived from rule 108 of the Magistrates' Courts Rules 1981.*]

37.11   Duty of court officer receiving statutory declaration under section 14(1) of the Magistrates' Courts Act 1980

Where a magistrates' court officer receives a statutory declaration which complies with section 14(1) of the Magistrates' Courts Act 1980 (accused did not know of proceedings), he shall –

(a)   note the receipt of the declaration in the register; and

(b)   inform the prosecutor and, if the prosecutor is not a constable, the chief officer of police, of the receipt of the declaration.

[*Note: Formerly rule 7.4 of these Rules, which derived from rule 20 of the Magistrates' Courts Rules 1981. As to the requirement to keep a register, see rule 6.1.*]

PART 38   TRIAL OF CHILDREN AND YOUNG PERSONS

38.1   Application of this Part

(1)   This Part applies, subject to paragraph (3) of this rule, where proceedings to which paragraph (2) applies are brought in a magistrates' court in respect of a child or young person ("the relevant minor").

(2)   This paragraph applies to proceedings in which the relevant minor is charged with an offence, and, where he appears or is brought before the court, to proceedings under –

(a)   Paragraphs 1, 2, 5 and 6 of Schedule 7 to the Powers of Criminal Courts (Sentencing) Act 2000 (breach, revocation and amendment of supervision orders);

(b)   Part II, III or IV of Schedule 3 to the 2000 Act (breach, revocation and amendment of certain community orders);

(c)   Paragraphs 4, 5, 6 and 7 of Schedule 5 to the 2000 Act (breach, revocation and amendment of attendance centre orders); and

(d)   Schedule 8 to the 2000 Act (breach, revocation and amendment of action plan orders and reparation orders).

(3)   Where the court is inquiring into an offence as examining justices, only rules 38.2, 38.3 and 38.5(3) apply, and where the proceedings are of a kind mentioned in paragraph (2)(a), (b) or (c) rule 38.4 does not apply.

[*Formerly rule 4 of the Magistrates' Courts (Children and Young Persons) Rules 1992.*]

38.2   Assistance in conducting case

(1)   Except where the relevant minor is legally represented, the magistrates' court shall allow his parent or guardian to assist him in conducting his case.

(2)   Where the parent or guardian cannot be found or cannot in the opinion of the court reasonably be required to attend, the court may allow any relative or other responsible person to take the place of the parent or guardian for the purposes of this Part.

[*Formerly rule 5 of the Magistrates' Courts (Children and Young Persons) Rules 1992.*]

38.3   Duty of court to explain nature of proceedings etc

(1)   The magistrates' court shall explain to the relevant minor the nature of the proceedings and, where he is charged with an offence, the substance of the charge.

(2)   The explanation shall be given in simple language suitable to his age and understanding.

[*Formerly rule 6 of the Magistrates' Courts (Children and Young Persons) Rules 1992.*]

38.4   Duty of court to take plea to charge

Where the relevant minor is charged with an offence the magistrates' court shall, after giving the explanation required by rule 38.3, ask him whether he pleads guilty or not guilty to the charge.

[*Formerly rule 7 of the Magistrates' Courts (Children and Young Persons) Rules 1992.*]

38.5   Evidence in support of charge

(1) Where –

(a)   the relevant minor is charged with an offence and does not plead guilty, or

(b)   the proceedings are of a kind mentioned in rule 38.1(2)(a), (b) or (c),

the magistrates' court shall hear the witnesses in support of the charge or, as the case may be, the application.

(2) Except where –

(a)   the proceedings are of a kind mentioned in rule 38.1(2)(a), (b) or (c), and

(b)   the relevant minor is the applicant,

each witness may at the close of his evidence-in-chief be cross-examined by or on behalf of the relevant minor.

(3) If in any case where the relevant minor is not legally represented or assisted as provided by rule 38.2, the relevant minor, instead of asking questions by way of cross-examination, makes assertions, the court shall then put to the witness such questions as it thinks necessary on behalf of the relevant minor and may for this purpose question the relevant minor in order to bring out or clear up any point arising out of any such assertions.

[*Formerly rule 8 of the Magistrates' Courts (Children and Young Persons) Rules 1992.*]

38.6   Evidence in reply

If it appears to the magistrates' court after hearing the evidence in support of the charge or application that a prima facie case is made out, the relevant minor shall, if he is not the applicant and is not legally represented, be told that he may give evidence or address the court, and the evidence of any witnesses shall be heard.

[*Formerly rule 9 of the Magistrates' Courts (Children and Young Persons) Rules 1992.*]

PART 39   TRIAL ON INDICTMENT

39.1   Time limits for beginning of trials

The periods set out for the purposes of section 77(2)(a) and (b) of the Supreme Court Act 1981 shall be 14 days and 8 weeks respectively and accordingly the trial of a person committed by a magistrates' court –

(a)   shall not begin until the expiration of 14 days beginning with the date of his committal, except with his consent and the consent of the prosecution; and

(b)   shall, unless the Crown Court has otherwise ordered, begin not later than the expiration of 8 weeks beginning with the date of his committal.

[*Formerly rule 24 of the Crown Court Rules 1982.*]

39.2   Appeal against refusal to excuse from jury service or to defer attendance

(1) A person summoned under the Juries Act 1974 for jury service may appeal in accordance with the provisions of this rule against any refusal of the appropriate court officer to excuse him under section 9(2), or to defer his attendance under section 9A(1), of that Act.

(2) Subject to paragraph (3), an appeal under this rule shall be heard by the Crown Court.

(3) Where the appellant is summoned under the 1974 Act to attend before the High Court in Greater London the appeal shall be heard by a judge of the High Court and where the appellant is summoned under that Act to attend before the High Court outside Greater London or before a county court and the appeal has not been decided by the Crown Court before the day on which the appellant is required by the summons to attend, the appeal shall be heard by the court before which he is summoned to attend.

(4) An appeal under this rule shall be commenced by the appellant's giving notice of appeal to the appropriate court officer of the Crown Court or the High Court in Greater London, as the case may be, and such notice shall be in writing and shall specify the matters upon which the appellant relies as providing good reason why he should be excused from attending in pursuance of the summons or why his attendance should be deferred.

(5) The court shall not dismiss an appeal under this rule unless the appellant has been given an opportunity of making representations.

(6) Where an appeal under this rule is decided in the absence of the appellant, the appropriate court officer of the Crown Court or the High Court in Greater London, as the case may be, shall notify him of the decision without delay.

[*Note. Formerly rule 25 of the Crown Court Rules 1982.*]

39.3   Application to change a plea of guilty

(1) The defendant must apply as soon as practicable after becoming aware of the grounds for making an application to change a plea of guilty, and may only do so before the final disposal of the case, by sentence or otherwise.

(2) Unless the court otherwise directs, the application must be in writing and it must –

   (a)   set out the reasons why it would be unjust for the guilty plea to remain unchanged;

   (b)   indicate what, if any, evidence the defendant wishes to call;

   (c)   identify any proposed witness; and

   (d)   indicate whether legal professional privilege is waived, specifying any material name and date.

(3) The defendant must serve the written application on –

   (a)   the court officer; and

   (b)   the prosecutor.

PART 40   TAINTED ACQUITTALS

40.1   Time of certification

Where a person is convicted of an offence as referred to in section 54(1)(b) of the Criminal Procedure and Investigations Act 1996 and it appears to the court before which the conviction has taken place that the provisions of section 54(2) are satisfied, the court shall make the certification referred to in section 54(2) at any time following conviction but no later than –

   (a)   immediately after the court sentences or otherwise deals with that person in respect of the offence; or

   (b)   where the court, being a magistrates' court, commits that person to the Crown Court, or remits him to another magistrates' court, to be dealt with in respect of the offence, immediately after he is so committed or remitted, as the case may be; or

   (c)   where that person is a child or young person and the court, being the Crown Court, remits him to a youth court to be dealt with in respect of the offence, immediately after he is so remitted.

[*Formerly rule 2 of the Magistrates' Courts (Criminal Procedure and Investigations Act 1996) (Tainted Acquittals) Rules 1997 and rule 2 of the Crown Court (Criminal Procedure and Investigations Act 1996) (Tainted Acquittals) Rules 1997.*]

40.2   Form of certification in the Crown Court

A certification referred to in section 54(2) of the Criminal Procedure and Investigations Act 1996 by the Crown Court shall be drawn up in the form set out in the Practice Direction.

[*Formerly rule 3 of the Crown Court (Criminal Procedure and Investigations Act 1996) (Tainted Acquittals) Rules 1997.*]

40.3   Service of a copy of the certification

(1)   Where a magistrates' court or the Crown Court makes a certification as referred to in section 54(2) of the Criminal Procedure and Investigations Act 1996, the court officer shall, as soon as practicable after the drawing up of the form, serve a copy on the acquitted person referred to in the certification, on the prosecutor in the proceedings which led to the acquittal, and, where the acquittal has taken place before a court other than, or at a different place to, the court where the certification has been made, on –

(a)   the clerk of the magistrates' court before which the acquittal has taken place; or
(b)   the Crown Court officer at the place where the acquittal has taken place.

(2)   [Revoked]
(3)   [Revoked]
(4)   [Revoked]

[*This rule derives in part from rule 4 of the Magistrates' Courts (Criminal Procedure and Investigations Act 1996) (Tainted Acquittals) Rules 1997 and rule 4 of the Crown Court (Criminal Procedure and Investigations Act 1996) (Tainted Acquittals) Rules 1997.*]

40.4   Entry in register or records in relation to the conviction which occasioned certification

A clerk of a magistrates' court or an officer of a Crown Court which has made a certification under section 54(2) of the Criminal Procedure and Investigations Act 1996 shall enter in the register or records, in relation to the conviction which occasioned the certification, a note of the fact that certification has been made, the date of certification, the name of the acquitted person referred to in the certification, a description of the offence of which the acquitted person has been acquitted, the date of the acquittal, and the name of the court before which the acquittal has taken place.

[*Formerly rule 5 of the Magistrates' Courts (Criminal Procedure and Investigations Act 1996) (Tainted Acquittals) Rules 1997 and rule 5 of the Crown Court (Criminal Procedure and Investigations Act 1996) (Tainted Acquittals) Rules 1997. As to the requirement for a magistrates' court to keep a register, see rule 6.1.*]

40.5   Entry in the register or records in relation to the acquittal

The court officer of the court before which an acquittal has taken place shall, as soon as practicable after receipt of a copy of a form recording a certification under section 54(2) of the Criminal Procedure and Investigations Act 1996 relating to the acquittal, enter in the register or records a note that the certification has been made, the date of the certification, the name of the court which has made the certification, the name of the person whose conviction occasioned the making of the certification, and a description of the offence of which that person has been convicted. Where the certification has been made by the same court as the court before which the acquittal has occurred, sitting at the same place, the entry shall be made as soon as practicable after the making of the certification. In the case of an acquittal before a magistrates' court the entry in the register shall be signed by the clerk of the court.

[Formerly rule 6 of the Magistrates' Courts (Criminal Procedure and Investigations Act 1996) (Tainted Acquittals) Rules 1997 and rule 6 of the Crown Court (Criminal Procedure and Investigations Act 1996) (Tainted Acquittals) Rules 1997. As to the requirement for a magistrates' court to keep a register, see rule 6.1.]

40.6   Display of copy certification form

(1) Where a court makes a certification as referred to in section 54(2) of the Criminal Procedure and Investigations Act 1996, the court officer shall, as soon as practicable after the drawing up of the form, display a copy of that form at a prominent place within court premises to which place the public has access.

(2) Where an acquittal has taken place before a court other than, or at a different place to, the court which has made the certification under section 54(2) of the 1996 Act in relation to the acquittal, the court officer at the court where the acquittal has taken place shall, as soon as practicable after receipt of a copy of the form recording the certification, display a copy of it at a prominent place within court premises to which place the public has access.

(3) The copy of the form referred to in paragraph (1), or the copy referred to in paragraph (2), shall continue to be displayed as referred to, respectively, in those paragraphs at least until the expiry of 28 days from, in the case of paragraph (1), the day on which the certification was made, or, in the case of paragraph (2), the day on which the copy form was received at the court.

[Formerly rule 7 of the Magistrates' Courts (Criminal Procedure and Investigations Act 1996) (Tainted Acquittals) Rules 1997 and rule 7 of the Crown Court (Criminal Procedure and Investigations Act 1996) (Tainted Acquittals) Rules 1997.]

40.7   Entry in the register or records in relation to decision of High Court

(1) The court officer at the court where an acquittal has taken place shall, on receipt from the Administrative Court Office of notice of an order made under section 54(3) of the Criminal Procedure and Investigations Act 1996 quashing the acquittal, or of a decision not to make such an order, enter in the register or records, in relation to the acquittal, a note of the fact that the acquittal has been quashed by the said order, or that a decision has been made not to make such an order, as the case may be.

(2) The court officer of the court which has made a certification under section 54(2) of the 1996 Act shall, on receipt from the Administrative Court Office of notice of an order made under section 54(3) of that Act quashing the acquittal referred to in the certification, or of a decision not to make such an order, enter in the register or records, in relation to the conviction which occasioned the certification, a note that the acquittal has been quashed by the said order, or that a decision has been made not to make such an order, as the case may be.

(3) The entries in the register of a magistrates' court referred to, respectively, in paragraphs (1) and (2) above shall be signed by the magistrates' court officer.

[Formerly rule 8 of the Magistrates' Courts (Criminal Procedure and Investigations Act 1996) (Tainted Acquittals) Rules 1997 and rule 8 of the Crown Court (Criminal Procedure and Investigations Act 1996) (Tainted Acquittals) Rules 1997. As to the requirement on a magistrates' court to keep a register, see rule 6.1. As to the procedure to be followed in the High Court, see RSC Order 116 in Schedule 1 to the Civil Procedure Rules 1998.]

40.8   Display of copy of notice received from High Court

(1) Where the court officer of a court which has made a certification under section 54(2) of the Criminal Procedure and Investigations Act 1996 or before which an acquittal has occurred to which such a certification refers, receives from the Administrative Court Office notice of an order quashing the acquittal concerned, or notice of a decision not to

make such an order, he shall, as soon as practicable after receiving the notice, display a copy of it at a prominent place within court premises to which place the public has access.

(2) The copy notice referred to in paragraph (1) shall continue to be displayed as referred to in that paragraph at least until the expiry of 28 days from the day on which the notice was received at the court.

[*Formerly rule 9 of the Magistrates' Courts (Criminal Procedure and Investigations Act 1996) (Tainted Acquittals) Rules 1997 and rule 9 of the Crown Court (Criminal Procedure and Investigations Act 1996) (Tainted Acquittals) Rules 1997. As to the procedure to be followed in the High Court, see RSC Order 116 in Schedule 1 to the Civil Procedure Rules 1998.*]

PART 41   RETRIAL FOLLOWING ACQUITTAL FOR SERIOUS OFFENCE

41.1   Interpretation

In this Part:

"business day" means any day other than a Saturday, Sunday, Christmas Day, Good Friday or a bank holiday under the Banking and Financial Dealings Act 1971, in England and Wales; and

"section 76 application" means an application made by a prosecutor under section 76(1) or (2) of the Criminal Justice Act 2003.

41.2   Notice of a section 76 application

(1) A prosecutor who wants to make a section 76 application must serve notice of that application in the form set out in the Practice Direction on the Registrar and the acquitted person.

(2) That notice shall, where practicable, be accompanied by –

    (a)   relevant witness statements which are relied upon as forming new and compelling evidence of guilt of the acquitted person as well as any relevant witness statements from the original trial;

    (b)   any unused statements which might reasonably be considered capable of undermining the section 76 application or of assisting an acquitted person's application to oppose that application under rule 41.3;

    (c)   a copy of the indictment and paper exhibits from the original trial;

    (d)   copies of the transcript of the summing up and any other relevant transcripts from the original trial; and

    (e)   any other documents relied upon to support the section 76 application.

(3) The prosecutor must, as soon as practicable after service of that notice on the acquitted person, file with the Registrar a witness statement or certificate of service which exhibits a copy of that notice.

41.3   Response of the acquitted person

(1) An acquitted person who wants to oppose a section 76 application must serve a response in the form set out in the Practice Direction on the Registrar and the prosecutor which –

    (a)   indicates if he is also seeking an order under section 80(6) of the Criminal Justice Act 2003 for –

        (i)   the production of any document, exhibit or other thing, or

        (ii)   a witness to attend for examination and to be examined before the Court of Appeal; and

    (b)   exhibits any relevant documents.

(2) The acquitted person must serve that response not more than 28 days after receiving notice under rule 41.2.

(3) The Court of Appeal may extend the period for service under paragraph (2), either before or after that period expires.

41.4   Examination of witnesses or evidence by the Court of Appeal

(1) Prior to the hearing of a section 76 application, a party may apply to the Court of Appeal for an order under section 80(6) of the Criminal Justice Act 2003 for –

  (a)   the production of any document, exhibit or other thing; or

  (b)   a witness to attend for examination and to be examined before the Court of Appeal.

(2) An application under paragraph (1) must be in the form set out in the Practice Direction and must be sent to the Registrar and a copy sent to each party to the section 76 application.

(3) An application must set out the reasons why the order was not sought from the Court when –

  (a)   the notice was served on the Registrar under rule 41.2, if the application is made by the prosecutor; or

  (b)   the response was served on the Registrar under rule 41.3, if the application is made by the acquitted person.

(4) An application must be made at least 14 days before the day of the hearing of the section 76 application.

(5) If the Court of Appeal makes an order under section 80(6) of the 2003 Act on its own motion or on application from the prosecutor, it must serve notice and reasons for that order on all parties to the section 76 application.

41.5   Bail or custody hearings in the Crown Court

(1) Rules 19.18, 19.22 and 19.23 shall apply where a person is to appear or be brought before the Crown Court pursuant to sections 88 or 89 of the Criminal Justice Act 2003 (with the modification as set out in paragraph (2)), as if they were applications under rule 19.18(1).

(2) Substitute the following for Rule 19.18:

  "Where a person is to appear or be brought before the Crown Court pursuant to sections 88 or 89 of the Criminal Justice Act 2003, the prosecutor must serve notice of the need for such a hearing on the court officer."

(3) Where a person is to appear or be brought before the Crown Court pursuant to sections 88 or 89 of the 2003 Act the Crown Court may order that the person shall be released from custody on entering into a recognizance, with or without sureties, or giving other security before –

  (a)   the Crown Court officer; or

  (b)   any other person authorised by virtue of section 119(1) of the Magistrates' Courts Act 1980 to take a recognizance where a magistrates' court having power to take the recognizance has, instead of taking it, fixed the amount in which the principal and his sureties, if any, are to be bound.

(4) The court officer shall forward to the Registrar a copy of any record made in pursuance of section 5(1) of the Bail Act 1976.

41.6   Further provisions regarding bail and custody in the Crown Court

(1) The prosecutor may only apply to extend or further extend the relevant period before it expires and that application must be served on the Crown Court officer and the acquitted person.

(2) A prosecutor's application for a summons or a warrant under section 89(3)(a) or (b) of the Criminal Justice Act 2003 must be served on the court officer and the acquitted person.

41.7 Bail or custody orders in the Court of Appeal

Rules 68.8 and 68.9 shall apply to bail or custody orders made in the Court of Appeal under section 90 of the Criminal Justice Act 2003 as if they were orders made pursuant to an application under rule 68.7.

41.8 Application for restrictions on publication

(1) An application by the Director of Public Prosecutions, under section 82 of the Criminal Justice Act 2003, for restrictions on publication must be in the form set out in the Practice Direction and be served on the Registrar and the acquitted person.

(2) If notice of a section 76 application has not been given and the Director of Public Prosecution has indicated that there are reasons why the acquitted person should not be notified of the application for restrictions on publication, the Court of Appeal may order that service on the acquitted person is not to be effected until notice of a section 76 application is served on that person.

(3) If the Court of Appeal makes an order for restrictions on publication of its own motion or on application of the Director of Public Prosecutions, the Registrar must serve notice and reasons for that order on all parties, unless paragraph (2) applies.

41.9 Variation or revocation of restrictions on publication

(1) A party who wants to vary or revoke an order for restrictions on publication, under section 82(7) of the Criminal Justice Act 2003, may apply to the Court of Appeal in writing at any time after that order was made.

(2) A copy of the application to vary or revoke shall be sent to all parties to the section 76 application unless paragraph (3) applies.

(3) If the application to vary or revoke is made by the Director of Public Prosecutions and –

   (a)   the notice of a section 76 application has not been given under rule 41.2; and
   (b)   the Director of Public Prosecutions has indicted that there are reasons why the acquitted person should not be notified of an application for restrictions on publication,

the Court of Appeal may order that service on the acquitted person is not to be effected until notice of a section 76 application is served on that person.

(4) If the Court of Appeal varies or revokes an order for restrictions on publication of its own motion or on application, it must serve notice and reasons for that order on all parties, unless paragraph (3) applies.

41.10 Powers exercisable by a single judge of the Court of Appeal

(1) The following powers under the Criminal Justice Act 2003 and under this Part may be exercised by a single judge in the same manner as they may be exercised by the Court of Appeal and subject to the same provisions, namely to –

   (a)   order the production of any document, exhibit or thing under section 80(6)(a) of the 2003 Act;
   (b)   order any witness who would be a compellable witness in proceedings pursuant to an order or declaration made on the application to attend for examination and be examined before the Court of Appeal under section 80(6)(b) of the 2003 Act;
   (c)   extend the time for service under rule 41.3(2); and
   (d)   delay the requirement of service on the acquitted person of an application for restrictions on publication under rules 41.8(2) and 41.9(3).

(2) A single judge may, for the purposes of exercising any of the powers specified in paragraph (1), sit in such place as he appoints and may sit otherwise than in open court.

(3) Where a single judge exercises one of the powers set out in paragraph (1), the Registrar must serve notice of the single judge's decision on all parties to the section 76 application.

41.11   Powers exercisable by the Registrar

(1) The Registrar may require the Crown Court at the place of original trial to provide the Court of Appeal with any assistance or information which it may require for the purposes of exercising its jurisdiction under Part 10 of the Criminal Justice Act 2003 or this Part.

(2) The following powers may be exercised by the Registrar in the same manner as the Court of Appeal and subject to the same provisions –

    (a)   order the production of any document, exhibit or thing under section 80(6)(a) of the 2003 Act;

    (b)   order any witness who would be a compellable witness in proceedings pursuant to an order or declaration made on the application to attend for examination and be examined before the Court of Appeal under section 80(6)(b) of the 2003 Act; and

    (c)   extend the time for service under rule 41.3(2).

(3) Where the Registrar exercises one of the powers set out in paragraph (2) the Registrar must serve notice of that decision on all parties to the section 76 application.

(4) Where the Registrar has refused an application to exercise any of the powers referred to in paragraph (2), the party making the application may have it determined by a single judge by serving a renewal in the form set out in the Practice Direction within 14 days of the day on which notice of the Registrar's decision is served on the party making the application, unless that period is extended by the Court of Appeal.

41.12   Determination by full court

(1) Where a single judge has refused an application to exercise any of the powers referred to in rule 41.10, the applicant may have that application determined by the Court of Appeal by serving a notice of renewal in the form set out in the Practice Direction.

(2) A notice under paragraph (1) must be served on the Registrar within 14 days of the day on which notice of the single judge's decision is served on the party making the application, unless that period is extended by the Court of Appeal.

(3) If a notice under paragraph (1) is not served on the Registrar within the period specified in paragraph (2) or such extended period as the Court of Appeal has allowed, the application shall be treating as having been refused by the Court of Appeal.

41.13   Notice of the determination of the application

(1) The Court of Appeal may give its determination of the section 76 application at the conclusion of the hearing.

(2) If determination is reserved, the Registrar shall as soon as practicable, serve notice of the determination on the parties to the section 76 application.

(3) If the Court of Appeal orders under section 77 of the Criminal Justice Act 2003 that a retrial take place, the Registrar must as soon as practicable, serve notice on the Crown Court officer at the appropriate place of retrial.

41.14   Notice of application to set aside order for retrial

(1) If an acquitted person has not been arraigned before the end of 2 months after the date of an order under section 77 of the Criminal Justice Act 2003 he may apply in the form set out in the Practice Direction to the Court of Appeal to set aside the order.

(2) An application under paragraph (1) must be served on the Registrar and the prosecutor.

41.15   Leave to arraign

(1) If the acquitted person has not been arraigned before the end of 2 months after the date of an order under section 77 of the Criminal Justice Act 2003, the prosecutor may apply in the form set out in the Practice Direction to the Court of Appeal for leave to arraign.

(2) An application under paragraph (1) must be served on the Registrar and the acquitted person.

41.16   Abandonment of the application

(1) A section 76 application may be abandoned by the prosecutor before the hearing of that application by serving a notice in the form set out in the Practice Direction on the Registrar and the acquitted person.

(2) The Registrar must, as soon as practicable, after receiving a notice under paragraph (1) send a copy of it endorsed with the date of receipt to the prosecutor and acquitted person.

41.17   [Revoked]

PART 42   REMITTAL FROM ONE MAGISTRATES' COURT TO ANOTHER FOR SENTENCE

42.1   Remittal for sentence

(1) Where a magistrates' court remits an offender to some other magistrates' court under section 10 of the Powers of Criminal Courts (Sentencing) Act 2000 after convicting him of an offence, the court officer for the convicting court shall send to the court officer for the other court –

   (a)   a copy signed by the court officer for the convicting court of the minute or memorandum of the conviction and remittal entered in the register;

   (b)   a copy of any note of the evidence given at the trial of the offender, any written statement tendered in evidence and any deposition;

   (c)   such documents and articles produced in evidence before the convicting court as have been retained by that court;

   (d)   any report relating to the offender considered by the convicting court;

   (e)   if the offender is remitted on bail, a copy of the record made by the convicting court in pursuance of section 5 of the Bail Act 1976 relating to such bail and also any recognizance entered into by any person as his surety;

   (f)   if the convicting court makes an order under section 148 of the 2000 Act (restitution orders), a copy signed by the court officer for the convicting court of the minute or memorandum of the order entered in the register;

   (g)   a copy of any representation order previously made in the same case; and

   (h)   a copy of any application for a representation order.

(2) Where a magistrates' court remits an offender to some other magistrates' court as aforesaid and the other court remits him back to the convicting court under section 10(5) of the 2000 Act, the court officer for the other court shall send to the court officer for the convicting court –

   (a)   a copy signed by the court officer for the other court of the minute or memorandum of the remittal back entered in the register;

   (b)   if the offender is remitted back on bail, a copy of the record made by the other court in pursuance of section 5 of the Bail Act 1976 relating to such bail and also any recognizance entered into by any person as his surety; and

   (c)   all documents and articles sent in pursuance of paragraph (1) of this rule.

(3) In this rule "the offender", "the convicting court" and "the other court" have the same meanings as in section 10 of the 2000 Act.

[Formerly rule 19 of the Magistrates' Courts Rules 1981.]

PART 43   Committal to the Crown Court for sentence

43.1   Committals for sentence, etc

(1) Where a magistrates' court commits an offender to the Crown Court under the Vagrancy Act 1824, sections 3, 6, 116(3)(b) or 120(2)(a) of the Powers of Criminal Courts (Sentencing) Act 2000 or section 6 of the Bail Act 1976 after convicting him of an offence, the magistrates' court officer shall send to the Crown Court officer –

  (a)   a copy signed by the magistrates' court officer of the minute or memorandum of the conviction entered in the register;

  (b)   copy of any note of the evidence given at the trial of the offender, any written statement tendered in evidence and any deposition;

  (c)   such documents and articles produced in evidence before the court as have been retained by the court;

  (d)   any report relating to the offender considered by the court;

  (e)   if the offender is committed on bail, a copy of the record made in pursuance of section 5 of the 1976 Act relating to such bail and also any recognizance entered into by any person as his surety;

  (f)   if the court imposes under section 26 of the Road Traffic Offenders Act 1988 an interim disqualification for holding or obtaining a licence under Part III of the Road Traffic Act 1988, a statement of the date of birth and sex of the offender;

  (g)   if the court makes an order under section 148 of the 2000 Act (restitution orders), a copy signed by the clerk of the convicting court of the minute or memorandum of the order entered in the register; and

  (h)   any documents relating to an appeal by the prosecution against the granting of bail.

(2) Where a magistrates' court commits an offender to the Crown Court under the Vagrancy Act 1824 or sections 3, 6 or 120(2) of the 2000 Act and the magistrates' court on that occasion imposes, under section 26 of the Road Traffic Offenders Act 1988, an interim disqualification for holding or obtaining a licence under Part III of the Road Traffic Act 1988, the magistrates' court officer shall give notice of the interim disqualification to the Crown Court officer.

(3) Where a magistrates' court commits a person on bail to the Crown Court under any of the enactments mentioned in paragraph (2) of this rule or under section 6 of the Bail Act 1976 the magistrates' court officer shall give notice thereof in writing to the governor of the prison to which persons of the sex of the person committed are committed by that court if committed in custody for trial and also, if the person committed is under the age of 21, to the governor of the remand centre to which he would have been committed if the court had refused him bail.

[Formerly rule 17 of the Magistrates' Courts Rules 1981. See also direction V.52 in the Practice Direction.]

43.2   Committal to Crown Court for order restricting discharge, etc

Where a magistrates' court commits an offender to the Crown Court either –

  (a)   under section 43 of the Mental Health Act 1983 with a view to the making of a hospital order with an order restricting his discharge; or

  (b)   under section 3 of the Powers of Criminal Courts (Sentencing) Act 2000, as modified by section 43(4) of the 1983 Act, with a view to the passing of a more severe sentence than the magistrates' court has power to inflict if such an order is not made,

The magistrates' court officer shall send to the Crown Court officer –

> (i)　　the copies, documents and articles specified in rule 43.1,
>
> (ii)　　any written evidence about the offender given by a medical practitioner under section 37 of the 1983 Act or a copy of a note of any oral evidence so given,
>
> (iii)　　the name and address of the hospital the managers of which have agreed to admit the offender if a hospital order is made, and
>
> (iv)　　if the offender has been admitted to a hospital under section 37 of the 1983 Act, the name and address of that hospital.

[*Formerly rule 18 of the Magistrates' Courts Rules 1981.*]

PART 44　SENTENCING CHILDREN AND YOUNG PERSONS

44.1　Procedure after finding against minor in a magistrates' court

(1) This rule applies where –

(a)　the relevant minor (as defined in rule 38.1) is found guilty by a magistrates' court of an offence, whether after a plea of guilty or otherwise; or

(b)　in proceedings of a kind mentioned in rule 38.1(2)(a), (b) or (c) the court is satisfied that the case for the applicant –

　(i)　if the relevant minor is not the applicant, has been made out, or

　(ii)　if he is the applicant, has not been made out.

(2) Where this rule applies –

(a)　the relevant minor and his parent or guardian, if present, shall be given an opportunity of making a statement;

(b)　the court shall take into consideration all available information as to the general conduct, home surroundings, school record and medical history of the relevant minor and, in particular, shall take into consideration such information as aforesaid which is provided in pursuance of section 9 of the Children and Young Persons Act 1969;

(c)　if such information as aforesaid is not fully available, the court shall consider the desirability of adjourning the proceedings for such inquiry as may be necessary;

(d)　any written report of a probation officer, local authority, educational establishment or registered medical practitioner may be received and considered by the court without being read aloud; and

(e)　if the court considers it necessary in the interests of the relevant minor, it may require him or his parent or guardian, if present, to withdraw from the court.

(3) The court shall arrange for copies of any written report before the court to be made available to –

(a)　the legal representative, if any, of the relevant minor;

(b)　any parent or guardian of the relevant minor who is present at the hearing; and

(c)　the relevant minor, except where the court otherwise directs on the ground that it appears to it impracticable to disclose the report having regard to his age and understanding or undesirable to do so having regard to potential serious harm which might thereby be suffered by him.

(4) In any case in which the relevant minor is not legally represented and where a report which has not been made available to him in accordance with a direction under paragraph (3)(c) has been considered without being read aloud in pursuance of paragraph (2)(d) or where he or his parent or guardian has been required to withdraw from the court in pursuance of paragraph (2)(e), then –

(a)　the relevant minor shall be told the substance of any part of the information given to the court bearing on his character or conduct which the court considers to be material to the manner in which the case should be dealt with unless it appears to it impracticable so to do having regard to his age and understanding; and

(b)   the parent or guardian of the relevant minor, if present, shall be told the substance of any part of such information which the court considers to be material as aforesaid and which has reference to his character or conduct or to the character, conduct, home surroundings or health of the relevant minors, and if such a person, having been told the substance of any part of such information, desires to produce further evidence with reference thereto, the court, if it thinks the further evidence would be material, shall adjourn the proceedings for the production thereof and shall, if necessary in the case of a report, require the attendance at the adjourned hearing of the person who made the report.

[*Formerly rule 10 of the Magistrates' Courts (Children and Young Persons) Rules 1992.*]

44.2   Duty of magistrates' court to explain manner in which it proposes to deal with case and effect of order

(1)   Before finally disposing of the case or before remitting the case to another court in pursuance of section 8 of the Powers of Criminal Courts (Sentencing) Act 2000, the magistrates' court shall inform the relevant minor and his parent or guardian, if present, or any person assisting him in his case, of the manner in which it proposes to deal with the case and allow any of those persons so informed to make representations; but the relevant minor shall not be informed as aforesaid if the court considers it undesirable so to do.

(2)   On making any order, the court shall explain to the relevant minor the general nature and effect of the order unless, in the case of an order requiring his parent or guardian to enter into a recognizance, it appears to it undesirable so to do.

[*Formerly rule 11 of the Magistrates' Courts (Children and Young Persons) Rules 1992.*]

PART 45   DEFERRED SENTENCE

45.1   Further conviction in magistrates' court after sentence deferred

Where under section 1 of the Powers of Criminal Courts (Sentencing) Act 2000 a court has deferred passing sentence on an offender and before the expiration of the period of deferment he is convicted of any offence by a magistrates' court, the court officer for the convicting court shall, if the court which deferred passing sentence on the earlier occasion was another magistrates' court or the Crown Court, give notice of the conviction to the court officer for that court.

[*Formerly rule 27 of the Magistrates' Courts Rules 1981.*]

PART 46   CUSTODIAL SENTENCES

[*There are currently no rules in this Part.*]

PART 47   SUSPENDED SENTENCES OF IMPRISONMENT

47.1   Entries in magistrates' court register in respect of suspended sentences

(1)   Where under section 119 of the Powers of Criminal Courts (Sentencing) Act 2000 a magistrates' court deals with a person in respect of a suspended sentence otherwise than by making an order under section 119(1)(a), the court shall cause to be entered in the register its reasons for its opinion that it would be unjust to make such an order.

(2) Where an offender is dealt with under section 119 of the 2000 Act in respect of a suspended sentence passed by a magistrates' court, the court officer shall note this in the register, or where the suspended sentence was not passed by that court, shall notify the court officer for the court by which it was passed who shall note it in the register.

[Formerly rule 29 of the Magistrates' Court Rules 1981. As to the requirement to keep a register, see rule 6.1.]

47.2   Suspended sentence supervision orders

(1) Where a magistrates' court makes an order under section 119(1)(a) or (b) of the Powers of Criminal Courts (Sentencing) Act 2000 in respect of a person who is subject to a suspended sentence supervision order, the court officer shall note this in the register, or where that order was not made by that court, shall –

  (a)   if the order was made by another magistrates' court, notify the court officer for that court who shall note the court register accordingly; or
  (b)   if the order was made by the Crown Court, notify the Crown Court officer.

(2) Where a magistrates' court discharges a suspended sentence supervision order under section 124(1) of the 2000 Act, the court officer shall note this in the register, or where that order was not made by that court, shall –

  (a)   if the order was made by another magistrates' court, notify the court officer for that court who shall note the court register accordingly; or
  (b)   if the order was made by the Crown Court, notify the Crown Court officer.

(3) Where a magistrates' court fines a person under section 123 of the 2000 Act for breach of the requirements of a suspended sentence supervision order which was not made by that court, the court officer shall –

  (a)   if the order was made by another magistrates' court, notify the court officer for that court; or
  (b)   if the order was made by the Crown Court, notify the Crown Court officer.

[Formerly rule 30 of the Magistrates' Court Rules 1981. As to the requirement to keep a register, see rule 6.1.]

PART 48   COMMUNITY PENALTIES

48.1   Curfew order or requirement with electronic monitoring requirement

(1) This rule applies where the Crown Court makes –

  (a)   a curfew order with an electronic monitoring requirement under section 35 of the Crime (Sentences) Act 1997 or under sections 37 and 36B of the Powers of Criminal Courts (Sentencing) Act 2000; or
  (b)   a community rehabilitation order with curfew and electronic monitoring requirements under section 41 of and paragraph 7 of Schedule 2 to the 2000 Act.

(2) The court officer shall serve notice of the order on the person in respect of whom it is made by way of pages 1 and 2 of the form set out in the Practice Direction.
(3) The court officer shall serve notice of the order on the person responsible for electronically monitoring compliance with it by way of the form set out in the Practice Direction.
(4) Where any community order additional to the curfew order has been made in respect of the offender, the court officer shall serve a copy of the notice required by paragraph (3) on the local probation board or Youth Offending Team responsible for the offender.

[Formerly rules 37 and 37A of the Crown Court Rules 1982.]

PART 49   HOSPITAL AND GUARDIANSHIP ORDERS

49.1   Remand by magistrates' court for medical inquiries

On exercising the powers conferred by section 11 of the Powers of Criminal Courts (Sentencing) Act 2000 a magistrates' court shall –

(a)   where the accused is remanded in custody, send to the institution or place to which he is committed; or

(b)   where the accused is remanded on bail, send to the institution or place at which, or the person by whom, he is to be examined,

a statement of the reasons why the court is of opinion that an inquiry ought to be made into his physical or mental condition and of any information before the court about his physical or mental condition.

[*Formerly rule 24 of the Magistrates' Courts Rules 1981.*]

49.2   Hospital or guardianship order imposed by a magistrates' court

(1)   The magistrates' court by which a hospital order is made under section 37 of the Mental Health Act 1983 shall send to the hospital named in the order such information in the possession of the court as it considers likely to be of assistance in dealing with the patient to whom the order relates, and in particular such information about the mental condition, character and antecedents of the patient and the nature of the offence.

(2)   The magistrates' court by which a guardianship order is made under section 37 of the 1983 Act shall send to the local health authority named therein as guardian or, as the case may be, the local health authority for the area in which the person so named resides, such information in the possession of the court as it considers likely to be of assistance in dealing with the patient to whom the order relates and in particular such information about the mental condition, character and antecedents of the patient and the nature of the offence.

(3)   The magistrates' court by which an offender is ordered to be admitted to hospital under section 44 of the 1983 Act shall send to the hospital such information in the possession of the court as it considers likely to assist in the treatment of the offender until his case is dealt with by the Crown Court.

[*Formerly rule 31 of the Magistrates' Court Rules 1981.*]

PART 50   CIVIL BEHAVIOUR ORDERS AFTER VERDICT OR FINDING

[*Note. The rules in this Part derive in part from those contained in rule 114 of the Magistrates' Courts Rules 1981, rule 38 of the Crown Court Rules 1982, rules 2 to 5 of the Magistrates' Courts (Hearsay Evidence in Civil Proceedings) Rules 1999, rules 5 and 6 of the Magistrates' Courts (Anti-Social Behaviour Orders) Rules 2002, rules 7, 8 and 9 of the Magistrates' Courts (Parenting Orders) Rules 2004 and rule 4 of the Magistrates' Courts (Sexual Offences Prevention Orders) Rules 2004.*

See Part 3 for the court's general powers to consider an application and to give directions.]

50.1   When this Part applies

(1)   This Part applies in magistrates' courts and in the Crown Court where the court could decide to make, vary or revoke a civil order –

(a)   under a power that the court can exercise after reaching a verdict or making a finding, and

(b)   that requires someone to do, or not do, something.

(2) A reference to a "behaviour order" in this Part is a reference to any such order.

(3) A reference to "hearsay evidence" in this Part is a reference to evidence consisting of hearsay within the meaning of section 1(2) of the Civil Evidence Act 1995.

[Note. In the circumstances set out in the Acts listed, the court can make a behaviour order:

(a) on conviction, under –

- *Football Spectators Act 1989, section 14A (football banning orders),*
- *Protection from Harassment Act 1997, section 5 (restraining orders),*
- *Crime and Disorder Act 1998, sections 1C and 1D (anti-social behaviour orders and interim anti-social behaviour orders),*
- *Crime and Disorder Act 1998, sections 8 and 9 (parenting orders),*
- *Sexual Offences Act 2003, section 104 (sexual offences prevention orders),*
- *Serious Crime Act 2007, section 19 (serious crime prevention orders),*

(b) on acquittal, under –

- *Protection from Harassment Act 1997, section 5A (restraining orders on acquittal), and*

(c) on the making of a finding of (i) not guilty by reason of insanity, or (ii) disability, under –

- *Sexual Offences Act 2003, section 104 (sexual offences prevention orders).*

Section 1(2) of the Civil Evidence Act 1995 defines hearsay as meaning "a statement made otherwise than by a person while giving oral evidence in the proceedings which is tendered as evidence of the matters stated". Section 13 of that Act defines a statement as meaning "any representation of fact or opinion, however made".]

50.2 Behaviour orders: general rules

(1) The court must not make a behaviour order unless the person to whom it is directed has had an opportunity –

(a)   to consider what order is proposed and why; and

(b)   to make representations at a hearing (whether or not that person in fact attends).

(2) That restriction does not apply to making an interim behaviour order.

(3) But an interim behaviour order has no effect unless the person to whom it is directed –

(a)   is present when it is made; or

(b)   is handed a document recording the order not more than 7 days after it is made.

[Note. The Acts listed in the note to rule 50.1 impose requirements specific to each different type of behaviour order. Not all allow the court to make an interim behaviour order.]

50.3 Application for behaviour order: special rules

(1) This rule applies where a prosecutor wants the court to make –

(a)   an anti-social behaviour order; or

(b)   a serious crime prevention order,

if the defendant is convicted.

(2) The prosecutor must serve a notice of intention to apply for such an order on –

(a)   the court officer;

(b)   the defendant against whom the prosecutor wants the court to make the order; and

(c)   any person on whom the order would be likely to have a significant adverse effect, as soon as practicable (without waiting for the verdict).

(3)   The notice must be in the form set out in the Practice Direction and must –

  (a)   summarise the relevant facts;
  (b)   identify the evidence on which the prosecutor relies in support;
  (c)   attach any written statement that the prosecutor has not already served; and
  (d)   specify the order that the prosecutor wants the court to make.

(4)   The defendant must then –

  (a)   serve written notice of any evidence on which the defendant relies on –

    (i)   the court officer, and
    (ii)   the prosecutor,

    as soon as practicable (without waiting for the verdict); and

  (b)   in the notice, identify that evidence and attach any written statement that has not already been served.

(5)   This rule does not apply to an application for an interim anti-social behaviour order.

[*Note. Under section 8 of the Serious Crime Act 2007 a serious crime prevention order may be made only on an application by the Director of Public Prosecutions, the Director of Revenue and Customs Prosecutions, or the Director of the Serious Fraud Office. See also paragraphs 2, 7 and 13 of Schedule 2 to the 2007 Act.*

If a party relies on hearsay evidence, see also rules 50.6, 50.7, and 50.8.]

50.4   Evidence to assist the court: special rules

(1)   This rule applies where the court indicates that it may make on its own initiative –

  (a)   a football banning order;
  (b)   a restraining order;
  (c)   an anti-social behaviour order; or
  (d)   a drinking banning order.

(2)   A party who wants the court to take account of any particular evidence before making that decision must –

  (a)   serve notice in writing on –

    (i)   the court officer, and
    (ii)   every other party,

    as soon as practicable (without waiting for the verdict); and

  (b)   in that notice identify that evidence and attach any written statement that has not already been served.

[*Note. If a party relies on hearsay evidence, see also rules 50.6, 50.7, and 50.8.*]

50.5   Application to vary or revoke behaviour order

(1)   The court may vary or revoke a behaviour order if –

  (a)   the legislation under which it is made allows the court to do so; and
  (b)   one of the following applies –

    (i)   the prosecutor,
    (ii)   the person to whom the order is directed,
    (iii)   any other person mentioned in the order,
    (iv)   the relevant authority or responsible officer,
    (v)   the relevant Chief Officer of Police, or
    (vi)   the Director of Public Prosecutions.

(2) A person applying under this rule must –

  (a) apply in writing as soon as practicable after becoming aware of the grounds for doing so, explaining why the order should be varied or revoked; and

  (b) serve the application, and any notice under paragraph (3), on the court officer and, as appropriate, anyone listed in paragraph (1)(b).

(3) A party who wants the court to take account of any particular evidence before making its decision must, as soon as practicable –

  (a) serve notice in writing on –

    (i)   the court officer, and

    (ii) as appropriate, anyone listed in paragraph (1)(b); and

  (b) in that notice identify the evidence and attach any written statement that has not already been served.

(4) The court may decide an application under this rule with or without a hearing.

(5) But the court must not –

  (a) dismiss an application under this rule unless the applicant has had an opportunity to make representations at a hearing (whether or not the applicant in fact attends); or

  (b) allow an application under this rule unless everyone served with the application has had at least 14 days in which to make representations, including representations about whether there should be a hearing.

(6) Where a person applies under this rule to a magistrates' court –

  (a) the application must be by complaint; and

  (b) the court officer must give notice by summons of any hearing.

[*Note. The legislation that gives the court power to make a behaviour order may limit the circumstances in which it may be varied or revoked and may require a hearing.*

If a party relies on hearsay evidence, see also rules 50.6, 50.7 and 50.8.]

50.6   Notice of hearsay evidence

(1) A party who wants to introduce hearsay evidence must –

  (a) serve notice in writing on –

    (i)   the court officer, and

    (ii) every other party directly affected; and

  (b) in that notice –

    (i)   explain that it is a notice of hearsay evidence,

    (ii)   identify that evidence,

    (iii) identify the person who made the statement which is hearsay, or explain why if that person is not identified, and

    (iv)   explain why that person will not be called to give oral evidence.

(2) A party may serve one notice under this rule in respect of more than one statement and more than one witness.

[*Note. For the time within which to serve a notice of hearsay evidence, see rule 50.3(2) to (4), rule 50.4(2) and rule 50.5(3). See also the requirement in section 2 of the Civil Evidence Act 1995 for reasonable and practicable notice of a proposal to introduce hearsay evidence.*

Rules 50.6, 50.7 and 50.8 broadly correspond with rules 3, 4 and 5 of the Magistrates' Courts (Hearsay Evidence in Civil Proceedings) Rules 1999, which apply in civil proceedings in magistrates' courts. Rule 3 of the magistrates' courts rules however includes a time limit, which may be varied by the court, or a justices' clerk, of 21 days before the date fixed for the hearing, for service of a hearsay notice.]

50.7   Cross-examination of maker of hearsay statement

(1)   This rule applies where a party wants the court's permission to cross-examine a person who made a statement which another party wants to introduce as hearsay.

(2)   The party who wants to cross-examine that person must –

(a)   apply in writing, with reasons, not more than 7 days after service of the notice of hearsay evidence; and

(b)   serve the application on –

(i)   the court officer,

(ii)   the party who served the hearsay evidence notice, and

(iii)   every party on whom the hearsay evidence notice was served.

(3)   The court may decide an application under this rule with or without a hearing.

(4)   But the court must not –

(a)   dismiss an application under this rule unless the applicant has had an opportunity to make representations at a hearing (whether or not the applicant in fact attends); or

(b)   allow an application under this rule unless everyone served with the application has had at least 7 days in which to make representations, including representations about whether there should be a hearing.

[*Note. See also section 3 of the Civil Evidence Act 1995.*]

50.8   Credibility and consistency of maker of hearsay statement

(1)   This rule applies where a party wants to challenge the credibility or consistency of a person who made a statement which another party wants to introduce as hearsay.

(2)   The party who wants to challenge the credibility or consistency of that person must –

(a)   serve a written notice of intention to do so on –

(i)   the court officer, and

(ii)   the party who served the notice of hearsay evidence

not more than 7 days after service of that hearsay evidence notice; and

(b)   in the notice, identify any statement or other material on which that party relies.

(3)   The party who served the hearsay notice –

(a)   may call that person to give oral evidence instead; and

(b)   if so, must serve a notice of intention to do so on –

(i)   the court officer, and

(ii)   every party on whom he served the hearsay notice

not more than 7 days after service of the notice under paragraph (2).

[*Note. Section 5(2) of the Civil Evidence Act 1995 describes the procedure for challenging the credibility of the maker of a statement of which hearsay evidence is introduced. See also section 6 of that Act. The 1995 Act does not allow the introduction of evidence of a previous inconsistent statement otherwise than in accordance with sections 5, 6 and 7 of the Criminal Procedure Act 1865.*]

50.9   Court's power to vary requirements under this Part

The court may –

(a)   shorten a time limit or extend it (even after it has expired);

(b)   allow a notice or application to be given in a different form, or presented orally.

PART 51   FINES

[*There are currently no rules in this Part.*]

PART 52   ENFORCEMENT OF FINES

52.1   Notice to defendant of fine or forfeited recognizance

(1) Where under section 140(1) of the Powers of Criminal Courts (Sentencing) Act 2000 or section 67(2) of the Criminal Justice Act 1988 a magistrates' court is required to enforce payment of a fine imposed or recognizance forfeited by the Crown Court or where a magistrates' court allows time for payment of a sum adjudged to be paid by a summary conviction, or directs that the sum be paid by instalments, or where the offender is absent when a sum is adjudged to be paid by a summary conviction, the magistrates' court officer shall serve on the offender notice in writing stating the amount of the sum and, if it is to be paid by instalments, the amount of the instalments, the date on which the sum, or each of the instalments, is to be paid and the places and times at which payment may be made; and a warrant of distress or commitment shall not be issued until the preceding provisions of this rule have been complied with.

(2) [Revoked]

[*This rule derives in part from rule 46 of the Magistrates' Courts Rules 1981.*]

52.2   Payment of fine to be made to magistrates' court officer

(1) A person adjudged by the conviction of a magistrates' court to pay any sum shall, unless the court otherwise directs, pay that sum, or any instalment of that sum, to the court officer.

(2) Where payment of any sum or instalment of any sum adjudged to be paid by the conviction or order of a magistrates' court is made to any person other than the court officer, that person, unless he is the person to whom the court has directed payment to be made or, in the case of a child, is the person with whom the child has his home, shall, as soon as may be, account for and, if the court officer so requires, pay over the sum or instalment to the court officer.

(3) Where payment of any sum adjudged to be paid by the conviction or order of a magistrates' court, or any instalment of such a sum, is directed to be made to the court officer for another court, the court officer for the court that adjudged the sum to be paid shall pay over any sums received by him on account of the said sum or instalment to the court officer for that other court.

[*Formerly rule 48 of the Magistrates' Courts Rules 1981.*]

52.3   Duty of magistrates' court officer to give receipt

The court officer for a magistrates' court shall give or send a receipt to any person who makes a payment to him in pursuance of a conviction or order of a magistrates' court and who asks for a receipt.

[*Formerly rule 49 of the Magistrates' Courts Rules 1981.*]

52.4   Application to magistrates' court for further time

An application under section 75(2) of the Magistrates' Courts Act 1980 (further time to pay) may, unless the court requires the applicant to attend, be made in writing.

[Formerly rule 51 of the Magistrates' Courts Rules 1981.]

52.5   [Revoked]

52.6   Review of terms of postponement of warrant of commitment by magistrates' court

An application under section 77(5) of the Magistrates' Courts Act 1980 may be made in writing or in person.

[This rule derives in part from rule 52A of the Magistrates' Courts Rules 1981.]

52.7   Notice to defendant before enforcing magistrates' court order

(1)   A warrant of commitment shall not be issued for disobedience to an order of a magistrates' court unless the defendant has been previously served with a copy of the minute of the order, or the order was made in his presence and the warrant is issued on that occasion:
Provided that this paragraph shall not apply to an order to pay money.
(2)   [Revoked]

[This rule derives in part from rule 53 of the Magistrates' Courts Rules 1981.]

52.8   Execution of magistrates' court distress warrant

(1)   A warrant of distress issued for the purpose of levying a sum adjudged to be paid by a summary conviction or order –

(a)   shall name or otherwise describe the person against whom the distress is to be levied;

(b)   shall be directed to the constables of the police area in which the warrant is issued or to the civilian enforcement officers for the area in which they are employed, or to a person named in the warrant and shall, subject to, and in accordance with, the provisions of this rule, require them to levy the said sum by distress and sale of the goods belonging to the said person; and

(c)   may where it is directed to the constables of a police area, instead of being executed by any of those constables, be executed by any person under the direction of a constable.

(2)   The warrant shall authorise the person charged with the execution of it to take as well any money as any goods of the person against whom the distress is levied; and any money so taken shall be treated as if it were the proceeds of the sale of goods taken under the warrant.

(3)   The warrant shall require the person charged with the execution to pay the sum to be levied to the court officer for the court that issued the warrant.

(4)   A warrant to which this rule applies may be executed by the persons to whom it was directed or by any of the following persons, whether or not the warrant was directed to them –

(a)   A constable for any police area in England and Wales, acting in his own police area;

(b)   where the warrant is one to which section 125A of the Magistrates' Courts Act 1980 applies, a civilian enforcement officer within the meaning of section 125A of the 1980 Act; and

(c)   where the warrant is one to which section 125A of the 1980 Act applies, any of the individuals described in section 125B(1) of the 1980 Act;

and in this rule any reference to the person charged with the execution of a warrant includes any of the above persons who is for the time being authorised to execute the warrant, whether or not they have the warrant in their possession at the time.

(5)   A person executing a warrant of distress shall –

    (a)   either –

        (i)   if he has the warrant with him, show it to the person against whom the distress is levied, or

        (ii)   otherwise, state where the warrant is and what arrangements may be made to allow the person against whom distress is levied to inspect it;

    (b)   explain, in ordinary language, the sum for which distress is levied and the reason for the distress;

    (c)   where the person executing the warrant is one of the persons referred to in paragraph (4)(b) or (c) above, show the person against whom distress is levied a written statement under section 125A(4) of 125B(4) as appropriate; and

    (d)   in any case, show documentary proof of his identity.

(6)   There shall not be taken under the warrant the clothing or bedding of any person or his family or the tools, books, vehicles or other equipment which he personally needs to use in his employment, business or vocation, provided that in this paragraph the word "person" shall not include a corporation.

(7)   The distress levied under any such warrant as aforesaid shall be sold within such period beginning not earlier than the 6th day after the making of the distress as may be specified in the warrant, or if no period is specified in the warrant, within a period beginning on the 6th day and ending on the 14th day after the making of the distress:
Provided that with the consent in writing of the person against whom the distress is levied the distress may be sold before the beginning of the said period.

(8)   The clerk of the court which issued the warrant may, on the application of the person charged with the execution of it, extend the period within which the distress must be sold by any number of days not exceeding 60; but following the grant of such an application there shall be no further variation or extension of that period.

(9)   The said distress shall be sold by public auction or in such other manner as the person against whom the distress is levied may in writing allow.

(10) Notwithstanding anything in the preceding provisions of this rule, the said distress shall not be sold if the sum for which the warrant was issued and the charges of taking and keeping the distress have been paid.

(11) Subject to any direction to the contrary in the warrant, where the distress is levied on household goods, the goods shall not, without the consent in writing of the person against whom the distress is levied, be removed from the house until the day of sale; and so much of the goods shall be impounded as is in the opinion of the person executing the warrant sufficient to satisfy the distress, by affixing to the articles impounded a conspicuous mark.

(12) The person charged with the execution of any such warrant as aforesaid shall cause the distress to be sold, and may deduct out of the amount realised by the sale all costs and charges incurred in effecting the sale; and he shall return to the owner the balance, if any, after retaining the amount of the sum for which the warrant was issued and the proper costs and charges of the execution of the warrant.

(13) The person charged with the execution of any such warrant as aforesaid shall as soon as practicable send to the court officer for the court that issued it a written account of the costs and charges incurred in executing it; and the court officer shall allow the person against whom the distress was levied to inspect the account within one month after the levy of the distress at any reasonable time to be appointed by the court.

(14) If any person pays or tenders to the person charged with the execution of any such warrant as aforesaid the sum mentioned in the warrant, or produces a receipt for that sum given by the court officer for the court that issued the warrant, and also pays the

amount of the costs and charges of the distress up to the time of the payment or tender or the production of the receipt, the person as aforesaid shall not execute the warrant, or shall cease to execute it, as the case may be.

[Formerly rule 54 of the Magistrates' Courts Rules 1981.]

52.9   Payment after imprisonment imposed by magistrates' court

(1) The persons authorised for the purposes of section 79(2) of the Magistrates' Courts Act 1980 to receive a part payment are –

  (a)   unless there has been issued a warrant of distress or commitment, the court officer for the court enforcing payment of the sum, or any person appointed under section 88 of that Act to supervise the offender;

  (b)   where the issue of a warrant of commitment has been suspended on conditions which provide for payment to be made to the court officer for another magistrates' court, that court officer;

  (c)   any constable holding a warrant of distress or commitment or, where the warrant is directed to some other person, that person; and

  (d)   the governor or keeper of the prison or place in which the defaulter is detained, or other person having lawful custody of the defaulter:
Provided that –

    (i)   the said governor or keeper shall not be required to accept any sum tendered in part payment under the said section 79(2) of the 1980 Act except on a week-day between 9 o'clock in the morning and 5 o'clock in the afternoon, and

    (ii)   no person shall be required to receive in part payment under the said subsection (2) an amount which, or so much of an amount as, will not procure a reduction of the period for which the defaulter is committed or ordered to be detained.

(2) Where a person having custody of a defaulter receives payment of any sum he shall note receipt of the sum on the warrant of commitment.

(3) Where the magistrates' court officer for a court other than the court enforcing payment of the sums receives payment of any sum he shall inform the magistrates' court officer for the other court.

(4) Where a person appointed under section 88 of the 1980 Act to supervise an offender receives payment of any sum, he shall send it forthwith to the magistrates' court officer for the court which appointed him.

[Formerly rule 55 of the Magistrates' Courts Rules 1981.]

52.10   Order for supervision made by magistrates' court

(1) Unless an order under section 88(1) of the Magistrates' Courts Act 1980 is made in the offender's presence, the court officer for the court making the order shall deliver to the offender, or serve on him by post, notice in writing of the order.

(2) It shall be the duty of any person for the time being appointed under the said section to advise and befriend the offender with a view to inducing him to pay the sum adjudged to be paid and thereby avoid committal to custody and to give any information required by a magistrates' court about the offender's conduct and means.

[Formerly rule 56 of the Magistrates' Courts Rules 1981.]

52.11   Transfer of magistrates' court fine order

(1) The court officer for a magistrates' court which has made a transfer of fine order under

section 89 or 90 or section 90 as applied by section 91 of the Magistrates' Courts Act 1980 shall send to the clerk of the court having jurisdiction under the order a copy of the order.

(2) Where a magistrates' court has made a transfer of fine order in respect of a sum adjudged to be paid by a court in Scotland or in Northern Ireland the court officer shall send a copy of the order to the clerk of the Scottish court or to the clerk of the Northern Irish court, as the case may be.

(3) Where a court officer receives a copy of a transfer of fine order (whether made in England and Wales, or in Scotland or in Northern Ireland) specifying his court as the court by which payment of the sum in question is to be enforceable, he shall thereupon, if possible, deliver or send by post to the offender notice in writing.

(4) Where under a transfer of fine order a sum adjudged to be paid by a Scottish court or by a Northern Irish court is enforceable by a magistrates' court –

(a)   if the sum is paid, the court officer shall send it to the clerk of the Scottish court or to the clerk of the Northern Irish court, as the case may be; or

(b)   if the sum is not paid, the court officer shall inform the clerk of the Scottish court or the clerk of the Northern Irish court, as the case may be, of the manner in which the adjudication has been satisfied or that the sum, or any balance thereof, appears to be irrecoverable.

[*Formerly rule 57 of the Magistrates' Courts Rules 1981.*]

52.12   Directions by magistrates' court that money found on defaulter shall not be applied in satisfaction of debt

Where the defaulter is committed to, or ordered to be detained in, a prison or other place of detention, any direction given under section 80(2) of the Magistrates' Courts Act 1980 shall be endorsed on the warrant of commitment.

[*Formerly rule 64 of the Magistrates' Courts Rules 1981.*]

52.13   Particulars of fine enforcement to be entered in magistrates' court register

(1) Where the court on the occasion of convicting an offender of an offence issues a warrant of commitment for a default in paying a sum adjudged to be paid by the conviction or, having power to issue such a warrant, fixes a term of imprisonment under section 77(2) of the Magistrates' Courts Act 1980, the reasons for the court's action shall be entered in the register, or any separate record kept for the purpose of recording particulars of fine enforcement.

(2) There shall be entered in the register, or any such record, particulars of any –

(a)   means inquiry under section 82 of the 1980 Act;

(b)   hearing under subsection (5) of the said section 82;

(c)   allowance of further time for the payment of a sum adjudged to be paid by a conviction;

(d)   direction that such a sum shall be paid by instalments including any direction varying the number of instalments payable, the amount of any instalments payable and the date on which any instalment becomes payable;

(e)   distress for the enforcement of such a sum;

(f)   attachment of earnings order for the enforcement of such a sum;

(g)   decision of the Secretary of State to make deductions from income support under section 24 of the Criminal Justice Act 1991;

(h)   order under the 1980 Act placing a person under supervision pending payment of such a sum;

(i)   order under section 85(1) of the 1980 Act remitting the whole or any part of a fine;

(j)   order under section 120(4) of the 1980 Act remitting the whole or any part of any sum enforceable under that section (forfeiture of recognizance);

(k)   authority granted under section 87(3) of the 1980 Act authorising the taking of proceedings in the High Court or county court for the recovery of any sum adjudged to be paid by a conviction;

(l)   transfer of fine order made by the court;

(m)   order transferring a fine to the court;

(n)   order under section 140(1) of the Powers of Criminal Courts (Sentencing) Act 2000 specifying the court for the purpose of enforcing a fine imposed or a recognizance forfeited by the Crown Court; and

(o)   any fine imposed or recognizance forfeited by a coroner which has to be treated as imposed or forfeited by the court;

(p)   reference by a justice of the peace of an application under section 77(5) of the 1980 Act for a review of the terms on which a warrant of commitment is postponed; or

(q)   order under section 77(3) of the 1980 Act varying the time for which or the conditions subject to which a warrant of commitment is postponed.

[*Formerly rule 65 of the Magistrates' Courts Rules 1981. As to the requirement to keep a register, see rule 6.1.*]

52.14   Attendance Centre Order imposed by magistrates' court in default of payment of a financial penalty

(1)   Where any person is ordered, under section 60 of the Powers of Criminal Courts (Sentencing) Act 2000, to attend at an attendance centre in default of payment of a sum of money, payment may thereafter be made –

(a)   of the whole of the said sum, to the court officer for the magistrates' court which made the order, or

(b)   of the whole or, subject to paragraph (2), any part of the said sum, to the officer in charge of the attendance centre specified in the order ("the officer in charge").

(2)   The officer in charge may not accept a part payment that would not secure the reduction by one or more complete hours of the period of attendance specified in the order.

(3)   On receiving a payment under paragraph (1) the court officer shall forthwith notify the officer in charge.

(4)   The officer in charge shall pay any money received by him under paragraph (1) above to the court officer and shall note the receipt of the money in the register maintained at the attendance centre.

[*Formerly rule 3 of the Magistrates' Courts (Attendance Centre) Rules 1992 and rule 27 of the Magistrates' Courts (Children and Young Persons) Rules 1992.*]

PART 53   COMPENSATION ORDERS

53.1   Review of compensation order made by a magistrates' court

(1)   An application under section 133 of the Powers of Criminal Courts (Sentencing) Act 2000 for the review of a compensation order shall be by complaint.

(2)   The court officer for the magistrates' court to which the complaint is made shall send a letter to the person for whose benefit the compensation order was made, inviting him to make observations and to attend any hearing of the complaint and advising him of his right to be heard.

[*This rule derives in part from rule 104 Magistrates' Courts Rules 1981.*]

PART 54 CONDITIONAL DISCHARGE

54.1 Further offence committed after offender conditionally discharged by a magistrates' court

(1) Where a magistrates' court deals with a person under section 13 of the Powers of Criminal Courts (Sentencing) Act 2000 in relation to an order for conditional discharge which was not made by that court the court officer shall give notice of the result of the proceedings to the court officer for the court by which the order was made.

(2) The court officer for a magistrates' court receiving a notice under this rule shall note the decision of the other court in the register.

[Formerly rule 28 of the Magistrates' Courts Rules 1981. For the requirement to keep a register, see rule 6.1.]

PART 55 ROAD TRAFFIC PENALTIES

55.1 Endorsement of driving licence by magistrates' court

(1) Where a magistrates' court convicts a person of an offence and, under section 44 of the Road Traffic Offenders Act 1988 orders that particulars of the conviction, and, if the court orders him to be disqualified, particulars of the disqualification, shall be endorsed on any licence held by him, the particulars to be endorsed shall include –

   (a) the name of the local justice area for which the court is acting;
   (b) the date of the conviction and the date on which sentence was passed (if different);
   (c) particulars of the offence including the date on which it was committed; and
   (d) particulars of the sentence of the court (including the period of disqualification, if any).

(2) Where a magistrates' court orders that the licence of an offender be endorsed as mentioned in paragraph (1) or imposes an interim disqualification as mentioned in rule 43.1(1)(f) and the court officer knows or is informed of the date of birth and sex of the offender, the court officer shall send the information to the licensing authority which granted the licence.

[Formerly rule 32 of the Magistrates' Courts Rules 1981.]

55.2 Application to magistrates' court for removal of disqualification

(1) An application under section 42 of the Road Traffic Offenders Act 1988 or paragraph 7 of Schedule 4 to the Road Traffic (Consequential Provisions) Act 1988 for an order removing a disqualification or disqualifications for holding or obtaining a licence shall be by complaint.

(2) The justice to whom the complaint is made shall issue a summons directed to the chief officer of police requiring him to appear before a magistrates' court to show cause why an order should not be made on the complaint.

(3) Where a magistrates' court makes an order under either of the provisions mentioned in paragraph (1) the court shall cause notice of the making of the order and a copy of the particulars of the order endorsed on the licence, if any, previously held by the applicant for the order to be sent to the licensing authority to which notice of the applicant's disqualification was sent.

[Formerly rule 101 of the Magistrates' Courts Rules 1981.]

55.3 Application to magistrates' court for review of course organiser's refusal to issue certificate of satisfactory completion of driving course

(1) An application to the supervising court under section 34B(6) or (7) of the Road Traffic

Offenders Act 1988 shall be served on the court officer within 28 days after the date specified in an order under section 34A(2) of the1988 Act, where that date falls on or after 24th May 1993.

(2)   An application under section 34B(6) of the 1988 Act shall be accompanied by the notice under section 34B(5) of the 1988 Act.

(3)   Where such an application is served on the court officer –

    (a)   he shall fix a date and time for the hearing of the application; and

    (b)   he shall –

        (i)   serve a copy of the application on the course organiser, and

        (ii)   serve notice of the hearing on the applicant and course organiser.

(4)   If the course organiser fails to appear or be represented at the hearing of the application without reasonable excuse, the court may proceed to decide the application in his absence.

(5)   In this rule, "course organiser" and "supervising court" have the meanings assigned to them in England and Wales by section 34C of the 1988 Act.

[Formerly rule 101A of the Magistrates' Courts Rules 1981.]

55.4   Statutory declaration under section 72 or 73 of the Road Traffic Offenders Act 1988

Where a magistrates' court officer receives a statutory declaration under section 72 or 73 of the Road Traffic Offenders Act 1988 (fixed penalty notice or notice fixed to vehicle invalid) he shall send a copy of it to the appropriate chief officer of police.

[Note. Formerly rule 7.6 of these Rules, which derived from rule 112 of the Magistrates' Courts Rules 1981.]

PART 56   CRIMINAL PROCEEDINGS UNDER THE CRIMINAL JUSTICE ACT 1988 AND THE DRUG TRAFFICKING ACT 1994

56.1   Statements etc, relevant to making confiscation orders

(1)   Where a prosecutor or defendant –

    (a)   tenders to a magistrates' court any statement or other document under section 73 of the Criminal Justice Act 1988 in any proceedings in respect of an offence listed in Schedule 4 to that Act; or

    (b)   tenders to the Crown Court any statement or other document under section 11 of the Drug Trafficking Act 1994 or section 73 of the 1988 Act in any proceedings in respect of a drug trafficking offence or in respect of an offence to which Part VI of the 1988 Act applies,

he must serve a copy as soon as practicable on the defendant or the prosecutor, as the case may be.

(2)   Any statement tendered by the prosecutor to the magistrates' court under section 73 of the 1988 Act or to the Crown Court under section 11(1) of the 1994 Act or section 73(1A) of the 1988 Act shall include the following particulars –

    (a)   the name of the defendant;

    (b)   the name of the person by whom the statement is made and the date on which it was made;

    (c)   where the statement is not tendered immediately after the defendant has been convicted, the date on which and the place where the relevant conviction occurred; and

(d)   such information known to the prosecutor as is relevant to the determination as to whether or not the defendant has benefited from drug trafficking or relevant criminal conduct and to the assessment of the value of his proceeds of drug trafficking or, as the case may be, benefit from relevant criminal conduct.

(3) Where, in accordance with section 11(7) of the 1994 Act or section 73(1C) of the 1988 Act, the defendant indicates the extent to which he accepts any allegation contained within the prosecutor's statement, if he indicates the same in writing to the prosecutor, he must serve a copy of that reply on the court officer.

(4) Expressions used in this rule shall have the same meanings as in the 1994 Act or, where appropriate, the 1988 Act.

[*Formerly rule 104A of the Magistrates' Courts Rules 1981 and rule 25A of the Crown Court Rules 1982. The relevant provisions of the 1988 and 1994 Acts were repealed on 24th March 2003, but they continue to have effect in respect of proceedings for offences committed before that date.*]

56.2   Postponed determinations

(1) Where an application is made by the defendant or the prosecutor –

(a)   to a magistrates' court under section 72A(5)(a) of the Criminal Justice Act 1988 asking the court to exercise its powers under section 72A(4) of that Act; or

(b)   to the Crown Court under section 3(5)(a) of the Drug Trafficking Act 1994 asking the Court to exercise its powers under section 3(4) of that Act, or under section 72A(5)(a) of the 1988 Act asking the court to exercise its powers under section 72A(4) of the 1988 Act,

the application must be made in writing and a copy must be served on the prosecutor or the defendant, as the case may be.

(2) A party served with a copy of an application under paragraph (1) shall, within 28 days of the date of service, notify the applicant and the court officer, in writing, whether or not he proposes to oppose the application, giving his reasons for any opposition.

(3) After the expiry of the period referred to in paragraph (2), the court shall determine whether an application under paragraph (1) is to be dealt with –

(a)   without a hearing; or

(b)   at a hearing at which the parties may be represented.

[*Formerly rule 104B of the Magistrates' Courts Rules 1981 and rule 34 of the Crown Court Rules 1982. The relevant provisions of the 1988 and 1994 Acts were repealed on 24th March 2003, but they continue to have effect in respect of proceedings for offences committed before that date.*]

56.3   Confiscation orders – revised assessments

(1) Where the prosecutor makes an application under section 13, 14 or 15 of the Drug Trafficking Act 1994 or section 74A, 74B or 74C of the Criminal Justice Act 1988, the application must be in writing and a copy must be served on the defendant.

(2) The application must include the following particulars –

(a)   the name of the defendant;

(b)   the date on which and the place where any relevant conviction occurred;

(c)   the date on which and the place where any relevant confiscation order was made or, as the case may be, varied;

(d)   the grounds on which the application is made; and

(e)   an indication of the evidence available to support the application.

[*Formerly rule 104C of the Magistrates' Courts Rules 1981 and rule 35 of the Crown Court Rules 1982. The relevant provisions of the 1988 and 1994 Acts were repealed on 24th March 2003, but they continue to have effect in respect of proceedings for offences committed before that date.*]

56.4   Application to Crown Court to discharge or vary order to make material available

(1) Where an order under section 93H of the Criminal Justice Act 1988 (order to make material available), section 55 of the Drug Trafficking Act 1994 (order to make material available), or section 345 of the Proceeds of Crime Act 2002 (production orders) has been made by the Crown Court, any person affected by it may apply in writing to the court officer for the order to be discharged or varied, and on hearing such an application a circuit judge or, in the case of an order under the 2002 Act, a judge entitled to exercise the jurisdiction of the Crown Court may discharge the order or make such variations to it as he thinks fit.

(2) Subject to paragraph (3), where a person proposes to make an application under paragraph (1) for the discharge or variation of an order, he shall give a copy of the application, not later than 48 hours before the making of the application –

   (a)   to a constable at the police station specified in the order; or
   (b)   where the application for the order was made under the 2002 Act and was not made by a constable, to the office of the appropriate officer who made the application, as specified in the order,

   in either case together with a notice indicating the time and place at which the application for discharge or variation is to be made.

(3) A circuit judge or, in the case of an order under the 2002 Act, a judge entitled to exercise the jurisdiction of the Crown Court may direct that paragraph (2) need not be complied with if he is satisfied that the person making the application has good reason to seek a discharge or variation of the order as soon as possible and it is not practicable to comply with that paragraph.

(4) In this rule:

   "appropriate officer" has the meaning given to it by section 378 of the 2002 Act;

   "constable" includes a person commissioned by the Commissioners for Her Majesty's Revenue and Customs;

   "police station" includes a place for the time being occupied by Her Majesty's Revenue and Customs.

[*This rule derives in part from rule 25B of the Crown Court Rules 1982. For further rules applicable to investigations under the 2002 Act, see Part 62. The relevant provision of the 1988 Act was repealed on 24th February 2003, but it continues to have effect in respect of proceedings for offences committed before that date.*]

56.5   Application to Crown Court for increase in term of imprisonment in default of payment of a confiscation order

(1) This rule applies to applications made, or that have effect as made, to the Crown Court under section 10 of the Drug Trafficking Act 1994 and section 75A of the Criminal Justice Act 1988 (interest on sums unpaid under confiscation orders).

(2) Notice of an application to which this rule applies to increase the term of imprisonment or detention fixed in default of payment of a confiscation order by a person ("the defendant") shall be made by the prosecutor in writing to the court officer. (3) A notice under paragraph (2) shall –

   (a)   state the name and address of the defendant;
   (b)   specify the grounds for the application;
   (c)   give details of the enforcement measures taken, if any; and
   (d)   include a copy of the confiscation order.

(4) On receiving a notice under paragraph (2), the court officer shall –

   (a)   forthwith send to the defendant and the magistrates' court required to enforce payment of the confiscation order under section 140(1) of the Powers of Criminal Courts (Sentencing) Act 2000, a copy of the said notice; and

(b)   notify in writing the applicant and the defendant of the date, time and place appointed for the hearing of the application.

(5)   Where the Crown Court makes an order pursuant to an application mentioned in paragraph (1) above, the court officer shall send forthwith a copy of the order –

(a)   to the applicant;

(b)   to the defendant;

(c)   where the defendant is at the time of the making of the order in custody, to the person having custody of him; and

(d)   to the magistrates' court mentioned in paragraph (4)(a).

[*Formerly rule 33 of the Crown Court Rules 1982. The relevant provisions of the 1988 and 1994 Acts were repealed on 24th March 2003, but they continue to have effect in respect of proceedings for offences committed before that date.*]

56.6   Drug trafficking – compensation on acquittal in Crown Court

Where a Crown Court cancels a confiscation order under section 22(2) of the Drug Trafficking Act 1994, the court officer shall serve notice to that effect on the High Court and on the magistrates' court which has responsibility for enforcing the order.

[*Formerly rule 36 of the Crown Court Rules 1982. The relevant provision of the 1994 Act was repealed on 24th March 2003, but it continues to have effect in respect of proceedings for offences committed before that date.*]

PART 57   PROCEEDS OF CRIME ACT 2002 – RULES APPLICABLE TO ALL PROCEEDINGS

57.1   Interpretation

In this Part and in Parts 58, 59, 60 and 61:

"business day" means any day other than a Saturday, Sunday, Christmas Day or Good Friday, or a bank holiday under the Banking and Financial Dealings Act 1971, in England and Wales;

"document" means anything in which information of any description is recorded;

"hearsay evidence" means evidence consisting of hearsay within the meaning of section 1(2) of the Civil Evidence Act 1995;

"restraint proceedings" means proceedings under sections 42 and 58(2) and (3) of the Proceeds of Crime Act 2002;

"receivership proceedings" means proceedings under sections 48, 49, 50, 51, 54(4), 59(2) and (3), 62 and 63 of the 2002 Act;

"witness statement" means a written statement signed by a person which contains the evidence, and only that evidence, which that person would be allowed to give orally; and

words and expressions used have the same meaning as in Part 2 of the 2002 Act.

[*This rule derives from rule 2 of the Crown Court (Confiscation, Restraint and Receivership) Rules 2003.*]

57.2   Calculation of time

(1)   This rule shows how to calculate any period of time for doing any act which is specified by this Part and Parts 58, 59, 60 and 61 for the purposes of any proceedings under Part 2

of the Proceeds of Crime Act 2002 or by an order of the Crown Court in restraint proceedings or receivership proceedings.

(2) A period of time expressed as a number of days shall be computed as clear days.

(3) In this rule "clear days" means that in computing the number of days –

(a)   the day on which the period begins; and
(b)   if the end of the period is defined by reference to an event, the day on which that event occurs are not included.

(4) Where the specified period is five days or less and includes a day which is not a business day that day does not count.

[*Formerly rule 3 of the Crown Court (Confiscation, Restraint and Receivership) Rules 2003.*]

57.3   Court office closed

When the period specified by this Part or Parts 58, 59, 60 and 61, or by an order of the Crown Court under Part 2 of the Proceeds of Crime Act 2002, for doing any act at the court office falls on a day on which the office is closed, that act shall be in time if done on the next day on which the court office is open.

[*Formerly rule 4 of the Crown Court (Confiscation, Restraint and Receivership) Rules 2003.*]

57.4   Application for registration of Scottish or Northern Ireland Order

(1) This rule applies to an application for registration of an order under article 6 of the Proceeds of Crime Act 2002 (Enforcement in different parts of the United Kingdom) Order 2002.

(2) The application may be made without notice.

(3) The application must be in writing and may be supported by a witness statement which must –

(a)   exhibit the order or a certified copy of the order; and
(b)   to the best of the witness's ability, give full details of the realisable property located in England and Wales in respect of which the order was made and specify the person holding that realisable property.

(4) If the court registers the order, the applicant must serve notice of the registration on –

(a)   any person who holds realisable property to which the order applies; and
(b)   any other person whom the applicant knows to be affected by the order.

(5) The permission of the Crown Court under rule 57.13 is not required to serve the notice outside England and Wales.

[*Formerly rule 30 of the Crown Court (Confiscation, Restraint and Receivership) Rules 2003.*]

57.5   Application to vary or set aside registration

(1) An application to vary or set aside registration of an order under article 6 of the Proceeds of Crime Act 2002 (Enforcement in different parts of the United Kingdom) Order 2002 may be made to the Crown Court by –

(a)   any person who holds realisable property to which the order applies; and
(b)   any other person affected by the order.

(2) The application must be in writing and may be supported by a witness statement.

(3) The application and any witness statement must be lodged with the Crown Court.

(4) The application must be served on the person who applied for registration at least seven days before the date fixed by the court for hearing the application, unless the Crown Court specifies a shorter period.

(5) No property in England and Wales may be realised in pursuance of the order before the Crown Court has decided the application.

[*Formerly rule 31 of the Crown Court (Confiscation, Restraint and Receivership) Rules 2003.*]

57.6   Register of orders

(1) The Crown Court must keep, under the direction of the Lord Chancellor, a register of the orders registered under article 6 of the Proceeds of Crime Act 2002 (Enforcement in different parts of the United Kingdom) Order 2002.

(2) The register must include details of any variation or setting aside of a registration under rule 57.5 and of any execution issued on a registered order.

(3) If the person who applied for registration of an order which is subsequently registered notifies the Crown Court that the court which made the order has varied or discharged the order, details of the variation or discharge, as the case may be, must be entered in the register.

[*Formerly rule 32 of the Crown Court (Confiscation, Restraint and Receivership) Rules 2003.*]

57.7   Statements of truth

(1) Any witness statement required to be served by this Part or by Parts 58, 59, 60 or 61 must be verified by a statement of truth contained in the witness statement.

(2) A statement of truth is a declaration by the person making the witness statement to the effect that the witness statement is true to the best of his knowledge and belief and that he made the statement knowing that, if it were tendered in evidence, he would be liable to prosecution if he wilfully stated in it anything which he knew to be false or did not believe to be true.

(3) The statement of truth must be signed by the person making the witness statement.

(4) If the person making the witness statement fails to verify the witness statement by a statement of truth, the Crown Court may direct that it shall not be admissible as evidence.

[*Formerly rule 54 of the Crown Court (Confiscation, Restraint and Receivership) Rules 2003.*]

57.8   Use of witness statements for other purposes

(1) Except as provided by this rule, a witness statement served in proceedings under Part 2 of the Proceeds of Crime Act 2002 may be used only for the purpose of the proceedings in which it is served.

(2) Paragraph (1) does not apply if and to the extent that –

(a)   the witness gives consent in writing to some other use of it;

(b)   the Crown Court gives permission for some other use; or

(c)   the witness statement has been put in evidence at a hearing held in public.

[*Formerly rule 55 of the Crown Court (Confiscation, Restraint and Receivership) Rules 2003.*]

57.9   Expert evidence

(1) A party to proceedings under Part 2 of the Proceeds of Crime Act 2002 who wishes to adduce expert evidence (whether of fact or opinion) in the proceedings must, as soon as practicable –

(a)   serve on the other parties a statement in writing of any finding or opinion which he proposes to adduce by way of such evidence; and

(b)   serve on any party who requests it in writing, a copy of (or if it appears to the party proposing to adduce the evidence to be more practicable, a reasonable opportunity to examine) –

(i)   the record of any observation, test, calculation or other procedure on which the finding or opinion is based, and

(ii)   any document or other thing or substance in respect of which the observation, test, calculation or other procedure mentioned in paragraph (1)(b)(i) has been carried out.

(c)   A party may serve notice in writing waiving his right to be served with any of the matters mentioned in paragraph (1) and, in particular, may agree that the statement mentioned in paragraph (1)(a) may be given to him orally and not served in writing.

(d)   If a party who wishes to adduce expert evidence in proceedings under Part 2 of the 2002 Act fails to comply with this rule he may not adduce that evidence in those proceedings without the leave of the court, except where rule 57.10 applies.

[*Formerly rule 56 of the Crown Court (Confiscation, Restraint and Receivership) Rules 2003.*]

57.10   Exceptions to procedure for expert evidence

(1)   If a party has reasonable grounds for believing that the disclosure of any evidence in compliance with rule 57.9 might lead to the intimidation, or attempted intimidation, of any person on whose evidence he intends to rely in the proceedings, or otherwise to the course of justice being interfered with, he shall not be obliged to comply with those requirements in relation to that evidence, unless the Crown Court orders otherwise.

(2)   Where, in accordance with paragraph (1), a party considers that he is not obliged to comply with the requirements imposed by rule 57.9 with regard to any evidence in relation to any other party, he must serve notice in writing on that party stating –

(a)   that the evidence is being withheld; and

(b)   the reasons for withholding the evidence.

[*Formerly rule 57 of the Crown Court (Confiscation, Restraint and Receivership) Rules 2003.*]

57.11   Service of documents

(1)   Part 4 and rule 32.1 (notice required to accompany process served outside the United Kingdom and translations) shall not apply in restraint proceedings and receivership proceedings.

(2)   Where this Part or Parts 58, 59, 60 or 61 requires service of a document, then, unless the Crown Court directs otherwise, the document may be served by any of the following methods –

(a)   in all cases, by delivering the document personally to the party to be served;

(b)   if no solicitor is acting for the party to be served by delivering the document at, or by sending it by first class post to, his residence or his last-known residence; or

(c)   if a solicitor is acting for the party to be served –

(i)   by delivering the document at, or sending it by first class post to, the solicitor's business address, or

(ii)   where the solicitor's business address includes a numbered box at a document exchange, by leaving the document at that document exchange or at a document exchange which transmits documents on every business day to that document exchange, or

(iii) if the solicitor has indicated that he is willing to accept service by facsimile transmission, by sending a legible copy of the document by facsimile transmission to the solicitor's office.

(3) A document shall, unless the contrary is proved, be deemed to have been served –

(a)   in the case of service by first class post, on the second business day after posting;

(b)   in the case of service in accordance with paragraph (2)(c)(ii), on the second business day after the day on which it is left at the document exchange; and

(c)   in the case of service in accordance with paragraph (2)(c)(iii), where it is transmitted on a business day before 4 p.m., on that day and in any other case, on the next business day.

(4) An order made in restraint proceedings or receivership proceedings may be enforced against the defendant or any other person affected by it notwithstanding that service of a copy of the order has not been effected in accordance with this rule if the Crown Court is satisfied that the person had notice of the order by being present when the order was made.

[This rule derives in part from rule 58 of the Crown Court (Confiscation, Restraint and Receivership) Rules 2003.]

57.12   Service by an alternative method

(1) Where it appears to the Crown Court that there is a good reason to authorise service by a method not otherwise permitted by rule 57.11, the court may make an order permitting service by an alternative method.

(2) An application for an order permitting service by an alternative method –

(a)   must be supported by evidence; and

(b)   may be made without notice.

(3) An order permitting service by an alternative method must specify –

(a)   the method of service; and

(b)   the date when the document will be deemed to be served.

[Formerly rule 59 of the Crown Court (Confiscation, Restraint and Receivership) Rules 2003.]

57.13   Service outside the jurisdiction

(1) Where this Part requires a document to be served on someone who is outside England and Wales, it may be served outside England and Wales with the permission of the Crown Court.

(2) Where a document is to be served outside England and Wales it may be served by any method permitted by the law of the country in which it is to be served.

(3) Nothing in this rule or in any court order shall authorise or require any person to do anything in the country where the document is to be served which is against the law of that country.

(4) Where this Part requires a document to be served a certain period of time before the date of a hearing and the recipient does not appear at the hearing, the hearing must not take place unless the Crown Court is satisfied that the document has been duly served.

[Formerly rule 60 of the Crown Court (Confiscation, Restraint and Receivership) Rules 2003.]

57.14   Certificates of service

(1) Where this Part requires that the applicant for an order in restraint proceedings or receivership proceedings serve a document on another person, the applicant must lodge a certificate of service with the Crown Court within seven days of service of the document.

(2) The certificate must state –

    (a)   the method of service;
    (b)   the date of service; and
    (c)   if the document is served under rule 57.12, such other information as the court may require when making the order permitting service by an alternative method.

(3) Where a document is to be served by the Crown Court in restraint proceedings and receivership proceedings and the court is unable to serve it, the court must send a notice of non-service stating the method attempted to the party who requested service.

[*Formerly rule 61 of the Crown Court (Confiscation, Restraint and Receivership) Rules 2003.*]

57.15   External requests and orders

(1) The rules in this Part and in Parts 59 to 61 and 71 apply with the necessary modifications to proceedings under the Proceeds of Crime Act 2002 (External Requests and Orders) Order 2005 in the same way that they apply to corresponding proceedings under Part 2 of the Proceeds of Crime Act 2002.

(2) This table shows how provisions of the 2005 Order correspond with provisions of the 2002 Act.

Article of the Proceeds of Crime Act 2002 (External Requests and Orders) Order 2005	Section of the Proceeds of Crime Act 2002
B3	41
B4	42
B5	43
B6	44
B10	48
B11	49
B12	58
B18	31
B22	50
B24	51
B25	52
B26	53
B29	55
B31	57
B36	62
B37	63
B39	65
B40	66

PART 58   PROCEEDS OF CRIME ACT 2002 – RULES APPLICABLE ONLY TO CONFISCATION PROCEEDINGS

58.1   Statements in connection with confiscation orders

(1)   When the prosecutor is required, under section 16 of the Proceeds of Crime Act 2002, to give a statement to the Crown Court, the prosecutor must also, as soon as practicable, serve a copy of the statement on the defendant.

(2)   Any statement given to the Crown Court by the prosecutor under section 16 of the 2002 Act must, in addition to the information required by the 2002 Act, include the following information –

(a)   the name of the defendant;

(b)   the name of the person by whom the statement is made and the date on which it is made; and

(c)   where the statement is not given to the Crown Court immediately after the defendant has been convicted, the date on which and the place where the relevant conviction occurred.

(3)   Where, under section 17 of the 2002 Act, the Crown Court orders the defendant to indicate the extent to which he accepts each allegation in a statement given by the prosecutor, the defendant must indicate this in writing to the prosecutor and must give a copy to the Crown Court.

(4)   Where the Crown Court orders the defendant to give to it any information under section 18 of the 2002 Act, the defendant must provide the information in writing and must, as soon as practicable, serve a copy of it on the prosecutor.

[Note. This rule derives from rule 5 of the Crown Court (Confiscation, Restraint and Receivership) Rules 2003.]

58.2   Postponement of confiscation proceedings

The Crown Court may grant a postponement under section 14(1)(b) of the Proceeds of Crime Act 2002 without a hearing.

[Note. Formerly rule 6 of the Crown Court (Confiscation, Restraint and Receivership) Rules 2003.]

58.3   Application for reconsideration

(1)   This rule applies where the prosecutor makes an application under section 19, 20 or 21 of the Proceeds of Crime Act 2002.

(2)   The application must be in writing and give details of –

(a)   the name of the defendant;

(b)   the date on which and the place where any relevant conviction occurred;

(c)   the date on which and the place where any relevant confiscation order was made or varied;

(d)   the grounds for the application; and

(e)   an indication of the evidence available to support the application.

(3)   The application must be lodged with the Crown Court.

(4)   The application must be served on the defendant at least seven days before the date fixed by the court for hearing the application, unless the Crown Court specifies a shorter period.

[Note. This rule derives from rule 7 of the Crown Court (Confiscation, Restraint and Receivership) Rules 2003.]

58.4   Application for new calculation of available amount

(1) This rule applies where the prosecutor or a receiver makes an application under section 22 of the Proceeds of Crime Act 2002 for a new calculation of the available amount.
(2) The application must be in writing and may be supported by a witness statement.
(3) The application and any witness statement must be lodged with the Crown Court.
(4) The application and any witness statement must be served on –

(a)   the defendant;
(b)   the receiver, if the prosecutor is making the application and a receiver has been appointed under section 50 of the 2002 Act; and
(c)   the prosecutor, if the receiver is making the application,

at least seven days before the date fixed by the court for hearing the application, unless the Crown Court specifies a shorter period.

[Note. This rule derives from rule 8 of the Crown Court (Confiscation, Restraint and Receivership) Rules 2003.]

58.5   Variation of confiscation order due to inadequacy of available amount

(1) This rule applies where the defendant or a receiver makes an application under section 23 of the Proceeds of Crime Act 2002 for the variation of a confiscation order.
(2) The application must be in writing and may be supported by a witness statement.
(3) The application and any witness statement must be lodged with the Crown Court.
(4) The application and any witness statement must be served on –

(a)   the prosecutor;
(b)   the defendant, if the receiver is making the application; and
(c)   the receiver, if the defendant is making the application and a receiver has been appointed under section 50 of the 2002 Act,

at least seven days before the date fixed by the court for hearing the application, unless the Crown Court specifies a shorter period.

[Note. This rule derives from rule 9 of the Crown Court (Confiscation, Restraint and Receivership) Rules 2003.]

58.6   Application by magistrates' court officer to discharge confiscation order

(1) This rule applies where a magistrates' court officer makes an application under section 24 or 25 of the Proceeds of Crime Act 2002 for the discharge of a confiscation order.
(2) The application must be in writing and give details of –

(a)   the confiscation order;
(b)   the amount outstanding under the order; and
(c)   the grounds for the application.

(3) The application must be served on –

(a)   the defendant;
(b)   the prosecutor; and
(c)   any receiver appointed under section 50 of the 2002 Act.

(4) The Crown Court may determine the application without a hearing unless a person listed in paragraph (3) indicates, within seven days after the application was served on him, that he would like to make representations.
(5) If the Crown Court makes an order discharging the confiscation order, the court must, at once, send a copy of the order to –

(a)   the magistrates' court officer who applied for the order;
(b)   the defendant;
(c)   the prosecutor; and
(d)   any receiver appointed under section 50 of the 2002 Act.

[*Note. Formerly rule 10 of the Crown Court (Confiscation, Restraint and Receivership) Rules 2003.*]

58.7   Application for variation of confiscation order made against an absconder

(1) This rule applies where the defendant makes an application under section 29 of the Proceeds of Crime Act 2002 for the variation of a confiscation order made against an absconder.
(2) The application must be in writing and supported by a witness statement which must give details of –

(a)   the confiscation order made against an absconder under section 6 of the 2002 Act as applied by section 28 of the 2002 Act;
(b)   the circumstances in which the defendant ceased to be an absconder;
(c)   the defendant's conviction of the offence or offences concerned; and
(d)   the reason why he believes the amount required to be paid under the confiscation order was too large.

(3) The application and witness statement must be lodged with the Crown Court.
(4) The application and witness statement must be served on the prosecutor at least seven days before the date fixed by the court for hearing the application, unless the Crown Court specifies a shorter period.

[*Note. This rule derives from rule 11 of the Crown Court (Confiscation, Restraint and Receivership) Rules 2003.*]

58.8   Application for discharge of confiscation order made against an absconder

(1) This rule applies if the defendant makes an application under section 30 of the Proceeds of Crime Act 2002 for the discharge of a confiscation order.
(2) The application must be in writing and supported by a witness statement which must give details of –

(a)   the confiscation order made under section 28 of the 2002 Act;
(b)   the date on which the defendant ceased to be an absconder;
(c)   the acquittal of the defendant if he has been acquitted of the offence concerned; and
(d)   if the defendant has not been acquitted of the offence concerned –

  (i)   the date on which the defendant ceased to be an absconder,
  (ii)   the date on which the proceedings taken against the defendant were instituted and a summary of steps taken in the proceedings since then, and
  (iii)   any indication given by the prosecutor that he does not intend to proceed against the defendant.

(3) The application and witness statement must be lodged with the Crown Court.
(4) The application and witness statement must be served on the prosecutor at least seven days before the date fixed by the court for hearing the application, unless the Crown Court specifies a shorter period.
(5) If the Crown Court orders the discharge of the confiscation order, the court must serve notice on the magistrates' court responsible for enforcing the order.

[*Note. This rule derives from rule 12 of the Crown Court (Confiscation, Restraint and Receivership) Rules 2003.*]

58.9   Application for increase in term of imprisonment in default

(1) This rule applies where the prosecutor makes an application under section 39(5) of the Proceeds of Crime Act 2002 to increase the term of imprisonment in default of payment of a confiscation order.

(2) The application must be made in writing and give details of –

  (a)   the name and address of the defendant;
  (b)   the confiscation order;
  (c)   the grounds for the application; and
  (d)   the enforcement measures taken, if any.

(3) On receipt of the application, the court must –

  (a)   at once, send to the defendant and the magistrates' court responsible for enforcing the order, a copy of the application; and
  (b)   fix a time, date and place for the hearing and notify the applicant and the defendant of that time, date and place.

(4) If the Crown Court makes an order increasing the term of imprisonment in default, the court must, at once, send a copy of the order to –

  (a)   the applicant;
  (b)   the defendant;
  (c)   where the defendant is in custody at the time of the making of the order, the person having custody of the defendant; and
  (d)   the magistrates' court responsible for enforcing the order.

[*Note. This rule derives from rule 13 of the Crown Court (Confiscation, Restraint and Receivership) Rules 2003.*]

58.10   Compensation – general

(1) This rule applies to an application for compensation under section 72 of the Proceeds of Crime Act 2002.

(2) The application must be in writing and may be supported by a witness statement.

(3) The application and any witness statement must be lodged with the Crown Court.

(4) The application and any witness statement must be served on –

  (a)   the person alleged to be in default; and
  (b)   the person by whom the compensation would be payable under section 72(9) of the 2002 Act (or if the compensation is payable out of a police fund under section 72(9)(a), the chief officer of the police force concerned),

at least seven days before the date fixed by the court for hearing the application, unless the Crown Court directs otherwise.

[*Note. Formerly rule 14 of the Crown Court (Confiscation, Restraint and Receivership) Rules 2003.*]

58.11   Compensation – confiscation order made against absconder

(1) This rule applies to an application for compensation under section 73 of the Proceeds of Crime Act 2002.

(2) The application must be in writing and supported by a witness statement which must give details of –

(a)   the confiscation order made under section 28 of the 2002 Act;
(b)   the variation or discharge of the confiscation order under section 29 or 30 of the 2002 Act;
(c)   the realisable property to which the application relates; and
(d)   the loss suffered by the applicant as a result of the confiscation order.

(3) The application and witness statement must be lodged with the Crown Court.
(4) The application and witness statement must be served on the prosecutor at least seven days before the date fixed by the court for hearing the application, unless the Crown Court specifies a shorter period.

[*Note. This rule derives from rule 15 of the Crown Court (Confiscation, Restraint and Receivership) Rules 2003.*]

58.12   Payment of money in bank or building society account in satisfaction of confiscation order

(1) An order under section 67 of the Proceeds of Crime Act 2002 requiring a bank or building society to pay money to a magistrates' court officer ("a payment order") shall –
(a)   be directed to the bank or building society in respect of which the payment order is made;
(b)   name the person against whom the confiscation order has been made;
(c)   state the amount which remains to be paid under the confiscation order;
(d)   state the name and address of the branch at which the account in which the money ordered to be paid is held and the sort code of that branch, if the sort code is known;
(e)   state the name in which the account in which the money ordered to be paid is held and the account number of that account, if the account number is known;
(f)   state the amount which the bank or building society is required to pay to the court officer under the payment order;
(g)   give the name and address of the court officer to whom payment is to be made; and
(h)   require the bank or building society to make payment within a period of seven days beginning on the day on which the payment order is made, unless it appears to the court that a longer or shorter period would be appropriate in the particular circumstances.

(2) The payment order shall be served on the bank or building society in respect of which it is made by leaving it at, or sending it by first class post to, the principal office of the bank or building society.
(3) A payment order which is served by first class post shall, unless the contrary is proved, be deemed to have been served on the second business day after posting.
(4) In this rule "confiscation order" has the meaning given to it by section 88(6) of the Proceeds of Crime Act 2002.

[*Note. Formerly rule 57A of the Magistrates' Courts Rules 1981.*]

PART 59   PROCEEDS OF CRIME ACT 2002 – RULES APPLICABLE ONLY TO RESTRAINT PROCEEDINGS

59.1   Application for restraint order

(1) This rule applies where the prosecutor or an accredited financial investigator makes an application for a restraint order under section 42 of the Proceeds of Crime Act 2002.
(2) The application may be made without notice.

(3)   The application must be in writing and supported by a witness statement which must –

    (a)   give the grounds for the application;

    (b)   to the best of the witness's ability, give full details of the realisable property in respect of which the applicant is seeking the order and specify the person holding that realisable property;

    (c)   give the grounds for, and full details of, any application for an ancillary order under section 41(7) of the 2002 Act for the purposes of ensuring that the restraint order is effective; and

    (d)   where the application is made by an accredited financial investigator, include a statement that he has been authorised to make the application under section 68 of the 2002 Act.

[*This rule derives from rule 16 of the Crown Court (Confiscation, Restraint and Receivership) Rules 2003.*]

59.2   Restraint orders

(1)   The Crown Court may make a restraint order subject to exceptions, including, but not limited to, exceptions for reasonable living expenses and reasonable legal expenses, and for the purpose of enabling any person to carry on any trade, business or occupation.

(2)   But the Crown Court must not make an exception for legal expenses where this is prohibited by section 41(4) of the Proceeds of Crime Act 2002.

(3)   An exception to a restraint order may be made subject to conditions.

(4)   The Crown Court must not require the applicant for a restraint order to give any undertaking relating to damages sustained as a result of the restraint order by a person who is prohibited from dealing with realisable property by the restraint order.

(5)   The Crown Court may require the applicant for a restraint order to give an undertaking to pay the reasonable expenses of any person, other than a person who is prohibited from dealing with realisable property by the restraint order, which are incurred in complying with the restraint order.

(6)   A restraint order must include a statement that disobedience of the order, either by a person to whom the order is addressed, or by another person, may be contempt of court and the order must include details of the possible consequences of being held in contempt of court.

(7)   Unless the Crown Court directs otherwise, a restraint order made without notice has effect until the court makes an order varying or discharging the restraint order.

(8)   The applicant for a restraint order must –

    (a)   serve copies of the restraint order and of the witness statement made in support of the application on the defendant and any person who is prohibited from dealing with realisable property by the restraint order; and

    (b)   notify any person whom the applicant knows to be affected by the restraint order of the terms of the restraint order.

[*Formerly rule 17 of the Crown Court (Confiscation, Restraint and Receivership) Rules 2003.*]

59.3   Application for discharge or variation of restraint order by person affected by order

(1)   This rule applies where a person affected by a restraint order makes an application to the Crown Court under section 42(3) of the Proceeds of Crime Act 2002 to discharge or vary the restraint order or any ancillary order made under section 41(7) of the Act.

(2)   The application must be in writing and may be supported by a witness statement.

(3)   The application and any witness statement must be lodged with the Crown Court.

(4) The application and any witness statement must be served on the person who applied for the restraint order and any person who is prohibited from dealing with realisable property by the restraint order (if he is not the person making the application) at least two days before the date fixed by the court for hearing the application, unless the Crown Court specifies a shorter period.

[*Formerly rule 18 of the Crown Court (Confiscation, Restraint and Receivership) Rules 2003.*]

59.4   Application for variation of restraint order by the person who applied for the order

(1) This rule applies where the applicant for a restraint order makes an application under section 42(3) of the Proceeds of Crime Act 2002 to the Crown Court to vary the restraint order or any ancillary order made under section 41(7) of the 2002 Act (including where the court has already made a restraint order and the applicant is seeking to vary the order in order to restrain further realisable property).

(2) The application may be made without notice if the application is urgent or if there are reasonable grounds for believing that giving notice would cause the dissipation of realisable property which is the subject of the application.

(3) The application must be in writing and must be supported by a witness statement which must –

(a) give the grounds for the application;

(b) where the application is for the inclusion of further realisable property in the order give full details, to the best of the witness's ability, of the realisable property in respect of which the applicant is seeking the order and specify the person holding that realisable property; and

(c) where the application is made by an accredited financial investigator, include a statement that he has been authorised to make the application under section 68 of the 2002 Act.

(4) The application and witness statement must be lodged with the Crown Court.

(5) Except where, under paragraph (2), notice of the application is not required to be served, the application and witness statement must be served on any person who is prohibited from dealing with realisable property by the restraint order at least 2 days before the date fixed by the court for hearing the application, unless the Crown Court specifies a shorter period.

(6) If the court makes an order for the variation of a restraint order, the applicant must serve copies of the order and of the witness statement made in support of the application on –

(a) the defendant;

(b) any person who is prohibited from dealing with realisable property by the restraint order (whether before or after the variation); and

(c) any other person whom the applicant knows to be affected by the order.

[*Formerly rule 19 of the Crown Court (Confiscation, Restraint and Receivership) Rules 2003.*]

59.5   Application for discharge of a restraint order by the person who applied for the order

(1) This rule applies where the applicant for a restraint order makes an application under section 42(3) of the Proceeds of Crime Act 2002 to discharge the order or any ancillary order made under section 41(7) of the 2002 Act.

(2) The application may be made without notice.

(3) The application must be in writing and must state the grounds for the application.

(4) If the court makes an order for the discharge of a restraint order, the applicant must serve copies of the order on –

  (a)   the defendant;
  (b)   any person who is prohibited from dealing with realisable property by the restraint order (whether before or after the discharge); and
  (c)   any other person whom the applicant knows to be affected by the order.

[*Formerly rule 20 of the Crown Court (Confiscation, Restraint and Receivership) Rules 2003.*]

PART 60   PROCEEDS OF CRIME ACT 2002 – RULES APPLICABLE ONLY TO RECEIVERSHIP PROCEEDINGS

60.1   Application for appointment of a management or an enforcement receiver

(1) This rule applies to an application for the appointment of a management receiver under section 48(1) of the Proceeds of Crime Act 2002 and an application for the appointment of an enforcement receiver under section 50(1) of the 2002 Act.

(2) The application may be made without notice if –

  (a)   the application is joined with an application for a restraint order under rule 59.1;
  (b)   the application is urgent; or
  (c)   there are reasonable grounds for believing that giving notice would cause the dissipation of realisable property which is the subject of the application.

(3) The application must be in writing and must be supported by a witness statement which must –

  (a)   give the grounds for the application;
  (b)   give full details of the proposed receiver;
  (c)   to the best of the witness' ability, give full details of the realisable property in respect of which the applicant is seeking the order and specify the person holding that realisable property;
  (d)   where the application is made by an accredited financial investigator, include a statement that he has been authorised to make the application under section 68 of the 2002 Act; and
  (e)   if the proposed receiver is not a member of staff of the Crown Prosecution Service or the Revenue and Customs Prosecutions Office and the applicant is asking the court to allow the receiver to act –

    (i)   without giving security, or
    (ii)   before he has given security or satisfied the court that he has security in place,

  explain the reasons why that is necessary.

(4) Where the application is for the appointment of an enforcement receiver, the applicant must provide the Crown Court with a copy of the confiscation order made against the defendant.

(5) The application and witness statement must be lodged with the Crown Court.

(6) Except where, under paragraph (2), notice of the application is not required to be served, the application and witness statement must be lodged with the Crown Court and served on –

  (a)   the defendant;
  (b)   any person who holds realisable property to which the application relates; and
  (c)   any other person whom the applicant knows to be affected by the application,

at least seven days before the date fixed by the court for hearing the application, unless the Crown Court specifies a shorter period.

(7) If the court makes an order for the appointment of a receiver, the applicant must serve copies of the order and of the witness statement made in support of the application on –

   (a)   the defendant;
   (b)   any person who holds realisable property to which the order applies; and
   (c)   any other person whom the applicant knows to be affected by the order.

[*Note. This rule derives from rule 21 of the Crown Court (Confiscation, Restraint and Receivership) Rules 2003.*]

60.2   Application for conferral of powers on management receiver or enforcement receiver

(1) This rule applies to an application for the conferral of powers on a management receiver under section 49(1) of the Proceeds of Crime Act 2002 or an enforcement receiver under section 51(1) of the 2002 Act.

(2) The application may be made without notice if the application is to give the receiver power to take possession of property and –

   (a)   the application is joined with an application for a restraint order under rule 59.1;
   (b)   the application is urgent; or
   (c)   there are reasonable grounds for believing that giving notice would cause the dissipation of the property which is the subject of the application.

(3) The application must be made in writing and supported by a witness statement which must –

   (a)   give the grounds for the application;
   (b)   give full details of the realisable property in respect of which the applicant is seeking the order and specify the person holding that realisable property; and
   (c)   where the application is made by an accredited financial investigator, include a statement that he has been authorised to make the application under section 68 of the 2002 Act.

(4) Where the application is for the conferral of powers on an enforcement receiver, the applicant must provide the Crown Court with a copy of the confiscation order made against the defendant.

(5) The application and witness statement must be lodged with the Crown Court.

(6) Except where, under paragraph (2), notice of the application is not required to be served, the application and witness statement must be served on –

   (a)   the defendant;
   (b)   any person who holds realisable property in respect of which a receiver has been appointed or in respect of which an application for a receiver has been made;
   (c)   any other person whom the applicant knows to be affected by the application; and
   (d)   the receiver (if one has already been appointed),

at least seven days before the date fixed by the court for hearing the application, unless the Crown Court specifies a shorter period.

(7) If the court makes an order for the conferral of powers on a receiver, the applicant must serve copies of the order on –

   (a)   the defendant;
   (b)   any person who holds realisable property in respect of which the receiver has been appointed; and

(c)   any other person whom the applicant knows to be affected by the order.

[*Note. This rule derives from rule 22 of the Crown Court (Confiscation, Restraint and Receivership) Rules 2003.*]

60.3   Applications for discharge or variation of receivership orders and applications for other orders

(1)   This rule applies to applications under section 62(3) of the Proceeds of Crime Act 2002 for orders (by persons affected by the action of receivers) and applications under section 63(1) of the 2002 Act for the discharge or variation of orders relating to receivers.

(2)   The application must be made in writing and lodged with the Crown Court.

(3)   The application must be served on the following persons (except where they are the person making the application) –

    (a)   the person who applied for appointment of the receiver;
    (b)   the defendant;
    (c)   any person who holds realisable property in respect of which the receiver has been appointed;
    (d)   the receiver; and
    (e)   any other person whom the applicant knows to be affected by the application,

at least seven days before the date fixed by the court for hearing the application, unless the Crown Court specifies a shorter period.

(4)   If the court makes an order for the discharge or variation of an order relating to a receiver under section 63(2) of the 2002 Act, the applicant must serve copies of the order on any persons whom he knows to be affected by the order.

[*Note. Formerly rule 23 of the Crown Court (Confiscation, Restraint and Receivership) Rules 2003.*]

60.4   Sums in the hands of receivers

(1)   This rule applies where the amount payable under a confiscation order has been fully paid and any sums remain in the hands of an enforcement receiver.

(2)   The receiver must make an application to the Crown Court for directions as to the distribution of the sums in his hands.

(3)   The application and any evidence which the receiver intends to rely on in support of the application must be served on –

    (a)   the defendant; and
    (b)   any other person who held (or holds) interests in any property realised by the receiver,

at least seven days before the date fixed by the court for hearing the application, unless the Crown Court specifies a shorter period.

(4)   If any of the provisions listed in paragraph (5) (provisions as to the vesting of funds in a trustee in bankruptcy) apply, then the Crown Court must make a declaration to that effect.

(5)   These are the provisions –

    (a)   section 31B of the Bankruptcy (Scotland) Act 1985;
    (b)   section 306B of the Insolvency Act 1986; and
    (c)   article 279B of the Insolvency (Northern Ireland) Order 1989.

[*Note. This rule derives from rule 24 of the Crown Court (Confiscation, Restraint and Receivership) Rules 2003.*]

60.5   Security

(1) This rule applies where the Crown Court appoints a receiver under section 48 or 50 of the Proceeds of Crime Act 2002 and the receiver is not a member of staff of the Crown Prosecution Service or the Revenue and Customs Prosecutions Office (and it is immaterial whether the receiver is a permanent or temporary member or he is on secondment from elsewhere).

(2) The Crown Court may direct that before the receiver begins to act, or within a specified time, he must either –

   (a)   give such security as the Crown Court may determine; or
   (b)   file with the Crown Court and serve on all parties to any receivership proceedings evidence that he already has in force sufficient security,

   to cover his liability for his acts and omissions as a receiver.

(3) The Crown Court may terminate the appointment of a receiver if he fails to –

   (a)   give the security; or
   (b)   satisfy the court as to the security he has in force,

   by the date specified.

[*Note. This rule derives in part from rule 25 of the Crown Court (Confiscation, Restraint and Receivership) Rules 2003.*]

60.6   Remuneration

(1) This rule applies where the Crown Court appoints a receiver under section 48 or 50 of the Proceeds of Crime Act 2002 and the receiver is not a member of staff of the Crown Prosecution Service or of the Revenue and Customs Prosecutions Office (and it is immaterial whether the receiver is a permanent or temporary member or he is on secondment from elsewhere).

(2) The receiver may only charge for his services if the Crown Court –

   (a)   so directs; and
   (b)   specifies the basis on which the receiver is to be remunerated.

(3) Unless the Crown Court orders otherwise, in determining the remuneration of the receiver, the Crown Court shall award such sum as is reasonable and proportionate in all the circumstances and which takes into account –

   (a)   the time properly given by him and his staff to the receivership;
   (b)   the complexity of the receivership;
   (c)   any responsibility of an exceptional kind or degree which falls on the receiver in consequence of the receivership;
   (d)   the effectiveness with which the receiver appears to be carrying out, or to have carried out, his duties; and
   (e)   the value and nature of the subject matter of the receivership.

(4) The Crown Court may refer the determination of a receiver's remuneration to be ascertained by the taxing authority of the Crown Court and rules 78.4 to 78.7 shall have effect as if the taxing authority was ascertaining costs.

(5) A receiver appointed under section 48 of the 2002 Act is to receive his remuneration by realising property in respect of which he is appointed, in accordance with section 49(2)(d) of the 2002 Act.

(6) A receiver appointed under section 50 of the 2002 Act is to receive his remuneration by applying to the magistrates' court officer for payment under section 55(4)(b) of the 2002 Act.

[Note. This rule derives from rule 26 of the Crown Court (Confiscation, Restraint and Receivership) Rules 2003.]

60.7   Accounts

(1) The Crown Court may order a receiver appointed under section 48 or 50 of the Proceeds of Crime Act 2002 to prepare and serve accounts.

(2) A party to receivership proceedings served with such accounts may apply for an order permitting him to inspect any document in the possession of the receiver relevant to those accounts.

(3) Any party to receivership proceedings may, within 14 days of being served with the accounts, serve notice on the receiver –

  (a)   specifying any item in the accounts to which he objects;

  (b)   giving the reason for such objection; and

  (c)   requiring the receiver within 14 days of receipt of the notice, either –

    (i)   to notify all the parties who were served with the accounts that he accepts the objection, or

    (ii)   if he does not accept the objection, to apply for an examination of the accounts in relation to the contested item.

(4) When the receiver applies for the examination of the accounts he must at the same time lodge with the Crown Court –

  (a)   the accounts; and

  (b)   a copy of the notice served on him under this section of the rule.

(5) If the receiver fails to comply with paragraph (3)(c) of this rule, any party to receivership proceedings may apply to the Crown Court for an examination of the accounts in relation to the contested item.

(6) At the conclusion of its examination of the accounts the court will certify the result.

[Note. This rule derives from rule 27 of the Crown Court (Confiscation, Restraint and Receivership) Rules 2003.]

60.8   Non-compliance by receiver

(1) If a receiver appointed under section 48 or 50 of the Proceeds of Crime Act 2002 fails to comply with any rule, practice direction or direction of the Crown Court, the Crown Court may order him to attend a hearing to explain his non-compliance.

(2) At the hearing, the Crown Court may make any order it considers appropriate, including –

  (a)   terminating the appointment of the receiver;

  (b)   reducing the receiver's remuneration or disallowing it altogether; and

  (c)   ordering the receiver to pay the costs of any party.

[Note. This rule derives from rule 28 of the Crown Court (Confiscation, Restraint and Receivership) Rules 2003.]

PART 61   PROCEEDS OF CRIME ACT 2002 – RULES APPLICABLE TO RESTRAINT AND RECEIVERSHIP PROCEEDINGS

61.1   Distress and forfeiture

(1) This rule applies to applications under sections 58(2) and (3) and 59(2) and (3) of the Proceeds of Crime Act 2002 for leave of the Crown Court to levy distress against property or exercise a right of forfeiture by peaceable re-entry in relation to a tenancy, in

circumstances where the property or tenancy is the subject of a restraint order or a receiver has been appointed in respect of the property or tenancy.

(2) The application must be made in writing to the Crown Court.

(3) The application must be served on –

(a)   the person who applied for the restraint order or the order appointing the receiver; and

(b)   any receiver appointed in respect of the property or tenancy,

at least seven days before the date fixed by the court for hearing the application, unless the Crown Court specifies a shorter period.

[*This rule derives from rule 29 of the Crown Court (Confiscation, Restraint and Receivership) Rules 2003.*]

61.2   Joining of applications

An application for the appointment of a management receiver or enforcement receiver under rule 60.1 may be joined with –

(a)   an application for a restraint order under rule 59.1; and

(b)   an application for the conferral of powers on the receiver under rule 60.2.

[*Formerly rule 33 of the Crown Court (Confiscation, Restraint and Receivership) Rules 2003.*]

61.3   Applications to be dealt with in writing

Applications in restraint proceedings and receivership proceedings are to be dealt with without a hearing, unless the Crown Court orders otherwise.

[*Formerly rule 34 of the Crown Court (Confiscation, Restraint and Receivership) Rules 2003.*]

61.4   Business in chambers

Restraint proceedings and receivership proceedings may be heard in chambers.

[*Formerly rule 35 of the Crown Court (Confiscation, Restraint and Receivership) Rules 2003.*]

61.5   Power of court to control evidence

(1) When hearing restraint proceedings and receivership proceedings, the Crown Court may control the evidence by giving directions as to –

(a)   the issues on which it requires evidence;

(b)   the nature of the evidence which it requires to decide those issues; and

(c)   the way in which the evidence is to be placed before the court.

(2) The court may use its power under this rule to exclude evidence that would otherwise be admissible.

(3) The court may limit cross-examination in restraint proceedings and receivership proceedings.

[*Formerly rule 36 of the Crown Court (Confiscation, Restraint and Receivership) Rules 2003.*]

61.6   Evidence of witnesses

(1) The general rule is that, unless the Crown Court orders otherwise, any fact which needs to be proved in restraint proceedings or receivership proceedings by the evidence of a witness is to be proved by their evidence in writing.

(2) Where evidence is to be given in writing under this rule, any party may apply to the Crown Court for permission to cross-examine the person giving the evidence.

(3) If the Crown Court gives permission under paragraph (2) but the person in question does not attend as required by the order, his evidence may not be used unless the court gives permission.

[Formerly rule 37 of the Crown Court (Confiscation, Restraint and Receivership) Rules 2003.]

61.7   Witness summons

(1) Any party to restraint proceedings or receivership proceedings may apply to the Crown Court to issue a witness summons requiring a witness to –

    (a)   attend court to give evidence; or
    (b)   produce documents to the court.

(2) Rule 28.3 applies to an application under this rule as it applies to an application under section 2 of the Criminal Procedure (Attendance of Witnesses) Act 1965.

[Formerly rule 38 of the Crown Court (Confiscation, Restraint and Receivership) Rules 2003.]

61.8   Hearsay evidence

Section 2(1) of the Civil Evidence Act 1995 (duty to give notice of intention to rely on hearsay evidence) does not apply to evidence in restraint proceedings and receivership proceedings.

[Formerly rule 39 of the Crown Court (Confiscation, Restraint and Receivership) Rules 2003.]

61.9   Disclosure and inspection of documents

(1) This rule applies where, in the course of restraint proceedings or receivership proceedings, an issue arises as to whether property is realisable property.

(2) The Crown Court may make an order for disclosure of documents.

(3) Part 31 of the Civil Procedure Rules 1998 as amended from time to time shall have effect as if the proceedings were proceedings in the High Court.

[Formerly rule 40 of the Crown Court (Confiscation, Restraint and Receivership) Rules 2003.]

61.10   Court documents

(1) Any order which the Crown Court issues in restraint proceedings or receivership proceedings must –

    (a)   state the name and judicial title of the person who made it;
    (b)   bear the date on which it is made; and
    (c)   be sealed by the Crown Court.

(2) The Crown Court may place the seal on the order –

    (a)   by hand; or
    (b)   by printing a facsimile of the seal on the order whether electronically or otherwise.

(3) A document purporting to bear the court's seal shall be admissible in evidence without further proof.

[Formerly rule 41 of the Crown Court (Confiscation, Restraint and Receivership) Rules 2003.]

61.11   Consent orders

(1) This rule applies where all the parties to restraint proceedings or receivership proceedings agree the terms in which an order should be made.

(2) Any party may apply for a judgment or order in the terms agreed.

(3) The Crown Court may deal with an application under paragraph (2) without a hearing.

(4) Where this rule applies –

    (a)   the order which is agreed by the parties must be drawn up in the terms agreed;

    (b)   it must be expressed as being "By Consent"; and

    (c)   it must be signed by the legal representative acting for each of the parties to whom the order relates or by the party if he is a litigant in person.

(5) Where an application is made under this rule, then the requirements of any other rule as to the procedure for making an application do not apply.

[Formerly rule 42 of the Crown Court (Confiscation, Restraint and Receivership) Rules 2003.]

61.12   Slips and omissions

(1) The Crown Court may at any time correct an accidental slip or omission in an order made in restraint proceedings or receivership proceedings.

(2) A party may apply for a correction without notice.

[Formerly rule 43 of the Crown Court (Confiscation, Restraint and Receivership) Rules 2003.]

61.13   Supply of documents from court records

(1) No document relating to restraint proceedings or receivership proceedings may be supplied from the records of the Crown Court for any person to inspect or copy unless the Crown Court grants permission.

(2) An application for permission under paragraph (1) must be made on notice to the parties to the proceedings.

[Formerly rule 44 of the Crown Court (Confiscation, Restraint and Receivership) Rules 2003.]

61.14   Disclosure of documents in criminal proceedings

(1) This rule applies where –

    (a)   proceedings for an offence have been started in the Crown Court and the defendant has not been either convicted or acquitted on all counts; and

    (b)   an application for a restraint order under section 42(1) of the Proceeds of Crime Act 2002 has been made.

(2) The judge presiding at the proceedings for the offence may be supplied from the records of the Crown Court with documents relating to restraint proceedings and any receivership proceedings.

(3) Such documents must not otherwise be disclosed in the proceedings for the offence.

[Formerly rule 45 of the Crown Court (Confiscation, Restraint and Receivership) Rules 2003.]

61.15   Preparation of documents

(1) Every order in restraint proceedings or receivership proceedings will be drawn up by the Crown Court unless –

    (a)   the Crown Court orders a party to draw it up;

    (b)   a party, with the permission of the Crown Court, agrees to draw it up; or

    (c)   the order is made by consent under rule 61.10.

(2) The Crown Court may direct that –

    (a)   an order drawn up by a party must be checked by the Crown Court before it is sealed; or

    (b)   before an order is drawn up by the Crown Court, the parties must lodge an agreed statement of its terms.

(3) Where an order is to be drawn up by a party –

  (a)   he must lodge it with the Crown Court no later than seven days after the date on which the court ordered or permitted him to draw it up so that it can be sealed by the Crown Court; and

  (b)   if he fails to lodge it within that period, any other party may draw it up and lodge it.

(4) Nothing in this rule shall require the Crown Court to accept a document which is illegible, has not been duly authorised, or is unsatisfactory for some other similar reason.

[Formerly rule 46 of the Crown Court (Confiscation, Restraint and Receivership) Rules 2003.]

61.16   Change of solicitor

(1) This rule applies where –

  (a)   a party for whom a solicitor is acting in restraint proceedings or receivership proceedings wants to change his solicitor;

  (b)   a party, after having represented himself in such proceedings, appoints a solicitor to act on his behalf (except where the solicitor is appointed only to act as an advocate for a hearing); or

  (c)   a party, after having been represented by a solicitor in such proceedings, intends to act in person.

(2) Where this rule applies, the party or his solicitor (where one is acting) must –

  (a)   lodge notice of the change at the Crown Court; and

  (b)   serve notice of the change on every other party and, where paragraph (1)(a) or (c) applies, on the former solicitor.

(3) The notice lodged at the Crown Court must state that notice has been served as required by paragraph (2)(b).

(4) Subject to paragraph (5), where a party has changed his solicitor or intends to act in person, the former solicitor will be considered to be the party's solicitor unless and until –

  (a)   notice is served in accordance with paragraph (2); or

  (b)   the Crown Court makes an order under rule 61.17 and the order is served as required by paragraph (3) of that rule.

(5) Where the certificate of a LSC funded client is revoked or discharged –

  (a)   the solicitor who acted for that person will cease to be the solicitor acting in the proceedings as soon as his retainer is determined under regulation 4 of the Community Legal Service (Costs) Regulations 2000; and

  (b)   if that person wishes to continue, where he appoints a solicitor to act on his behalf paragraph (2) will apply as if he had previously represented himself in the proceedings.

(6) "Certificate" in paragraph (5) means a certificate issued under the Funding Code (approved under section 9 of the Access to Justice Act 1999) and "LSC funded client" means an individual who receives services funded by the Legal Services Commission as part of the Community Legal Service within the meaning of Part I of the 1999 Act.

[Formerly rule 47 of the Crown Court (Confiscation, Restraint and Receivership) Rules 2003.]

61.17   Application by solicitor for declaration that solicitor has ceased to act

(1) A solicitor may apply to the Crown Court for an order declaring that he has ceased to be the solicitor acting for a party to restraint proceedings or receivership proceedings.

(2) Where an application is made under this rule –

    (a)   notice of the application must be given to the party for whom the solicitor is acting, unless the Crown Court directs otherwise; and

    (b)   the application must be supported by evidence.

(3) Where the Crown Court makes an order that a solicitor has ceased to act, the solicitor must serve a copy of the order on every party to the proceedings.

[Formerly rule 48 of the Crown Court (Confiscation, Restraint and Receivership) Rules 2003.]

61.18   Application by other party for declaration that solicitor has ceased to act

(1) Where –

    (a)   a solicitor who has acted for a party to restraint proceedings or receivership proceedings –

        (i)   has died,

        (ii)   has become bankrupt,

        (iii)   has ceased to practise, or

        (iv)   cannot be found, and

    (b)   the party has not given notice of a change of solicitor or notice of intention to act in person as required by rule 61.16,

any other party may apply to the Crown Court for an order declaring that the solicitor has ceased to be the solicitor acting for the other party in the proceedings.

(2) Where an application is made under this rule, notice of the application must be given to the party to whose solicitor the application relates unless the Crown Court directs otherwise.

(3) Where the Crown Court makes an order under this rule, the applicant must serve a copy of the order on every other party to the proceedings.

[Formerly rule 49 of the Crown Court (Confiscation, Restraint and Receivership) Rules 2003.]

61.19   Order for costs

(1) This rule applies where the Crown Court is deciding whether to make an order for costs under rule 78.1 in restraint proceedings or receivership proceedings.

(2) The court has discretion as to –

    (a)   whether costs are payable by one party to another;

    (b)   the amount of those costs; and

    (c)   when they are to be paid.

(3) If the court decides to make an order about costs –

    (a)   the general rule is that the unsuccessful party will be ordered to pay the costs of the successful party; but

    (b)   the court may make a different order.

(4) In deciding what order (if any) to make about costs, the court must have regard to all of the circumstances, including –

    (a)   the conduct of all the parties; and

    (b)   whether a party has succeeded on part of an application, even if he has not been wholly successful.

(5) The orders which the court may make under rule 78.1 include an order that a party must pay –

    (a)   a proportion of another party's costs;

    (b)   a stated amount in respect of another party's costs;

(c)   costs from or until a certain date only;
(d)   costs incurred before proceedings have begun;
(e)   costs relating to particular steps taken in the proceedings;
(f)   costs relating only to a distinct part of the proceedings; and
(g)   interest on costs from or until a certain date, including a date before the making of an order.

(6) Where the court would otherwise consider making an order under paragraph (5)(f), it must instead, if practicable, make an order under paragraph (5)(a) or (c).

(7) Where the court has ordered a party to pay costs, it may order an amount to be paid on account before the costs are assessed.

[Formerly rule 50 of the Crown Court (Confiscation, Restraint and Receivership) Rules 2003.]

61.20   Assessment of costs

(1) Where the Crown Court has made an order for costs in restraint proceedings or receivership proceedings it may either –

(a)   make an assessment of the costs itself; or
(b)   order assessment of the costs under rule 78.3.

(2) In either case, the Crown Court or the taxing authority, as the case may be, must –

(a)   only allow costs which are proportionate to the matters in issue; and
(b)   resolve any doubt which it may have as to whether the costs were reasonably incurred or reasonable and proportionate in favour of the paying party.

(3) The Crown Court or the taxing authority, as the case may be, is to have regard to all the circumstances in deciding whether costs were proportionately or reasonably incurred or proportionate and reasonable in amount.

(4) In particular, the Crown Court or the taxing authority must give effect to any orders which have already been made.

(5) The Crown Court or the taxing authority must also have regard to –

(a)   the conduct of all the parties, including in particular, conduct before, as well as during, the proceedings;
(b)   the amount or value of the property involved;
(c)   the importance of the matter to all the parties;
(d)   the particular complexity of the matter or the difficulty or novelty of the questions raised;
(e)   the skill, effort, specialised knowledge and responsibility involved;
(f)   the time spent on the application; and
(g)   the place where and the circumstances in which work or any part of it was done.

[Formerly rule 51 of the Crown Court (Confiscation, Restraint and Receivership) Rules 2003.]

61.21   Time for complying with an order for costs

(1) A party to restraint proceedings or receivership proceedings must comply with an order for the payment of costs within 14 days of –

(a)   the date of the order if it states the amount of those costs;
(b)   if the amount of those costs is decided later under rule 78.3, the date of the taxing authority's decision; or
(c)   in either case, such later date as the Crown Court may specify.

[Formerly rule 52 of the Crown Court (Confiscation, Restraint and Receivership) Rules 2003.]

61.22   Application of costs rules

Rules 61.19, 61.20 and 61.21 do not apply to the assessment of costs in proceedings to the extent that section 11 of the Access to Justice Act 1999 applies and provisions made under that Act make different provision.

[*Formerly rule 53 of the Crown Court (Confiscation, Restraint and Receivership) Rules 2003.*]

PART 62   PROCEEDS OF CRIME ACT 2002 – RULES APPLICABLE TO INVESTIGATIONS

62.1   Account monitoring orders under the Terrorism Act 2000 and the Proceeds of Crime Act 2002

(1) Where a circuit judge makes an account monitoring order under paragraph 2(1) of Schedule 6A to the Terrorism Act 2000 the court officer shall give a copy of the order to the financial institution specified in the application for the order.

(2) Where any person other than the person who applied for the account monitoring order proposes to make an application under paragraph 4(1) of Schedule 6A to the 2000 Act or section 375(2) of the Proceeds of Crime Act 2002 for the discharge or variation of an account monitoring order, he shall give a copy of the proposed application, not later than 48 hours before the application is to be made –

    (a)   to a police officer at the police station specified in the account monitoring order; or

    (b)   where the application for the account monitoring order was made under the 2002 Act and was not made by a constable, to the office of the appropriate officer who made the application, as specified in the account monitoring order,

in either case together with a notice indicating the time and place at which the application for discharge or variation is to be made.

(3) In this rule –

"appropriate officer" has the meaning given to it by section 378 of the 2002 Act; and

references to the person who applied for an account monitoring order must be construed in accordance with section 375(4) and (5) of the 2002 Act.

[*Note. Formerly rule 25C of the Crown Court Rules 1982.*]

62.2   Customer information orders under the Proceeds of Crime Act 2002

(1) Where any person other than the person who applied for the customer information order proposes to make an application under section 369(3) of the Proceeds of Crime Act 2002 for the discharge or variation of a customer information order, he shall, not later than 48 hours before the application is to be made, give a copy of the proposed application –

    (a)   to a police officer at the police station specified in the customer information order; or

    (b)   where the application for the customer information order was not made by a constable, to the office of the appropriate officer who made the application, as specified in the customer information order,

in either case together with a notice indicating the time and place at which the application for a discharge or variation is to be made.

(2) In this rule:

"appropriate officer" has the meaning given to it by section 378 of the 2002 Act; and references to the person who applied for the customer information order must be construed in accordance with section 369(5) and (6) of the 2002 Act.

[*Note. Formerly rule 25D of the Crown Court Rules 1982.*]

62.3   Proof of identity and accreditation

(1)   This rule applies where –

(a)   an appropriate officer makes an application under section 345 (production orders), section 363 (customer information orders) or section 370 (account monitoring orders) of the Proceeds of Crime Act 2002 for the purposes of a confiscation investigation or a money laundering investigation; or

(b)   a prosecutor makes an application under section 357 of the 2002 Act (disclosure orders) for the purposes of a confiscation investigation.

(2)   Subject to sections 449 and 449A of the 2002 Act (which make provision for a member of –

(a)   the Serious Organised Crime Agency's staff; and

(b)   the staff of the relevant Director,

to use pseudonyms),

the appropriate officer or an authorised person, as the case may be, must provide the judge with proof of his identity and, if he is an accredited financial investigator, his accreditation under section 3 of the 2002 Act.

(3)   In this rule:

"appropriate officer" has the meaning given to it by section 378 of the 2002 Act; and

"confiscation investigation" and "money laundering investigation" have the meanings given to them by section 341 of the 2002 Act.

[*Note. This rule derives in part from rule 25E of the Crown Court Rules 1982. For applications to discharge or vary a production order see also Part 56.4.*]

PART 63   APPEAL TO THE CROWN COURT

63.1   When this Part applies

(1)   This Part applies where –

(a)   a defendant wants to appeal under –

(i)   section 108 of the Magistrates' Courts Act 1980,

(ii)   section 45 of the Mental Health Act 1983,

(iii)   paragraph 10 of Schedule 3 to the Powers of Criminal Courts (Sentencing) Act 2000;

(b)   the Criminal Cases Review Commission refers a defendant's case to the Crown Court under section 11 of the Criminal Appeal Act 1995;

(c)   a prosecutor wants to appeal under –

(i)   section 14A(5A) of the Football Spectators Act 1989, or

(ii)   section 147(3) of the Customs and Excise Management Act 1979; or

(d)   a person wants to appeal under –

(i)   section 1 of the Magistrates' Courts (Appeals from Binding Over Orders) Act 1956,

(ii)   section 12(5) of the Contempt of Court Act 1981,

(iii)   regulation 3C or 3H of the Costs in Criminal Cases (General) Regulations 1986, or

(iv)   section 22 of the Football Spectators Act 1989.

(2)   A reference to an "appellant" in this Part is a reference to such a party or person.

[*Note. An appeal to the Crown Court is by way of re-hearing: see section 79(3) of the Supreme Court Act 1981. For the powers of the Crown Court on an appeal, see section 48 of that Act.*

A defendant may appeal from a magistrates' court to the Crown Court –

(a)   *under section 108 of the Magistrates' Courts Act 1980, against sentence after a guilty plea and after a not guilty plea against conviction, against a finding of guilt or against sentence;*

(b)   *under section 45 of the Mental Health Act 1983, where the magistrates' court makes a hospital order or guardianship order without convicting the defendant;*

(c)   *under paragraph 10 of Schedule 3 to the Powers of Criminal Courts (Sentencing) Act 2000, where the magistrates' court revokes a community order and deals with the defendant in another way.*

See section 13 of the Criminal Appeal Act 1995 for the circumstances in which the Criminal Cases Review Commission may refer a conviction or sentence to the Crown Court.

Under section 14A(5A) of the Football Spectators Act 1989, a prosecutor may appeal to the Crown Court against a failure by a magistrates' court to make a football banning order.

Under section 147(3) of the Customs and Excise Management Act 1979, a prosecutor may appeal to the Crown Court against any decision of a magistrates' court in proceedings for an offence under any Act relating to customs or excise.

Under section 1 of the Magistrates' Courts (Appeals from Binding Over Orders) Act 1956, a person bound over to keep the peace or be of good behaviour by a magistrates' court may appeal to the Crown Court.

Under section 12(5) of the Contempt of Court Act 1981, a person detained, committed to custody or fined by a magistrates' court for insulting a member of the court or another participant in the case, or for interrupting the proceedings, may appeal to the Crown Court.

Under regulation 3C of the Costs in Criminal Cases (General) Regulations 1986, a legal representative against whom a magistrates' court makes a wasted costs order under section 19A of the Prosecution of Offences Act 1985 and regulation 3B may appeal against that order to the Crown Court.

Under regulation 3H of the Costs in Criminal Cases (General) Regulations 1986, a third party against whom a magistrates' court makes a costs order under section 19B of the Prosecution of Offences Act 1985 and regulation 3F may appeal against that order to the Crown Court.

Under section 22 of the Football Spectators Act 1989, any person aggrieved by the decision of a magistrates' court making a football banning order may appeal to the Crown Court.]

63.2   Service of appeal notice

(1)   An appellant must serve an appeal notice on –

(a)   the magistrates' court officer; and
(b)   every other party.

(2)   The appellant must serve the appeal notice –

(a)   as soon after the decision appealed against as the appellant wants; but
(b)   not more than 21 days after –

(i)   sentence or the date sentence is deferred, whichever is earlier, if the appeal is against conviction or against a finding of guilt,
(ii)   sentence, if the appeal is against sentence, or

> > (iii)   the order or failure to make an order about which the appellant wants to appeal, in any other case.

(3)   The appellant must –

> (a)   serve with the appeal notice any application for an extension of the time limit under this rule; and
>
> (b)   in that application, explain why the appeal notice is late.

[*Note. Under section 1(1) of the Powers of Criminal Courts (Sentencing) Act 2000, a magistrates' court may defer passing sentence for up to 6 months.*]

63.3   Form of appeal notice

The appeal notice must be in writing and must –

> (a)   specify –
>
> > (i)   the conviction or finding of guilt,
> > (ii)   the sentence, or
> > (iii)   the order, or the failure to make an order
>
> > about which the appellant wants to appeal;
>
> (b)   summarise the issues;
> (c)   in an appeal against conviction –
>
> > (i)   identify the prosecution witnesses whom the appellant will want to question if they are called to give oral evidence, and
> > (ii)   say how long the trial lasted in the magistrates' court and how long the appeal is likely to last in the Crown Court;
>
> (d)   in an appeal against a finding that the appellant insulted someone or interrupted proceedings in the magistrates' court, attach –
>
> > (i)   the magistrates' court's written findings of fact, and
> > (ii)   the appellant's response to those findings;
>
> (e)   say whether the appellant has asked the magistrates' court to reconsider the case; and
> (f)   include a list of those on whom the appellant has served the appeal notice.

[*Note. The Practice Direction sets out a form of appeal notice for use in connection with this rule.*

In some cases, a magistrates' court can reconsider a conviction, sentence or other order and make a fresh decision. See section 142 of the Magistrates' Courts Act 1980.

See also rule 3.10 (conduct of a trial or an appeal).]

63.4   Duty of magistrates' court officer

The magistrates' court officer must –

> (a)   as soon as practicable serve on the Crown Court officer –
>
> > (i)   the appeal notice and any accompanying application served by the appellant,
> > (ii)   details of the parties including their addresses,
> > (iii)   a copy of each magistrates' court register entry relating to the decision under appeal and to any application for bail pending appeal, and
> > (iv)   any report received for the purposes of sentencing;
>
> (b)   keep any document or object exhibited in the proceedings in the magistrates' court, or arrange for it to be kept by some other appropriate person, until –
>
> > (i)   6 weeks after the conclusion of those proceedings, or

      (ii)   the conclusion of any proceedings in the Crown Court that begin within that 6 weeks; and

(c)   provide the Crown Court with any document, object or information for which the Crown Court officer asks, within such period as the Crown Court officer may require.

63.5   Duty of person keeping exhibit

A person who, under arrangements made by the magistrates' court officer, keeps a document or object exhibited in the proceedings in the magistrates' court must –

(a)   keep that exhibit until –

      (i)   6 weeks after the conclusion of those proceedings, or

      (ii)   the conclusion of any proceedings in the Crown Court that begin within that six weeks,

    unless the magistrates' court or the Crown Court otherwise directs; and

(b)   provide the Crown Court with any such document or object for which the Crown Court officer asks, within such period as the Crown Court officer may require.

63.6   Reference by the Criminal Cases Review Commission

(1)   The Crown Court officer must, as soon as practicable, serve a reference by the Criminal Cases Review Commission on –

(a)   the appellant;

(b)   every other party; and

(c)   the magistrates' court officer.

(2)   The appellant may serve an appeal notice on –

(a)   the Crown Court officer; and

(b)   every other party,

not more than 21 days later.

(3)   The Crown Court must treat the reference as the appeal notice if the appellant does not serve an appeal notice.

63.7   Hearings and decisions

(1)   The Crown Court as a general rule must hear in public an appeal or reference to which this Part applies, but –

(a)   may order any hearing to be in private; and

(b)   where a hearing is about a public interest ruling, must hold that hearing in private.

(2)   The Crown Court officer must give as much notice as reasonably practicable of every hearing to –

(a)   the parties;

(b)   any party's custodian; and

(c)   any other person whom the Crown Court requires to be notified.

(3)   The Crown Court officer must serve every decision on –

(a)   the parties;

(b)   any other person whom the Crown Court requires to be served; and

(c)   the magistrates' court officer and any party's custodian, where the decision determines an appeal.

(4) But where a hearing or decision is about a public interest ruling, the Crown Court officer must not –

(a)   give notice of that hearing to; or
(b)   serve that decision on,

anyone other than the prosecutor who applied for that ruling, unless the court otherwise directs.

[*Note. See also Part 25 (Applications for Public Interest Immunity and specific disclosure).*]

63.8   Abandoning an appeal

(1) The appellant –

(a)   may abandon an appeal without the Crown Court's permission, by serving a notice of abandonment on –

(i)   the magistrates' court officer,
(ii)   the Crown Court officer, and
(iii)   every other party

before the hearing of the appeal begins; but

(b)   after the hearing of the appeal begins, may only abandon the appeal with the Crown Court's permission.

(2) A notice of abandonment must be signed by or on behalf of the appellant.

(3) Where an appellant who is on bail pending appeal abandons an appeal –

(a)   the appellant must surrender to custody as directed by the magistrates' court officer; and
(b)   any conditions of bail apply until then.

[*Note. The Practice Direction sets out a form of notice of abandonment for use in connection with this rule.*

Where an appellant abandons an appeal to the Crown Court, both the Crown Court and the magistrates' court have power to make a costs order against that appellant in favour of the respondent: see section 52 of the Supreme Court Act 1981 and section 109 of the Magistrates' Courts Act 1980. Part 78 contains rules about costs on abandoning an appeal.]

63.9   Court's power to vary requirements under this Part

The Crown Court may –

(a)   shorten or extend (even after it has expired) a time limit under this Part;
(b)   allow an appellant to vary an appeal notice that that appellant has served;
(c)   direct that an appeal notice be served on any person;
(d)   allow an appeal notice or a notice of abandonment to be in a different form to one set out in the Practice Direction, or to be presented orally.

63.10   Constitution of the Crown Court

On the hearing of an appeal –

(a)   the general rule is that the Crown Court must comprise –

(i)   a judge of the High Court, a Circuit judge or a Recorder, and
(ii)   no less than two and no more than four justices of the peace, none of whom took part in the decision under appeal; and

(b)   if the appeal is from a youth court –

(i)   each justice of the peace must be qualified to sit as a member of a youth court, and

      (ii)   the Crown Court must include a man and a woman; but

(c)   the Crown Court may include only one justice of the peace and need not include both a man and a woman if –

      (i)   the presiding judge decides that otherwise the start of the appeal hearing will be delayed unreasonably, or

      (ii)   one or more of the justices of the peace who started hearing the appeal is absent.

[*Note. See sections 73 and 74 of the Supreme Court Act 1981, section 45 of the Children and Young Persons Act 1933 and section 9 of the Courts Act 2003.*]

PART 64   APPEAL TO THE HIGH COURT BY WAY OF CASE STATED

64.1   Application to a magistrates' court to state a case

(1) An application under section 111(1) of the Magistrates' Courts Act 1980 shall be made in writing and signed by or on behalf of the applicant and shall identify the question or questions of law or jurisdiction on which the opinion of the High Court is sought.

(2) Where one of the questions on which the opinion of the High Court is sought is whether there was evidence on which the magistrates' court could come to its decision, the particular finding of fact made by the magistrates' court which it is claimed cannot be supported by the evidence before the magistrates' court shall be specified in such application.

(3) Any such application shall be sent to a court officer for the magistrates' court whose decision is questioned.

[*Formerly rule 76 of the Magistrates' Courts Rules 1981. As to the procedure to be followed in the High Court, see Part 52 of the Civil Procedure Rules 1998.*]

64.2   Consideration of a draft case by a magistrates' court

(1) Within 21 days after receipt of an application made in accordance with rule 64.1, a court officer for the magistrates' court whose decision is questioned shall, unless the justices refuse to state a case under section 111(5) of the Magistrates' Courts Act 1980, send a draft case in which are stated the matters required under rule 64.6 (content of case stated) to the applicant or his legal representative and shall send a copy thereof to the respondent or his legal representative.

(2) Within 21 days after receipt of the draft case under paragraph (1), each party may make representations thereon. Any such representations shall be in writing and signed by or on behalf of the party making them and shall be sent to the magistrates' court officer.

(3) Where the justices refuse to state a case under section 111(5) of the 1980 Act and they are required by a mandatory order of the High Court under section 111(6) to do so, this rule shall apply as if in paragraph (1) –

(a)   for the words "receipt of an application made in accordance with rule 64.1" there were substituted the words "the date on which a mandatory order under section 111(6) of the 1980 Act is made"; and

(b)   the words "unless the justices refuse to state a case under section 111(5) of the 1980 Act" were omitted.

[*Formerly rule 77 of the Magistrates' Courts Rules 1981.*]

64.3   Preparation and submission of final case to a magistrates' court

(1) Within 21 days after the latest day on which representations may be made under rule

64.2, the justices whose decision is questioned shall make such adjustments, if any, to the draft case prepared for the purposes of that rule as they think fit, after considering any such representations, and shall state and sign the case.

(2)   A case may be stated on behalf of the justices whose decision is questioned by any 2 or more of them and may, if the justices so direct, be signed on their behalf by the justices' clerk.

(3)   Forthwith after the case has been stated and signed a court officer for the court shall send it to the applicant or his legal representative, together with any statement required by rule 64.4.

[*Formerly rule 78 of the Magistrates' Courts Rules 1981.*]

64.4   Extension of time limits by a magistrates' court

(1)   If a magistrates' court officer is unable to send to the applicant a draft case under rule 64.2(1) within the time required by that paragraph, he shall do so as soon as practicable thereafter and the provisions of that rule shall apply accordingly; but in that event a court officer shall attach to the draft case, and to the final case when it is sent to the applicant or his legal representative under rule 64.3(3), a statement of the delay and the reasons for it.

(2)   If a magistrates' court officer receives an application in writing from or on behalf of the applicant or the respondent for an extension of the time within which representations on the draft case may be made under rule 64.2(2), together with reasons in writing for it, the justices' clerk may, by notice in writing sent to the applicant, or respondent as the case may be, by the magistrates' court officer, extend the time and the provisions of that paragraph and of rule 64.3 shall apply accordingly; but in that event the court officer shall attach to the final case, when it is sent to the applicant or his legal representative under rule 64.3(3), a statement of the extension and the reasons for it.

(3)   If the justices are unable to state a case within the time required by rule 64.3(1), they shall do so as soon as practicable thereafter and the provisions of that rule shall apply accordingly; but in that event a court officer shall attach to the final case, when it is sent to the applicant or his legal representative under rule 64.3(3), a statement of the delay and the reasons for it.

[*Formerly rule 79 of the Magistrates' Courts Rules 1981.*]

64.5   [Revoked]

64.6   Content of case stated by a magistrates' courts

(1)   A case stated by the magistrates' court shall state the facts found by the court and the question or questions of law or jurisdiction on which the opinion of the High Court is sought.

(2)   Where one of the questions on which the opinion of the High Court is sought is whether there was evidence on which the magistrates' court could come to its decision, the particular finding of fact which it is claimed cannot be supported by the evidence before the magistrates' court shall be specified in the case.

(3)   Unless one of the questions on which the opinion of the High Court is sought is whether there was evidence on which the magistrates' court could come to its decision, the case shall not contain a statement of evidence.

[*Formerly rule 81 of the Magistrates' Courts Rules 1981.*]

64.7   Application to the Crown Court to state a case

(1)   An application under section 28 of the Supreme Court Act 1981 to the Crown Court to

state a case for the opinion of the High Court shall be made in writing to a court officer within 21 days after the date of the decision in respect of which the application is made.

(2) The application shall state the ground on which the decision of the Crown Court is questioned.

(3) After making the application, the applicant shall forthwith send a copy of it to the parties to the proceedings in the Crown Court.

(4) On receipt of the application, the Crown Court officer shall forthwith send it to the judge who presided at the proceedings in which the decision was made.

(5) On receipt of the application, the judge shall inform the Crown Court officer as to whether or not he has decided to state a case and that officer shall give notice in writing to the applicant of the judge's decision.

(6) If the judge considers that the application is frivolous, he may refuse to state a case and shall in that case, if the applicant so requires, cause a certificate stating the reasons for the refusal to be given to him.

(7) If the judge decides to state a case, the procedure to be followed shall, unless the judge in a particular case otherwise directs, be the procedure set out in paragraphs (8) to (12) of this rule.

(8) The applicant shall, within 21 days of receiving the notice referred to in paragraph (5), draft a case and send a copy of it to the Crown Court officer and to the parties to the proceedings in the Crown Court.

(9) Each party to the proceedings in the Crown Court shall, within 21 days of receiving a copy of the draft case under paragraph (8), either –

    (a)   give notice in writing to the applicant and the Crown Court officer that he does not intend to take part in the proceedings before the High Court;

    (b)   indicate in writing on the copy of the draft case that he agrees with it and send the copy to a court officer; or

    (c)   draft an alternative case and send it, together with the copy of the applicant's case, to the Crown Court officer.

(10) The judge shall consider the applicant's draft case and any alternative draft case sent to the Crown Court officer under paragraph (9)(c).

(11) If the Crown Court so orders, the applicant shall, before the case is stated and delivered to him, enter before the Crown Court officer into a recognizance, with or without sureties and in such sum as the Crown Court considers proper, having regard to the means of the applicant, conditioned to prosecute the appeal without delay.

(12) The judge shall state and sign a case within 14 days after either –

    (a)   the receipt of all the documents required to be sent to a court officer under paragraph (9); or

    (b)   the expiration of the period of 21 days referred to in that paragraph,

whichever is the sooner.

(13) A case stated by the Crown Court shall state the facts found by the Crown Court, the submissions of the parties (including any authorities relied on by the parties during the course of those submissions), the decision of the Crown Court in respect of which the application is made and the question on which the opinion of the High Court is sought.

(14) Any time limit referred to in this rule may be extended either before or after it expires by the Crown Court.

(15) If the judge decides not to state a case but the stating of a case is subsequently required by a mandatory order of the High Court, paragraphs (7) to (14) shall apply to the stating of the case save that –

(a)   in paragraph (7) the words "If the judge decides to state a case" shall be omitted; and

(b)   in paragraph (8) for the words "receiving the notice referred to in paragraph (5)" there shall be substituted the words "the day on which the mandatory order was made".

[Formerly rule 26 of the Crown Court Rules 1982.]

PART 65   APPEAL TO THE COURT OF APPEAL: GENERAL RULES

65.1   When this Part applies

(1)   This Part applies to all the applications, appeals and references to the Court of Appeal to which Parts 66, 67, 68, 69, 70 and 74 apply.

(2)   In this Part and in those, unless the context makes it clear that something different is meant –

"court" means the Court of Appeal or any judge of that court;

"Registrar" means the Registrar of Criminal Appeals or a court officer acting with the Registrar's authority.

[Note. See rule 2.2 for the usual meaning of "court".

Under section 53 of the Supreme Court Act 1981 the criminal division of the Court of Appeal exercises jurisdiction in the appeals and references to which Parts 66, 67, 68, 69 and 70 apply. Under section 55 of that Act the Court of Appeal must include at least two judges, and for some purposes at least three. For the powers of the Court of Appeal that may be exercised by one judge of that court or by the Registrar, see sections 31, 31A, 31B, 31C and 44 of the Criminal Appeal Act 1968; section 49 of the Criminal Justice Act 2003; the Criminal Justice Act 2003 (Mandatory Life Sentences: Appeals in Transitional Cases) Order 2005; the Serious Organised Crime and Police Act 2005 (Appeals under Section 74) Order 2006; the Serious Crime Act 2007 (Appeals under Section 24) Order 2008 and the power conferred by section 53(4) of the 1981 Act.]

65.2   Case management in the Court of Appeal

(1)   The court and the parties have the same duties and powers as under Part 3 (case management).

(2)   The Registrar –

(a)   must fulfil the duty of active case management under rule 3.2; and

(b)   in fulfilling that duty may exercise any of the powers of case management under –

(i)   rule 3.5 (the court's general powers of case management),

(ii)   rule 3.9(3) (requiring a certificate of readiness), and

(iii)   rule 3.10 (requiring a party to identify intentions and anticipated requirements)

subject to the directions of the court.

(3)   The Registrar must nominate a case progression officer under rule 3.4.

65.3   Power to vary requirements

The court or the Registrar may –

(a)   shorten a time limit or extend it (even after it has expired) unless that is inconsistent with other legislation;

(b)   allow a party to vary any notice that that party has served;

(c)   direct that a notice or application be served on any person;

(d)   allow a notice or application to be in a different form, or presented orally.

[*Note. The time limit for serving an appeal notice –*

(a) *under section 18 of the Criminal Appeal Act 1968 on an appeal against conviction or sentence, and*

(b) *under section 18A of that Act on an appeal against a finding of contempt of court*

may be extended but not shortened: see rule 68.2.

The time limit for serving an application for permission to refer a sentencing case under section 36 of the Criminal Justice Act 1988 may be neither extended nor shortened: see rule 70.2(2).

The time limits in rule 74.2 for applying to the Court of Appeal for permission to appeal or refer a case to the House of Lords may be extended or shortened only as explained in the note to that rule.]

65.4   Application for extension of time

A person who wants an extension of time within which to serve a notice or make an application must –

    (a)   apply for that extension of time when serving that notice or making that application; and

    (b)   give the reasons for the application for an extension of time.

65.5   Renewing an application refused by a judge or the Registrar

(1) This rule applies where a party with the right to do so wants to renew –

    (a)   to a judge of the Court of Appeal an application refused by the Registrar; or

    (b)   to the Court of Appeal an application refused by a judge of that court.

(2) That party must –

    (a)   renew the application in the form set out in the Practice Direction, signed by or on behalf of the applicant;

    (b)   serve the renewed application on the Registrar not more than 14 days after –

        (i)   the refusal of the application that the applicant wants to renew; or

        (ii)   the Registrar serves that refusal on the applicant, if the applicant was not present in person or by live link when the original application was refused.

[*Note. The time limit of 14 days under this rule is reduced to 5 days where Parts 66, 67 or 69 apply: see rules 66.7, 67.10 and 69.7.*

For the right to renew an application to a judge or to the Court of Appeal, see sections 31(3), 31C and 44 of the Criminal Appeal Act 1968, the Criminal Justice Act 2003 (Mandatory Life Sentences: Appeals in Transitional Cases) Order 2005, the Serious Organised Crime and Police Act 2005 (Appeals under Section 74) Order 2006 and the Serious Crime Act 2007 (Appeals under Section 24) Order 2008.

A party has no right under section 31C of the 1968 Act to renew to the Court of Appeal an application for procedural directions refused by a judge, but in some circumstances a case management direction may be varied: see rule 3.6.

If an applicant does not renew an application that a judge has refused, including an application for permission to appeal, the Registrar will treat it as if it had been refused by the Court of Appeal.

Under section 22 of the Criminal Appeal Act 1968, the Court of Appeal may direct that an appellant who is in custody is to attend a hearing by live link.]

65.6   Hearings

(1) The general rule is that the Court of Appeal must hear in public –

(a)   an application, including an application for permission to appeal; and

(b)   an appeal or reference,

but it may order any hearing to be in private.

(2) Where a hearing is about a public interest ruling that hearing must be in private unless the court otherwise directs.

(3) Where the appellant wants to appeal against an order restricting public access to a trial the court must decide without a hearing –

(a)   an application, including an application for permission to appeal; and

(b)   an appeal.

(4) Where the appellant wants to appeal or to refer a case to the House of Lords the court –

(a)   may decide without a hearing an application –

(i)   for permission to appeal or to refer a sentencing case, or

(ii)   to refer a point of law; but

(b)   must announce its decision on such an application at a hearing in public.

(5) A judge of the Court of Appeal and the Registrar may exercise any of their powers –

(a)   at a hearing in public or in private; or

(b)   without a hearing.

[*Note. For the procedure on an appeal against an order restricting public access to a trial, see Part 69.*]

65.7   Notice of hearings and decisions

(1) The Registrar must give as much notice as reasonably practicable of every hearing to –

(a)   the parties;

(b)   any party's custodian;

(c)   any other person whom the court requires to be notified; and

(d)   the Crown Court officer, where Parts 66, 67 or 69 apply.

(2) The Registrar must serve every decision on –

(a)   the parties;

(b)   any other person whom the court requires to be served; and

(c)   the Crown Court officer and any party's custodian, where the decision determines an appeal or application for permission to appeal.

(3) But where a hearing or decision is about a public interest ruling, the Registrar must not –

(a)   give notice of that hearing to; or

(b)   serve that decision on,

anyone other than the prosecutor who applied for that ruling, unless the court otherwise directs.

65.8   Duty of Crown Court officer

(1) The Crown Court officer must provide the Registrar with any document, object or information for which the Registrar asks within such period as the Registrar may require.

(2) Unless the Crown Court otherwise directs, where someone may appeal to the Court of Appeal the Crown Court officer must –

(a)   arrange for the recording of the proceedings in the Crown Court;

(b)   arrange for the transcription of such a recording if –

(i)   the Registrar wants such a transcript, or

       (ii)   anyone else wants such a transcript (but that is subject to the restrictions in rule 65.9(2)); and

(c)   arrange for any document or object exhibited in the proceedings in the Crown Court to be kept there, or kept by some other appropriate person, until 6 weeks after the conclusion of those proceedings.

(3) Where Part 66 applies (appeal to the Court of Appeal against ruling at preparatory hearing), the Crown Court officer must as soon as practicable serve on the appellant a transcript or note of –

    (a)   each order or ruling against which the appellant wants to appeal; and

    (b)   the decision by the Crown Court judge on any application for permission to appeal.

(4) Where Part 67 applies (appeal to the Court of Appeal against ruling adverse to prosecution), the Crown Court officer must as soon as practicable serve on the appellant a transcript or note of –

    (a)   each ruling against which the appellant wants to appeal;

    (b)   the decision by the Crown Court judge on any application for permission to appeal; and

    (c)   the decision by the Crown Court judge on any request to expedite the appeal.

(5) Where Part 68 applies (appeal to the Court of Appeal about conviction or sentence), the Crown Court officer must as soon as practicable serve on the Registrar –

    (a)   the appeal notice and any accompanying application that the appellant serves on the Crown Court officer;

    (b)   any Crown Court judge's certificate that the case is fit for appeal;

    (c)   the decision on any application at the Crown Court centre for bail pending appeal;

    (d)   such of the Crown Court case papers as the Registrar requires; and

    (e)   such transcript of the Crown Court proceedings as the Registrar requires.

(6) Where Part 69 applies (appeal to the Court of Appeal regarding reporting or public access) and an order is made restricting public access to a trial, the Crown Court officer must –

    (a)   immediately notify the Registrar of that order, if the appellant has given advance notice of intention to appeal; and

    (b)   as soon as practicable provide the applicant for that order with a transcript or note of the application.

[Note. See also rules 65.9 (duty of person transcribing record of proceedings in the Crown Court) and 65.10 (duty of person keeping exhibit).]

65.9   Duty of person transcribing proceedings in the Crown Court

(1) A person who transcribes a recording of proceedings in the Crown Court under arrangements made by the Crown Court officer must provide the Registrar with any transcript for which the Registrar asks within such period as the Registrar may require.

(2) Unless the Crown Court otherwise directs, such a person –

    (a)   must not provide anyone else with a transcript of a public interest ruling or of an application for such a ruling;

    (b)   subject to that, must provide anyone else with any transcript for which that person asks –

        (i)   in accordance with the transcription arrangements made by the Crown Court officer, and

        (ii)   on payment by that person of any charge fixed by the Treasury.

[*Note. Section 32 of the Criminal Appeal Act 1968 deals with the recording of proceedings in the Crown Court, the transcription of such a recording and the charge for providing such a transcript. See also rule 65.8(2) (duty of Crown Court officer).*]

65.10   Duty of person keeping exhibit

A person who under arrangements made by the Crown Court officer keeps a document or object exhibited in the proceedings in the Crown Court must –

    (a)   keep that exhibit until –

        (i)   6 weeks after the conclusion of the Crown Court proceedings, or

        (ii)   the conclusion of any appeal proceedings that begin within that 6 weeks,

        unless the court, the Registrar or the Crown Court otherwise directs; and

    (b)   provide the Registrar with any such document or object for which the Registrar asks within such period as the Registrar may require.

[*Note. See also rule 65.8(2) (duty of Crown Court officer).*]

65.11   Registrar's duty to provide copy documents for appeal or reference

Unless the court otherwise directs, for the purposes of an appeal or reference –

    (a)   the Registrar must –

        (i)   provide a party with a copy of any document or transcript held by the Registrar for such purposes, or

        (ii)   allow a party to inspect such a document or transcript,

        on payment by that party of any charge fixed by the Treasury; but

    (b)   the Registrar must not provide a copy or allow the inspection of –

        (i)   a document provided only for the court and the Registrar, or

        (ii)   a transcript of a public interest ruling or of an application for such a ruling.

[*Note. Section 21 of the Criminal Appeal Act 1968 requires the Registrar to collect, prepare and provide documents needed by the court.*]

65.12   Declaration of incompatibility with a Convention right

(1)   This rule applies where a party –

    (a)   wants the court to make a declaration of incompatibility with a Convention right under section 4 of the Human Rights Act 1998; or

    (b)   raises an issue that the Registrar thinks may lead the court to make such a declaration.

(2)   The Registrar must serve notice on –

    (a)   the relevant person named in the list published under section 17(1) of the Crown Proceedings Act 1947; or

    (b)   the Treasury Solicitor, if it is not clear who is the relevant person.

(3)   That notice must include or attach details of –

    (a)   the legislation affected and the Convention right concerned;

    (b)   the parties to the appeal; and

    (c)   any other information or document that the Registrar thinks relevant.

(4)   A person who has a right under the 1998 Act to become a party to the appeal must –

    (a)   serve notice on –

        (i)   the Registrar, and

        (ii)   the other parties,

        if that person wants to exercise that right; and

   (b)   in that notice –

        (i)   indicate the conclusion that that person invites the court to reach on the question of incompatibility, and

        (ii)   identify each ground for that invitation, concisely outlining the arguments in support.

(5) The court must not make a declaration of incompatibility –

   (a)   less than 21 days after the Registrar serves notice under paragraph (2); and

   (b)   without giving any person who serves a notice under paragraph (4) an opportunity to make representations at a hearing.

65.13   Abandoning an appeal

(1) This rule applies where an appellant wants to –

   (a)   abandon –

        (i)   an application to the court for permission to appeal, or
        (ii)   an appeal; or

   (b)   reinstate such an application or appeal after abandoning it.

(2) The appellant –

   (a)   may abandon such an application or appeal without the court's permission by serving a notice of abandonment on –

        (i)   the Registrar, and
        (ii)   any respondent

        before any hearing of the application or appeal; but

   (b)   at any such hearing, may only abandon that application or appeal with the court's permission.

(3) A notice of abandonment must be in the form set out in the Practice Direction, signed by or on behalf of the appellant.

(4) On receiving a notice of abandonment the Registrar must –

   (a)   date it;
   (b)   serve a dated copy on –

        (i)   the appellant,
        (ii)   the appellant's custodian, if any,
        (iii)   the Crown Court officer, and
        (iv)   any other person on whom the appellant or the Registrar served the appeal notice; and

   (c)   treat the application or appeal as if it had been refused or dismissed by the Court of Appeal.

(5) An appellant who wants to reinstate an application or appeal after abandoning it must –

   (a)   apply in writing, with reasons; and
   (b)   serve the application on the Registrar.

[*Note. The Court of Appeal has power only in exceptional circumstances to allow an appellant to reinstate an application or appeal that has been abandoned.*]

65.14   Abandoning a ground of appeal or opposition

(1) This rule applies where a party wants to abandon –

(a)   a ground of appeal identified in an appeal notice; or
(b)   a ground of opposition identified in a respondent's notice.

(2) Such a party must give written notice to –

(a)   the Registrar; and
(b)   every other party,

before any hearing at which that ground will be considered by the court.

PART 66   APPEAL TO THE COURT OF APPEAL AGAINST RULING AT PREPARATORY HEARING

66.1   When this Part applies

(1) This Part applies where a party wants to appeal under –

(a)   section 9(11) of the Criminal Justice Act 1987 or section 35(1) of the Criminal Procedure and Investigations Act 1996; or
(b)   section 47(1) of the Criminal Justice Act 2003.

(2) A reference to an "appellant" in this Part is a reference to such a party.

[*Note. Under section 9(11) of the Criminal Justice Act 1987 (which applies to serious or complex fraud cases) and under section 35(1) of the Criminal Procedure and Investigations Act 1996 (which applies to other complex, serious or long cases) a party may appeal to the Court of Appeal against an order made at a preparatory hearing in the Crown Court.*

Under section 47(1) of the Criminal Justice Act 2003 a party may appeal to the Court of Appeal against an order in the Crown Court that because of jury tampering a trial will continue without a jury or that there will be a new trial without a jury.

Part 15 contains rules about preparatory hearings.

The rules in Part 65 also apply where this Part applies.]

66.2   Service of appeal notice

(1) An appellant must serve an appeal notice on –

(a)   the Crown Court officer;
(b)   the Registrar; and
(c)   every party directly affected by the order or ruling against which the appellant wants to appeal.

(2) The appellant must serve the appeal notice not more than 5 business days after –

(a)   the order or ruling against which the appellant wants to appeal; or
(b)   the Crown Court judge gives or refuses permission to appeal.

66.3   Form of appeal notice

(1) An appeal notice must be in the form set out in the Practice Direction.
(2) The appeal notice must –

(a)   specify each order or ruling against which the appellant wants to appeal;
(b)   identify each ground of appeal on which the appellant relies, numbering them consecutively (if there is more than one) and concisely outlining each argument in support;
(c)   summarise the relevant facts;
(d)   identify any relevant authorities;
(e)   include or attach any application for the following, with reasons –

    (i)   permission to appeal, if the appellant needs the court's permission,

>   (ii)   an extension of time within which to serve the appeal notice,
>   (iii)   a direction to attend in person a hearing that the appellant could attend
>   by live link, if the appellant is in custody;

(f)   include a list of those on whom the appellant has served the appeal notice; and

(g)   attach –

>   (i)   a transcript or note of each order or ruling against which the appellant
>   wants to appeal,
>   (ii)   all relevant skeleton arguments considered by the Crown Court judge,
>   (iii)   any written application for permission to appeal that the appellant made
>   to the Crown Court judge,
>   (iv)   a transcript or note of the decision by the Crown Court judge on any
>   application for permission to appeal, and
>   (v)   any other document or thing that the appellant thinks the court will need
>   to decide the appeal.

[*Note. An appellant needs the court's permission to appeal in every case to which this Part applies unless the Crown Court judge gives permission.*]

66.4   Crown Court judge's permission to appeal

(1)   An appellant who wants the Crown Court judge to give permission to appeal must –

(a)   apply orally, with reasons, immediately after the order or ruling against which
       the appellant wants to appeal; or

(b)   apply in writing and serve the application on –

>   (i)   the Crown Court officer, and
>   (ii)   every party directly affected by the order or ruling

not more than 2 business days after that order or ruling.

(2)   A written application must include the same information (with the necessary adaptations) as an appeal notice.

[*Note. For the Crown Court judge's power to give permission to appeal, see section 9(11) of the Criminal Justice Act 1987, section 35(1) of the Criminal Procedure and Investigations Act 1996 and section 47(2) of the Criminal Justice Act 2003.*]

66.5   Respondent's notice

(1)   A party on whom an appellant serves an appeal notice may serve a respondent's notice, and must do so if –

(a)   that party wants to make representations to the court; or

(b)   the court so directs.

(2)   Such a party must serve the respondent's notice on –

(a)   the appellant;
(b)   the Crown Court officer;
(c)   the Registrar; and
(d)   any other party on whom the appellant served the appeal notice.

(3)   Such a party must serve the respondent's notice not more than 5 business days after –

(a)   the appellant serves the appeal notice; or
(b)   a direction to do so.

(4)   The respondent's notice must be in the form set out in the Practice Direction.

(5)   The respondent's notice must –

(a)   give the date on which the respondent was served with the appeal notice;

(b)   identify each ground of opposition on which the respondent relies, numbering them consecutively (if there is more than one), concisely outlining each argument in support and identifying the ground of appeal to which each relates;

(c)   summarise any relevant facts not already summarised in the appeal notice;

(d)   identify any relevant authorities;

(e)   include or attach any application for the following, with reasons –

  (i)   an extension of time within which to serve the respondent's notice,

  (ii)   a direction to attend in person any hearing that the respondent could attend by live link, if the respondent is in custody;

(f)   identify any other document or thing that the respondent thinks the court will need to decide the appeal.

66.6   Powers of Court of Appeal judge

A judge of the Court of Appeal may give permission to appeal as well as exercising the powers given by other legislation (including these Rules).

[*Note. See section 31 of the Criminal Appeal Act 1968 and section 49 of the Criminal Justice Act 2003.*]

66.7   Renewing applications

Rule 65.5 (renewing an application refused by a judge or the Registrar) applies with a time limit of 5 business days.

66.8   Right to attend hearing

(1)   A party who is in custody has a right to attend a hearing in public.

(2)   The court or the Registrar may direct that such a party is to attend a hearing by live link.

[*Note. See rule 65.6 (hearings).*]

PART 67   APPEAL TO THE COURT OF APPEAL AGAINST RULING ADVERSE TO PROSECUTION

67.1   When this Part applies

(1)   This Part applies where a prosecutor wants to appeal under section 58(2) of the Criminal Justice Act 2003.

(2)   A reference to an "appellant" in this Part is a reference to such a prosecutor.

[*Note. Under section 58(2) of the Criminal Justice Act 2003 a prosecutor may appeal to the Court of Appeal against a ruling in the Crown Court. See also sections 57 and 59 to 61 of the 2003 Act.*

The rules in Part 65 also apply where this Part applies.]

67.2   Decision to appeal

(1)   An appellant must tell the Crown Court judge of any decision to appeal –

(a)   immediately after the ruling against which the appellant wants to appeal; or

(b)   on the expiry of the time to decide whether to appeal allowed under paragraph (2).

(2)   If an appellant wants time to decide whether to appeal –

(a)   the appellant must ask the Crown Court judge immediately after the ruling; and

(b)   the general rule is that the judge must not require the appellant to decide there and then but instead must allow until the next business day.

[*Note. If the ruling against which the appellant wants to appeal is a ruling that there is no case to answer, the appellant may appeal against earlier rulings as well: see section 58(7) of the Criminal Justice Act 2003.*

Under section 58(8) of the 2003 Act the appellant must agree that a defendant directly affected by the ruling must be acquitted if the appellant (a) does not get permission to appeal or (b) abandons the appeal.

The Crown Court judge may give permission to appeal and may expedite the appeal: see rules 67.5 and 67.6.]

67.3   Service of appeal notice

(1)   An appellant must serve an appeal notice on –

    (a)   the Crown Court officer;
    (b)   the Registrar; and
    (c)   every defendant directly affected by the ruling against which the appellant wants to appeal.

(2)   The appellant must serve the appeal notice not later than –

    (a)   the next business day after telling the Crown Court judge of the decision to appeal, if the judge expedites the appeal; or
    (b)   5 business days after telling the Crown Court judge of that decision, if the judge does not expedite the appeal.

[*Note. If the ruling against which the appellant wants to appeal is a public interest ruling, see rule 67.8.*]

67.4   Form of appeal notice

(1)   An appeal notice must be in the form set out in the Practice Direction.

(2)   The appeal notice must –

    (a)   specify each ruling against which the appellant wants to appeal;
    (b)   identify each ground of appeal on which the appellant relies, numbering them consecutively (if there is more than one) and concisely outlining each argument in support;
    (c)   summarise the relevant facts;
    (d)   identify any relevant authorities;
    (e)   include or attach any application for the following, with reasons –

        (i)   permission to appeal, if the appellant needs the court's permission,
        (ii)   an extension of time within which to serve the appeal notice,
        (iii)   expedition of the appeal, or revocation of a direction expediting the appeal;

    (f)   include a list of those on whom the appellant has served the appeal notice;
    (g)   attach –

        (i)   a transcript or note of each ruling against which the appellant wants to appeal,
        (ii)   all relevant skeleton arguments considered by the Crown Court judge,
        (iii)   any written application for permission to appeal that the appellant made to the Crown Court judge,
        (iv)   a transcript or note of the decision by the Crown Court judge on any application for permission to appeal,
        (v)   a transcript or note of the decision by the Crown Court judge on any request to expedite the appeal, and

        (vi)   any other document or thing that the appellant thinks the court will need to decide the appeal; and

(h)   attach a form of respondent's notice for any defendant served with the appeal notice to complete if that defendant wants to do so.

[*Note. An appellant needs the court's permission to appeal unless the Crown Court judge gives permission: see section 57(4) of the Criminal Justice Act 2003. For "respondent's notice" see rule 67.7.*]

67.5   Crown Court judge's permission to appeal

(1)   An appellant who wants the Crown Court judge to give permission to appeal must –

    (a)   apply orally, with reasons, immediately after the ruling against which the appellant wants to appeal; or

    (b)   apply in writing and serve the application on –

        (i)   the Crown Court officer, and

        (ii)   every defendant directly affected by the ruling

on the expiry of the time allowed under rule 67.2 to decide whether to appeal.

(2)   A written application must include the same information (with the necessary adaptations) as an appeal notice.

(3)   The Crown Court judge must allow every defendant directly affected by the ruling an opportunity to make representations.

(4)   The general rule is that the Crown Court judge must decide whether or not to give permission to appeal on the day that the application for permission is made.

[*Note. For the Crown Court judge's power to give permission to appeal, see section 57(4) of the Criminal Justice Act 2003.*

Rule 67.5(3) does not apply where the appellant wants to appeal against a public interest ruling: see rule 67.8(5).]

67.6   Expediting an appeal

(1)   An appellant who wants the Crown Court judge to expedite an appeal must ask, giving reasons, on telling the judge of the decision to appeal.

(2)   The Crown Court judge must allow every defendant directly affected by the ruling an opportunity to make representations.

(3)   The Crown Court judge may revoke a direction expediting the appeal unless the appellant has served the appeal notice.

[*Note. For the Crown Court judge's power to expedite the appeal, see section 59 of the Criminal Justice Act 2003.*

Rule 67.6(2) does not apply where the appellant wants to appeal against a public interest ruling: see rule 67.8(5).]

67.7   Respondent's notice

(1)   A defendant on whom an appellant serves an appeal notice may serve a respondent's notice, and must do so if –

    (a)   the defendant wants to make representations to the court; or

    (b)   the court so directs.

(2)   Such a defendant must serve the respondent's notice on –

    (a)   the appellant;

(b)   the Crown Court officer;

(c)   the Registrar; and

(d)   any other defendant on whom the appellant served the appeal notice.

(3) Such a defendant must serve the respondent's notice –

(a)   not later than the next business day after –

(i)   the appellant serves the appeal notice, or

(ii)   a direction to do so

if the Crown Court judge expedites the appeal; or

(b)   not more than 5 business days after –

(i)   the appellant serves the appeal notice, or

(ii)   a direction to do so

if the Crown Court judge does not expedite the appeal.

(4) The respondent's notice must be in the form set out in the Practice Direction.

(5) The respondent's notice must –

(a)   give the date on which the respondent was served with the appeal notice;

(b)   identify each ground of opposition on which the respondent relies, numbering them consecutively (if there is more than one), concisely outlining each argument in support and identifying the ground of appeal to which each relates;

(c)   summarise any relevant facts not already summarised in the appeal notice;

(d)   identify any relevant authorities;

(e)   include or attach any application for the following, with reasons –

(i)   an extension of time within which to serve the respondent's notice,

(ii)   a direction to attend in person any hearing that the respondent could attend by live link, if the respondent is in custody;

(f)   identify any other document or thing that the respondent thinks the court will need to decide the appeal.

67.8   Public interest ruling

(1) This rule applies where the appellant wants to appeal against a public interest ruling.

(2) The appellant must not serve on any defendant directly affected by the ruling –

(a)   any written application to the Crown Court judge for permission to appeal; or

(b)   an appeal notice

if the appellant thinks that to do so in effect would reveal something that the appellant thinks ought not be disclosed.

(3) The appellant must not include in an appeal notice –

(a)   the material that was the subject of the ruling; or

(b)   any indication of what sort of material it is

if the appellant thinks that to do so in effect would reveal something that the appellant thinks ought not be disclosed.

(4) The appellant must serve on the Registrar with the appeal notice an annex –

(a)   marked to show that its contents are only for the court and the Registrar;

(b)   containing whatever the appellant has omitted from the appeal notice, with reasons; and

(c)   if relevant, explaining why the appellant has not served the appeal notice.

(5) Rules 67.5(3) and 67.6(2) do not apply.

[Note. Rules 67.5(3) and 67.6(2) require the Crown Court judge to allow a defendant to make representations about (i) giving permission to appeal and (ii) expediting an appeal.]

67.9   Powers of Court of Appeal judge

A judge of the Court of Appeal may –

(a)   give permission to appeal;

(b)   revoke a Crown Court judge's direction expediting an appeal; and

(c)   where an appellant abandons an appeal, order a defendant's acquittal, his release from custody and the payment of his costs,

as well as exercising the powers given by other legislation (including these Rules).

[Note. See section 73 of the Criminal Justice Act 2003.]

67.10   Renewing applications

Rule 65.5 (renewing an application refused by a judge or the Registrar) applies with a time limit of 5 business days.

67.11   Right to attend hearing

(1)   A respondent who is in custody has a right to attend a hearing in public.

(2)   The court or the Registrar may direct that such a respondent is to attend a hearing by live link.

[Note. See rule 65.6 (hearings).]

PART 68   APPEAL TO THE COURT OF APPEAL ABOUT CONVICTION OR SENTENCE

68.1   When this Part applies

(1)   This Part applies where –

(a)   a defendant wants to appeal under –

(i)   Part 1 of the Criminal Appeal Act 1968, or

(ii)   paragraph 14 of Schedule 22 to the Criminal Justice Act 2003;

(b)   the Criminal Cases Review Commission refers a case to the Court of Appeal under section 9 of the Criminal Appeal Act 1995;

(c)   a prosecutor wants to appeal to the Court of Appeal under section 14A(5A) of the Football Spectators Act 1989;

(d)   a party wants to appeal under section 74(8) of the Serious Organised Crime and Police Act 2005;or

(e)   a person found to be in contempt of court wants to appeal under section 13 of the Administration of Justice Act 1960 and section 18A of the Criminal Appeal Act 1968; or.

(f)   a person wants to appeal to the Court of Appeal under –

(i)   section 24 of the Serious Crime Act 2007, or

(ii)   regulation 3C or 3H of the Costs in Criminal Cases (General) Regulations 1986.

(2)   A reference to an "appellant" in this Part is a reference to such a party or person.

[Note. Under Part 1 (sections 1 to 32) of the Criminal Appeal Act 1968 a defendant may appeal against –

■   *a conviction (section 1)*

- *a sentence (sections 9 and 10: see section 50 for the meaning of "sentence")*
- *a verdict of not guilty by reason of insanity (section 12)*
- *a finding of disability (section 15)*
- *a hospital order, interim hospital order or supervision order under section 5(14) or 5A(15) of the Criminal Procedure (Insanity) Act 1964 (section 16A of the 1968 Act).*

Under paragraph 14 of Schedule 22 to the Criminal Justice Act 2003 a defendant sentenced to life imprisonment may appeal against the minimum term fixed on review by a High Court judge in certain cases.

See section 13 of the Criminal Appeal Act 1995 for the circumstances in which the Criminal Cases Review Commission may refer a conviction, sentence, verdict or finding to the Court of Appeal.

Under section 14A(5A) of the Football Spectators Act 1989 a prosecutor may appeal against a failure by the Crown Court to make a football banning order.

Under section 74(8) of the Serious Organised Crime and Police Act 2005 a prosecutor or defendant may appeal against a review by a Crown Court judge of a sentence that was reduced because the defendant assisted the investigator or prosecutor.

Under section 13 of the Administration of Justice Act 1960 a person punished by the Crown Court for contempt of court may appeal to the Court of Appeal.

Under section 24 of the Serious Crime Act 2007 a person who is the subject of a serious crime prevention order, or the relevant applicant authority, may appeal to the Court of Appeal against a decision of the Crown Court in relation to that order. In addition, any person who was given an opportunity to make representations in the proceedings by virtue of section 9(4) of the Act may appeal to the Court of Appeal against a decision of the Crown Court to make, vary or not vary a serious crime prevention order.

Under regulation 3C of the Costs in Criminal Cases (General) Regulations 1986, a legal representative against whom the Crown Court makes a wasted costs order under section 19A of the Prosecution of Offences Act 1985 and regulation 3B may appeal against that order to the Court of Appeal.

Under regulation 3H of the Costs in Criminal Cases (General) Regulations 1986, a third party against whom the Crown Court makes a costs order under section 19B of the Prosecution of Offences Act 1985 and regulation 3F may appeal against that order to the Court of Appeal.

The rules in Part 65 also apply where this Part applies.]

68.2   Service of appeal notice

(1) The general rule is that an appellant must serve an appeal notice –

    (a) on the Crown Court officer at the Crown Court centre where there occurred –

        (i) the conviction, verdict, or finding,

        (ii) the sentence, or

        (iii) the order, or the failure to make an order

        about which the appellant wants to appeal; and

    (b) not more than –

        (i) 28 days after that occurred, or

        (ii) 21 days after the order, in a case in which the appellant appeals against a wasted or third party costs order.

(2) But an appellant must serve an appeal notice –

    (a) on the Registrar instead where –

        (i) the appeal is against a minimum term review decision under paragraph 14 of Schedule 22 to the Criminal Justice Act 2003, or

          (ii)   the Criminal Cases Review Commission refers the case to the court; and

(b)   not more than –

          (i)   28 days after such a decision, or after the Registrar serves notice that the Commission has referred a sentence, or

          (ii)   56 days after the Registrar serves notice that the Commission has referred a conviction.

[*Note. The time limit for serving an appeal notice (a) on an appeal under Part 1 of the Criminal Appeal Act 1968 and (b) on an appeal against a finding of contempt of court is prescribed by sections 18 and 18A of the Criminal Appeal Act 1968. It may be extended but not shortened.*

For service of a reference by the Criminal Cases Review Commission, see rule 68.5.]

68.3   Form of appeal notice

(1) An appeal notice must be in the form set out in the Practice Direction.

(2) The appeal notice must –

(a)   specify –

          (i)   the conviction, verdict, or finding,
          (ii)   the sentence, or
          (iii) the order, or the failure to make an order

    about which the appellant wants to appeal;

(b)   identify each ground of appeal on which the appellant relies, numbering them consecutively (if there is more than one) and concisely outlining each argument in support;

(c)   identify the transcript that the appellant thinks the court will need, if the appellant wants to appeal against a conviction;

(d)   identify the relevant sentencing powers of the Crown Court, if sentence is in issue;

(e)   where the Criminal Cases Review Commission refers a case to the court, explain how each ground of appeal relates (if it does) to the reasons for the reference;

(f)   summarise the relevant facts;

(g)   identify any relevant authorities;

(h)   include or attach any application for the following, with reasons –

          (i)   permission to appeal, if the appellant needs the court's permission,
          (ii)   an extension of time within which to serve the appeal notice,
          (iii)   bail pending appeal,
          (iv)   a direction to attend in person a hearing that the appellant could attend by live link, if the appellant is in custody,
          (v)   the introduction of evidence, including hearsay evidence and evidence of bad character,
          (vi)   an order requiring a witness to attend court,
          (vii) a direction for special measures for a witness,
          (viii) a direction for special measures for the giving of evidence by the appellant;

(i)   identify any other document or thing that the appellant thinks the court will need to decide the appeal.

[*Note. In some legislation, including the Criminal Appeal Act 1968, permission to appeal is described as "leave to appeal".*

An appellant needs the court's permission to appeal in every case to which this Part applies, except where –

- *the Criminal Cases Review Commission refers the case*
- *the appellant appeals against –*

  - *a finding of contempt of court*
  - *a wasted or third party costs order*

- *the Crown Court judge certifies under sections 1(2)(a), 11(1A), 12(b), 15(2)(b) or 16A(2)(b) of the Criminal Appeal Act 1968, under section 81(1B) of the Supreme Court Act 1981, under section 14A(5B) of the Football Spectators Act 1989 or under section 24(4) of the Serious Crime Act 2007, that a case is fit for appeal.*

A judge of the Court of Appeal may give permission to appeal under section 31 of the Criminal Appeal Act 1968.]

68.4   Crown Court judge's certificate that case is fit for appeal

(1) An appellant who wants the Crown Court judge to certify that a case is fit for appeal must –

  (a)   apply orally, with reasons, immediately after there occurs –

    (i)   the conviction, verdict, or finding,
    (ii)   the sentence, or
    (iii)   the order, or the failure to make an order

    about which the appellant wants to appeal; or

  (b)   apply in writing and serve the application on the Crown Court officer not more than 14 days after that occurred.

(2) A written application must include the same information (with the necessary adaptations) as an appeal notice.

[Note. The Crown Court judge may certify that a case is fit for appeal under sections 1(2)(b), 11(1A), 12(b), 15(2)(b) or 16A(2)(b) of the Criminal Appeal Act 1968, under section 81(1B) of the Supreme Court Act 1981, under section 14A(5B) of the Football Spectators Act 1989 or under section 24(4) of the Serious Crime Act 2007.

See also rule 68.2 (service of appeal notice in all cases).]

68.5   Reference by Criminal Cases Review Commission

(1) The Registrar must serve on the appellant a reference by the Criminal Cases Review Commission.

(2) The court must treat that reference as the appeal notice if the appellant does not serve such a notice under rule 68.2.

68.6   Respondent's notice

(1) The Registrar –

  (a)   may serve an appeal notice on any party directly affected by the appeal; and
  (b)   must do so if the Criminal Cases Review Commission refers a conviction, verdict, finding or sentence to the court.

(2) Such a party may serve a respondent's notice, and must do so if –

  (a)   that party wants to make representations to the court; or
  (b)   the court or the Registrar so directs.

(3) Such a party must serve the respondent's notice on –

  (a)   the appellant;
  (b)   the Registrar; and
  (c)   any other party on whom the Registrar served the appeal notice.

(4)   Such a party must serve the respondent's notice not more than 14 days after the Registrar serves –

    (a)   the appeal notice; or
    (b)   a direction to do so.

(5)   The respondent's notice must be in the form set out in the Practice Direction.

(6)   The respondent's notice must –

    (a)   give the date on which the respondent was served with the appeal notice;
    (b)   identify each ground of opposition on which the respondent relies, numbering them consecutively (if there is more than one), concisely outlining each argument in support and identifying the ground of appeal to which each relates;
    (c)   identify the relevant sentencing powers of the Crown Court, if sentence is in issue;
    (d)   summarise any relevant facts not already summarised in the appeal notice;
    (e)   identify any relevant authorities;
    (f)   include or attach any application for the following, with reasons –

        (i)   an extension of time within which to serve the respondent's notice,
        (ii)   bail pending appeal,
        (iii)   a direction to attend in person a hearing that the respondent could attend by live link, if the respondent is in custody,
        (iv)   the introduction of evidence, including hearsay evidence and evidence of bad character,
        (v)   an order requiring a witness to attend court,
        (vi)   a direction for special measures for a witness; and

    (g)   identify any other document or thing that the respondent thinks the court will need to decide the appeal.

[Note. Part II of the Practice Direction sets out the circumstances in which the Registrar usually will serve a defendant's appeal notice on the prosecutor.]

68.7   Adaptation of rules about introducing evidence

(1)   The following Parts apply with such adaptations as the court or the Registrar may direct –

    (a)   Part 29 (special measures directions);
    (b)   Part 30 (use of live television link other than for vulnerable witnesses);
    (c)   Part 34 (hearsay evidence);
    (d)   Part 35 (evidence of bad character); and
    (e)   Part 36 (evidence of a complainant's previous sexual behaviour).

(2)   But the general rule is that –

    (a)   a respondent who opposes an appellant's application to which one of those Parts applies must do so in the respondent's notice, with reasons;
    (b)   an appellant who opposes a respondent's application to which one of those Parts applies must serve notice, with reasons, on –

        (i)   the Registrar, and
        (ii)   the respondent

    not more than 14 days after service of the respondent's notice; and

    (c)   the court or the Registrar may give directions with or without a hearing.

[Note. An application to introduce evidence or for directions about evidence must be included in, or attached to, an appeal notice or a respondent's notice: see rule 68.3 and 68.6(6).

Under section 23 of the Criminal Appeal Act 1968 the Court of Appeal may allow the introduction of evidence that was not introduced at trial.

See also Part 27 (witness statements) and Part 33 (expert evidence).]

68.8   Application for bail pending appeal or retrial

(1) This rule applies where a party wants to make an application to the court about bail pending appeal or retrial.

(2) That party must serve an application in the form set out in the Practice Direction on –

    (a)   the Registrar, unless the application is with the appeal notice; and

    (b)   the other party.

(3) The court must not decide such an application without giving the other party an opportunity to make representations, including representations about any condition or surety proposed by the applicant.

[Note. See section 19 of the Criminal Appeal Act 1968 and section 3(8) of the Bail Act 1976. An application about bail or about the conditions of bail may be made either by an appellant or respondent.

Under section 81(1) of the Supreme Court Act 1981 a Crown Court judge may grant bail pending appeal only (a) if that judge gives a certificate that the case is fit for appeal (see rule 68.4) and (b) not more than 28 days after the conviction or sentence against which the appellant wants to appeal.]

68.9   Conditions of bail pending appeal or retrial

(1) This rule applies where the court grants a party bail pending appeal or retrial subject to any condition that must be met before that party is released.

(2) The court may direct how such a condition must be met.

(3) The Registrar must serve a certificate in the form set out in the Practice Direction recording any such condition and direction on –

    (a)   that party;

    (b)   that party's custodian; and

    (c)   any other person directly affected by any such direction.

(4) A person directly affected by any such direction need not comply with it until the Registrar serves that person with that certificate.

(5) Unless the court otherwise directs, if any such condition or direction requires someone to enter into a recognizance it must be –

    (a)   in the form set out in the Practice Direction and signed before –

        (i)   the Registrar,

        (ii)   the custodian, or

        (iii)   someone acting with the authority of the Registrar or custodian;

    (b)   copied immediately to the person who enters into it; and

    (c)   served immediately by the Registrar on the appellant's custodian or vice versa, as appropriate.

(6) Unless the court otherwise directs, if any such condition or direction requires someone to make a payment, surrender a document or take some other step –

    (a)   that payment, document or step must be made, surrendered or taken to or before –

        (i)   the Registrar,

        (ii)   the custodian, or

(iii)   someone acting with the authority of the Registrar or custodian;

(b)   the Registrar or the custodian, as appropriate, must serve immediately on the other a statement that the payment, document or step has been made, surrendered or taken, as appropriate.

(7) The custodian must release the appellant where it appears that any condition ordered by the court has been met.

(8) For the purposes of section 5 of the Bail Act 1976 (record of decision about bail), the Registrar must keep a copy of –

(a)   any certificate served under paragraph (3);
(b)   a notice of hearing given under rule 65.7(1); and
(c)   a notice of the court's decision served under rule 65.7(2).

(9) Where the court grants bail pending retrial the Registrar must serve on the Crown Court officer copies of the documents kept under paragraph (8).

68.10   Forfeiture of a recognizance given as a condition of bail

(1) This rule applies where –

(a)   the court grants a party bail pending appeal or retrial; and
(b)   the bail is subject to a condition that that party provides a surety to guarantee that he will surrender to custody as required; but
(c)   that party does not surrender to custody as required.

(2) The Registrar must serve notice on –

(a)   the surety; and
(b)   the prosecutor

of the hearing at which the court may order the forfeiture of the recognizance given by that surety.

(3) The court must not forfeit a surety's recognizance –

(a)   less than 7 days after the Registrar serves notice under paragraph (2); and
(b)   without giving the surety an opportunity to make representations at a hearing.

[Note. If the purpose for which a recognizance is entered is not fulfilled, that recognizance may be forfeited by the court. If the court forfeits a surety's recognizance, the sum promised by that person is then payable to the Crown.]

68.11   Right to attend hearing

(1) A party who is in custody has a right to attend a hearing in public unless –

(a)   it is a hearing preliminary or incidental to an appeal, including the hearing of an application for permission to appeal; or
(b)   that party is in custody in consequence of –

(i)   a verdict of not guilty by reason of insanity, or
(ii)   a finding of disability.

[Note. See rule 65.6 (hearings) and section 22 of the Criminal Appeal Act 1968. There are corresponding provisions in the Criminal Justice Act 2003 (Mandatory Life Sentences: Appeals in Transitional Cases) Order 2005 and in the Serious Organised Crime and Police Act 2005 (Appeals under section 74) Order 2006. Under section 22 of the 1968 Act the court may direct that an appellant who is in custody is to attend a hearing by live link.]

68.12   Power to vary determination of appeal against sentence

(1) This rule applies where the court decides an appeal affecting sentence in a party's absence.

(2)   The court may vary such a decision if it did not take account of something relevant because that party was absent.

(3)   A party who wants the court to vary such a decision must –

(a)   apply in writing, with reasons;

(b)   serve the application on the Registrar not more than 7 days after –

(i)   the decision, if that party was represented at the appeal hearing, or

(ii)   the Registrar serves the decision, if that party was not represented at that hearing.

[*Note. Section 22(3) of the Criminal Appeal Act 1968 allows the court to sentence in an appellant's absence. There are corresponding provisions in the Criminal Justice Act 2003 (Mandatory Life Sentences: Appeals in Transitional Cases) Order 2005 and in the Serious Organised Crime and Police Act 2005 (Appeals under section 74) Order 2006.*]

68.13   Directions about re-admission to hospital on dismissal of appeal

(1)   This rule applies where –

(a)   an appellant subject to –

(i)   an order under section 37(1) of the Mental Health Act 1983 (detention in hospital on conviction), or

(ii)   an order under section 5(2) of the Criminal Procedure (Insanity) Act 1964 (detention in hospital on finding of insanity or disability)

has been released on bail pending appeal; and

(b)   the court –

(i)   refuses permission to appeal,

(ii)   dismisses the appeal, or

(iii)   affirms the order under appeal.

(2)   The court must give appropriate directions for the appellant's –

(a)   re-admission to hospital; and

(b)   if necessary, temporary detention pending re-admission.

68.14   Renewal or setting aside of order for retrial

(1)   This rule applies where –

(a)   a prosecutor wants a defendant to be arraigned more than 2 months after the court ordered a retrial under section 7 of the Criminal Appeal Act 1968; or

(b)   a defendant wants such an order set aside after 2 months have passed since it was made.

(2)   That party must apply in writing, with reasons, and serve the application on –

(a)   the Registrar;

(b)   the other party.

[*Note. Section 8(1) and (1A) of the Criminal Appeal Act 1968 set out the criteria for making an order on an application to which this rule applies.*]

PART 69   APPEAL TO THE COURT OF APPEAL REGARDING REPORTING OR PUBLIC ACCESS RESTRICTION

69.1   When this Part applies

(1)   This Part applies where a person directly affected by an order to which section 159(1) of the Criminal Justice Act 1988 applies wants to appeal against that order.

(2) A reference to an "appellant" in this Part is a reference to such a party.

[Note. Section 159(1) of the Criminal Justice Act 1988 gives a "person aggrieved" (in this Part described as a person directly affected) a right of appeal to the Court of Appeal against a Crown Court judge's order –

- *under section 4 or 11 of the Contempt of Court Act 1981*
- *under section 58(7) of the Criminal Procedure and Investigations Act 1996*
- *restricting public access to any part of a trial for reasons of national security or for the protection of a witness or other person*
- *restricting the reporting of any part of a trial.*

See Rule 16.10 for the procedure on an application to restrict public access to a trial.

The rules in Part 65 also apply where this Part applies.]

69.2   Service of appeal notice

(1) An appellant must serve an appeal notice on –

    (a)   the Crown Court officer;
    (b)   the Registrar;
    (c)   the parties; and
    (d)   any other person directly affected by the order against which the appellant wants to appeal.

(2) The appellant must serve the appeal notice not later than –

    (a)   the next business day after an order restricting public access to the trial;
    (b)   10 business days after an order restricting reporting of the trial.

69.3   Form of appeal notice

(1) An appeal notice must be in the form set out in the Practice Direction.

(2) The appeal notice must –

    (a)   specify the order against which the appellant wants to appeal;
    (b)   identify each ground of appeal on which the appellant relies, numbering them consecutively (if there is more than one) and concisely outlining each argument in support;
    (c)   summarise the relevant facts;
    (d)   identify any relevant authorities;
    (e)   include or attach, with reasons –

        (i)   an application for permission to appeal,
        (ii)   any application for an extension of time within which to serve the appeal notice,
        (iii)   any application for a direction to attend in person a hearing that the appellant could attend by live link, if the appellant is in custody,
        (iv)   any application for permission to introduce evidence, and
        (v)   a list of those on whom the appellant has served the appeal notice; and

    (f)   attach any document or thing that the appellant thinks the court will need to decide the appeal.

[Note. An appellant needs the court's permission to appeal in every case to which this Part applies.

A Court of Appeal judge may give permission to appeal under section 31(2B) of the Criminal Appeal Act 1968.]

69.4   Advance notice of appeal against order restricting public access

(1) This rule applies where the appellant wants to appeal against an order restricting public access to a trial.

(2)   The appellant may serve advance written notice of intention to appeal against any such order that may be made.

(3)   The appellant must serve any such advance notice –

    (a)   on –

        (i)   the Crown Court officer,

        (ii)   the Registrar,

        (iii)   the parties, and

        (iv)   any other person who will be directly affected by the order against which the appellant intends to appeal, if it is made; and

    (b)   not more than 5 business days after the Crown Court officer displays notice of the application for the order.

(4)   The advance notice must include the same information (with the necessary adaptations) as an appeal notice.

(5)   The court must treat that advance notice as the appeal notice if the order is made.

69.5   Duty of applicant for order restricting public access

(1)   This rule applies where the appellant wants to appeal against an order restricting public access to a trial.

(2)   The party who applied for the order must serve on the Registrar –

    (a)   a transcript or note of the application for the order; and

    (b)   any other document or thing that that party thinks the court will need to decide the appeal.

(3)   That party must serve that transcript or note and any such other document or thing as soon as practicable after –

    (a)   the appellant serves the appeal notice; or

    (b)   the order, where the appellant served advance notice of intention to appeal.

69.6   Respondent's notice on appeal against reporting restriction

(1)   This rule applies where the appellant wants to appeal against an order restricting the reporting of a trial.

(2)   A person on whom an appellant serves an appeal notice may serve a respondent's notice, and must do so if –

    (a)   that person wants to make representations to the court; or

    (b)   the court so directs.

(3)   Such a person must serve the respondent's notice on –

    (a)   the appellant;

    (b)   the Crown Court officer;

    (c)   the Registrar;

    (d)   the parties; and

    (e)   any other person on whom the appellant served the appeal notice.

(4)   Such a person must serve the respondent's notice not more than 3 business days after –

    (a)   the appellant serves the appeal notice; or

    (b)   a direction to do so.

(5)   The respondent's notice must be in the form set out in the Practice Direction.

(6)   The respondent's notice must –

    (a)   give the date on which the respondent was served with the appeal notice;

    (b)   identify each ground of opposition on which the respondent relies, numbering

them consecutively (if there is more than one), concisely outlining each
argument in support and identifying the ground of appeal to which each relates;

(c)   summarise any relevant facts not already summarised in the appeal notice;
(d)   identify any relevant authorities;
(e)   include or attach any application for the following, with reasons –

  (i)   an extension of time within which to serve the respondent's notice,
  (ii)   a direction to attend in person any hearing that the respondent could
         attend by live link, if the respondent is in custody,
  (iii) permission to introduce evidence; and

(f)   identify any other document or thing that the respondent thinks the court will
       need to decide the appeal.

69.7   Renewing applications

Rule 65.5 (renewing an application refused by a judge or the Registrar) applies with a time
limit of 5 business days.

69.8   Right to introduce evidence

No person may introduce evidence without the court's permission.

[Note. Section 159(4) of the Criminal Justice Act 1988 entitles the parties to give evidence, subject
to procedure rules.]

69.9   Right to attend hearing

(1)   A party who is in custody has a right to attend a hearing in public of an appeal against an
      order restricting the reporting of a trial.

(2)   The court or the Registrar may direct that such a party is to attend a hearing by live link.

[Note. See rule 65.6 (hearings). The court must decide an application and an appeal without a
hearing where the appellant wants to appeal against an order restricting public access to a trial:
rule 65.6(3).]

PART 70   REFERENCE TO THE COURT OF APPEAL OF POINT OF LAW OR UNDULY LENIENT SENTENCING

70.1   When this Part applies

(1)   This Part applies where the Attorney General wants to –

(a)   refer a point of law to the Court of Appeal under section 36 of the Criminal
       Justice Act 1972; or
(b)   refer a sentencing case to the Court of Appeal under section 36 of the Criminal
       Justice Act 1988.

[Note. Under section 36 of the Criminal Justice Act 1972, where a defendant is acquitted in the
Crown Court the Attorney General may refer to the Court of Appeal a point of law in the case.

Under section 36 of the Criminal Justice Act 1988, if the Attorney General thinks the sentencing of
a defendant in the Crown Court is unduly lenient he may refer the case to the Court of Appeal: but
only if the sentence is one to which Part IV of the 1988 Act applies, and only if the Court of Appeal
gives permission. See also section 35 of the 1988 Act and the Criminal Justice Act 1988 (Reviews of
Sentencing) Order 2006.

The rules in Part 65 also apply where this Part applies.]

70.2   Service of notice of reference and application for permission

(1)   The Attorney General must –

(a)   serve on the Registrar –

    (i)   any notice of reference, and

    (ii)   any application for permission to refer a sentencing case; and

(b)   with a notice of reference of a point of law, give the Registrar details of –

    (i)   the defendant affected,

    (ii)   the date and place of the relevant Crown Court decision, and

    (iii)   the relevant verdict and sentencing.

(2) The Attorney General must serve an application for permission to refer a sentencing case not more than 28 days after the last of the sentences in that case.

[*Note. The time limit for serving an application for permission to refer a sentencing case is prescribed by paragraph 1 of Schedule 3 to the Criminal Justice Act 1988. It may be neither extended nor shortened.*]

70.3   Form of notice of reference and application for permission

(1) A notice of reference and an application for permission to refer a sentencing case must be in the appropriate form set out in the Practice Direction, giving the year and number.

(2) A notice of reference of a point of law must –

(a)   specify the point of law in issue and indicate the opinion that the Attorney General invites the court to give;

(b)   identify each ground for that invitation, numbering them consecutively (if there is more than one) and concisely outlining each argument in support;

(c)   exclude any reference to the defendant's name and any other reference that may identify the defendant;

(d)   summarise the relevant facts; and

(e)   identify any relevant authorities.

(3) An application for permission to refer a sentencing case must –

(a)   give details of –

    (i)   the defendant affected,

    (ii)   the date and place of the relevant Crown Court decision, and

    (iii)   the relevant verdict and sentencing;

(b)   explain why that sentencing appears to the Attorney General unduly lenient, concisely outlining each argument in support; and

(c)   include the application for permission to refer the case to the court.

(4) A notice of reference of a sentencing case must –

(a)   include the same details and explanation as the application for permission to refer the case;

(b)   summarise the relevant facts; and

(c)   identify any relevant authorities.

(5) Where the court gives the Attorney General permission to refer a sentencing case, it may treat the application for permission as the notice of reference.

70.4   Registrar's notice to defendant

(1) The Registrar must serve on the defendant –

(a)   a notice of reference;

(b)   an application for permission to refer a sentencing case.

(2) Where the Attorney General refers a point of law, the Registrar must give the defendant notice that –

    (a)   the outcome of the reference will not make any difference to the outcome of the trial; and

    (b)   the defendant may serve a respondent's notice.

(3) Where the Attorney General applies for permission to refer a sentencing case, the Registrar must give the defendant notice that –

    (a)   the outcome of the reference may make a difference to that sentencing, and in particular may result in a more severe sentence; and

    (b)   the defendant may serve a respondent's notice.

70.5   Respondent's notice

(1) A defendant on whom the Registrar serves a reference or an application for permission to refer a sentencing case may serve a respondent's notice, and must do so if –

    (a)   the defendant wants to make representations to the court; or

    (b)   the court so directs.

(2) Such a defendant must serve the respondent's notice on –

    (a)   the Attorney General; and

    (b)   the Registrar.

(3) Such a defendant must serve the respondent's notice –

    (a)   where the Attorney General refers a point of law, not more than 28 days after –

        (i)   the Registrar serves the reference, or

        (ii)   a direction to do so;

    (b)   where the Attorney General applies for permission to refer a sentencing case, not more than 14 days after –

        (i)   the Registrar serves the application, or

        (ii)   a direction to do so.

(4) Where the Attorney General refers a point of law, the respondent's notice must –

    (a)   identify each ground of opposition on which the respondent relies, numbering them consecutively (if there is more than one), concisely outlining each argument in support and identifying the Attorney General's ground or reason to which each relates;

    (b)   summarise any relevant facts not already summarised in the reference;

    (c)   identify any relevant authorities; and

    (d)   include or attach any application for the following, with reasons –

        (i)   an extension of time within which to serve the respondent's notice,

        (ii)   permission to attend a hearing that the respondent does not have a right to attend,

        (iii) a direction to attend in person a hearing that the respondent could attend by live link, if the respondent is in custody.

(5) Where the Attorney General applies for permission to refer a sentencing case, the respondent's notice must –

    (a)   say if the respondent wants to make representations at the hearing of the application or reference; and

    (b)   include or attach any application for the following, with reasons –

        (i)   an extension of time within which to serve the respondent's notice,

        (ii)   permission to attend a hearing that the respondent does not have a right to attend,

        (iii) a direction to attend in person a hearing that the respondent could attend by live link, if the respondent is in custody.

70.6   Variation or withdrawal of notice of reference or application for permission

(1)   This rule applies where the Attorney General wants to vary or withdraw –

    (a)   a notice of reference; or

    (b)   an application for permission to refer a sentencing case.

(2)   The Attorney General –

    (a)   may vary or withdraw the notice or application without the court's permission by serving notice on –

        (i)   the Registrar, and

        (ii)   the defendant

    before any hearing of the reference or application; but

    (b)   at any such hearing, may only vary or withdraw that notice or application with the court's permission.

70.7   Right to attend hearing

(1)   A respondent who is in custody has a right to attend a hearing in public unless it is a hearing preliminary or incidental to a reference, including the hearing of an application for permission to refer a sentencing case.

(2)   The court or the Registrar may direct that such a respondent is to attend a hearing by live link.

[*Note. See rule 65.6 (hearings) and paragraphs 6 and 7 of Schedule 3 to the Criminal Justice Act 1988. Under paragraph 8 of that Schedule the Court of Appeal may sentence in the absence of a defendant whose sentencing is referred.*]

70.8   Anonymity of defendant on reference of point of law

Where the Attorney General refers a point of law, the court must not allow anyone to identify the defendant during the proceedings unless the defendant gives permission.

PART 71   APPEAL TO THE COURT OF APPEAL UNDER THE PROCEEDS OF CRIME ACT 2002 – GENERAL RULES

71.1   Extension of time

(1)   An application to extend the time limit for giving notice of application for leave to appeal under Part 2 of the Proceeds of Crime Act 2002 must –

    (a)   be included in the notice of appeal; and

    (b)   state the grounds for the application.

(2)   The parties may not agree to extend any date or time limit set by this Part, Part 72 or Part 73, or by the Proceeds of Crime Act 2002 (Appeals under Part 2) Order 2003.

[*Note. Formerly rule 13 of the Criminal Appeal (Confiscation, Restraint and Receivership) Rules 2003.*]

71.2   Other applications

(1)   Rule 68.3(2)(h) (form of appeal notice) applies in relation to an application –

    (a)   by a party to an appeal under Part 2 of the Proceeds of Crime Act 2002 that, under article 7 of the Proceeds of Crime Act 2002 (Appeals under Part 2) Order 2003, a witness be ordered to attend or that the evidence of a witness be received by the Court of Appeal; or

(b)   by the defendant to be given leave by the court to be present at proceedings for which leave is required under article 6 of the 2003 Order,

as it applies in relation to applications under Part I of the Criminal Appeal Act 1968 and the form in which rule 68.3 requires notice to be given may be modified as necessary.

[*Note. This rule derives from rule 14 of the Criminal Appeal (Confiscation, Restraint and Receivership) Rules 2003.*]

71.3   Examination of witness by court

Rule 65.7 (notice of hearings and decisions) applies in relation to an order of the court under article 7 of the Proceeds of Crime Act 2002 (Appeals under Part 2) Order 2003 to require a person to attend for examination as it applies in relation to such an order of the court under Part I of the Criminal Appeal Act 1968.

[*Note. This rule derives from rule 15 of the Criminal Appeal (Confiscation, Restraint and Receivership) Rules 2003.*]

71.4   Supply of documentary and other exhibits

Rule 65.11 (Registrar's duty to provide copy documents for appeal or reference) applies in relation to an appellant or respondent under Part 2 of the Proceeds of Crime Act 2002 as it applies in relation to an appellant and respondent under Part I of the Criminal Appeal Act 1968.

[*Note. This rule derives from rule 16 of the Criminal Appeal (Confiscation, Restraint and Receivership) Rules 2003.*]

71.5   Registrar's power to require information from court of trial

The Registrar may require the Crown Court to provide the Court of Appeal with any assistance or information which they may require for the purposes of exercising their jurisdiction under Part 2 of the Proceeds of Crime Act 2002, the Proceeds of Crime Act 2002 (Appeals under Part 2) Order 2003, this Part or Parts 72 and 73.

[*Note. Formerly rule 17 of the Criminal Appeal (Confiscation, Restraint and Receivership) Rules 2003.*]

71.6   Hearing by single judge

Rule 65.6(4) (hearings) applies in relation to a judge exercising any of the powers referred to in article 8 of the Proceeds of Crime Act 2002 (Appeals under Part 2) Order 2003 or the powers in rules 72.2(3) and (4) (respondent's notice), 73.2(2) (notice of appeal) and 73.3(6) (respondent's notice), as it applies in relation to a judge exercising the powers referred to in section 31(2) of the Criminal Appeal Act 1968.

[*Note. This rule derives from rule 18 of the Criminal Appeal (Confiscation, Restraint and Receivership) Rules 2003.*]

71.7   Determination by full court

Rule 65.5 (renewing an application refused by a judge or the registrar) shall apply where a single judge has refused an application by a party to exercise in his favour any of the powers listed in article 8 of The Proceeds of Crime Act 2002 (Appeals under Part 2) Order 2003, or the power in rule 72.2(3) or (4) as it applies where the judge has refused to exercise the powers referred to in section 31(2) of the Criminal Appeal Act 1968.

[*Note. This rule derives from rule 19 of the Criminal Appeal (Confiscation, Restraint and Receivership) Rules 2003.*]

71.8   Notice of determination

(1)   This rule applies where a single judge or the Court of Appeal has determined an application or appeal under the Proceeds of Crime Act 2002 (Appeals under Part 2) Order 2003 or under Part 2 of the Proceeds of Crime Act 2002.

(2)   The Registrar must, as soon as practicable, serve notice of the determination on all of the parties to the proceedings.

(3)   Where a single judge or the Court of Appeal has disposed of an application for leave to appeal or an appeal under section 31 of the 2002 Act, the registrar must also, as soon as practicable, serve the order on a court officer of the court of trial and any magistrates' court responsible for enforcing any confiscation order which the Crown Court has made.

[*Note. Formerly rule 20 of the Criminal Appeal (Confiscation, Restraint and Receivership) Rules 2003.*]

71.9   Record of proceedings and transcripts

Rule 65.8(2)(a) and (b) (duty of Crown Court officer – arranging recording of proceedings in Crown Court and arranging transcription) and rule 65.9 (duty of person transcribing proceedings in the Crown Court) apply in relation to proceedings in respect of which an appeal lies to the Court of Appeal under Part 2 of the Proceeds of Crime Act 2002 as they apply in relation to proceedings in respect of which an appeal lies to the Court of Appeal under Part I of the Criminal Appeal Act 1968.

[*Note. This rule derives from rule 21 of the Criminal Appeal (Confiscation, Restraint and Receivership) Rules 2003.*]

71.10   Appeal to House of Lords

(1)   An application to the Court of Appeal for leave to appeal to the House of Lords under Part 2 of the Proceeds of Crime Act 2002 must be made –

    (a)   orally after the decision of the Court of Appeal from which an appeal lies to the House of Lords; or

    (b)   in the form set out in the Practice Direction, in accordance with article 12 of the Proceeds of Crime Act 2002 (Appeals under Part 2) Order 2003 and served on the Registrar.

(2)   The application may be abandoned at any time before it is heard by the Court of Appeal by serving notice in writing on the Registrar.

(3)   Rule 65.6(5) (hearings) applies in relation to a single judge exercising any of the powers referred to in article 15 of the 2003 Order, as it applies in relation to a single judge exercising the powers referred to in section 31(2) of the Criminal Appeal Act 1968.

(4)   Rule 65.5 (renewing an application refused by a judge or the Registrar) applies where a single judge has refused an application by a party to exercise in his favour any of the powers listed in article 15 of the 2003 Order as they apply where the judge has refused to exercise the powers referred to in section 31(2) of the 1968 Act.

(5)   The form in which rule 65.5(2) requires an application to be made may be modified as necessary.

[*Note. This rule derives from rule 22 of the Criminal Appeal (Confiscation, Restraint and Receivership) Rules 2003.*]

PART 72   APPEAL TO THE COURT OF APPEAL UNDER PROCEEDS OF CRIME ACT 2002 – PROSECUTOR'S APPEAL REGARDING CONFISCATION

72.1   Notice of appeal

(1) Where an appellant wishes to apply to the Court of Appeal for leave to appeal under section 31 of the Proceeds of Crime Act 2002, he must serve a notice of appeal in the form set out in the Practice Direction on –

  (a)   the Crown Court officer; and
  (b)   the defendant.

(2) When the notice of the appeal is served on the defendant, it must be accompanied by a respondent's notice in the form set out in the Practice Direction for the defendant to complete and a notice which –

  (a)   informs the defendant that the result of an appeal could be that the Court of Appeal would increase a confiscation order already imposed on him, make a confiscation order itself or direct the Crown Court to hold another confiscation hearing;
  (b)   informs the defendant of any right he has under article 6 of the Proceeds of Crime Act 2002 (Appeals under Part 2) Order 2003 to be present at the hearing of the appeal, although he may be in custody;
  (c)   invites the defendant to serve notice on the registrar if he wishes –

    (i)   to apply to the Court of Appeal for leave to be present at proceedings for which leave is required under article 6 of the 2003 Order, or
    (ii)   to present any argument to the Court of Appeal on the hearing of the application or, if leave is given, the appeal, and whether he wishes to present it in person or by means of a legal representative;

  (d)   draws to the defendant's attention the effect of rule 71.4 (supply of documentary and other exhibits); and
  (e)   advises the defendant to consult a solicitor as soon as possible.

(3) The appellant must provide a Crown Court officer with a certificate of service stating that he has served the notice of appeal on the defendant in accordance with paragraph (1) or explaining why he has been unable to effect service.

[*Formerly rule 3 of the Criminal Appeal (Confiscation, Restraint and Receivership)Rules 2003.*]

72.2   Respondent's notice

(1) This rule applies where a defendant is served with a notice of appeal under rule 72.1.

(2) If the defendant wishes to oppose the application for leave to appeal, he must, not later than 14 days after the date on which he received the notice of appeal, serve on the Registrar and on the appellant a notice in the form set out in the Practice Direction –

  (a)   stating the date on which he received the notice of appeal;
  (b)   summarising his response to the arguments of the appellant; and
  (c)   specifying the authorities which he intends to cite.

(3) The time for giving notice under this rule may be extended by the Registrar, a single judge or by the Court of Appeal.

(4) Where the Registrar refuses an application under paragraph (3) for the extension of time, the defendant shall be entitled to have his application determined by a single judge.

(5) Where a single judge refuses an application under paragraph (3) or (4) for the extension of time, the defendant shall be entitled to have his application determined by the Court of Appeal.

[Formerly rule 4 of the Criminal Appeal (Confiscation, Restraint and Receivership) Rules 2003.]

72.3   Amendment and abandonment of appeal

(1)   The appellant may amend a notice of appeal served under rule 72.1 or abandon an appeal under section 31 of the Proceeds of Crime Act 2002 –

    (a)   without the permission of the Court at any time before the Court of Appeal have begun hearing the appeal; and

    (b)   with the permission of the Court after the Court of Appeal have begun hearing the appeal,

by serving notice in writing on the Registrar.

(2)   Where the appellant serves a notice abandoning an appeal under paragraph (1), he must send a copy of it to –

    (a)   the defendant;

    (b)   a court officer of the court of trial; and

    (c)   the magistrates' court responsible for enforcing any confiscation order which the Crown Court has made.

(3)   Where the appellant serves a notice amending a notice of appeal under paragraph (1), he must send a copy of it to the defendant.

(4)   Where an appeal is abandoned under paragraph (1), the application for leave to appeal or appeal shall be treated, for the purposes of section 85 of the 2002 Act (conclusion of proceedings), as having been refused or dismissed by the Court of Appeal.

[Formerly rule 5 of the Criminal Appeal (Confiscation, Restraint and Receivership) Rules 2003.]

PART 73   APPEAL TO THE COURT OF APPEAL UNDER POCA 2002 – RESTRAINT OR RECEIVERSHIP ORDERS

73.1   Leave to appeal

(1)   Leave to appeal to the Court of Appeal under section 43 or section 65 of the Proceeds of Crime Act 2002 will only be given where –

    (a)   the Court of Appeal considers that the appeal would have a real prospect of success; or

    (b)   there is some other compelling reason why the appeal should be heard.

(2)   An order giving leave may limit the issues to be heard and be made subject to conditions.

[Formerly rule 6 of the Criminal Appeal (Confiscation, Restraint and Receivership) Rules 2003.]

73.2   Notice of appeal

(1)   Where an appellant wishes to apply to the Court of Appeal for leave to appeal under section 43 or 65 of the Proceeds of Crime Act 2002 Act, he must serve a notice of appeal in the form set out in the Practice Direction on the Crown Court officer.

(2)   Unless the Registrar, a single judge or the Court of Appeal directs otherwise, the appellant must serve the notice of appeal, accompanied by a respondent's notice in the form set out in the Practice Direction for the respondent to complete, on –

    (a)   each respondent;

    (b)   any person who holds realisable property to which the appeal relates; and

    (c)   any other person affected by the appeal,

as soon as practicable and in any event not later than 7 days after the notice of appeal is served on a Crown Court officer.

(3)   The appellant must serve the following documents with his notice of appeal –

    (a)   four additional copies of the notice of appeal for the Court of Appeal;

    (b)   four copies of any skeleton argument;

    (c)   one sealed copy and four unsealed copies of any order being appealed;

    (d)   four copies of any witness statement or affidavit in support of the application for leave to appeal;

    (e)   four copies of a suitable record of the reasons for judgment of the Crown Court; and

    (f)   four copies of the bundle of documents used in the Crown Court proceedings from which the appeal lies.

(4)   Where it is not possible to serve all of the documents referred to in paragraph (3), the appellant must indicate which documents have not yet been served and the reasons why they are not currently available.

(5)   The appellant must provide a Crown Court officer with a certificate of service stating that he has served the notice of appeal on each respondent in accordance with paragraph (2) and including full details of each respondent or explaining why he has been unable to effect service.

[Formerly rule 7 of the Criminal Appeal (Confiscation, Restraint and Receivership) Rules 2003.]

73.3   Respondent's notice

(1)   This rule applies to an appeal under section 43 or 65 of the Proceeds of Crime Act 2002.

(2)   A respondent may serve a respondent's notice on the Registrar.

(3)   A respondent who –

    (a)   is seeking leave to appeal from the Court of Appeal; or

    (b)   wishes to ask the Court of Appeal to uphold the decision of the Crown Court for reasons different from or additional to those given by the Crown Court,

must serve a respondent's notice on the Registrar.

(4)   A respondent's notice must be in the form set out in the Practice Direction and where the respondent seeks leave to appeal to the Court of Appeal it must be requested in the respondent's notice.

(5)   A respondent's notice must be served on the Registrar not later than 14 days after –

    (a)   the date the respondent is served with notification that the Court of Appeal has given the appellant leave to appeal; or

    (b)   the date the respondent is served with notification that the application for leave to appeal and the appeal itself are to be heard together.

(6)   Unless the Registrar, a single judge or the Court of Appeal directs otherwise, the respondent serving a respondent's notice must serve the notice on the appellant and any other respondent –

    (a)   as soon as practicable; and

    (b)   in any event not later than seven days,

after it is served on the Registrar.

[Formerly rule 8 of the Criminal Appeal (Confiscation, Restraint and Receivership) Rules 2003.]

73.4   Amendment and abandonment of appeal

(1)   The appellant may amend a notice of appeal served under rule 73.2 or abandon an appeal under section 43 or 65 of the Proceeds of Crime Act 2002 –

(a) without the permission of the Court at any time before the Court of Appeal have begun hearing the appeal; and

(b) with the permission of the Court after the Court of Appeal have begun hearing the appeal,

by serving notice in writing on the Registrar.

(2) Where the appellant serves a notice under paragraph (1), he must send a copy of it to each respondent.

[*Formerly rule 9 of the Criminal Appeal (Confiscation, Restraint and Receivership) Rules 2003.*]

73.5   Stay

Unless the Court of Appeal or the Crown Court orders otherwise, an appeal under section 43 or 65 of the Proceeds of Crime Act 2002 shall not operate as a stay of any order or decision of the Crown Court.

[*Formerly rule 10 of the Criminal Appeal (Confiscation, Restraint and Receivership) Rules 2003.*]

73.6   Striking out appeal notices and setting aside or imposing conditions on leave to appeal

(1) The Court of Appeal may –

(a) strike out the whole or part of a notice of appeal served under rule 73.2; or

(b) impose or vary conditions upon which an appeal under section 43 or 65 of the Proceeds of Crime Act 2002 may be brought.

(2) The Court of Appeal will only exercise its powers under paragraph (1) where there is a compelling reason for doing so.

(3) Where a party is present at the hearing at which leave to appeal was given, he may not subsequently apply for an order that the Court of Appeal exercise its powers under paragraph (1)(b).

[*Formerly rule 11 of the Criminal Appeal (Confiscation, Restraint and Receivership) Rules 2003.*]

73.7   Hearing of appeals

(1) This rule applies to appeals under section 43 or 65 of the Proceeds of Crime Act 2002.

(2) Every appeal will be limited to a review of the decision of the Crown Court unless the Court of Appeal considers that in the circumstances of an individual appeal it would be in the interests of justice to hold a re-hearing.

(3) The Court of Appeal will allow an appeal where the decision of the Crown Court was –

(a) wrong; or

(b) unjust because of a serious procedural or other irregularity in the proceedings in the Crown Court.

(4) The Court of Appeal may draw any inference of fact which it considers justified on the evidence.

(5) At the hearing of the appeal a party may not rely on a matter not contained in his notice of appeal unless the Court of Appeal gives permission.

[*Formerly rule 12 of the Criminal Appeal (Confiscation, Restraint and Receivership) Rules 2003.*]

PART 74   APPEAL OR REFERENCE TO THE HOUSE OF LORDS

74.1   When this Part applies

(1) This Part applies where –

  (a)   a party wants to appeal to the House of Lords after –

    (i)   an application to the Court of Appeal to which Part 41 applies (retrial following acquittal for serious offence), or

    (ii)   an appeal to the Court of Appeal to which applies Part 66 (appeal to the Court of Appeal against ruling at preparatory hearing), Part 67 (appeal to the Court of Appeal against ruling adverse to prosecution), or Part 68 (appeal to the Court of Appeal about conviction or sentence); or

  (b)   a party wants to refer a case to the House of Lords after a reference to the Court of Appeal to which Part 70 applies (reference to the Court of Appeal of point of law or unduly lenient sentencing).

(2) A reference to an "appellant" in this Part is a reference to such a party.

[Note. Under section 33 of the Criminal Appeal Act 1968 a party may appeal to the House of Lords from a decision of the Court of Appeal on –

(a) an application to the court under section 76 of the Criminal Justice Act 2003 (prosecutor's application for retrial after acquittal for serious offence). See also Part 41.

(b) an appeal to the court under –

    (i)   section 9 of the Criminal Justice Act 1987 or section 35 of the Criminal Procedure and Investigations Act 1996 (appeal against order at preparatory hearing). See also Part 66.

    (ii)   section 47 of the Criminal Justice Act 2003 (appeal against order for non-jury trial after jury tampering.) See also Part 66.

    (iii)   Part 9 of the Criminal Justice Act 2003 (prosecutor's appeal against adverse ruling). See also Part 67.

    (iv)   Part 1 of the Criminal Appeal Act 1968 (defendant's appeal against conviction, sentence, etc.). See also Part 68.

Under section 13 of the Administration of Justice Act 1960 a person found to be in contempt of court may appeal to the House of Lords from a decision of the Court of Appeal on an appeal to the court under that section. See also Part 68.

Under article 12 of the Criminal Justice Act 2003 (Mandatory Life Sentence: Appeals in Transitional Cases) Order 2005 a party may appeal to the House of Lords from a decision of the Court of Appeal on an appeal to the court under paragraph 14 of Schedule 22 to the Criminal Justice Act 2003 (appeal against minimum term review decision). See also Part 68.

Under article 15 of the Serious Organised Crime and Police Act 2005 (Appeals under Section 74) Order 2006 a party may appeal to the House of Lords from a decision of the Court of Appeal on an appeal to the court under section 74 of the Serious Organised Crime and Police Act 2005 (appeal against sentence review decision). See also Part 68.

Under section 24 of the Serious Crime Act 2007 a party may appeal to the House of Lords from a decision of the Court of Appeal on an appeal to that court under that section (appeal about a serious crime prevention order). See also Part 68.

Under section 36(3) of the Criminal Justice Act 1972 the Court of Appeal may refer to the House of Lords a point of law referred by the Attorney General to the court. See also Part 70.

Under section 36(5) of the Criminal Justice Act 1988 a party may refer to the House of Lords a sentencing decision referred by the Attorney General to the court. See also Part 70.

When section 40 of the Constitutional Reform Act 2005 and Schedule 9, paragraphs 16, 23 and 48 of that Act come into force the Supreme Court will take over the jurisdiction of the House of Lords under the provisions listed above. When that happens, references in this Part to the House of Lords must be read as references to the Supreme Court.

Under section 33(3) of the Criminal Appeal Act 1968 there is no appeal to the House of Lords –

(a) *from a decision of the Court of Appeal on an appeal under section 14A(5A) of the Football Spectators Act 1989 (prosecutor's appeal against failure to make football banning order). See Part 68.*

(b) *from a decision of the Court of Appeal on an appeal under section 159(1) of the Criminal Justice Act 1988 (appeal about reporting or public access restriction). See Part 69.*

The rules in Part 65 also apply where this Part applies.]

74.2   Application for permission or reference

(1)   An appellant must –

    (a)   apply orally to the Court of Appeal –

        (i)   for permission to appeal or to refer a sentencing case, or

        (ii)   to refer a point of law

        immediately after the court gives the reasons for its decision; or

    (b)   apply in writing and serve the application on the Registrar and every other party not more than –

        (i)   14 days after the court gives the reasons for its decision if that decision was on a sentencing reference to which Part 70 applies (Attorney General's reference of sentencing case), or

        (ii)   28 days after the court gives those reasons in any other case.

(2)   An application for permission to appeal or to refer a sentencing case must –

    (a)   identify the point of law of general public importance that the appellant wants the court to certify is involved in the decision; and

    (b)   give reasons why –

        (i)   that point of law ought to be considered by the House of Lords, and

        (ii)   the court ought to give permission to appeal.

(3)   An application to refer a point of law must give reasons why that point ought to be considered by the House of Lords.

(4)   An application must include or attach any application for the following, with reasons –

    (a)   an extension of time within which to make the application for permission or for a reference,

    (b)   bail pending appeal,

    (c)   permission to attend any hearing in the House of Lords, if the appellant is in custody.

(5)   A written application must be in the form set out in the Practice Direction.

[Note. In some legislation, including the Criminal Appeal Act 1968, permission to appeal is described as "leave to appeal".

Under the provisions listed in the note to rule 74.1, except section 36(3) of the Criminal Justice Act 1972 (Attorney General's reference of point of law), an appellant needs permission to appeal or to refer a sentencing case. Under those provisions the Court of Appeal must not give permission unless it first certifies that –

(a) *a point of law of general public importance is involved in the decision, and*

(b)   it appears to the court that the point is one which the House of Lords ought to consider.

If the Court of Appeal gives such a certificate but refuses permission, an appellant may apply for such permission to the House of Lords.

Under section 36(3) of the Criminal Justice Act 1972 an appellant needs no such permission. The Court of Appeal may refer the point of law to the House of Lords or may refuse to do so.

For the power of the court or the Registrar to shorten or extend a time limit, see rule 65.3. The time limit in this rule –

(a)   for applying for permission to appeal under section 33 of the Criminal Appeal Act 1968 (28 days) is prescribed by section 34 of that Act. That time limit may be extended but not shortened by the court. But it may be extended on an application by a prosecutor only after an application to which Part 41 applies (retrial after acquittal for serious offence).
(b)   for applying for permission to refer a case under section 36(5) of the Criminal Justice Act 1988 (Attorney General's reference of sentencing decision: 14 days) is prescribed by paragraph 4 of Schedule 3 to that Act. That time limit may be neither extended nor shortened.
(c)   for applying for permission to appeal under article 12 of the Criminal Justice Act 2003 (Mandatory Life Sentence: Appeals in Transitional Cases) Order 2005 (28 days) is prescribed by article 13 of that Order. That time limit may be extended but not shortened.
(d)   for applying for permission to appeal under article 15 of the Serious Organised Crime and Police Act 2005 (Appeals under Section 74) Order 2006 (28 days) is prescribed by article 16 of that Order. That time limit may be extended but not shortened.

For the power of the Court of Appeal to grant bail pending appeal to the House of Lords, see –

(a)   section 36 of the Criminal Appeal Act 1968.
(b)   article 18 of the Serious Organised Crime and Police Act 2005 (Appeals under Section 74) Order 2006.

For the right of an appellant in custody to attend a hearing in the House of Lords, see –

(a)   section 38 of the Criminal Appeal Act 1968.
(b)   paragraph 9 of Schedule 3 to the Criminal Justice Act 1988.
(c)   article 15 of the Criminal Justice Act 2003 (Mandatory Life Sentences: Appeals in Transitional Cases) Order 2005).
(d)   article 20 of the Serious Organised Crime and Police Act 2005 (Appeals under Section 74) Order 2006.]

74.3   Determination of detention pending appeal, etc.

(1)   On an application for permission to appeal the Court of Appeal must –

(a)   decide whether to order the detention of a defendant who would have been liable to be detained but for the decision of the court; and
(b)   determine any application for –

(i)   bail pending appeal,
(ii)   permission to attend any hearing in the House of Lords, or
(iii)   a representation order.

[Note. For the liability of a defendant to be detained pending a prosecutor's appeal to the House of Lords and afterwards, see –

(a)   section 37 of the Criminal Appeal Act 1968.
(b)   article 19 of the Serious Organised Crime and Police Act 2005 (Appeals under Section 74) Order 2006.

For the grant of a representation order for proceedings in the House of Lords, see –

(a)   *Access to Justice Act 1999, sections 12 and 14 and Schedule 3, and*
(b)   *The Criminal Defence Service (General) (No. 2) Regulations 2001.*]

74.4   Bail pending appeal

Rules 68.8 (Application for bail pending appeal or retrial), 68.9 (Conditions of bail pending appeal or re-trial) and 68.10 (Forfeiture of a recognizance given as a condition of bail) apply.

PART 75   Reference to the European Court

75.1   Reference to the European Court

(1) In this rule "order" means an order referring a question to the European Court for a preliminary ruling under Article 234 of the Treaty establishing the European Community, Article 150 of the Treaty establishing Euratom or Article 41 of the Treaty establishing the Coal and Steel Community.
(2) An order may be made –

(a)   by the Crown Court of its own motion or on application by a party to proceedings in the Crown Court; or
(b)   by the Court of Appeal, on application or otherwise, at any time before the determination of an appeal or application for leave to appeal under Part I of the Criminal Appeal Act 1968.

(3) An order shall set out in a schedule the request for the preliminary ruling of the European Court, and the court making the order may give directions as to the manner and form in which the schedule is to be prepared.
(4) When an order has been made, a copy shall be sent to the senior master of the Supreme Court (Queen's Bench Division) for transmission to the Registrar of the European Court.
(5) The Crown Court proceedings in which an order is made shall, unless the Crown Court otherwise determines, be adjourned until the European Court has given a preliminary ruling on the question referred to it.
(6) Nothing in paragraph (5) above shall be taken as preventing the Crown Court from deciding any preliminary or incidental question that may arise in the proceedings after an order is made and before a preliminary ruling is given by the European Court.
(7) No appeal or application for leave to appeal, in the course of which an order is made, shall, unless the Court of Appeal otherwise orders, be determined until the European Court has given a preliminary ruling on the question referred to it.

[*Formerly rule 29 of the Crown Court Rules 1982 and rules 3–5 of the Criminal Appeal (References to the European Court) Rules 1972. See also Practice Direction (ECJ references: procedure) 1999 1 Cr App R 452 and the House of Lords Practice Directions and Standing Orders applicable to Criminal Appeals (November 2003), paragraphs 31.1–31.7*]

PART 76   REPRESENTATION ORDERS

[*There are currently no rules in this Part.*]

PART 77   RECOVERY OF DEFENCE COSTS ORDERS

[*There are currently no rules in this Part.*]

PART 78   COSTS ORDERS AGAINST THE PARTIES

78.1   Crown Court's jurisdiction to award costs in appeal from magistrates' court

(1)   Subject to the provisions of section 109(1) of the Magistrates' Courts Act 1980 (power of magistrates' courts to award costs on abandonment of appeals from magistrates' courts), no party shall be entitled to recover any costs of any proceedings in the Crown Court from any other party to the proceedings except under an order of the Court.

(2)   Subject to the following provisions of this rule, the Crown Court may make such order for costs as it thinks just.

(3)   [Revoked]

(4)   Without prejudice to the generality of paragraph (2), the Crown Court may make an order for costs on dismissing an appeal where the appellant has failed to proceed with the appeal or on the abandonment of an appeal.

[Formerly rule 12 of the Crown Court Rules 1982. See also the relevant provisions of the Prosecution of Offences Act 1985 and the Costs in Criminal Cases (General) Regulations 1986. As to costs in restraint or receivership proceedings under Part 2 of the Proceeds of Crime Act 2002 see rules 61.19 to 61.22.]

78.2   Crown Court's jurisdiction to award costs in magistrates' court proceedings from which appeal is brought

Where an appeal is brought to the Crown Court from the decision of a magistrates' court and the appeal is successful, the Crown Court may make any order as to the costs of the proceedings in the magistrates' court which that court had power to make.

[Formerly rule 13 of the Crown Court Rules 1982. See also the relevant provisions of the Prosecution of Offences Act 1985 and the Costs in Criminal Cases (General) Regulations 1986.]

78.3   Taxation of Crown Court costs

(1)   Where under these Rules the Crown Court has made an order for the costs of any proceedings to be paid by a party and the Court has not fixed a sum, the amount of the costs to be paid shall be ascertained as soon as practicable by the Crown Court officer (hereinafter referred to as the taxing authority).

(2)   On a taxation under the preceding paragraph there shall be allowed the costs reasonably incurred in or about the prosecution and conviction or the defence, as the case may be.

[Formerly rule 14 of the Crown Court Rules 1982. See also the relevant provisions of the Prosecution of Offences Act 1985 and the Costs in Criminal Cases (General) Regulations 1986.]

78.4   Review of Crown Court costs by taxing authority

(1)   Any party dissatisfied with the taxation of any costs by the taxing authority under rule 78.3 may apply to the taxing authority to review his decision.

(2)   The application shall be made by giving notice to the taxing authority and to any other party to the taxation within 14 days of the taxation, specifying the items in respect of which the application is made and the grounds of objection.

(3)   Any party to whom notice is given under the preceding paragraph may within 14 days of the service of the notice deliver to the taxing authority answers in writing to the objections specified in that notice to the taxing authority and, if he does, shall send copies to the applicant for the review and to any other party to the taxation.

(4)   The taxing authority shall reconsider his taxation in the light of the objections and answers, if any, of the parties and any oral representations made by or on their behalf and shall notify them of the result of his review.

[Formerly rule 15 of the Crown Court Rules 1982. See also the relevant provisions of the Prosecution of Offences Act 1985 and the Costs in Criminal Cases (General) Regulations 1986.]

78.5   Further review of Crown Court costs by Taxing Master

(1)   Any party dissatisfied with the result of a review of taxation under rule 78.4 may, within 14 days of receiving notification thereof, request the taxing authority to supply him with reasons in writing for his decision and may within 14 days of the receipt of such reasons apply to the Chief Taxing Master for a further review and shall, in that case, give notice of the application to the taxing authority and to any other party to the taxation, to whom he shall also give a copy of the reasons given by the taxing authority.

(2)   Such application shall state whether the application wishes to appear or be represented, or whether he will accept a decision given in his absence and shall be accompanied by a copy of the notice given under rule 78.4, of any answer which may have been given under paragraph (3) thereof and of the reasons given by the taxing authority for his decision, together with the bill of costs and full supporting documents.

(3)   A party to the taxation who receives notice of an application under this rule shall inform the Chief Taxing Master whether he wishes to appear or be represented at a further review, or whether he will accept a decision given in his absence.

(4)   The further review shall be conducted by a Taxing Master and if the applicant or any other party to the taxation has given notice of his intention to appear or be represented, the Taxing Master shall inform the parties (or their agents) of the date on which the further review will take place.

(5)   Before reaching his decision the Taxing Master may consult the judge who made the order for costs and the taxing authority and, unless the Taxing Master otherwise directs, no further evidence shall be received on the hearing of the further review; and no ground of objection shall be valid which was not raised on the review under rule 78.4.

(6)   In making his review, the Taxing Master may alter the assessment of the taxing authority in respect of any sum allowed, whether by increase or decrease.

(7)   The Taxing Master shall communicate the result of the further review to the parties and to the taxing authority.

[Formerly rule 16 of the Crown Court Rules 1982. See also the relevant provisions of the Prosecution of Offences Act 1985 and the Costs in Criminal Cases (General) Regulations 1986.]

78.6   Appeal to High Court judge after review of Crown Court costs

(1)   Any party dissatisfied with the result of a further review under rule 78.5 may, within 14 days of receiving notification thereof, appeal by originating summons to a judge of the Queen's Bench Division of the High Court if, and only if, the Taxing Master certifies that the question to be decided involves a point of principle of general importance.

(2)   On the hearing of the appeal the judge may reverse, affirm or amend the decision appealed against or make such other order as he thinks appropriate.

[Formerly rule 17 of the Crown Court Rules 1982. See also the relevant provisions of the Prosecution of Offences Act 1985 and the Costs in Criminal Cases (General) Regulations 1986.]

78.7   Supplementary provisions on Crown Court costs

(1)   On a further review or an appeal to a judge of the High Court the Taxing Master or judge may make such order as he thinks just in respect of the costs of the hearing of the further review or the appeal, as the case may be.

(2)   The time set out by rules 78.4, 78.5 and 78.6 may be extended by the taxing authority, Taxing Master or judge of the High Court on such terms as he thinks just.

[*Formerly rule 18 of the Crown Court Rules 1982. See also the relevant provisions of the Prosecution of Offences Act 1985 and the Costs in Criminal Cases (General) Regulations 1986.*]

Section B

ANNEX E TO THE CONSOLIDATED PRACTICE DIRECTION: CASE MANAGEMENT FORMS AND GUIDANCE NOTES

THE CASE MANAGEMENT FORMS (PART 3 OF THE CRIMINAL PROCEDURE RULES)

Plea and Case Management Hearing
Crown Court Preliminary Hearing
Magistrates' Court – Directions for Case Committed to the Crown Court
Magistrates' Court – Directions for Case Sent to the Crown Court
Magistrates' Court – Case Progression
Youth Court – Directions for Case Committed to the Crown Court
Youth Court – Directions for Case Sent to the Crown Court
Youth Court – Case Progression

Plea and case management hearing form: guidance notes

How to use the form

The parties should complete only one form for each case. **The form should be used in every Crown Court centre, without any local exception or variation.**

The form may be completed in manuscript or electronically.

Questions 1 to 14 must be answered in every case. Questions 15–35 need only be answered if they are relevant.

The advocate may be asked by the court to expand upon or explain an entry, or to account for the absence of an entry, where one is required. The judge will record on the template any orders made and, if practicable, issue a copy to the parties before the hearing ends. The parties must obtain a copy of that record and comply with the orders made by the date given.

Accessing the form

The current version of the form is available on the Court Service web-site at **http://www.hmcourts-service.gov.uk/HMCSCourtFinder**. Please note that the form will be updated from time to time. When you open the file, a box will appear with the options of disabling or enabling macros. Choosing "enable macros" will produce a fully operational e-form. Choosing "disable macros" may cause some of the functions to be lost, including the option of altering the number of defendants or using a screen reader.

Next will appear the box giving the option of a screen reader. This is software which translates text into speech.

The next box asks for the number of defendants in the case. This can be altered later by clicking on "Add Def" in the toolbar at the top of the screen.

The Crown Court

Case Number   D1 [ ]

Date of trial [ ]

Fixed ☐
Warned ☐

Plea and Case Management Hearing

Advocates Questionnaire

■Parties must complete this form.
■This form is to be used at all Crown Court Centres, without local variation.
There is an electronic version of the form which contains answer boxes that expand. The form is at:
http://www.hmcourts-service.gov.uk/HMCSCourtFinder

---

1   Date of PCMH [ ]   PTI URN [ ]

Judge [ ]   Estimated length of trial [ ]

2   **Parties' details**

	Parties name	Age	Remand status	CTL expires	Advocate at PCMH	Trial advocate (if known)
P						
D1			C ☐ B ☐			

3   **Contact details**

3.1   Parties

P   Office
Name	Phone
Email	

Advocate
Name	Phone
Email	

D1   Solicitor
Name	Phone
Email	

Advocate
Name	Phone
Email	

3.2

Case progression officers

P

Name	Phone
Email	

D1

Name	Phone
Email	

Court

Name	Phone
Email	

4   Which orders made at the magistrates' court have not been complied with?

5

D1   Has the defendant been advised that he or she will receive credit for a guilty plea?   ☐ No ☐ Yes

6

D1   Has the defendant been warned that the case may proceed in his or her absence?   ☐ No ☐ Yes

7   What plea(s) is/are the defendant(s) offering?

D1

8   Should the case be referred to the Resident Judge for a trial judge to be allocated?   ☐ No ☐ Yes

9   Give details of any issues relating to the fitness to plead or to stand trial.

D1

10

10.1   Has the prosecution made statutory disclosure?

P

D1

10.2   Has a defence statement been served?

D1

10.3   Does it comply with the statutory requirements?

P

10.4   If not clear from the defence statement, what are the real issues?

D1

10.5

D1   Has / will the defence made/make an application in writing under
        section 8 of the Criminal Procedure and Investigations Act 1996?   ☐ No ☐ Yes

11   What further evidence is to be served by the prosecution?
          By when is it reasonably practicable to serve this?

P

12

12.1   Give details of any expert evidence likely to be relied upon, including
        why it is required and by when it is reasonably practicable to serve this.

P

D1

12.2   Is a note of agreement / disagreement required?

13

13.1

D1   Has the defence completed the Witness List (see **36**)?   ☐ No ☐ Yes

13.2   Is any witness summons necessary?

13.3

D1   Is a timetable for the calling of witnesses required (see **30**)?   ☐ No ☐ Yes

14

14.1

D1   Is a certificate for a litigator sought?   ☐ No ☐ Yes

14.2   If **Yes**, why and for how long?

D1

For 15 to 35, answer the relevant questions only

---

15   Admissions, schedules etc.

What matters can usefully be admitted or put into schedules, diagrams, visual aids etc.?

16   Case summary

P   Is it proposed to serve a case summary or note of opening?   ☐ No ☐ Yes

17   Special measures

17.1   Give details of any special measures application to be made.

17.2

Can any order be made now?   ☐ No   ☐ Yes

17.3   What other arrangements are needed for any young/vulnerable/ ntimidated witness?

18   Young defendants

Are any arrangements needed for any young defendant?

D1

19   Reporting restrictions

State type and grounds of any reporting restriction sought.

P

D1

20   Third party material

20.1   What third party material is sought, from whom, and why?

P

D1

20.2   If the material can be obtained without a court order, by whom and by when?

P

D1

20.3   Should any person adversely affected by an order be notified?

21   Defendant's interview(s)

21.1   Is there an issue in relation to the accuracy of the transcript/admissibility of the defendant's interview?

D1

21.2   What proposals are made for any editing required?

D1

21.3   What proposals are made to summarise the interview(s)?

D1

22   Video Evidence

22.1   Is there video evidence of any young / vulnerable / intimidated witness yet to be served?

22.2   Has each video been transcribed?

22.3   Is there an issue in relation to the accuracy/admissibility/quality of any video or transcript?

23   Witness interview(s)

23.1   Are there any videos / audio tapes of witness interviews which, if they meet the disclosure test, are yet to be disclosed as unused material?

23.2   If so, is any application made for that video/audio tape to be transcribed and, if so, why?

24   CCTV evidence

24.1   Are there any outstanding issues in relation to service disclosure of CCTV footage?
If the material is in the possession of a third party, complete 20 instead.

24.2   Is an edited version to be served/used?

25   Electronic equipment

25.1   Give details of any special equipment (e.g. CCTV, live link, audio recordings, DVD)
required in the trial courtroom.

P

D1

25.2   Is the evidence in its present form compatible with the equipment in court?

26   Cross-examination on sexual history

If an application has not already been made, does the defence intend to make an application under section 41
of the Youth Justice and Criminal Evidence Act 1999 to cross-examine a witness about his or her sexual
history?

D1

27   Bad character

Are any directions necessary in relation to bad character applications?
Are there to be any further applications?

P

D1

28   Hearsay

Are any directions necessary in relation to hearsay applications? Are there to be any further applications?

P

D1

29   Admissibility and legal issues

What points on admissibility / other legal issues are to be taken? Is it necessary for any to be resolved before trial?

P

D1

30   Timetable of trial

Are there matters which need to be determined on the day of trial, which may affect the timetable of trial? If so, when will (1) the jury and (2) the witnesses be required?

P

31   Public interest immunity

Is any 'on notice' public interest immunity application to be made?

P

32   Jury bundle

What proposals do the prosecution make for a jury bundle?

P

33   Concurrent family proceedings

Give details of any concurrent family proceedings.

34   Other special arrangements

Give details of any special arrangements (e.g., interpreter, intermediary, wheelchair access, hearing loop system) needed for anyone attending the trial.

35   Linked criminal proceedings

Are there other criminal proceedings against the defendant or otherwise linked?

36   Witness List

The defence should indicate here which prosecution witnesses are required to give evidence at trial. The attendance of any witness is subject to the judge's direction.

Name of witness	Page No.	Type of witness: *Provide specific details of the type of witness. For example: eye witness, police officer, firearms expert, continuity*	Required by

Once this question has been answered, the form that is produced is ready for completion.

The space available to answer any question expands to accommodate the text inserted. The Tab button can be used to jump to the next box. Alternatively, the arrow keys will move the cursor backwards or forwards.

Transmitting the form

If you complete the form on the screen, it can still be printed off and used in hard copy. Alternatively, it can be emailed; the process for this differs depending on whether Outlook is available.

In order to send the form by email, click on the "e-mail" button on the toolbar at the top of the screen and follow the instructions. If the document is to be emailed using Outlook, that programme must be open at the time. Following the instructions will produce an e-mail window with the form attached. If Outlook is not used, the file must be saved and can then be attached in the usual way.

THE NEED FOR AN EFFECTIVE PCMH

The public, and all those concerned in or affected by a criminal case, have a right to expect that the business of the courts will be conducted fairly but also efficiently and effectively. Delays cost money and adversely impact on the quality of justice. The Plea and Case Management Hearing offers the best, and often the only, opportunity for the judge properly and effectively to manage the case before it is listed for trial. Other hearings – formerly called "mentions"– are expensive and should actively be discouraged; nearly everything formerly done at a "mention" can – and should – be done in some other way (usually by telephone or on paper or by an exchange of email, as permitted by CrimPR 3.5(2)(d)). An effective PCMH is therefore vital.

Advocates should attend the hearing fully prepared to deal with the issues that are likely to arise, and the listing officer should consider reasonable requests to list the PCMH to enable trial counsel to attend.

Since an effective PCMH can only take place after the defence have had a proper opportunity to consider the papers, it is suggested that at least four weeks should elapse between the service and listing of the PCMH.

The short guidance given here is intended to be followed in every case but, of course, it is not possible to cover exhaustively all the situations which may be relevant to achieving an effective PCMH. See also Consolidated Criminal Practice Direction (CCPD) IV.41, Management of Cases to be Heard in the Crown Court; V.56 Case Management in Magistrates' Courts and Criminal Case Management Framework (available on-line at **www.cjsonline.gov.uk/framework**).

CONTENTS OF THE FORM

Date of trial and custody time limits

The date of trial should normally be fixed at the PCMH (or before). Any application to extend the Custody Time Limit is best dealt with at the PCMH, when the reasons for fixing a case beyond the time limits will be clear; otherwise there will be the avoidable expense of another hearing.

1,2 and 3 details of case and parties

This section must be fully completed. The parties must be able to contact one another as must case progression officers and the court. Any change in the details must immediately be notified to the other parties and to the court. See CrimPR 3.4.

4 Compliance with the directions given by magistrates' courts

The standard/specific directions given by magistrates' courts should be complied with (CrimPR 3.5(3)). The court will need to know which orders have not been complied with, and why.

5 Credit for guilty plea

Defendants are entitled to be given the advice that credit is given for guilty pleas and the earlier the plea is entered, the greater is the credit given. The judge needs to know that this advice has been given.

6 Trial in absence

Defendants need to be warned that if they waive their right to attend, the trial may proceed in their absence. No one can engineer an adjournment simply by absconding. Those who claim to be ill must support that claim by medical evidence to the effect that they are unfit to attend their trial; it is unlikely that a medical certificate merely suggesting that they are unfit to work will be sufficient. See CCPD, I.13; CrimPR 3.8(2)(a).

7 The pleas which the defendant is offering

Recording in writing pleas offered to alternative offences which the prosecution are initially unwilling to accept will be advantageous to the defendant if the prosecution subsequently changes its position. In such circumstances, it will be easier for a defendant to claim maximum credit if that offer has been recorded. Pleas offered to counts on the indictment must similarly be recorded before credit is claimed.

8 Allocation of the case

Most courts have a system to identify before the PCMH those cases which require allocation to a particular judge; this question is intended to seek out those cases which have been missed.

9 Fitness to plead

This is self explanatory but the judge will need assistance to fix a timetable for the service of experts' reports and for the issue to be tried.

10 Disclosure and defence statement

The parties must identify any outstanding disclosure points. The defence must serve a detailed defence statement setting out the issues in the trial; any failure to do so may be the subject of adverse comment at the trial and the judge may issue a warning to this effect, under section 11(3) of the Criminal Procedure and Investigations Act 1996. Pending service of a defence statement, question 10.4 allows the defence to give some notification of the defence. The practice of appending long "shopping lists" to vague and unspecific defence statements has no legal foundation; any application for further disclosure should be made by way of formal application under section 8 of the Criminal Procedure and Investigations Act 1996 (as amended). The judge will expect reference to and compliance with the Disclosure Protocol: A Protocol for the Control and Management of Unused Material in the Crown Court.

11 and 12 Timetable of further evidence and expert evidence

Advocates should have available proper information as to what remains to be served, together with a realistic timetable for compliance. Parties should be prepared to provide realistic time estimates and not rely on a standard time period of, for example, 28 days if this has little bearing on the true amount of time likely to be required. The court needs detailed and accurate information as to when the evidence will be available. These enquiries should be made before the hearing. Failure to do so is likely to cause unnecessary adjournments. Consideration should be given to CrimPR 33.5 and whether (now or later) the experts should be asked to confer to identify the real areas of dispute.

13 Witness list (see also 36)

The mere fact of warning a witness to attend may cause him or her anxiety. Furthermore, the warning of witnesses is time consuming and expensive. The court may decline to order the attendance of witnesses unless their presence is really necessary. Consideration should therefore also be given to those witnesses in respect of whom a summons is required. See CrimPR Part 28 for rules on witness summonses. Thought should always be given to the staggering of witnesses to eliminate or reduce waiting times. The witnesses' availability must be known at the PCMH to ensure that the trial date is convenient.

14 Certificate for a litigator

Attendance by a litigator is not a matter of right and should always be justified by reference to the facts of the particular case.

15 Admissions

Properly drafted admissions can save a great deal of court time and proposals should be made in most cases.

16 Case Summary

Case Summaries should have been provided before the PCMH in all Class 1 cases and in any other case of complexity, but they may be needed in other cases as well.

17 Special measures

In accordance with CrimPR Part 29, special measures applications should have been made by the parties and considered by the court before the PCMH, but this question serves to remind advocates and judges of any outstanding applications.

18 Young and other vulnerable defendants

The needs of young and other vulnerable defendants must be identified in advance of the trial so that the necessary arrangements can be made. See CCPD III.30.

19 Reporting restrictions

Reporting restrictions need to be carefully considered and balanced against the rights of the press and other interested parties. The judge is likely to require assistance before making any order. See CCPD I.3.

20 Third party material and applications to produce documents

Such applications must comply with CrimPR Part 28. Careful thought needs to go into identifying the witness to be served, the material sought and the reason that it is said to be relevant to an issue in the case. Any person whose right of confidentiality might be adversely affected must also be identified and information provided as to how and by whom they are to be notified, how they are to be permitted to make representations and when and by whom any rulings are to be made. It is important that such applications are made no later than the PCMH to avoid adjournments at a later stage arising out of delayed applications.

21 Defendant's interviews

Inaccuracies within transcriptions and likely submissions as to admissibility must be identified. Furthermore, the police may interview suspects at length, producing bundles of transcripts, the volume of which may make them unsuitable to put before a jury. The parties must consider producing summaries. The production of the first draft is primarily the responsibility of the advocate for the prosecution. If practicable, interviews should be available in electronic form, so that editing, pagination and copying can be done without delay. Further guidance is given in CCPD IV.43.

22 Video evidence

These four questions, each of which raises a separate point, are self explanatory but failure to address them is a frequent source of adjournments. Accuracy, admissibility and quality are not the same. Errors of transcription or material on the tape that is indistinct or unclear, or which is alleged to be inadmissible, must be dealt with at PCMH. Editing takes time. It should not be done on the morning of the trial or the day beforehand. Only if these issues are addressed in advance can child witnesses be called as soon as they arrive at court. It is unacceptable to prolong the anxiety of vulnerable witnesses simply because these issues have not been resolved at PCMH. These matters are already addressed in the Supplementary Pre-trial Checklist for Cases Involving Young Witnesses. See also CrimPR Part 29 for rules on special measures directions; and CCPD IV.40.

23 Witness interviews

The issues raised in this question differ from those raised in question 22. There is a growing practice of recording interviews with witnesses before setting out their evidence in a written witness statement. If this is done, then, subject to the disclosure test, the video or audio recording should be disclosed as unused material. The prosecution advocate therefore needs to know if any witness was interviewed in this way (which may not be clear from the papers served). It will normally suffice for the video or audio recording itself to be disclosed. Transcripts are expensive and any claim for a transcript needs to be justified.

24 and 25 CCTV and electronic equipment

The prosecution only have duties to consider disclosure of CCTV footage in their possession. If the defence seek footage from third parties, it is for them to do so, rather than the prosecution. Furthermore, much CCTV footage is in a format (e.g. multiplex) which is unsuitable for showing in court without adaptation or editing. This must be sorted out before the trial. Many courts have simple VHS video and DVD playback facilities and the parties must ensure that the material which they want to play is compatible with the court equipment (if not, they must provide their own).

26 Cross-examination on sexual history

Section 41 of the Youth Justice and Criminal Evidence Act 1999 enacts an important principle and compliance with its requirements is vital to ensure that those who complain that they are victims of rape (and other sexual offences) receive the protection which the law affords to them. In accordance with CrimPR Part 36, applications should be made and considered – by the trial judge if possible – at or before the PCMH. Applications made on the day of the trial are strongly to be discouraged.

27 and 28 Bad character and hearsay

CrimPR 34.5 and 35.6 provide for detailed applications to be made in the prescribed forms. Questions 27 and 28 therefore only seek to identify any outstanding issues (or potential future applications).

29 Admissibility and legal issues

Issues of admissibility and legal issues should, where possible, be identified before the trial, so that the parties can exchange skeleton arguments and the judge can properly prepare for the hearing. See also section 7 of the Criminal Justice Act 1987; and sections 31 and 40 of the Criminal Procedure and Investigations Act 1996.

30 Timetable of the trial

If there are to be preliminary points taken, then consideration must be given to when a jury will be required and arrangements made to stagger the attendance of witnesses. No one should be asked to attend for a 10.30am start only to find that there is a lengthy legal argument before the case can even be opened. See CrimPR 3.10, which deals with, amongst other things, timetabling and witness arrangements.

31 PII claims

If a claim is to be made on notice, then the necessary arrangements must be made. See CrimPR Part 25.

32 Jury bundle

If a jury bundle will be needed at the trial, then its content will need to be agreed before the trial. Any outstanding issues need to be identified.

33 Concurrent family proceedings

It is important to identify those cases where there are concurrent family proceedings, so that the Designated Family Judge can be alerted.

34 Special arrangements

Any requirements for an interpreter or for those with a disability must be identified in advance, so that proper arrangements can be made. See CrimPR 10.5(1)(h) and 12.1(1)(e).

35 Linked criminal proceedings

These need to be identified, if possible with the court reference numbers.

TEMPLATE FOR ORDERS MADE AT PLEA AND CASE MANAGEMENT HEARING

*delete as appropriate

PCMH ques-tion	Description of order/ work required	Order made
	Trial date [*fixed for] [*warned for week commencing]	
1	Estimated length of hearing	
9	The defence to serve expert evidence (fitness to plead)	
9	The prosecution to serve expert evidence in response (fitness to plead)	

PCMH question	Description of order/ work required	Order made
10	The defence to serve any Defence Statement by	
10	Was a warning given that inferences may be drawn from failure to comply?	
10	The prosecution to make further disclosure by	
10	The defence to make any application under section 8 CPIA for disclosure by	
11	The prosecution to serve further evidence by	
12	The prosecution to serve expert evidence by	
12	The defence to serve any expert evidence on which they rely by	
13	Defence to serve a list of witnesses required at trial by	
13	Record any ruling that the judge has made that the attendance of any witness on that list is not required.	
14	Certificate for litigator granted for [*the first day] [*the whole trial]	
15	Prosecution to serve schedule of facts for agreement by	
16	Prosecution to serve case summary or note of opening by	
17	Prosecution to apply for special measures directions by	
17	Defence to apply for special measures directions by	
19	Reporting restrictions made in terms attached	
20	Prosecution to seek disclosure of third party material by	
20	Defence to seek disclosure of third party material by	
20	Person adversely affected [being] to be notified by	
21	Defence to notify editing required of defendant's interview by	
21	Prosecution to respond to same by	
21	Prosecution to prepare summaries for agreement by	
22	Prosecution to serve video tape of vulnerable witness by	
22	Prosecution to serve [*transcript][*summary] of evidence by	
22	Defence to notify editing required of defendant's interview by	
22	Prosecution to respond to same by	
23	Prosecution to serve tapes of witness interviews by	

PCMH ques-tion	Description of order/ work required	Order made
23	Prosecution to transcribe tapes of witness interviews by	
24	Prosecution to serve or disclose CCTV footage by	
24	Prosecution to serve edited version of CCTV footage by	
25	Prosecution to confirm that court equipment compatible with tape by	
26	Defence to serve application to cross-examine on sexual history by	
27	Prosecution to serve further bad character application by	
27	Defence to serve further bad character application by	
28	Prosecution to serve further hearsay application by	
28	Defence to serve further hearsay application by	
29	Defence to serve skeleton argument on legal points to be taken by	
29	Prosecution to respond by	
	*Other orders	
	*	
	*	

Judge's signature .... Date ....

Crown Court case progression preliminary hearing: guidance notes

GENERAL NOTES

These notes accompany the preliminary hearing form.

The parties must ensure that the Court has a copy of the "CASE SENT TO THE CROWN COURT UNDER SECTION 51 OF THE CRIME AND DISORDER ACT 1998" form completed in the Magistrates' Court.

The answers to the questions in bold must be filled in before the hearing. The proposed italicised orders should be filled in before the hearing, if possible (if there are more than five defendants, a further form should be filled in only so far as necessary).

Except where otherwise required, a direction in the form to "serve" material means serve on the other party(ies) and file with the Crown Court.

NOTES RELEVANT TO SPECIFIC SECTIONS

(1) Trial judge or nominated judge

If the case is due to last for more than 4 weeks or if it seems likely that a preparatory hearing will be ordered, the future case management should normally be under the supervision of the

CROWN COURT

CASE PROGRESSION

PRELIMINARY HEARING

Date of hearing: / /   Judge:

Prosecution advocate:				
D1		[bail] [custody]	represented by:	
D2		[bail] [custody]	represented by:	
D3		[bail] [custody]	represented by:	
D4		[bail] [custody]	represented by:	
D5		[bail] [custody]	represented by:	

No. of case in Crown Court: _____   URN: _____

Has the defendant been advised about credit for pleading guilty?

D1	D2	D3	D4	D5

Has the defendant been warned that if he is on bail and fails to attend, the proceedings may continue in his absence?

1) TRIAL JUDGE

Should the future management of the case be under the supervision of the trial judge or a nominated judge?   **YES/NO**

2) PLEA

a. **Is it likely that the case can be concluded by the defendant pleading guilty?**

D1	D2	D3	D4	D5

b. If yes and if the defendant cannot be sentenced at the preliminary hearing, go to 3) and/or 4) as appropriate

3) LIKELY GUILTY PLEA

a. *The defendant will be sentenced on: / / or at the plea and case management hearing*

b. *The directions made by the magistrates' court when the case was sent shall apply subject to the following amendments:*

c. *The pre-sentence report (if required) to be received by the Crown Court and made available to the defence and the prosecution by:*

d. *The defence to serve any material which it wishes the court to consider when sentencing by:*

e. **Does the defence intend to make "derogatory assertions" against a person's character in the course of mitigation?**

D1	D2	D3	D4	D5

f. *If yes, the court orders:*

g.   **Are there any other matters against a defendant which should be dealt with at the same time as the proceedings in this case (other offences/TIC's)?**

D1	D2	D3	D4	D5

h.   **If yes, give brief details:**

i.   *If there are other matters, the court orders:*

j.   *Further orders (e.g. orders re medical, psychiatric reports, confiscation proceedings or Newton hearings):*

4) DIRECTIONS FOR PLEA AND CASE MANAGEMENT HEARING

a.   *The directions made by the Magistrates' Court when the case was sent shall apply subject to the following amendments:*

b.   *Further orders:*

5) EXPERT EVIDENCE

a.   **Is this a case in which the parties will rely on expert evidence?**

P	D1	D2	D3	D4	D5

b.   *If yes, the court orders:*

6) TRIAL

a.   **Can the date of the trial or the period during which the trial will take place be fixed now?**   **YES/NO**

b.   *If yes, the trial will take place on:*
     or within the period of :
     and it is estimated that it will last:

trial judge or a nominated judge. It may also be desirable for the future case management to be under the supervision of the trial judge or a nominated judge in other cases where, for example there are difficult issues of law to be considered or where the prosecution intends to make a public interest immunity application.

If the case fits into this category, the court should normally make the necessary directions for the plea and case management hearing and then direct that the case be considered by the Resident Judge.

(2) Plea

If it is likely that the case can be concluded by all the defendants pleading guilty then 3) should be completed and there should be no need to make any orders under 4). Otherwise any appropriate orders under 3) should be made in respect of those defendants likely to plead guilty and 4) should be completed.

(3) Likely guilty plea

3b. The Crown Court has a greater power to vary the time limits than the magistrates' court.
3c. A pre-sentence report will not be required in every case.
3e. Advance notice of the fact that such an assertion is going to be made should be given to the prosecution to enable it to decide whether to challenge the assertion and to enable the sentencing court to consider whether to make an order restricting the publication of the assertion under sections 58–61 of the Criminal Procedure and Investigations Act 1996 ("CPIA").
3i. If the defendant is facing charges in other courts give brief details of offence, court and court number.

(4) Directions for plea and case management hearing

4a. The Crown Court has a greater power to vary the time limits than the Magistrates' Court.

(5) Expert evidence

The court should identify any issues in relation to which it is appropriate to call expert evidence and set a timetable for obtaining, serving, and (if possible) agreeing such evidence or identifying the issues in dispute. See also paragraph 15 of the guidance notes to the PCMH form.

The parties should consider whether orders being considered by the court will involve costs being incurred which may not be met by the Legal Services Commission.

(6) Trial

The court should consider whether it is possible and desirable to set the trial date or period because, for example, of the health, vulnerability or availability of a witness or the defendant or because the defendant falls within the definition of a persistent young offender, or because experts and/or leading counsel may have to be instructed and, before any such instructions can be expected, it is necessary to know the date.

MAGISTRATES' COURT

DIRECTIONS FOR CASE COMMITTED TO THE CROWN COURT

....Magistrates' Court

Date committed...

The Plea and Case Management Hearing will take place

on...................................at..…......Crown Court

Name of defendant	Case no	Remand status	Youth jointly charged with adult?	Represented by:
D1		Bail/cust/COM		
D2		Bail/cust/COM		
D3		Bail/cust/COM		
D4		Bail/cust/COM		

COM= in custody on other matters

Defence telephone numbers:
D1 .... (home) .... (mobile)   D1 solicitor .... (office)
D2 .... (home) .... (mobile)   D2 solicitor .... (office)
D3 .... (home) .... (mobile)   D3 solicitor .... (office)
D4 .... (home) .... (mobile)   D4 solicitor .... (office)

Prosecution telephone number...

CASE DETAILS

1. Has the defendant been advised that the case may proceed in his or her absence?

D1: Y ☐ N ☐   D2: Y ☐ N ☐

D3: Y ☐N ☐   D4: Y ☐ N ☐

2. Has the defendant been advised about credit for pleading guilty?

D1: Y ☐ N ☐   D2: Y ☐ N ☐

D3: Y ☐N ☐   D4: Y ☐ N ☐

3. What pleas, if any, are indicated?
D1: ....
D2: ....
D3: ....
D4: ....

NOTE: If the defendant decides to plead guilty after committal, the Crown Court must be notified immediately. The Crown Court will then list the case for a hearing as soon as possible.

4. Does the defence intend to make an application under section 41 of the Youth Justice and Criminal Evidence Act 1999 to cross-examine the complainant about his or her sexual history? .... be served within 28 days of primary/initial disclosure)

5. Please give details of any other matters which should be dealt with at the same time as these proceedings (e.g. other offences, offences to be taken into consideration)?
D1: ....   D2: ....
....
D3: ....   D4: ....
....

Insert committal date in blank box:

ACTION	TIME LIMITS	DIRECTIONS
1	Date committed	• Prosecution to serve provisional draft indictment, if not already done.
2	14 days after Action 1	• Prosecution to serve primary or initial disclosure • Defence to notify prosecution of witness requirements • Prosecution to serve any application for hearsay or defendant's bad character
3	28 days after Action 1	• Prosecution to serve final draft indictment and any special measures applications • Defence to serve any application under section 41 of the Youth Justice and Criminal Evidence Act 1999
4	14 days after Action 2	• Defence to serve: • (i) Defence statement* (including any alibi details) OR notification of guilty plea (ii) Any application for hearsay/bad character (iii) Response to hearsay/bad character application by prosecution
5	14 days after Action 3	• Defence to serve response to any prosecution application for special measures • Prosecution and defence to notify Crown Court of names of trial advocate and time estimate • Defence to notify Crown Court of non-availability of expert witnesses, with reasons • Witness Care Unit to notify Crown Court and prosecution of dates when witnesses required by defence are unavailable, with reasons.
6	14 days after Action 4	• Prosecution to serve responses to hearsay/bad character

NOTE: if any party seeks a subsequent variation in the timetable or further direction, a written application must be made to the Crown Court within 14 days of committal, and copies served on all other parties. A Crown Court judge may make directions as appropriate. If at any time either party is unable to comply with any direction, it must notify the case progression officer immediately and apply to the Crown Court for a variation.

* indicates those time limits which cannot be varied by a magistrates' court.

Please record any further directions here:

Received..(defence signature) ....(prosecution signature)

MAGISTRATES' COURT

DIRECTIONS FOR CASE SENT TO THE CROWN COURT

....Magistrates' Court
Date sent: ....

The Plea and Case Management Hearing will take place

on...................................at...Crown Court

Name of defendant	Case no	Remand status	Youth jointly charged with adult?	Represented by:
D1		Bail/cust/COM		
D2		Bail/cust/COM		
D3		Bail/cust/COM		
D4		Bail/cust/COM		

COM= in custody on other matters

Defence telephone numbers:
D1.............................. (home) .... (mobile)   D1 solicitor .... (office)
D2.............................. (home) .... (mobile)   D2 solicitor .... (office)
D3.............................. (home) .... (mobile)   D3 solicitor .... (office)
D4.............................. (home) .... (mobile)   D4 solicitor .... (office)

Prosecution telephone number..

CASE DETAILS

1. Has the defendant been advised that the case may proceed in his or her absence?

D1: Y ☐ N ☐   D2: Y ☐ N ☐

D3: Y ☐N ☐   D4: Y ☐ N ☐

2. Has the defendant been advised about credit for pleading guilty?

D1: Y ☐ N ☐   D2: Y ☐ N ☐

D3: Y ☐N ☐   D4: Y ☐ N ☐

3. What pleas, if any, are indicated?
D1: ....
D2: ....
D3: ....
D4: ....

NOTE: If the defendant decides to plead guilty after sending, the Crown Court must be notified immediately. The Crown Court will then list the case for a hearing as soon as possible.

4. Does the defence intend to make an application under section 41 of the Youth Justice and Criminal Evidence Act 1999 to cross-examine the complainant about his or her sexual history?
.... (to be served within 28 days of primary/initial disclosure)

5. Please give details of any other matters which should be dealt with at the same time as these proceedings (e.g. other offences, offences to be taken into consideration)?
D1: ....   D2: ....
....
D3: ....   D4: ....
....

Insert date by which Action 1 to be completed in blank box:

ACTION	TIME LIMITS	DIRECTIONS
1	Cust: 50 days after sent* Bail: 70 days after sent*	• Prosecution to serve draft indictment, case papers and primary or initial disclosure.
2	14 days after Action 1	• Defence to notify prosecution of witness requirements • Prosecution to serve any application for hearsay or defendant's bad character • Defence to serve: (i) Defence statement* (including any alibi details) OR notification of guilty plea (ii) Any application for hearsay/bad character (iii) Any notice of application to dismiss charges
3	28 days after Action 1	• Prosecution to serve final draft indictment and any special measures applications • Defence to serve any application under section 41 of the Youth Justice and Criminal Evidence Act 1999
4	14 days after Action 2	• Prosecution to serve responses to hearsay/bad character/dismissal of charges applications • Defence to serve response to hearsay/bad character application by prosecution
5	14 days after Action 3	• Defence to serve response to any prosecution application for special measures • Prosecution and defence to notify Crown Court of names of trial advocate and time estimate • Defence to notify Crown Court of non-availability of expert witnesses, with reasons • Witness Care Unit to notify Crown Court and prosecution of dates when witnesses required by defence are unavailable, with reasons

NOTE: if any party seeks a subsequent variation in the timetable or further direction, a written application must be made to the Crown Court within 14 days of date sent, and copies served on all other parties. A Crown Court judge may make directions as appropriate or fix a preliminary hearing. If at any time either party is unable to comply with any direction, it must notify the CPO immediately and apply to the Crown Court for a variation.

* indicates those time limits which cannot be varied by a magistrates' court.

Please record any further directions here:

Received .... (defence signature) .... (prosecution signature)

MAGISTRATES' COURT

CASE PROGRESSION

....Magistrates' Court

Date of hearing:..…..

Name of defendant	Case no	Remand status	Youth jointly charged with adult?	Represented by:
D1		Bail/cust/COM		
D2		Bail/cust/COM		
D3		Bail/cust/COM		
D4		Bail/cust/COM		

COM= in custody on other matters

Defence telephone numbers:

D1..............................(home) ....(mobile)   D1 solicitor ....(office)
D2..............................(home) ....(mobile)   D2 solicitor ....(office)
D3..............................(home) ....(mobile)   D3 solicitor ....(office)
D4..............................(home) ....(mobile)   D4 solicitor ....(office)

Prosecution telephone number..

CASE DETAILS

Date of trial:...   **Estimated length of trial:**...........................

Has the defendant been advised that the case may proceed in his or her absence?

D1: Y ☐ N ☐   D2: Y ☐ N ☐

D3: Y ☐N ☐   D4: Y ☐ N ☐

Has the defendant been advised about credit for pleading guilty?

D1: Y ☐ N ☐   D2: Y ☐ N ☐

D3: Y ☐N ☐   D4: Y ☐ N ☐

Trial issues (e.g. identification – please give details)

Applications to be made (e.g. special measures, bad character, hearsay)

Defence witnesses

Defendant	Likely no of witnesses	Type of witness* (e.g. 2 x civ; 1 x child)
D1		
D2		
D3		
D4		

Prosecution witnesses

Name of witness	Type of witness*	Required by which defendant	To be read s.9?

*P = police; Civ = civilian; Ex = expert; Child = child; VA = vulnerable adult

Note: parties must notify the court and the other party immediately if there is any change in witness availability or requirement to attend.

Give details of any special arrangements (e.g. interpreter, intermediary, wheelchair access, hearing loop system) for anyone attending the trial:

STANDARD DIRECTIONS APPLY UNLESS THE COURT DIRECTS OTHERWISE

A COPY OF THE STANDARD DIRECTIONS IS AVAILABLE FROM THE COURT

Please record any further directions here (e.g. in relation to bad character, hearsay, special measures, disclosure, expert evidence):

YOUTH COURT

DIRECTIONS FOR CASE COMMITTED TO THE CROWN COURT

....Youth Court

Date committed: ....

The Plea and Case Management Hearing will take place

on...............................at...Crown Court

Name of defendant	Case no	PYO	Remand status	Represented by:
D1		Y/N	Bail/cust/COM	
D2		Y/N	Bail/cust/COM	
D3		Y/N	Bail/cust/COM	
D4		Y/N	Bail/cust/COM	

COM= in custody on other matters

Defence telephone numbers:

D1.............................. (home) .... (mobile)   D1 solicitor .... (office)
D2.............................. (home) .... (mobile)   D2 solicitor .... (office)
D3.............................. (home) .... (mobile)   D3 solicitor .... (office)
D4.............................. (home) .... (mobile)   D4 solicitor .... (office)

Prosecution telephone number...

CASE DETAILS

1. Has the defendant been advised that the case may proceed in his or her absence?

D1: Y ☐ N ☐   D2: Y ☐ N ☐

D3: Y ☐N ☐   D4: Y ☐ N ☐

2. Has the defendant been advised about credit for pleading guilty?

D1: Y ☐ N ☐   D2: Y ☐ N ☐

D3: Y ☐N ☐   D4: Y ☐ N ☐

3. What pleas, if any, are indicated?
D1: ....
D2: ....
D3: ....
D4: ....

NOTE: If the defendant decides to plead guilty after committal, the Crown Court must be notified immediately. The Crown Court will then list the case for a hearing as soon as possible.

4. Does the defence intend to make an application under section 41 of the Youth Justice and Criminal Evidence Act 1999 to cross-examine the complainant about his or her sexual history? .... (to be served within 28 days of primary/initial disclosure)

5. Please give details of any other matters which should be dealt with at the same time as these proceedings (e.g. other offences, offences to be taken into consideration)?
D1: ....   D2: ....
....
D3: ....   D4: ....
....

Insert committal date in blank box:

ACTION	TIME LIMITS	DIRECTIONS
1	**Date committed**	• Prosecution to serve provisional draft indictment, if not already done.
2	**14 days after Action 1**	• Prosecution to serve primary or initial papers • Prosecution to serve any application for hearsay or defendant's bad character
3	**28 days after Action 1**	• Prosecution to serve final draft indictment and any special measures applications • Defence to serve any application under section 41 of the Youth Justice and Criminal Evidence Act 1999
4	**14 days after Action 2**	• Defence to notify prosecution of witness requirements • Defence to serve: • (i) Defence statement* (including any alibi details) OR notification of guilty plea (ii) Any application for hearsay/bad character (iii) Response to hearsay/bad character application by prosecution • (iv) Any notice of application to dismiss charges
5	**14 days after Action 3**	• Defence to serve response to any prosecution application for special measures • Prosecution and defence to notify Crown Court of names of trial advocate and time estimate • Defence to notify Crown Court of non-availability of expert witnesses, with reasons • Witness Care Unit to notify Crown Court and prosecution of dates when witnesses required by defence are unavailable, with reasons.
6	**14 days after Action 4**	• Prosecution to serve responses to hearsay/bad character/dismissal of charges applications

NOTE: if any party seeks a subsequent variation in the timetable or further direction, a written application must be made to the Crown Court within 14 days of committal, and copies served on all other parties. A Crown Court judge may make directions as appropriate or fix a preliminary hearing. If at any time either party is unable to comply with any direction, it must notify the case progression officer immediately and apply to the Crown Court for a variation.

* indicates those time limits which cannot be varied by a magistrates' court.

Please record any further directions here:

Received.......................................(defence signature) ....(prosecution signature)

YOUTH COURT

DIRECTIONS FOR CASE SENT TO THE CROWN COURT

....Youth Court

Date sent: ....

The Plea and Case Management Hearing will take place

on..............................at...Crown Court

Name of defendant	Case no	PYO	Remand status	Represented by:
D1		Y/N	Bail/cust/COM	
D2		Y/N	Bail/cust/COM	
D3		Y/N	Bail/cust/COM	
D4		Y/N	Bail/cust/COM	

COM= in custody on other matters

Defence telephone numbers:
D1............................. (home) .... (mobile)   D1 solicitor .... (office)
D2............................. (home) .... (mobile)   D2 solicitor .... (office)
D3............................. (home) .... (mobile)   D3 solicitor .... (office)
D4............................. (home) .... (mobile)   D4 solicitor .... (office)

Prosecution telephone number...

CASE DETAILS

1. Has the defendant been advised that the case may proceed in his or her absence?

D1: Y ☐ N ☐   D2: Y ☐ N ☐

D3: Y ☐N ☐   D4: Y ☐ N ☐

2. Has the defendant been advised about credit for pleading guilty?

D1: Y ☐ N ☐   D2: Y ☐ N ☐

D3: Y ☐N ☐   D4: Y ☐ N ☐

3. What pleas, if any, are indicated?
D1: ....
D2: ....
D3: ....
D4: ....

NOTE: If the defendant decides to plead guilty after sending, the Crown Court must be notified immediately. The Crown Court will then list the case for a hearing as soon as possible.

4. Does the defence intend to make an application under section 41 of the Youth Justice and Criminal Evidence Act 1999 to cross-examine the complainant about his or her sexual history? .... (to be served within 28 days of primary/initial disclosure)

5. Please give details of any other matters which should be dealt with at the same time as these proceedings (e.g. other offences, offences to be taken into consideration)?
D1: ....   D2: ....
....
D3: ....   D4: ....
....

Insert date by which Action 1 to be completed in blank box:

ACTION	TIME LIMITS	DIRECTIONS
1	Cust: 50 days after sent* Bail: 70 days after sent*	• Prosecution to serve draft indictment, case papers and primary or initial disclosure.
2	14 days after Action 1	• Defence to notify prosecution of witness requirements • Prosecution to serve any application for hearsay or defendant's bad character • Defence to serve: (i) Defence statement* (including any alibi details) OR notification of guilty plea (ii) Any application for hearsay/bad character (iii) Any notice of application to dismiss charges
3	28 days after Action 1	• Prosecution to serve final draft indictment and any special measures applications • Defence to serve any application under section 41 of the Youth Justice and Criminal Evidence Act 1999
4	14 days after Action 2	• Prosecution to serve responses to hearsay/bad character/dismissal of charges applications • Defence to serve response to hearsay/bad character application by prosecution
5	14 days after Action 3	• Defence to serve response to any prosecution application for special measures • Prosecution and defence to notify Crown Court of names of trial advocate and time estimate • Defence to notify Crown Court of non-availability of expert witnesses, with reasons • Witness Care Unit to notify Crown Court and prosecution of dates when witnesses required by defence are unavailable, with reasons

NOTE: if any party seeks a subsequent variation in the timetable or further direction, a written application must be made to the Crown Court within 14 days of date sent, and copies served on all other parties. A Crown Court judge may make directions as appropriate or fix a preliminary hearing. If at any time either party is unable to comply with any direction, it must notify the CPO immediately and apply to the Crown Court for a variation.

* indicates those time limits which cannot be varied by a magistrates' court.

Please record any further directions here:

Received.....................................(defence signature) ....(prosecution signature)

YOUTH COURT

CASE PROGRESSION

....Youth Court
Date of hearing:.......................................

Name of defendant	Case no	PYO	Remand status	Represented by:
D1		Y/N	Bail/cust/COM	
D2		Y/N	Bail/cust/COM	
D3		Y/N	Bail/cust/COM	
D4		Y/N	Bail/cust/COM	

COM= in custody on other matters

Defence telephone numbers:
D1.............................. (home) .... (mobile)   D1 solicitor .... (office)
D2.............................. (home) .... (mobile)   D2 solicitor .... (office)
D3.............................. (home) .... (mobile)   D3 solicitor .... (office)
D4.............................. (home) .... (mobile)   D4 solicitor .... (office)

Prosecution telephone number...

CASE DETAILS

Date of trial:...   **Estimated length of trial:**...........................

Has the defendant been advised that the case may proceed in his or her absence?

D1: Y ☐ N ☐   D2: Y ☐ N ☐

D3: Y ☐N ☐   D4: Y ☐ N ☐

Has the defendant been advised about credit for pleading guilty?

D1: Y ☐ N ☐   D2: Y ☐ N ☐

D3: Y ☐N ☐   D4: Y ☐ N ☐

Trial issues (e.g. identification – please give details)

Applications to be made (e.g. special measures, bad character, hearsay)

Defence witnesses

Defendant	Likely no of witnesses	Type of witness* (e.g. 2 x civ; 1 x child)
D1		
D2		
D3		
D4		

Prosecution witnesses

Name of witness	Type of witness*	Required by which defendant	To be read s.9?

*P = police; Civ = civilian; Ex = expert; Child = child; VA = vulnerable adult

Note: parties must notify the court and the other party immediately if there is any change in witness availability or requirement to attend.

Give details of any special arrangements (e.g. interpreter, intermediary, wheelchair access, hearing loop system) for anyone attending the trial:

STANDARD DIRECTIONS APPLY UNLESS THE COURT DIRECTS OTHERWISE

IF THE DEFENDANT IS A 'PYO' STANDARD DIRECTIONS MUST BE MODIFIED

A COPY OF THE STANDARD DIRECTIONS IS AVAILABLE FROM THE COURT

Please record any further directions here (e.g. in relation to bad character, hearsay, special measures, disclosure, expert evidence):

Section C
PROTOCOL FOR THE CONTROL AND MANAGEMENT OF HEAVY FRAUD AND OTHER COMPLEX CRIMINAL CASES

A Protocol issued by the Lord Chief Justice of England and Wales

22 March 2005

INTRODUCTION

There is a broad consensus that the length of fraud and trials of other complex crimes must be controlled within proper bounds in order:

(i) To enable the jury to retain and assess the evidence which they have heard. If the trial is so long that the jury cannot do this, then the trial is not fair either to the prosecution or the defence.

(ii) To make proper use of limited public resources: see *Jisl* [2004] EWCA Crim 696 at [113] – [121].

There is also a consensus that no trial should be permitted to exceed a given period, save in exceptional circumstances; some favour 3 months, others an outer limit of 6 months. Whatever view is taken, it is essential that the current length of trials is brought back to an acceptable and proper duration.

This Protocol supplements the Criminal Procedure Rules and summarises good practice which experience has shown may assist in bringing about some reduction in the length of trials of fraud and other crimes that result in complex trials. Flexibility of application of this Protocol according to the needs of each case is essential; it is designed to inform but not to prescribe.

This Protocol is primarily directed towards cases which are likely to last eight weeks or longer. It should also be followed, however, in all cases estimated to last more than four weeks. This Protocol applies to trials by jury, but many of the principles will be applicable if trials without a jury are permitted under s. 43 of the Criminal Justice Act 2003.

The best handling technique for a long case is continuous management by an experienced Judge nominated for the purpose. It is intended that this Protocol be kept up to date; any further practices or techniques found to be successful in the management of complex cases should be notified to the office of the Lord Chief Justice.

1. THE INVESTIGATION

(i) The role of the prosecuting authority and the judge

(a) Unlike other European countries, a judge in England and Wales does not directly control the investigative process; that is the responsibility of the Investigating Authority, and in turn the Prosecuting Authority and the prosecution advocate. Experience has shown that a prosecution lawyer (who must be of sufficient experience and who will be a member of the team at trial) and the prosecution advocate, if different, should be involved in the investigation as soon as it appears that a heavy fraud trial or other complex criminal trial is likely to ensue. The costs that this early preparation will incur will be saved many times over in the long run.

(b)   The judge can and should exert a substantial and beneficial influence by making it clear that, generally speaking, trials should be kept within manageable limits. In most cases 3 months should be the target outer limit, but there will be cases where a duration of 6 months, or in exceptional circumstances, even longer may be inevitable.

(ii)   Interviews

(a)   At present many interviews are too long and too unstructured. This has a knock-on effect on the length of trials. Interviews should provide an opportunity for suspects to respond to the allegations against them. They should not be an occasion to discuss every document in the case. It should become clear from judicial rulings that interviews of this kind are a waste of resources.

(b)   The suspect must be given sufficient information before or at the interview to enable them to meet the questions fairly and answer them honestly; the information is not provided to give the suspect the opportunity to manufacture a false story which fits undisputable facts.

(c)   It is often helpful if the principal documents are provided either in advance of the interview or shown as the interview progresses; asking detailed questions about events a considerable period in the past without reference to the documents is often not very helpful.

(iii)   The prosecution and defence teams

(a)   *The Prosecution Team*

While instructed, it is for the lead advocate for the prosecution to take all necessary decisions in the presentation and general conduct of the prosecution case in court. The prosecution lead advocate will be treated by the court as having that responsibility. However, in relation to policy decisions, the lead advocate for the prosecution must not give an indication or undertaking which binds the prosecution without first discussing the issue with the Director of the Prosecuting authority or other senior officer. "Policy" decisions should be understood as referring to non-evidential decisions on: the acceptance of pleas of guilty to lesser counts or groups of counts or available alternatives: offering no evidence on particular counts; consideration of a re-trial; whether to lodge an appeal; certification of a point of law; and the withdrawal of the prosecution as a whole (for further information see the "Farquharson Guidelines" on the role and responsibilities of the prosecution advocate).

(b)   *The Defence Team*

In each case, the lead advocate for the defence will be treated by the court as having responsibility to the court for the presentation and general conduct of the defence case.

(c)   In each case, a case progression officer must be assigned by the court, prosecution and defence from the time of the first hearing when directions are given (as referred to in paragraph 3 (iii)) until the conclusion of the trial.

(d)   In each case where there are multiple defendants, the LSC will need to consider carefully the extent and level of representation necessary.

(iv)   Initial consideration of the length of a case

If the prosecutor in charge of the case from the Prosecuting Authority or the lead advocate for the prosecution consider that the case as formulated is likely to last more than 8 weeks, the case should be referred in accordance with arrangements made by the Prosecuting Authority to a more senior prosecutor. The senior prosecutor will consider whether it is desirable for the case to be prosecuted in that way or whether some steps might be taken to reduce its likely length, whilst at the same time ensuring that the public interest is served.

Any case likely to last 6 months or more must be referred to the Director of the Prosecuting Authority so that similar considerations can take place.

(v)   Notification of cases likely to last more than 8 weeks

Special arrangements will be put in place for the early notification by the CPS and other Prosecuting Authorities, to the LSC and to a single designated officer of the Court in each Region (Circuit) of any case which the CPS or other Prosecuting Authority consider likely to last over 8 weeks.

(vi)   Venue

The court will allocate such cases and other complex cases likely to last 4 weeks or more to a specific venue suitable for the trial in question, taking into account the convenience to witnesses, the parties, the availability of time at that location, and all other relevant considerations.

2.   DESIGNATION OF THE TRIAL JUDGE

(i)   The assignment of a judge

(a)   In any complex case which is expected to last more than four weeks, the trial judge will be assigned under the direction of the Presiding Judges at the earliest possible moment.

(b)   Thereafter the assigned judge should manage that case "from cradle to grave"; it is essential that the same judge manages the case from the time of his assignment and that arrangements are made for him to be able to do so. It is recognised that in certain court centres with a large turnover of heavy cases (e.g. Southwark) this objective is more difficult to achieve. But in those court centres there are teams of specialist judges, who are more readily able to handle cases which the assigned judge cannot continue with because of unexpected events; even at such courts, there must be no exception to the principle that one judge must handle all the pre-trial hearings until the case is assigned to another judge.

3.   CASE MANAGEMENT

(i)   Objectives

(a)   The number, length and organisation of case management hearings will, of course, depend critically on the circumstances and complexity of the individual case. However, thorough, well-prepared and extended case management hearings will save court time and costs overall.

(b)   Effective case management of heavy fraud and other complex criminal cases requires the judge to have a much more detailed grasp of the case than may be necessary for many other Plea and Case Management Hearings (PCMHs). Though it is for the judge in each case to decide how much pre-reading time he needs so that the judge is on top of the case, it is not always a sensible use of judicial time to allocate a series of reading days, during which the judge sits alone in his room, working through numerous boxes of ring binders. See paragraph 3 (iv) (e) below.

(ii)   Fixing the trial date

Although it is important that the trial date should be fixed as early as possible, this may not always be the right course. There are two principal alternatives:

(a) The trial date should be fixed at the first opportunity – i.e. at the first (and usually short) directions hearing referred to in subparagraph (iii). From then on everyone must work to that date. All orders and pre-trial steps should be timetabled to fit in with that date. All advocates and the judge should take note of this date, in the expectation that the trial will proceed on the date determined.
(b) The trial date should not be fixed until the issues have been explored at a full case management hearing (referred to in subparagraph (iv), after the advocates on both sides have done some serious work on the case. Only then can the length of the trial be estimated.

Which is apposite must depend on the circumstances of each case, but the earlier it is possible to fix a trial date, by reference to a proper estimate and a timetable set by reference to the trial date, the better. It is generally to be expected that once a trial is fixed on the basis of the estimate provided, that it will be increased if, and only if, the party seeking to extend the time justifies why the original estimate is no longer appropriate.

(iii)   The first hearing for the giving of initial directions

At the first opportunity the assigned judge should hold a short hearing to give initial directions. The directions on this occasion might well include:

(a) That there should be a full case management hearing on, or commencing on, a specified future date by which time the parties will be properly prepared for a meaningful hearing and the defence will have full instructions.
(b) That the prosecution should provide an outline written statement of the prosecution case at least one week in advance of that case management hearing, outlining in simple terms:

(i)   The key facts on which it relies.
(ii)   The key evidence by which the prosecution seeks to prove the facts.

The statement must be sufficient to permit the judge to understand the case and for the defence to appreciate the basic elements of its case against each defendant. The prosecution may be invited to highlight the key points of the case orally at the case management hearing by way of a short mini-opening. The outline statement should not be considered binding, but it will serve the essential purpose in telling the judge, and everyone else, what the case is really about and identifying the key issues.

(c) That a core reading list and core bundle for the case management hearing should be delivered at least one week in advance.
(d) Preliminary directions about disclosure: see paragraph 4.

(iv)   The first Case Management Hearing

(a) At the first case management hearing:

(i)   The prosecution advocate should be given the opportunity to highlight any points from the prosecution outline statement of case (which will have been delivered at least a week in advance).
(ii)   Each defence advocate should be asked to outline the defence.

If the defence advocate is not in a position to say what is in issue and what is not in issue, then the case management hearing can be adjourned for a short and limited time and to a fixed date to enable the advocate to take instructions; such an adjournment should only be necessary in exceptional circumstances, as the defence advocate should be properly instructed by the time of the first case management hearing and in any event is under an obligation to take sufficient instructions to fulfil the obligations contained in S 33–39 of Criminal Justice Act 2003.

(b) There should then be a real dialogue between the judge and all advocates for the purpose of identifying:

    (i)   The focus of the prosecution case.

    (ii)   The common ground.

    (iii)   The real issues in the case. (Rule 3.2 of the Criminal Procedure Rules.)

(c) The judge will try to generate a spirit of co-operation between the court and the advocates on all sides. The expeditious conduct of the trial and a focussing on the real issues must be in the interests of all parties. It cannot be in the interests of any defendant for his good points to become lost in a welter of uncontroversial or irrelevant evidence.

(d) In many fraud cases the primary facts are not seriously disputed. The real issue is what each defendant knew and whether that defendant was dishonest. Once the judge has identified what is in dispute and what is not in dispute, the judge can then discuss with the advocate how the trial should be structured, what can be dealt with by admissions or agreed facts, what uncontroversial matters should be proved by concise oral evidence, what timetabling can be required under Rule 3.10 Criminal Procedure Rules, and other directions.

(e) In particularly heavy fraud or complex cases the judge may possibly consider it necessary to allocate a whole week for a case management hearing. If that week is used wisely, many further weeks of trial time can be saved. In the gaps which will inevitably arise during that week (for example while the advocates are exploring matters raised by the judge) the judge can do a substantial amount of informed reading. The case has come "alive" at this stage. Indeed, in a really heavy fraud case, if the judge fixes one or more case management hearings on this scale, there will be need for fewer formal reading days. Moreover a huge amount can be achieved in the pre-trial stage, if all trial advocates are gathered in the same place, focussing on the case at the same time, for several days consecutively.

(f) Requiring the defence to serve proper case statements may enable the court to identify:

    (i)   what is common ground and

    (ii)   the real issues.

It is therefore important that proper defence case statements be provided as required by the Criminal Procedure Rules; Judges will use the powers contained in ss 28–34 of the Criminal Proceedings and Evidence Act 1996 (and the corresponding provisions of the CJA 1987, ss. 33 and following of the Criminal Justice Act 2003) and the Criminal Procedure Rules to ensure that realistic defence case statements are provided.

(g) Likewise this objective may be achieved by requiring the prosecution to serve draft admissions by a specified date and by requiring the defence to respond within a specified number of weeks.

(v)   Further Case Management Hearings

(a) The date of the next case management hearing should be fixed at the conclusion of the hearing so that there is no delay in having to fix the date through listing offices, clerks and others.

(b) If one is looking at a trial which threatens to run for months, pre-trial case management on an intensive scale is essential.

(vi)   Consideration of the length of the trial

(a) Case management on the above lines, the procedure set out in paragraph 1 (iv), may still be insufficient to reduce the trial to a manageable length; generally a trial of 3 months should be the target, but there will be cases where a duration of 6 months or, in exceptional circumstances, even longer may be inevitable.

(b) If the trial is not estimated to be within a manageable length, it will be necessary for the judge to consider what steps should be taken to reduce the length of the trial, whilst still ensuring that the prosecution has the opportunity of placing the full criminality before the court.

(c) To assist the judge in this task,

  (i)   The lead advocate for the prosecution should be asked to explain why the prosecution have rejected a shorter way of proceeding; they may also be asked to divide the case into sections of evidence and explain the scope of each section and the need for each section.

  (ii)   The lead advocates for the prosecution and for the defence should be prepared to put forward in writing, if requested, ways in which a case estimated to last more than three months can be shortened, including possible severance of counts or defendants, exclusions of sections of the case or of evidence or areas of the case where admissions can be made.

(d) One course the judge may consider is pruning the indictment by omitting certain charges and/or by omitting certain defendants. The judge must not usurp the function of the prosecution in this regard, and he must bear in mind that he will, at the outset, know less about the case than the advocates. The aim is achieve fairness to all parties.

(e) Nevertheless, the judge does have two methods of pruning available for use in appropriate circumstances:

  (i)   Persuading the prosecution that it is not worthwhile pursuing certain charges and/or certain defendants.

  (ii)   Severing the indictment. Severance for reasons of case management alone is perfectly proper, although judges should have regard to any representations made by the prosecution that severance would weaken their case. Indeed the judge's hand will be strengthened in this regard by rule 1.1(2)(g) of the Criminal Procedure Rules. However, before using what may be seen as a blunt instrument, the judge should insist on seeing full defence statements of all affected defendants. Severance may be unfair to the prosecution if, for example, there is a cut-throat defence in prospect. For example, the defence of the principal defendant may be that the defendant relied on the advice of his accountant or solicitor that what was happening was acceptable. The defence of the professional may be that he gave no such advice. Against that background, it might be unfair to the prosecution to order separate trials of the two defendants.

(vii)   The exercise of the powers

(a) The Criminal Procedure Rules require the court to take a more active part in case management. These are salutary provisions which should bring to an end interminable criminal trials of the kind which the Court of Appeal criticised in Jisl [2004] EWCA 696 at [113] – [121].

(b) Nevertheless these salutary provisions do not have to be used on every occasion. Where the advocates have done their job properly, by narrowing the issues, pruning the evidence and so forth, it may be quite inappropriate for the judge to "weigh in" and start cutting out more evidence or more charges of his own volition. It behoves the judge to make a careful assessment of the degree of judicial intervention which is warranted in each case.

(c) The note of caution in the previous paragraph is supported by certain experience which has been gained of the Civil Procedure Rules (on which the Criminal Procedure Rules are based). The CPR contain valuable and efficacious provisions for case management by the judge on his own initiative which have led to huge savings of court time and costs. Surveys by the Law Society have shown that the CPR have been generally welcomed by court users and the profession, but there have been reported to have been isolated instances in which the parties to civil litigation have faithfully complied with both the letter and the spirit of the CPR, and have then been aggrieved by what was perceived to be unnecessary intermeddling by the court.

(viii)   **Expert Evidence**

(a)   Early identification of the subject matter of expert evidence to be adduced by the prosecution and the defence should be made as early as possible, preferably at the directions hearing.

(b)   Following the exchange of expert evidence, any areas of disagreement should be identified and a direction should generally be made requiring the experts to meet and prepare, after discussion, a joint statement identifying points of agreement and contention and areas where the prosecution is put to proof on matters of which a positive case to the contrary is not advanced by the defence. After the statement has been prepared it should be served on the court, the prosecution and the defence. In some cases, it might be appropriate to provide that to the jury.

(ix)   **Surveillance Evidence**

(a)   Where a prosecution is based upon many months' observation or surveillance evidence and it appears that it is capable of effective presentation based on a shorter period, the advocate should be required to justify the evidence of such observations before it is permitted to be adduced, either substantially or in its entirety.

(b)   Schedules should be provided to cover as much of the evidence as possible and admissions sought.

4.   DISCLOSURE

In fraud cases the volume of documentation obtained by the prosecution is liable to be immense. The problems of disclosure are intractable and have the potential to disrupt the entire trial process.

(i)   The prosecution lawyer (and the prosecution advocate if different) brought in at the outset, as set out in paragraph 1 (i)(a), each have a continuing responsibility to discharge the prosecution's duty of disclosure, either personally or by delegation, in accordance with the Attorney General's Guidelines on Disclosure.

(ii)   The prosecution should only disclose those documents which are relevant (i.e. likely to assist the defence or undermine the prosecution – see s. 3 (1) of CPIA 1996 and the provisions of the CJA 2003).

(iii)   It is almost always undesirable to give the "warehouse key" to the defence for two reasons:

(a)   This amounts to an abrogation of the responsibility of the prosecution;

(b)   The defence solicitors may spend a disproportionate amount of time and incur disproportionate costs trawling through a morass of documents.

The Judge should therefore try and ensure that disclosure is limited to what is likely to assist the defence or undermine the prosecution.

(iv)   At the outset the judge should set a timetable for dealing with disclosure issues. In particular, the judge should fix a date by which all defence applications for specific disclosure must be made. In this regard, it is relevant that the defendants are likely to be intelligent people, who know their own business affairs and who (for the most part) will know what documents or categories of documents they are looking for.

(v)   At the outset (and before the cut-off date for specific disclosure applications) the judge should ask the defence to indicate what documents they are interested in and from what source. A general list is not an acceptable response to this request. The judge should insist upon a list which is specific, manageable and realistic. The judge may also require justification of any request.

(vi)   In non-fraud cases, the same considerations apply, but some may be different:

(a)   It is not possible to approach many non-fraud cases on the basis that the defendant knows what is there or what they are looking for. But on the other hand this should not be turned into an excuse for a "fishing expedition"; the judge should insist on knowing the issue to which a request for disclosure applies.

(b)   If the bona fides of the investigation is called into question, a judge will be concerned to see that there has been independent and effective appraisal of the documents contained in the disclosure schedule and that its contents are adequate. In appropriate cases where this issue has arisen and there are grounds which show there is a real issue, consideration should be given to receiving evidence on oath from the senior investigating officer at an early case management hearing.

5.   ABUSE OF PROCESS

(i)   Applications to stay or dismiss for abuse of process have become a normal feature of heavy and complex cases. Such applications may be based upon delay and the health of defendants.

(ii)   Applications in relation to absent special circumstances tend to be unsuccessful and not to be pursued on appeal. For this reason there is comparatively little Court of Appeal guidance: but see: *Harris and Howells* [2003] EWCA Crim 486. It should be noted that abuse of process is not there to discipline the prosecution or the police.

(iii)   The arguments on both sides must be reduced to writing. Oral evidence is seldom relevant.

(iv)   The judge should direct full written submissions (rather than "skeleton arguments") on any abuse application in accordance with a timetable set by him; these should identify any element of prejudice the defendant is alleged to have suffered.

(v)   The Judge should normally aim to conclude the hearing within an absolute maximum limit of one day, if necessary in accordance with a timetable. The parties should therefore prepare their papers on this basis and not expect the judge to allow the oral hearing to be anything more than an occasion to highlight concisely their arguments and answer any questions the court may have of them; applications will not be allowed to drag on.

6.   THE TRIAL

(i)   The particular hazard of heavy fraud trials

A heavy fraud or other complex trial has the potential to lose direction and focus. This is a disaster for three reasons:

(a) The jury will lose track of the evidence, thereby prejudicing both prosecution and defence.

(b) The burden on the defendants, the judge and indeed all involved will become intolerable.

(c) Scarce public resources are wasted. Other prosecutions are delayed or – worse – may never happen. Fraud which is detected but not prosecuted (for resource reasons) undermines confidence.

(ii) Judicial mastery of the case

(a) It is necessary for the judge to exercise firm control over the conduct of the trial at all stages.

(b) In order to do this the judge must read the witness statements and the documents, so that the judge can discuss case management issues with the advocates on – almost – an equal footing.

(c) To this end, the judge should not set aside weeks or even days for pre-reading (see paragraph 3 (i)(b) above). Hopefully the judge will have gained a good grasp of the evidence during the case management hearings. Nevertheless, realistic reading time must be provided for the judge in advance of trial.

(d) The role of the judge in a heavy fraud or other complex criminal trial is different from his/her role in a "conventional" criminal trial. So far as possible, the judge should be freed from other duties and burdens, so that he/she can give the high degree of commitment which a heavy fraud trial requires. This will pay dividends in terms of saving weeks or months of court time.

(iii) The order of the evidence

(a) By the outset of the trial at the latest (and in most cases very much earlier) the judge must be provided with a schedule, showing the sequence of prosecution (and in an appropriate case defence) witnesses and the dates upon which they are expected to be called. This can only be prepared by discussion between prosecution and defence which the judge should expect, and say he/she expects, to take place: See: Criminal Procedure Rule 3.10. The schedule should, in so far as it relates to Prosecution witnesses, be developed in consultation with the witnesses, via the Witness Care Units, and with consideration given to their personal needs. Copies of the schedule should be provided for the Witness Service.

(b) The schedule should be kept under review by the trial judge and by the parties. If a case is running behind or ahead of schedule, each witness affected must be advised by the party who is calling that witness at the earliest opportunity.

(c) If an excessive amount of time is allowed for any witness, the judge can ask why. The judge may probe with the advocates whether the time envisaged for the evidence-in-chief or cross-examination (as the case may be) of a particular witness is really necessary.

(iv) Case management sessions

(a) The order of the evidence may have legitimately to be departed from. It will, however, be a useful for tool for monitoring the progress of the case. There should be periodic case management sessions, during which the judge engages the advocates upon a stock-taking exercise: asking, amongst other questions, "where are we going?" and "what is the relevance of the next three witnesses?". This will be a valuable means of keeping the case on track. Rule 3.10 of the Criminal Procedure Rules will again assist the judge.

(b) The judge may wish to consider issuing the occasional use of "case management notes" to the advocates, in order to set out the judge's tentative views on where the trial may be going off track, which areas of future evidence are relevant and which may have become irrelevant (e.g. because of concessions, admissions in cross-examination and so forth). Such notes from the judge plus written responses from the advocates can, cautiously used, provide a valuable focus for debate during the periodic case management reviews held during the course of the trial.

(v)   Controlling prolix cross-examination

(a) Setting rigid time limits in advance for cross-examination is rarely appropriate – as experience has shown in civil cases; but a timetable is essential so that the judge can exercise control and so that there is a clear target to aim at for the completion of the evidence of each witness. Moreover the judge can and should indicate when cross-examination is irrelevant, unnecessary or time wasting. The judge may limit the time for further cross-examination of a particular witness.

(vi)   Electronic presentation of evidence

(a) Electronic presentation of evidence (EPE) has the potential to save huge amounts of time in fraud and other complex criminal trials and should be used more widely.

(b) HMCS is providing facilities for the easier use of EPE with a standard audio visual facility. Effectively managed, the savings in court time achieved by EPE more than justify the cost.

(c) There should still be a core bundle of those documents to which frequent reference will be made during the trial. The jury may wish to mark that bundle or to refer back to particular pages as the evidence progresses. EPE can be used for presenting all documents not contained in the core bundle.

(d) Greater use of other modern forms of graphical presentations should be made wherever possible.

(vii)   Use of interviews

The Judge should consider extensive editing of self serving interviews, even when the defence want the jury to hear them in their entirety; such interviews are not evidence of the truth of their contents but merely of the defendant's reaction to the allegation.

(viii)   Jury Management

(a) The jury should be informed as early as possible in the case as to what the issues are in a manner directed by the Judge.

(b) The jury must be regularly updated as to the trial timetable and the progress of the trial, subject to warnings as to the predictability of the trial process.

(c) Legal argument should be heard at times that causes the least inconvenience to jurors.

(d) It is useful to consider with the advocates whether written directions should be given to the jury and, if so, in what form.

(ix)   Maxwell hours

(a) Maxwell hours should only be permitted after careful consideration and consultation with the Presiding Judge.

(b) Considerations in favour include:

   (i)   Legal argument can be accommodated without disturbing the jury;
   (ii)   There is a better chance of a representative jury;

    (iii)   Time is made available to the judge, advocates and experts to do useful work in the afternoons.

(c) Considerations against include:

    (i)   The lengthening of trials and the consequent waste of court time;

    (ii)   The desirability of making full use of the jury once they have arrived at court;

    (iii)   Shorter trials tend to diminish the need for special provisions e.g. there are fewer difficulties in empanelling more representative juries;

    (iv)   They are unavailable if any defendant is in custody.

(d) It may often be the case that a maximum of one day of Maxwell hours a week is sufficient; if so, it should be timetabled in advance to enable all submissions by advocates, supported by skeleton arguments served in advance, to be dealt with in the period after 1:30 pm on that day.

(x) Livenote

If Livenote is used, it is important that all users continue to take a note of the evidence, otherwise considerable time is wasted in detailed reading of the entire daily transcript.

7. OTHER ISSUES

(i) Defence representation and defence costs

(a) Applications for change in representation in complex trials need special consideration; the ruling of HH Judge Wakerley QC (as he then was) in *Asghar Ali* has been circulated by the JSB.

(b) Problems have arisen when the Legal Services Commission have declined to allow advocates or solicitors to do certain work; on occasions the matter has been raised with the judge managing or trying the case.

(c) The Legal Services Commission has provided guidance to judges on how they can obtain information from the LSC as to the reasons for their decisions; further information in relation to this can be obtained from Nigel Field, Head of the Complex Crime Unit, Legal Services Commission, 29–37 Red Lion Street, London, WC1R 4PP.

(ii) Assistance to the Judge

Experience has shown that in some very heavy cases, the judge's burden can be substantially offset with the provision of a Judicial Assistant or other support and assistance.

Section D
PROTOCOL FOR RAPE CASES IN THE YOUTH COURT

A protocol issued by the Senior Presiding Judge

INTRODUCTION

1. This protocol sets out the procedure regarding the hearing of rape cases in the Youth Court and has been written in consultation with HMCS and the Chief Magistrate.

COMMENCEMENT AND AMENDMENT

2. The protocol will take effect forthwith and may be amended as appropriate by the Senior Presiding Judge.

BACKGROUND

3. Historically, the position was that the Youth Court should never accept jurisdiction in a rape case.[1]
4. However, recent authorities have also suggested that the rule set out in Billam could now properly be modified so that in the case of very young defendants it may be appropriate to accept jurisdiction.[2]
5. Further, the Sexual Offences Act 2003 widened the definition of rape resulting in other circumstances in which it may be appropriate to try rape cases in the Youth Court.
6. The determination of venue in relation to Youth Court matters is governed by section 24 of the Magistrates' Courts Act 1980 which provides that the youth shall be tried summarily unless the defendant has been charged with such a grave crime that long term detention is a possibility.[3]
7. A series of cases provided further clarification of what amounts to a grave crime. In a recent case, it was stated that the court should ask itself whether there is a real prospect, having regard to the defendant's age, that he or she might require a sentence of, or in excess of, two years.[4]

PROCEDURE

8. In considering whether the Youth Court should retain jurisdiction in a rape case, the court will need to consider:

   (a) The suitability of the Youth Court as a venue.
   (b) The desirability of the case being heard by a Circuit Judge authorised to try serious sexual cases.

9. In the event that jurisdiction is retained, a request should be made to the regional listing co-ordinator for an authorised Circuit Judge to sit as a District Judge at the Youth Court.[5]

10. The listing co-ordinator will liaise with the Resident Judge and/or the Presiding Judge where appropriate in determining the Circuit Judge.
11. The Justices Clerk for the region should be consulted and kept informed of all developments.

November 2007

NOTES

1 *R v Billam* (1986) 1 All ER 985.
2 *R (on the application of B & others) v The Richmond on Thames Youth Court* (2006) EWHC 95 and *Stones Justices Manual.*
3 Section 24(1)(a) of the Magistrates Court Act 1980.
4 *R (on the application of H, A and O) v Southampton Youth Court* (2004) EHWC 2912 (Southampton Youth Court No 2).
5 Section 66 of the Courts Act 2003.

Section E
PROTOCOL FOR THE MANAGEMENT AND TRIAL OF TERRORISM CASES

Management of terrorism cases: A Protocol issued by the President of the Queen's Bench division

TERRORISM CASES

1. This protocol applies to "terrorism cases". For the purposes of this Protocol a case is a "terrorism case" where:

    (a) One of the offences charged against any of the defendants is indictable only and it is alleged by the prosecution that there is evidence that it took place during an act of terrorism or for the purposes of terrorism as defined in s1 of the Terrorism Act 2000. This may include, but is not limited to:

    - (i)   murder
    - (ii) manslaughter
    - (iii) an offence under section 18 of the Offences against the Person Act 1861 (wounding with intent)
    - (iv) an offence under section 23 or 24 of that Act (administering poison etc)
    - (v)   an offence under section 28 or 29 of that Act (explosives)
    - (vi) an offence under section 2,3 or 5 of the Explosive Substances Act 1883 (causing explosions)
    - (vii) an offence under section 1 (2) of the Criminal Damage Act 1971 (endangering life by damaging property)
    - (viii) an offence under section 1 of the Biological Weapons Act 1974 (biological weapons)
    - (ix) an offence under section 2 of the Chemical Weapons Act 1996 (chemical weapons)
    - (x)   an offence under section 56 of the Terrorism Act 2000 (directing a terrorist organisation)
    - (xi) an offence under section 59 of that Act (inciting terrorism overseas)
    - (xii) offences under (v), (vii) and (viii) above given jurisdiction by virtue of section 62 of that Act (terrorist bombing overseas)
    - (xiii) an offence under section 5 of the Terrorism Act 2006 (preparation of terrorism acts)

    (b) One of the offences charged is indictable only and includes an allegation by the prosecution of serious fraud that took place during an act of terrorism or for the purposes of terrorism as defined in s1 of the Terrorist Act 2000 and meets the test to be transferred to the Crown Court under section 4 of the Criminal Justice Act 1987.

    (c) One of the offences charged is indictable only includes an allegation that a defendant conspired, incited or attempted to commit an offence under sub paragraphs (1) a) or b) above.

(d)   It is a case (which can be indictable only or triable either way) that a judge of the terrorism cases list (see paragraph 2a) below) considers should be a terrorism case. In deciding whether a case not covered by subparagraphs (1) a), b) or c) above should be a terrorism case, the judge may hear representations from the Crown Prosecution Service.

THE TERRORISM CASES LIST

2. (a)   All terrorism cases, wherever they originate in England and Wales, will be managed in a list known as the "terrorism cases list" by the Presiding Judges of the South Eastern Circuit and such other judges of the High Court as are nominated by the President of the Queen's Bench Division.

    (b)   Such cases will be tried, unless otherwise directed by the President of the Queen's Bench Division, by a judge of the High Court as nominated by the President of the Queen's Bench Division.

3. The judges managing the terrorism cases referred to in paragraph (2) will be supported by the London and South Eastern Regional Co-ordinator's Office (the "Regional Co-ordinator's Office"). An official of that office or nominated by that office will act as the case progression officer for cases in that list for the purposes of part 3.4 of the Criminal Procedure Rules.

PROCEDURE AFTER CHARGE

4. Immediately after a person has been charged in a terrorism case, anywhere in England and Wales, a representative of the Crown Prosecution Service will notify the person on the 24 hour rota for special jurisdiction matters at Westminster Magistrates' Court of the following information:

    (a)   The full name of each defendant and the name of his solicitor of other legal representative, if known

    (b)   The charges laid

    (c)   The name and contact details of the Crown Prosecutor with responsibility for the case, if known.

    (d)   Confirmation that the case is a terrorism case

5. The person on the 24-hour rota will then ensure that all terrorism cases wherever they are charged in England and Wales are listed before the Chief Magistrate or other District Judge designated under the Terrorism Act 2000. Unless the Chief Magistrate or other District Judge designated under the Terrorism Act 2000 directs otherwise the first appearance of all defendants accused of terrorism offences will be listed at Westminster Magistrates' Court.

6. In order to comply with section 46 of the Police and Criminal Evidence Act 1984, if a defendant in a terrorism case is charged at a police station within the local justice area in which Westminster Magistrates' Court is situated the defendant must be brought before Westminster Magistrates' Court as soon as is practicable and in any event not later than the first sitting after he is charged with the offence. If a defendant in a terrorism case is charged at a police station outside the local justice area in which Westminster Magistrates' Court is situated, unless the Chief Magistrate or other designated judge directs otherwise, the defendant must be removed to that area as soon as is practicable. He must then be brought before Westminster Magistrates' Court as soon as is practicable after his arrival in the area and in any event not later than the first sitting of Westminster Magistrates' Court after his arrival in that area.

7. As soon as is practicable after charge a representative of the Crown Prosecution Service will also provide the Regional Listing Co-ordinator's Office with the information listed in paragraph 4 above.

8.   The Regional Co-ordinator's Office will then ensure that the Chief Magistrate and the Legal Services Commission have the same information.

CASES TO BE SENT TO THE CROWN COURT UNDER SECTION 51 OF THE CRIME AND DISORDER ACT 1998

9.   A preliminary hearing should normally be ordered by the Magistrates' Court in a terrorism case. The court should ordinarily direct that the preliminary hearing should take place about 14 days after charge.

10.   The sending Magistrates' Court should contact the Regional Listing Co-ordinator's Office who will be responsible for notifying the Magistrates' Court as to the relevant Crown Court to which to send the case.

11.   In all terrorism cases, the Magistrates' Court case progression form for cases sent to the Crown Court under section 51 of the Crime and Disorder Act 1998 should not be used. Instead of the automatic directions set out in that form, the Magistrates' Court shall make the following directions to facilitate the preliminary hearing at the Crown Court:

(a)   Three days prior to the preliminary hearing in the terrorism cases list, the prosecution must serve upon each defendant and the Regional Listing co-ordinator:

(i)   A preliminary summary of the case

(ii)   The names of those who are to represent the prosecution, if known.

(iii)   An estimate of the length of the trial

(iv)   A suggested provisional timetable which should generally include:

■   The general nature of further enquiries being made by the prosecution

■   The time needed for the completion of such enquiries

■   The time required by the prosecution to review the case

■   A timetable for the phased service of the evidence

■   The time for the provision by the Attorney General for his consent if necessary

■   The time for service of the detailed defence case statement

■   The date for the case management hearing

■   Estimated trial date

(v)   A preliminary statement of the possible disclosure issues setting out the nature and scale of the problem including the amount of unused material, the manner in which the prosecution seeks to deal with these matters and a suggested timetable for discharging their statutory duty.

(vi)   Any information relating to bail and custody time limits

(b)   One day prior to the preliminary hearing in the terrorist cases list, each defendant must serve in writing on the Regional Listing Co-ordinator and the prosecution:

(i)   The proposed representation

(ii)   Observations on the timetable

(iii)   An indication of plea and the general nature of the defence

CASES TO BE TRANSFERRED TO THE CROWN COURT UNDER SECTION 4(1) OF THE CRIMINAL JUSTICE ACT 1987

12.   If a terrorism case is to be transferred to the Crown Court the Magistrates' Court should proceed as if it is being sent to the Crown Court, as in paragraphs 9–11 above.

13.   When a terrorism case is so sent or transferred the case will go into the terrorism list and be managed by a judge as described in paragraph 2 above.

THE PRELIMINARY HEARING AT THE CROWN COURT

14. At the preliminary hearing, the judge will determine whether the case is one to remain in the terrorism list and if so give directions setting the provisional timetable.
15. The Legal Services Commission must attend the hearing by an authorised officer to assist the court.

USE OF VIDEO LINKS

17. Unless a judge otherwise directs, all Crown court hearings prior to the trial will be conducted by video link for all defendants in custody.

SECURITY

18. The police service and the prison service will provide the Regional Listing Co-ordinator's Office with an initial joint assessment of the security risks associated with any court appearance by the defendants within 14 days of charge. Any subsequent changes in circumstances or the assessment of risk which have the potential to impact upon the choice of trial venue will be notified to the Regional Listing Co-ordinator's Office immediately.

30 January 2007

Section F
ADULT CRIMINAL CASE MANAGEMENT FRAMEWORK

Part 1 The Magistrates' Courts

INTRODUCTION

What is the Criminal Case Management Framework?

It's a guide for participants involved in criminal case management to help them to prepare and conduct cases in compliance with the Criminal Procedure Rules[1] so that each case is brought to a fair conclusion as quickly as possible. It is not a substitute for the Criminal Procedure Rules or any part of them. The Rules (together with the provisions of the Consolidated Criminal Practice direction[2]) must be complied with

This is the third edition of the adult Framework. It incorporates practical improvements which have been tested by the Criminal Justice Simple Speedy Summary (CJSSS) programme which, in particular, promotes better initial preparation to achieve effective first hearings and the fair and early disposal of cases

This edition is issued in two parts:

(a) Part 1, the Magistrates' Courts (this document), refers to adult cases in magistrates' courts; and
(b) Part 2, the Crown Court, will follow later to cover adult cases in the Crown Court

This Framework does not cover cases involving offenders under the age of 18 years. A separate youth Framework will be issued. This Framework does not include cases started by summons which are outside the scope of CJSSS: Magistrates' Courts

The Framework does not cover every possible activity needed for a case to achieve a just and effective outcome. It principally addresses case management. So, for example, it covers the case management role of advocates but not advocacy itself. It seeks to give effect to the Criminal Procedure Rules and the provisions of the Consolidated Criminal Practice Direction. References are made to guidance which is to be found elsewhere in, for example, codes and circulars. The Framework is consistent with s.35(1) of The Interpretation Act 1976 where references to "he" imply "he or she"

What are the main changes?

■ This edition is shorter
■ The pre-charge and charge processes for police and CPS are dealt with together
■ Contested and uncontested cases are dealt with in one Part
■ It includes practices which have been assessed in the CJSSS pilots and which promote better initial preparation, effective first hearings, and the fair, early disposal of cases

- There is a new "Useful Links" page
- It is loose-leaf to enable the inclusion of updates

How has the Framework been produced?

The Framework has been produced by practitioners from CJS agencies based in OCJR, in consultation with members of the judiciary, the Law Society, the Bar, the Witness Service, and CJS agencies including the CPS, the police, HMCS and NOMS

Who will use the Framework?

- Participants, as they consider how better to prepare and conduct cases in compliance with the Criminal Procedure Rules. The term "participants"[3] includes defendants and their legal advisers. Nothing in the Framework affects the rights of defendants or the professional obligations of legal advisers towards their clients
- Local Criminal Justice Boards, as they produce their CJSSS local delivery schemes
- Inspectorates

How can I access the Framework?

It is available in hard copy from homeoffice@prologuk.com or by calling 0870 241 4680 and online at www.cjsonline.gov.uk/framework in printable pdf or interactive version

Comments on the Framework

If you have any comments or questions on the content of the Framework please email ccmf@cjs.gsi.gov.uk

NOTES

1 Crim PR Part 1: The Overriding Objective; Part 3: The Case Management Rules http://tinyurl.com/3cwal4
2 http://tinyurl.com/202jvs
3 Crim PR 1.2(2)

ABBREVIATIONS AND GLOSSARY

Action Plan	An Action Plan is completed by Duty Prosecutors when providing early investigative or charging advice to officers. It sets out what key evidence is outstanding and required before a Full Code Test can be carried out to enable a charging decision to be made. Action Plans should include agreed timetables for the completion of work
Advance Information (for anticipated not guilty plea case)/PSR pack	A defendant charged with an either-way offence is entitled to receive Advance Information (evidence on which the prosecution intend to rely or a summary of the facts) before deciding whether to elect trial at Crown Court or to consent to summary trial, or, if he is under 18, before entering a plea The Criminal Procedure Rules Part 21 requires the prosecution to serve on the defendant or his solicitor the evidence upon which the prosecution proposes to rely, or a summary thereof The principle has been extended to cover summary-only cases in CJSSS areas in association with the Attorney General's Guidelines

Bail	The release of a suspect (pre-charge) or defendant (postcharge) pending the completion of a criminal investigation or proceedings. The grant of bail in all criminal proceedings is governed by the Bail Act 1976 as amended. There is a statutory right to bail, subject to exceptions
Cautions	Disposals for adult offenders where it is in the public interest not to prosecute, but to issue a formal warning **Simple caution** A simple caution is a non-statutory citable disposal (for adult offenders) requiring a clear and reliable admission in accordance with Home Office guidelines. Such a caution may be decided on by the police in summary-only or either-way cases or be recommended by the CPS in indictable only cases **Conditional Caution** A Conditional Caution is a statutory citable disposal (for adult offenders) requiring a clear and reliable admission where a Crown Prosecutor considers that the full code test is met but the interests of the victim and community may be better served by the offender complying with suitable conditions
CC	Crown Court
CJS	Criminal Justice System. The CJS consists of these agencies: the police, CPS, Prison and Probation Services (NOMS), and the courts' administration (Her Majesty's Courts Service). The CJS does not include the judiciary (judges and magistrates) and the defence
CJSSS: Magistrates' Courts	**Simple Speedy Summary Justice in the Magistrates' Courts** A new way of working to encompass a simpler set of processes and procedures, that has been successfully piloted in magistrates' courts in four areas
Committal hearing	A procedure in the magistrates' courts where, in either-way cases, the defendant is committed to stand trial in the Crown Court, provided the court is satisfied on the evidence that the defendant has a case to answer
Contact Directory	A directory compiled by the Witness Care Unit that contains details of local or national organisations, offering support. This enables a full range of options to be considered by Witness Care Officers, when conducting a full needs assessment with a victim or witness
CPIA	Criminal Procedure and Investigations Act 1996
CPO	Case progression officer
CPS	Crown Prosecution Service
CPS Direct	CPS out-of-hours telephone service provided by a team of Duty Prosecutors for the purpose of providing charging decisions. CPS Direct operates on Monday – Friday from 5 pm to 9 am and 24 hours a day on Saturdays, Sundays and bank holidays

Crim PR	Criminal Procedure Rules
Crown Prosecutor	Crown Prosecutors are lawyers responsible for reviewing and, where appropriate, prosecuting criminal cases following investigation by the police. They also advise the police on matters relating to criminal investigations. In each case reviewed the prosecutor should consider whether there is sufficient evidence to pass the evidential test and, if so, whether the public interest requires a prosecution. Although Crown Prosecutors work closely with the police they are responsible to the Crown Prosecution Service, an independent governmental organisation
DCW	Designated caseworker. DCWs are CPS staff appointed by the Director of Public Prosecutions who are not lawyers but who are permitted to undertake specific case work and advocacy in the magistrates' courts
Director of Public Prosecution's Guidance on Charging	Guidance issued by the Director of Public Prosecutions to enable custody officers to decide whether a person should be charged
Director of Public Prosecution's Guidance on Conditional Cautioning	Guidance issued by the Director of Public Prosecutions to enable custody officers and Crown Prosecutors to decide whether a person should receive a Conditional Caution
Disclosure (defence)	Authorities relating to disclosure by the defence are: (i)Part 1 Criminal Procedure and Investigations Act 1996 and, for investigations begun on or after 4 April 2005, the 1996 Act as amended by the relevant provisions of Part 5, Criminal Justice Act 2003, CPI Act 1996 (Defence Disclosure Time Limits) Regulations 1997 (SI 1997 No 684) (ii)Attorney General's Guidelines on Disclosure 2005
Disclosure (prosecution)	Authorities relating to disclosure by the prosecution are: (i)Part 1, Criminal Procedure and Investigations Act 1996 and, for investigations begun on or after 4 April 2005, the 1996 Act as amended by the relevant provisions in Part 5 of Criminal Justice Act 2003 (ii) Attorney General's Guidelines on Disclosure 2005 (iii)Police-CPS Disclosure Manual
DNA Guidance	Advice to the police and CPS in relation to DNA evidence, available locally and on the ACPO and CPS intranets
Duty Prosecutor	Duty Prosecutors are Crown Prosecutors who attend police stations to provide guidance and advice to investigators and make charging decisions. Additionally an out of hours service operates nationally through CPS Direct
Either-way cases	Offences that can be tried either in the magistrates' courts or the Crown Court

Evidential/ Expedited file	Please see **Appendix B**
FTA	Failure to appear at court or at a police station
Full Code Test	Crown Prosecutors and custody officers must make charging decisions in accordance with the Full Code Test as set out in the Code for Crown Prosecutors and the Director's Guidance on Charging other than those limited circumstances where the Threshold Test applies The Full Code Test has two stages which must be met: (1) the evidential test (2) the public interest test Where a Crown Prosecutor makes a charging decision in accordance with the Threshold Test (see below), the case must be reviewed in accordance with the Full Code Test as soon as reasonably practicable, taking into account the progress of the investigation (See also Threshold Test)
Full file	Please see **Appendix B**
GP	Guilty plea
Indictable only cases	Offences which can be tried only in the Crown Court
LCJB	Local Criminal Justice Board
Manual of Guidance/ MOG	Information on the contents of case files can be found in Section 1 of the Manual of Guidance – A Guide to Case Building
MC	Magistrates' courts
MG forms	Forms referred to in the Manual of Guidance, see **Appendix B**
MOT	Mode of Trial: the decision-making process in the magistrates' courts in either-way cases, where a not guilty plea or no plea has been indicated, as to whether the trial is to take place in the magistrates' courts or Crown Court
Newton hearing (NH)	A Newton hearing is held when a defendant admits his guilt but disputes the prosecution's version of events and the court needs to determine the basis on which the defendant is to be sentenced
NG	Not guilty plea
Non-specified offences	Those traffic offences not included in The Prosecution of Offences Act 1985 (Specified Proceedings) Order 1999, SI 1999/904 made under the provisions of s.3(3) Prosecution of Offences Act 1985
Office for Criminal Justice Reform (OCJR)	OCJR is a cross-departmental organisation; it supports all criminal justice agencies in working together to provide an improved service to the public. The OCJR reports to Ministers in the Home Office, the Ministry of Justice and to the Office of the Attorney General
PBV	Plea before venue. A procedure in the magistrates' courts where, in an either-way case, a defendant is given the opportunity to indicate his or her likely plea

PNC	**Police National Computer**
	The Police National computer is a national information system, available to the police, criminal justice agencies and a variety of other non-policing organisations
POCA	Proceeds of Crime Act 2002
PSR	Pre Sentence Report
s.6(1) readout committal	A magistrates' court's enquiry into an offence as examining justices to determine whether there is sufficient evidence to commit a defendant to the Crown Court for trial
s.11(2) Magistrates' Courts Act 1980	The provision whereby a court can proceed in the absence of an accused when a summons has been issued and duly served and such service can be proved
s.12 Magistrates' Courts Act 1980	The provision whereby a court can proceed in the absence of a defendant who has pleaded guilty by post
Sent cases	Indictable only cases sent from the magistrates' courts directly to the Crown Court under s.51 of the Crime and Disorder Act 1998
Special measures	Measures which can be ordered by the court to improve the quality of the evidence given by a vulnerable witness
Specified offences	Specified offences are those so specified in the Prosecution of Offences Act 1985 (Specified Proceedings) Order 1999, SI 1999/904 made under the provisions of s.3 (3) Prosecution of Offences Act 1985
Summary cases	Offences that can be tried only in the magistrates' courts
Threshold Test	The Threshold Test is set out in the Code for Crown Prosecutors and Director's Guidance on Charging. The Test requires Crown Prosecutors to decide whether there is at least a reasonable suspicion that the suspect has committed an offence together with the likelihood that further evidence will become available within a reasonable time to meet the Full Code Test and that it is in the public interest to proceed. The public interest will be the same as under the Full Code Test but will be based on the information available at the time of the charge which may be limited
	Guidance on this is currently being revised
	(see also Full Code Test)
TICs	Offences to be taken into consideration
	A defendant may ask a court passing sentence to take into consideration other offences of a similar nature
Transfer	s.53 Criminal Justice Act 1991 (relating to some offences against children) and s4 Criminal Justice Act 1987 (serious fraud) provide for transfer of these cases to the Crown Court without committal proceedings
Victim	Any person who has made an allegation to the police, or has had an allegation made on his behalf, that he has been directly subjected to criminal conduct (*Para 3.1 The Code of Practice for Victims of Crime*). Therefore, the use of this term does not imply that a suspect or defendant is in fact guilty; nor does it imply that his case has been prejudged

Warrants
The court may consider issuing a warrant for the arrest of:
(i) a defendant who fails to answer to his bail; or
(ii) a non-attending witness who has been served with a witness summons
OCJR's "Getting Defendants to Court" – guidance is available to prosecutors, in relation to applications, and to the police, in relation to the swift execution
Copies are available upon request from
FTAWarrants@cjs.gsi.gov.uk

Witness Care Units
The role of the witness care unit is to provide a single point of contact to prosecution victims and witnesses, providing them with regular updates of the proceedings. In addition, they assess and meet the needs of victims and witnesses to support them in their attendance at court

USEFUL LINKS

We have made it easier for users to access electronic documents with lengthy web addresses by converting the web addresses to "Tiny URL" links. This does not in any way change the original web addresses; it just makes it easier to access information when typing it into your browser

Please enter the Tiny URL exactly as shown below

Attorney General's Guidelines on Disclosure	http://tinyurl.com/2wmgse
Case Management Forms (HMCS Website)	http://tinyurl.com/loob9
Code for Crown Prosecutors	http://tinyurl.com/26ogw2
Code of Practice for Victims of Crime	http://tinyurl.com/2pdumm
Consolidated Criminal Practice Direction	http://tinyurl.com/2o2jvs
Criminal Procedure Rules	http://tinyurl.com/3cwal4
CJS Online	http://tinyurl.com/32r7zp
CPS Homepage	http://tinyurl.com/29dhho
DPP's Guidance on Charging	http://tinyurl.com/3dsyfm
HMCS Homepage	http://tinyurl.com/ysbgph
Home Office Circulars	http://tinyurl.com/4lgme
Home Office guidance on the selection and treatment of interpreters within the CJS	http://tinyurl.com/34le2u
Home Office Homepage	http://tinyurl.com/4pgyj
MOJ Homepage	http://tinyurl.com/2cl726
Office of Public Sector Information website – Legislation	http://tinyurl.com/zl734
Penalty Notices for Disorder: Police Operational Guidance	http://tinyurl.com/2ycp55

Prosecution Team Guidance Offences to be taken into consideration	http://tinyurl.com/38t7l6
Prosecution Team Manual of Guidance 2004 Edition	http://tinyurl.com/337zkv
Sentencing Guidelines Council Homepage	http://tinyurl.com/2xahun
Victim Support – Going to Court leaflet for witnesses	http://tinyurl.com/ysf23y
Witness Security at Court guidance (Frontline Matters – an online resource for CJS practitioners)	http://tinyurl.com/yvvwom

The Route Map – (Anticipated) Guilty Plea Cases (non-traffic)

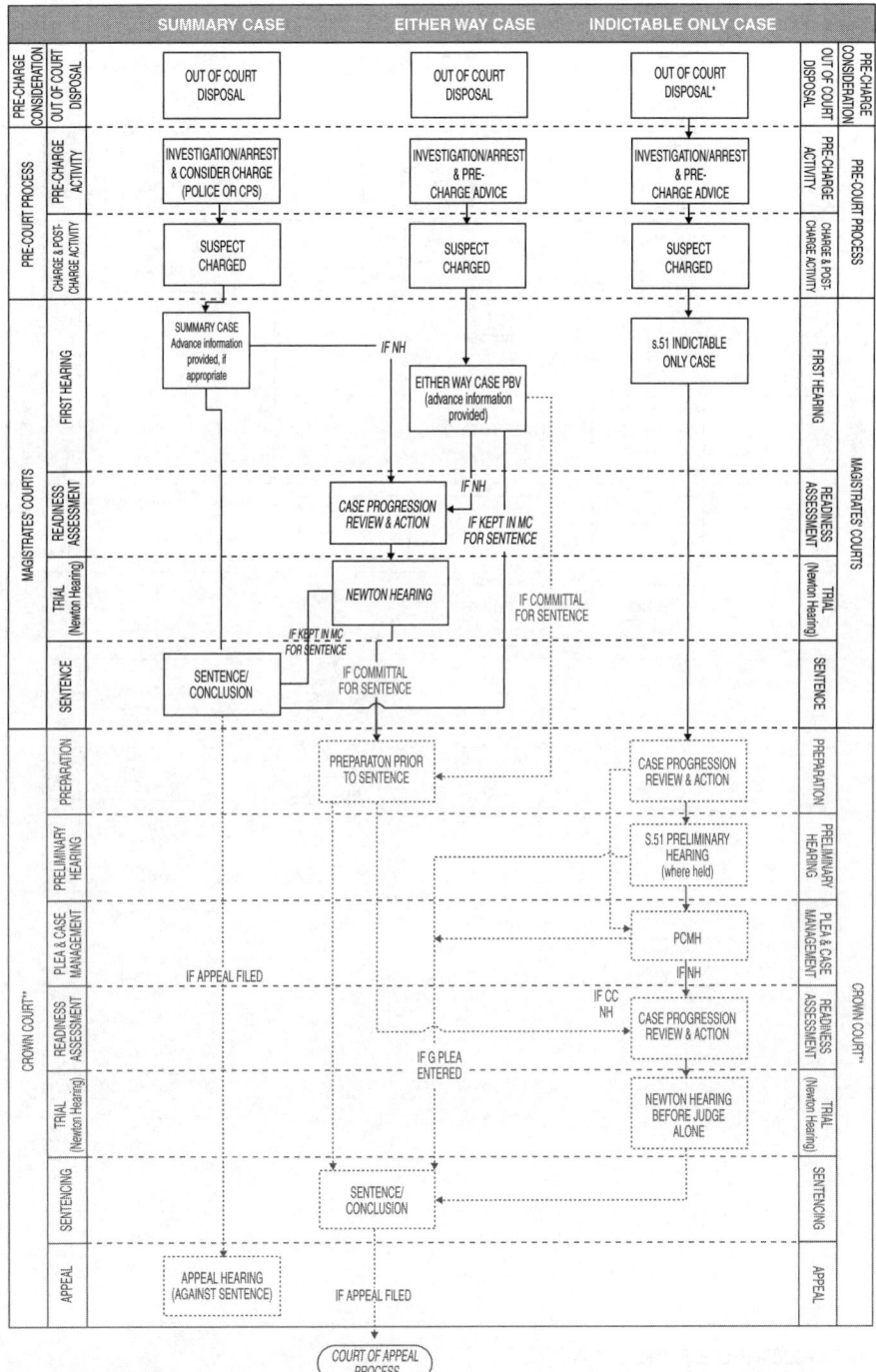

* A SIMPLE CAUTION IS THE ONLY OUT OF COURT DISPOSAL POSSIBLE IN INDICTABLE ONLY CASES AND MUST BE REFERRED TO THE CPS
** CROWN COURT PROCESS TO FOLLOW IN PART 2

The Route Map – Not Guilty Plea Cases (non-traffic)

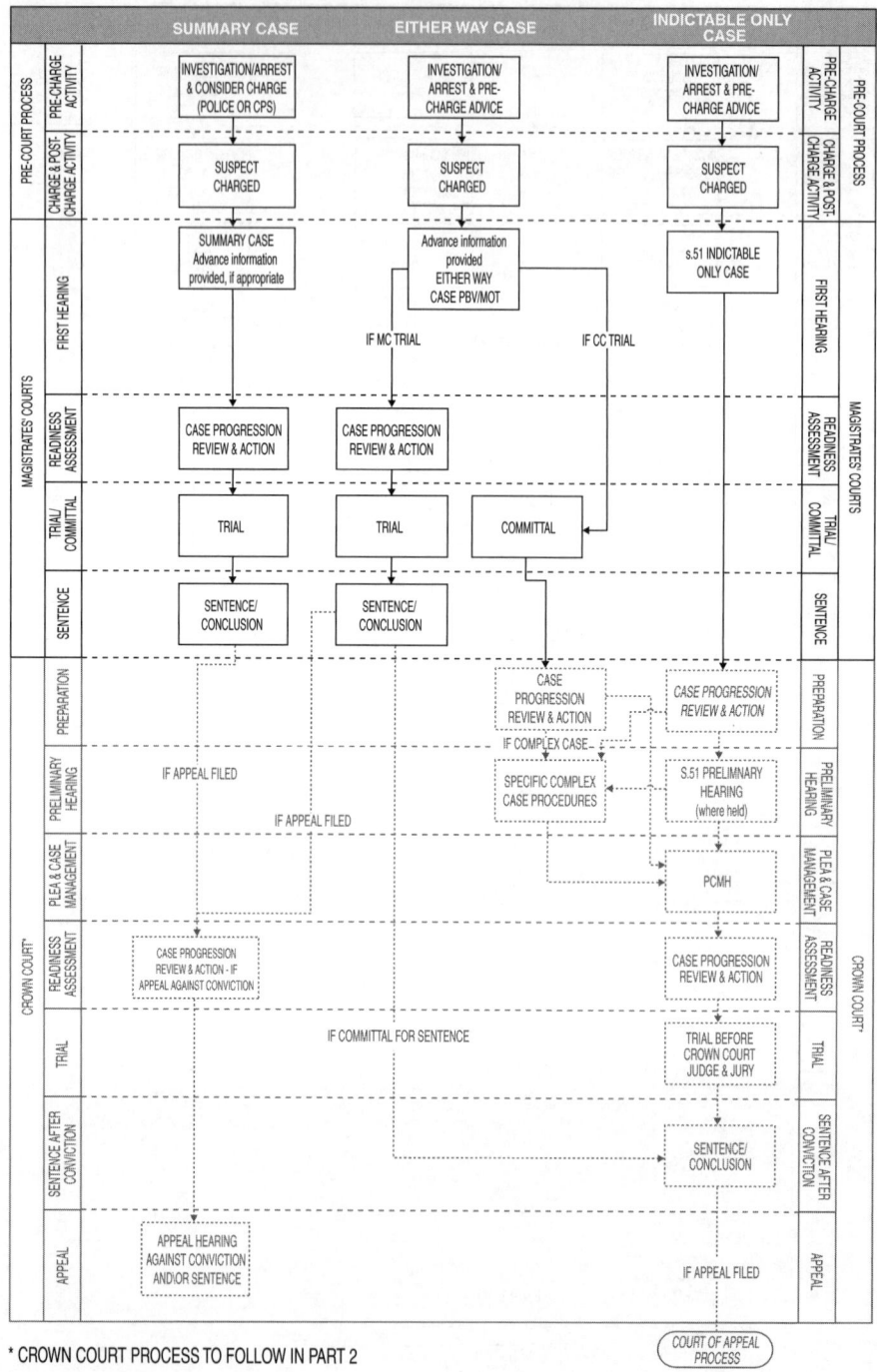

* CROWN COURT PROCESS TO FOLLOW IN PART 2

NOTE: PLEAS MAY CHANGE TO GUILTY AT ANY STAGE IN WHICH CASE REFER TO APPROPRIATE STEP OF THE GUILTY PLEA ROUTE MAP

Chapter 1   Pre-charge activity

OBJECTIVES

(a) Expeditiously to investigate and gather evidence in accordance with CPIA and the relevant codes, pursuing all reasonable lines of enquiry, whether these point towards or away from the suspect[1]
(b) The police and CPS to communicate effectively
(c) To assess as early and as reliably as possible:

    (i)   Whether to prosecute (which will include whether the case is unworthy of further investigation or whether it might be suitable for an out of court disposal)[2]

    (ii)   The legally correct and appropriate charge

    (iii)   The suspect's likely plea

    (iv)   The needs of victims and witnesses

    (v)   The needs of the suspect

ACTIONS

1.1 Investigation and Arrest

    (a)   The police should, as far as possible, investigate the case and obtain admissible evidence before or soon after arrest so that a properly informed decision can be taken in relation to charge/out of court disposal/taking the case no further. Where a suspect is arrested, his case must be dealt with expeditiously, and he must be released as soon as the need for detention no longer applies[3]

    (b)   Where a suspect can be released on bail he should be bailed if further evidence is to be obtained by the police. There are no set timescales for how long the suspect may remain on police bail as the nature and complexity of cases can vary significantly

    (c)   Where further evidence is required the CPS will prepare an Action Plan specifying in respect of each action how long the police should need to complete the action. Different actions will often require different timescales to complete

    (d)   Advice may be provided face to face which is normally preferable but, depending on local practices and limitations, telephone advice may be provided

    (e)   Locally agreed timescales may be shorter for cases meriting priority and, where agreed, the police may in those cases expedite their enquiries (e.g. by paying for earlier forensic analysis)

    (f)   Where it is clear that the suspect will contest the allegations, an evidential report should be submitted for a charging decision to be made within locally agreed timescales where relevant

    (g)   Where the CPS is satisfied that the suspect is not suitable for bail the case will be reviewed applying the Threshold Test (reasonable suspicion and likelihood of further evidence being obtained)

1.2 Consideration of Fixed Penalty Notices or Penalty Notices for Disorder[4]

Investigating officers should assess the seriousness of the matter and consider the issue of a fixed penalty notice or a penalty notice for disorder in appropriate cases

1.3 Consideration of an out of court disposal by custody officer

If there is sufficient evidence against a suspect, and guilt has been admitted, the custody officer should consider[5] the seriousness of an offence and the appropriateness of an out of court disposal, prior to referring the case to a prosecutor for a charging decision or proceeding to charge

1.4   Anticipated guilty plea cases suitable for disposal in the magistrates' courts

Anticipated guilty plea cases suitable for disposal in the magistrates' courts which do not require a CPS charging decision[6] should be charged by police at the earliest opportunity

1.5   Early consultation with Crown Prosecutor

(a)   In all cases requiring CPS advice for charging decisions, early consultation with a Crown Prosecutor should be undertaken to ensure the evidence is reviewed before the charging decision is made. An effective system which includes bail management should be employed to enable investigating officers to meet Crown Prosecutors and to obtain their legal advice or charging decisions promptly. Early consultation should identify:

(i)   whether the case is suitable for a simple/Conditional Caution or, if not
(ii)   the appropriate charges, the key evidence required to support them and the defendant's likely plea(s)

(b)   Crown Prosecutors should provide guidance and advice to investigators throughout the case or investigation and should be pro-active in identifying and, where possible, rectifying evidential difficulties and in bringing to an early conclusion those cases which do not meet the test of evidential sufficiency and cannot be strengthened by further investigation. Where a suspect is in police custody and a CPS charging decision is required, CPS Direct should be contacted outside local CPS office hours[7]

1.6   Referral to a Crown Prosecutor where Conditional Cautioning is to be considered

Cases appropriate for a Conditional Caution should be referred to a Crown Prosecutor for consideration in accordance with the Director's Guidance on Conditional Cautioning which specifies:

(i)   The information which must be sent to Crown Prosecutors to enable a Conditional Cautioning decision to be made and
(ii)   The practical arrangements for the referral of cases and for dealing with any non-compliance

1.7   Failure to comply with a caution or its conditions

(a)   Where a person declines a caution (simple or conditional) or does not attend to be cautioned, the case should be referred to the CPS for a charging decision
(b)   Where it appears to a custody officer or authorised person that the conditions of any Conditional Caution have not been complied with, the case should be referred to the CPS to consider a prosecution for the original offence

1.8   Anticipated not guilty plea cases

(a)   Those cases where the anticipated plea is one of not guilty and bail is appropriate must be investigated with a view to the key evidence being obtained before charge. This will include obtaining relevant key witness statements, seizing and viewing CCTV and pursuing all reasonable lines of enquiry
(b)   Those cases where the anticipated plea is one of not guilty and bail is inappropriate must be investigated with a view to the key evidence being obtained wherever possible before charge or, where it cannot be obtained, the Threshold Test will be applied (see **1.1(g)**)
(c)   Where bail is appropriate, expert evidence which is likely to be disputed and relied on at trial should be included by the police on any anticipated not guilty case file. A decision will be made by the police or CPS on whether to obtain expert evidence, if appropriate
(d)   Where the Threshold Test is met without the expert evidence but it is decided to obtain such evidence for trial, realistic deadlines should be agreed with the expert who will be instructed for inclusion in the Action Plan

(e)   Unused material, which may undermine the prosecution case or assist the case for the accused should be provided to the Duty Prosecutor by the police.[8] A disclosure schedule is not required at this stage

RESPONSIBILITIES

Police

1.9 The Police should:

(a)   Check the suspect's previous convictions against available PNC records and establish the particulars of any earlier out of court disposals involving the suspect prior to making a decision on whether an out of court disposal is appropriate

(b)   Notify vulnerable or intimidated victims of an out of court disposal within one working day and all other victims within 5 working days[9]

(c)   Ensure that an early consultation with a Duty Prosecutor takes place whenever the charging decision is to be undertaken by the CPS and promptly respond to all enquiries from prosecution or defence and deal with the actions identified in the Action Plan

(d)   Identify any cases that may be suitable for a Conditional Caution and consult the victim prior to making the decision, where appropriate

(e)   Appoint a disclosure officer in accordance with the disclosure manual

(f)   Prepare and submit an evidential report to CPS in accordance with the Manual of Guidance where it is anticipated that a case is to be contested

(g)   Fully complete the MG11, witness statement form, including the reverse (witness contact details, care and consent) in accordance with the Manual of Guidance

(h)   Identify any special measures required at or immediately after the taking of a witness statement or recorded interview, recording details on the MG2 (special measures assessment). In completing the MG2, police should consider the particular characteristics of the witness, the nature of the case, the evidence the witness can give and the range of different special measures which may be available. A detailed, reasoned assessment of the witness, specifically related to any special measure for which application is proposed, should be recorded on the MG2. The officer making that assessment should explain about the provision of special measures[10] to the victim and record any views the victim expresses about applying for special measures[11] while avoiding creating expectations which may not be fulfilled

(i)   Offer victims the opportunity to provide a victim personal statement;[12] such statements are not, however, compulsory

(j)   Having made a careful assessment of any particular needs (other than special measures) of any witness/victim, inform the prosecutor of them in writing on the rear of the MG11 (see 1.9 (g))

(k)   Consider the likelihood that a witness/victim might prove uncooperative at a later stage and whether a witness summons might be required

(l)   Prepare Records of Visual Interviews (ROVIs) at an early stage for investigative and CPS review purposes. A CPS specialist should be consulted where required in rape and serious sexual offence cases

Prosecution Team

1.10 The Prosecution

(a)   The CPS should ensure that investigators have access to appropriate prosecutors for consultation during the course of the investigation

(b)   The CPS should anticipate any offers of plea and whether these would be acceptable, wherever possible. In threshold test cases it is unlikely the prosecutor will be in a position to agree pleas until the full strength of the case can be determined. The prosecutor should have regard to the Attorney General's Guidelines on the Acceptance of Pleas and the Prosecutor's Role in the Sentencing Exercise

(c)   The Duty Prosecutor should be available for consultation with the Officer in the case, to consider the prosecution evidence and provide advice as appropriate. Alternatively, the police may submit an evidential report to the CPS office for a lawyer (not necessarily a Duty Prosecutor) to advise

(d)   If the Duty Prosecutor is not in a position to authorise charge owing to outstanding material being required he shall complete an Action Plan. This sets out what key evidence is outstanding and required before a Full Code Test can be carried out to enable a charging decision to be made. Action Plans should include agreed timetables for the completion of each action set out in the plan. These should be for no longer than are necessary to enable the evidence to be obtained. The suspect may be placed on pre-charge bail unless the Threshold Test is applied and the suspect is held in custody pending an application to remand him in custody. In bail cases, once the outstanding material has been obtained, the officer shall consult further with the Duty Prosecutor with a view to him authorising the appropriate charge

(e)   Police officers should endeavour to complete the work specified in the Action Plan as soon as practicable and within the timescales stated in the Action Plan. The date of the suspect's return on bail should be arranged to take account of the need to complete work on the Action Plan and for the officer to consult again with the Duty Prosecutor for a charging decision

(f)   Where a decision is made that no further action should be taken against the suspect the decision should be communicated to him and his representative in advance and his bail surrender should be cancelled. In addition, victims should be notified of the outcome[13]

Defence Team

1.11 The defence should:

If instructed to do so, ensure that all relevant considerations are made known to the prosecution team to enable a fully informed decision to be taken as to whether an out of court disposal is appropriate

NOTES

1 Criminal Procedure and Investigations Act 1996 Disclosure Code of Practice 3.5
2 In accordance with the Home Office Circular on Cautioning, the Director's Guidance on Conditional Cautioning, the Penalty Notices for Disorder – Police Operational Guidance. Also in accordance with Out of court disposals for Adults: A guide to alternatives to prosecution, which will be issued shortly
3 PACE Code C 1.1
4 Guidance for police is available at http://tinyurl.com/2ycp55
5 Out of court disposals for Adults: A guide to alternatives to prosecution, which will be issued shortly
6 In accordance with the Director of Public Prosecution's Guidance on Charging, the Police may charge with certain exceptions any summary or either way offence where the anticipated plea is guilty and also certain less serious offences even where the suspect may be expected to plead not guilty. These include Bail Act offences, less serious Road Traffic offences and offences punishable with no more than three months custody (unless specified that the CPS must charge)
7 CPS Direct is currently available for cases suitable under the DPP's guidance for advice and charging decisions. Decisions on Conditional Cautioning must be referred to the local Duty Prosecutor where appropriate
8 Director of Public Prosecution's Guidance on Charging
9 Crim PR 1.1(2)(d); 5.26 Code of Practice for Victims of Crime
10 Youth Justice and Criminal Evidence Act 1999

11 5.8 Code of Practice for victims of Crime
12 Consolidated Criminal Practice Direction III.28
13 5.15 Code of Practice for Victims of Crime

Chapter 2   Charge and post-charge activity

OBJECTIVES

(a) To charge the suspect with an appropriate offence which is legally correct, having regard to the available admissible evidence[1]
(b) To release the defendant on bail (subject to conditions, if appropriate) or to withhold bail, if an exception to the right to bail is justified
(c) To prepare the case so that the first hearing is effective in compliance with the Criminal Procedure Rules. In particular, to ensure that at the first hearing:

   (i)   The plea can be taken[2]
   (ii)   The real issue(s) are identified[3]
   (iii)   The case (including sentence) can be concluded there and then or, if it really cannot be concluded, directions[4] can be given so that it can be concluded at the next hearing or as soon as possible after that[5]

(d) To deal with the case proportionately[6]

ACTIONS

2.1 Charging Decision

Charging decisions should be made by the police (where appropriate) and the prosecutor (where appropriate), in accordance with the Director's Guidance on Charging and by applying the appropriate test as set out in the Code for Crown Prosecutors. Crown Prosecutors should ensure that full consideration is given to all current CPS policies when considering the appropriate charge

   (a)   In those cases where it is proposed to release the suspect on bail, the charging decision should be made by applying the Full Code test
   (b)   Where the Crown Prosecutor considers that the suspect should be kept in custody and where the Full Code test cannot be met, the charging decision should be made by applying the Threshold Test (see **1.1(g)**)
   (c)   The relevant file should be submitted by the police in accordance with the Manual of Guidance

2.2 Bail

   (a)   In those cases where the officer in the case opposes bail, he should make his representations to the custody officer. Where the decision to charge is for the police, the custody officer should consider any representations from the defendant, and from his legal representative, as well as from the officer in the case. The custody officer will grant unconditional bail unless satisfied that one of the exceptions (under the Bail Act 1976) applies. If he is satisfied that one of the exceptions to bail applies, he should consider whether bail should be granted with conditions and if so, grant conditional bail. The custody officer should only hold the defendant in custody to appear before the first available sitting of the magistrates' courts if satisfied that this is required
   (b)   Where the decision to charge is for the CPS, the procedure is the same except that if it is proposed to charge the suspect on the Threshold Test, the Duty Prosecutor should be consulted
   (c)   Where a defendant is granted bail after charge, under CJSSS: Magistrates'

Courts the period between the charge date and the first hearing should be subject to the listing practice set by the judicial members of the Justices' Issues Group

2.3 Securing attendance at court

The police should ensure that a defendant who is released on bail clearly understands any bail condition (clearly set out on form MG4A) and the possible consequences of breaching any bail condition or failing to answer to bail (which may be done by giving the defendant a leaflet). It may be necessary or appropriate to involve the defendant's legal representative and/or an appropriate adult in this

2.4 Representation

(a)   Where the defendant is unrepresented, the police should tell the defendant that if he wishes to be represented, he should consult a solicitor and apply for a representation order without delay (this should be reinforced by giving the defendant a leaflet)

(b)   When appropriate, the defence should complete an application for a representation order as soon as practicable after being instructed

2.5 Prior to the first hearing

(a)   The prosecution should serve advance information on the defence and on the court as early as possible in accordance with local CJSSS practice and at the latest by 9am on the day of the hearing. The content of advance information must comply with Crim PR 21.3(1)(a-b) and should be subject to a supervisory check before service

(b)   The defence should collect advance information promptly on the day of first hearing[7] and take instructions so that, in compliance with the Criminal Procedure Rules, the first hearing is effective (**see Objective C**)

(c)   Before the court sits the prosecutor should be available at a designated time and place, subject to local agreement, for consultation with defence

2.6 Local listing practice

The Justices' Issues Group (judicial membership) will decide on local listing practice, as set out in "**Listing of Cases**" guidance, issued in July 2005, (**see Appendix A**)

RESPONSIBILITIES

Police

2.7 The Police should:

(a)   Provide the prosecutor with the relevant file for the stage of the case, whether guilty/not guilty plea anticipated, in accordance with the Manual of Guidance

(b)   Ensure that key (i.e. evidence to be relied upon by the prosecution) CCTV evidence has been considered in good time and, where it is disclosable evidence it should be copied, particularly where it is the sole evidence to be relied upon

(c)   Ensure that the prosecution file (but not full disclosure) contains material on which a CPIA disclosure decision can be made, including material which may undermine the prosecution case or assist the case for the accused

(d)   Ensure that the witnesses' dates to avoid, and the reasons where available, have been ascertained and are available

(e)   Ensure completion of the reverse of the MG11 (witness statement)

(f)   Provide the MG2 (Special Measures Assessment form) to the CPS and to the Witness Care Unit including the Victim Personal Statement (if taken) to the CPS

(g)   Keep victims and witnesses informed of the progress of the case.[8] Where the police refer the case to a Crown Prosecutor for a charging decision it remains the responsibility of the police to notify the victim of the outcome.[9] If the suspect is to be charged, the police should contact[10] the victims and witnesses in accordance with the Code of Practice for Victims of Crime

(h)   Ensure that appropriate information will be available to the court when bail is considered. Complete the MG7 (remand application) in all cases where a remand in custody or conditional bail is sought and provide the MG7 to the CPS with supporting material

(i)   Ensure that an interpreter[11] has been booked to attend the first hearing where necessary

(j)   If the defendant wants any offences to be taken into consideration, prepare the MG18 Offences to be taken into consideration (TIC) form

2.8   The prosecution should:

(a)   Provide advance information, any TICs, and the defendant's antecedent history[12] to the court and the defence as early as possible in accordance with local CJSSS: Magistrates' Courts practice and at the latest by 9am on the morning of the first hearing

(b)   Prepare to open the case[13] so that the defendant can be sentenced after a plea of guilty

(c)   Prepare for the possibility that the defendant may be prepared to plead guilty to an alternative or lesser offence. Prosecution must be in a position to take a decision at court without recourse to an adjournment

(d)   Prepare to deal with plea before venue and mode of trial[14] (including assisting the court specifically in relation to the guidance set out in the Consolidated Criminal Practice Direction V.51.2-18) and any other matters concerning jurisdiction such as POCA and the dangerous offender provisions of the CJA 2003

(e)   Prepare to complete the prescribed case progression forms[15] in compliance with the Criminal Procedure Rules, Consolidated Criminal Practice Direction, and any guidance notes

(f)   Prepare to identify the real issue(s)[16] and apply for any direction[17] needed to achieve the overriding objective[18] and comply with the detailed requirements of Part 3 of the Criminal Procedure Rules

(g)   Prepare so that an early trial date can be fixed

(h)   Serve CCTV which is key evidence, relied on by the prosecution

(i)   Identify all unused material contained on the prosecution file

(j)   Prepare so that appropriate information, available to the prosecution, is available to the court[19] and any application for bail or to vary bail conditions can be dealt with without adjournment

Defence Team

2.9   The Defendant's legal representatives should:

(a)   Cause any application for a representation order to be made as soon as possible and in time for the defendant to be advised and represented before the first hearing

(b)   Take instructions, give advice, and prepare the case in compliance with the Criminal Procedure Rules so that the first hearing is effective (see Objective C). This will include: considering advance information, the defendant's antecedents, and any TICs; taking the defendant's instructions (including in relation to mitigation if there will or may be a guilty plea); and advising the defendant in relation to: the strength of the prosecution case, credit for pleading guilty,[20] whether to plead guilty to alternative or lesser offences, plea before venue and mode of trial and bail

(c)   Prepare to mitigate so that the defendant can be sentenced after a plea of guilty
(d)   Prepare to deal with plea before venue and mode of trial[21] (including assisting the court specifically in relation to the guidance set out in the Consolidated Criminal Practice Direction V.51.2-18) and any other matters concerning jurisdiction
(e)   Prepare to complete the prescribed case progression forms[22] in compliance with the Criminal Procedure Rules, Consolidated Criminal Practice Direction, and any guidance notes
(f)   Prepare to identify the real issue(s)[23] and apply for any direction[24] needed to achieve the overriding objective[25] and comply with the detailed requirements of Part 3 of the Criminal Procedure Rules
(g)   Prepare so that an early trial date can be fixed
(h)   Prepare so that appropriate information is available to the court[26] and any application for bail or to vary bail conditions can be dealt with without adjournment

Case Progression

2.10 The parties must:

(a)   Inform the court and the other party or parties of any significant failure (whoever is responsible for that failure) to take any procedural step required by the Rules, any practice direction, or any direction of the court. A failure is significant if it might hinder the court in furthering the overriding objective[27]
(b)   Be in a position to identify the individual who will be nominated as the case progression officer, who will be responsible for progressing the case and fulfilling the duties prescribed by Criminal Procedure Rule 3.4

National Offender Management Service – Productions from Prison Custody

2.11 PECS (or the Prison Service, in the case of Category A prisoners) should:

(a)   Ensure that all persons in custody are produced at the court when required and taken to each court room promptly
(b)   Notify the court administration immediately of any problems anticipated or arising in respect of the production of persons in custody

NOTES

1 The Code for Crown Prosecutors and the Director of Public Prosecution's Guidance on Charging
2 Crim PR 3.8(2)(b)
3 Crim PR 3.2(2)(a); 3.3(a)
4 Crim PR 3.2(3); 3.3(b); 3.5
5 Crim PR 3.8(1)
6 Crim PR 1.1(2)(g)
7 Under CJSSS: Magistrates' Courts advance information may be available before the day of first hearing subject to local agreement
8 Crim PR 1.1(2)(d)
9 5.20 Code of Practice For Victims of Crime
10 Contact should be made with the witness as agreed (e.g. use of telephone, email etc)
11 Guidance on the selection and treatment of interpreters within the criminal justice system can be found at the following site: http://tinyurl.com/34le2u
12 Consolidated Criminal Practice Direction III.27
13 Crim PR 1.1(2)(f); Consolidated Criminal Practice Direction III.26.1
14 Consolidated Criminal Practice Direction V.51
15 Crim PR 3.11(1); Consolidated Criminal Practice Direction V.56
16 Crim PR 3.2(2)(a); 3.3(a)
17 Crim PR 3.3(b)
18 That criminal cases be dealt with justly in accordance with Crim PR Part 1

19 Crim PR 1.1(2)(f)
20 Sentencing Guidelines Council, Reduction in Sentence for a Guilty plea providing guidelines in relation to guilty pleas in the Magistrates' and Crown Court. This can be found at http://tinyurl.com/2xahun
21 Consolidated Criminal Practice Direction V.51
22 Crim PR 3.11(1); Consolidated Criminal Practice Direction V.56
23 Crim PR 3.2(2)(a); 3.3(a)
24 Crim PR 3.3(b)
25 That criminal cases be dealt with justly in accordance with Crim PR Part 1
26 Crim PR 1.1(2)(f)
27 That criminal cases be dealt with justly in accordance with Crim PR Part 1

Chapter 3   First hearing

OBJECTIVES

(a) To achieve an effective first hearing in compliance with the Criminal Procedure Rules. In particular, to ensure that at the first hearing:

  (i)   The plea can be taken[1]
  (ii)   The appropriate venue is determined
  (iii)   The real issue(s) are identified[2]
  (iv)   The case (including sentence) can be concluded there and then or, if it really cannot be concluded, directions[3] can be given so that it can be concluded at the next hearing or as soon as possible after that[4]

(b) To enable directions to be given so that appropriate cases may be committed, sent, or transferred to the Crown Court as soon as possible, and so that such cases may be concluded there without undue delay

ACTIONS

3.1 Representation

  (a)   If he has not already done so and wishes to do so, the defendant should seek representation as soon as possible or see the duty solicitor on the day
  (b)   The court administration should determine all applications for legal representation within 48 hours of receipt

3.2 If the defendant does not attend

  (a)   Where the defendant does not attend court, the prosecution advocate will generally apply for a warrant not backed for bail and invite critical scrutiny of any material placed before the court on behalf of the defendant – in particular as to whether it appears to be reliable and relates specifically to the defendant's ability to attend court. A decision by the court not to issue a warrant will not prevent the later determination of whether the defendant has committed an offence contrary to s.6 of the Bail Act
  (b)   The overriding objective[5] and the case management obligations prescribed by the Criminal Procedure Rules apply whether the defendant is present or not.[6] The parties' advocates should prepare for the hearing accordingly and, at the hearing, actively assist the court even if the defendant is absent

3.3 Indictable Only Cases (s.51 Crime and Disorder Act 1998)

  (a)   The defence must expect to be required to give an indication of the likely plea[7] and prepare accordingly
  (b)   If a guilty plea is indicated, the parties may apply for directions in relation to the service of papers and indictment, the preparation of a PSR, and any other matters so that sentence may be passed at the first hearing in the Crown Court.

If the case requires management in the Crown Court (for example, to determine any issue arising out of a basis of plea or to decide whether a PSR is unnecessary) a party may apply for that matter to be decided, by hearing or otherwise, in accordance with local listing practice

(c)   Unless a preliminary hearing would automatically be held in accordance with the practice set by the Resident Judge, the parties should consider whether a preliminary hearing would further the overriding objective (having regard to any guidance notes accompanying the prescribed case progression form).[8] If it would, application should be made for a direction that a preliminary hearing be held on a date fixed in accordance with local listing practice

(d)   The parties should complete the prescribed case management forms[9] and actively consider, having particular regard to the real issue(s), whether the standard directions should be varied or supplemented and, if they should, make application accordingly[10]

3.4 Either-way cases[11]

(a)   **Plea and plea before venue**

   (i)   The Justices' Issues Group (judicial membership) will decide on local listing practice

   (ii)   The defence must expect that the court will, where relevant, take the defendant's plea or if no plea can be taken find out whether he is likely to plead guilty or not guilty and prepare accordingly

   (iii)   Where there is a not guilty plea, or no indication is given, it is for the court to determine the venue. (For guidance where a not guilty plea is indicated, the court accepts jurisdiction and the defendant consents to summary trial, see 3.5 (c))

   (iv)   Where a guilty plea is indicated, the court will consider the appropriate venue for sentence.[12] (For guidance where jurisdiction is retained, see 3.5 (b))

(b)   **Mode of Trial**

   Where the court declines jurisdiction or where the defendant elects Crown Court trial, unless the prosecution is able to proceed there and then, the prosecution shall apply for an adjournment for the service of papers and a committal hearing or transfer

(c)   **Committal or transfer to Crown Court for trial where appropriate**

   (See part 6 for detail on the committal and transfer processes)

3.5 Summary cases

(a)   The defendant must expect his plea to be taken[13] and the case must be prepared accordingly

(b)   Where a guilty plea is entered:

   (i)   The parties should be prepared for the court to pass sentence

   (ii)   If the defendant pleads guilty on a basis which is materially different to the prosecution case, the difference(s) should be clearly identified in a written basis of plea and served on the court and the prosecutor. The parties' advocates should be prepared to make submissions to the court in relation to the necessity of a Newton hearing

   (iii)   The parties should ask that any TICs (see 2.7(j), 2.8(a), 2.9(b)) be put. The police should be told which TICs are accepted. If a previously admitted offence is not accepted, the CPS file should be clearly marked and consideration given to prosecution

   (iv)   Whether to submit that a PSR should be prepared should be considered

with care. A PSR prepared for an earlier case involving the same defendant may provide enough information

(v)   If a PSR is ordered, the necessary information and assessment(s) should
be provided to the court by the Probation Service on the same day if
possible. An oral report may be appropriate

(vi)   If the court decides to commit the case to the Crown Court for sentence,
the defence should consider with care whether to apply there and then
for a PSR so that, if one is ordered, it is ready for the sentencing hearing.
This is subject to local practice set by the Resident Judge

(vii)   The court administration should ensure that the memorandum of conviction sent to the Crown Court is accurate

(viii) If sentence cannot be passed there and then, the parties should be able to
provide the court with the appropriate information concerning any
application for bail[14]

(c)   Where a plea of not guilty is entered or a Newton hearing has been ordered:

(i)   The parties should expect and prepare for the court to hold a case
management hearing there and then

(ii)   The parties should complete the prescribed case progression forms[15] and
consider whether the standard directions[16] should be varied or supplemented and, if they should, make application accordingly[17]

(iii)   The real issue(s) should be explicitly identified[18]

(iv)   Only those witnesses who are relevant to a real, disputed issue should be
required to attend the trial.[19] Each party should expect to be required to
justify the attendance of each and every witness by explicit reference to a
real, disputed issue

(v)   The parties should provide the dates to avoid (and reasons, where
available) in relation to the witnesses who are to attend the trial

(vi)   The parties should be able to provide a timetable for those steps which
are necessary for the case to be ready for trial so that the court may make
directions accordingly[20]

(vii)   The parties should be able to provide a timetable for the trial itself by
reference to estimates of the length of: the evidence of each witness (in
chief and in cross-examination); presenting agreed evidence; and submissions in relation to points of law

(viii) The trial will be fixed in accordance with local listing practice

(ix)   If a case management hearing cannot be held at first hearing, sub-
paragraphs (ii)–(vii) above apply to the subsequent case management
hearing

(x)   The parties should be able to provide to the court with appropriate
information when bail is considered[21]

3.6 The defendant's preparation of his case and attendance at subsequent hearings

(a)   It is the defendant's responsibility to prepare his case and attend hearings. Any
other practices to which this framework refers do not absolve him from those
responsibilities

(b)   The defendant or his advocate should be prepared to indicate to the court that
the defendant is aware of the importance of preparing his case, keeping
appointments with his solicitor, and attending court (knowing the consequences of not doing so)

(c)   The court administration should provide the defendant with a written notice of
the date of next hearing before the defendant leaves the court

(d)   Where agreed locally, the court administration may offer an additional
reminder service,[22] e.g. by text message/telephone, where appropriate

(e)   Agencies should consider the inter-agency agreement "Managing bail to ensure defendant attendance at court template"[23]

RESPONSIBILITIES

Prosecution Team

3.7 The Prosecution Advocate should:

(a)   Prepare and conduct the case to accomplish the actions set out above. Agents should have sufficient instructions and authority to do so

(b)   In the event of a guilty plea, ensure that the Probation Service is given a PSR pack there and then or as directed by local arrangements

(c)   Ensure that the nominated case progression officer and any other member of the prosecution team who is responsible for the conduct of the case know(s) what directions have been made

3.8 Prosecution Case Progression Officer

To comply with Crim PR 3.4(1), the prosecution must nominate an individual responsible for progressing the case and tell the other parties who he is and how to contact him

Police

3.9 The police

The police/court enforcement officer should execute warrants promptly

Witness Care Unit

3.10 The Witness Care Unit should:

(a)   Notify victims and prosecution witnesses of the outcome of the hearing and of the trial date set[24]

(b)   Share information about victims and prosecution witnesses (e.g. reluctance of witness to attend court or changes in availability) with the prosecution team

Defence Advocate

3.11 The defence should:

(a)   Prepare and conduct the case to accomplish the actions set out above

(b)   Ensure that the nominated case progression officer and any other member of the defence team who is responsible for the conduct of the case know(s) what directions have been made

Magistrates' Courts Administration

3.12 The court administration should:

(a)   Deal promptly with applications for representation

(b)   Deal promptly with the preparation and issue of warrants within local and/ or national targets

(c)   Deal promptly with the sending of cases to the Crown Court

(d)   Deal promptly with the preparation of court orders e.g. community orders

(e)   Send case progression forms, accurate memorandums of conviction, and any relevant case notes (committals for sentence)[25] to the Crown Court where necessary

Court Case Progression Officer (CPO)

3.13 Following the 1st hearing, for matters proceeding to trial/trial of issue, the court case progression officer should:

(a)   Record details of the prosecution and defence CPOs
(b)   Notify the parties of the name and contact details of the CPOs
(c)   Record the directions made and record the next date of hearing

National Offender Management Service – Probation Service

3.14 The Probation Service should:

(a)   In the event of a guilty plea, obtain a PSR pack from the prosecution and any appropriate information from the defence/defendant and report to the court on the same day if possible. An oral report may be appropriate

(b)   If a report (oral or written) really cannot be presented to the court on the same day, obtain a PSR pack from the prosecution and make an appointment with the defendant there and then (or make arrangements to see him in custody) so that the report is ready before the date fixed for sentence

NOTES

1 Crim PR 3.8(2)(b)
2 Crim PR 3.2(2)(a); 3.3(a)
3 Crim PR 3.2(3); 3.3(b); 3.5
4 Crim PR 3.8(1)
5 That criminal cases be dealt with justly in accordance with Crim PR Part 1
6 Crim PR 3.8(2)(a)
7 Crim PR 3.8(2)(b)
8 Consolidated Criminal Practice Direction V.56.4
9 Crim PR 3.11; Consolidated Criminal Practice Direction V.56.3
10 Crim PR 3.3(b); 3.5(3): "Magistrates' courts may give directions that will apply in the Crown Court if the case is to continue there"
11 s.19, 20 and 21 Magistrates' Courts Act 1980, as amended by part 6 schedule 3 Criminal Justice Act 2003 (when commenced) – allocation and sending of cases
12 Part 12 Chapter 5 Criminal Justice Act 2003 Chapter 44
13 Crim PR 3.8(2)(b)
14 Crim PR 1.1(2)(f)
15 Crim PR 3.11; Consolidated Criminal Practice Direction V.56.2: "The form, read with the notes, constitutes a case progression timetable for the effective preparation of the case"
16 Consolidated Criminal Practice Direction V.56.6: "All those directions apply to a case unless the court otherwise orders"
17 Crim PR 3.3(b); 3.5
18 Crim PR 3.2(2)(a); 3.3(a)
19 Crim PR 1.1(2)(d), (e); 3.2(2)(a), (e); 3.3
20 Crim PR 3.8(2)(c)
21 Crim PR 1.1(2)(f)
22 Guidance on reminder systems is available on the CJS Online secure site at http://tinyurl.com/36g7xa (CJS users can obtain the password by emailing ccmf@cjs.gsi.gov.uk)
23 The Managing bail to ensure defendant attendance at court template sets out the roles and responsibilities of each criminal justice agency in relation to the action to be taken when managing bail
24 Crim PR 1.1(2)(d); The Code of Practice for Victims of Crime
25 Consolidated Criminal Practice Direction V.52.1

Chapter 4   Preparation for hearings (trials, Newton hearings and sentence) in the magistrates' courts

READINESS ASSESSMENT

OBJECTIVES

(a) To ensure that everything is done so that the case can be concluded at the next hearing or as soon possible after that[1]
(b) To prepare the case according to the Rules and directions by the court[2]
(c) To tell the court and other parties of anything which might adversely affect the progress of the case and achievement of the overriding objective[3] and to apply promptly for any necessary directions[4]
(d) To certify readiness, if required by the court[5]

ACTIONS

4.1 Compliance with directions

(a)   The parties must comply with directions[6]
(b)   The parties' and the court's case progression officers must each: monitor compliance with all the directions (whether standard or not); make sure that the court is kept informed of events which may affect the progress of the case (including their own compliance or non-compliance with directions); make sure that they can be contacted promptly about the case during ordinary business hours; act promptly and reasonably in response to communications about the case; and, if unavailable, appoint a substitute[7]
(c)   The parties should only ask for a hearing if a problem cannot otherwise be resolved. Unnecessary hearings must be avoided.[8] Even if a matter cannot be resolved by agreement, a direction may be sought and/or made without a hearing[9]

4.2 Pre-sentence readiness check

(a)   Each party should review the statutory provisions relevant to the court's sentencing powers and any relevant Sentencing Guidelines Council guidance and guideline cases and consider, where appropriate, drawing them to the attention of the court
(b)   Prosecutors should undertake a review of the statutory provisions relating to any ancillary orders (such as anti-social behaviour orders, POCA orders, compensation orders) that might be relevant and consider, where appropriate, making applications to the court for such orders and providing drafts of such orders
(c)   If there are technical preconditions to the passing of a particular sentence and/or ancillary order, which will be submitted by a party to be an appropriate sentence and/or ancillary order, that party must ensure that the material to satisfy those preconditions will be available to the court on the day of sentence

4.3 Pre-trial readiness check

Each party must check that:[10]

(a)   All the court's directions (standard and case specific) have been complied with
(b)   Every reasonable step (including, where appropriate, seeking the issue of a witness summons) has been taken to make sure that his witnesses will attend when they are needed
(c)   Appropriate arrangements have been made for the presentation of written or other material

And[11]

- (d) Promptly inform the court and the other parties of anything that may affect the date or duration of the trial or appeal or significantly affect the progress of the case in any other way
- (e) Give a certificate of readiness if required by the court

RESPONSIBILITIES

Police

4.4 The Police should:

- (a) Ensure that the prosecution file is completed and submitted to the prosecutor in accordance with the Manual of Guidance
- (b) Ensure any actions or requests for information from within the prosecution team are acknowledged, responses are promptly given and any problems identified to the CPS immediately
- (c) Respond promptly to correspondence from prosecution

4.5 Prosecution Team

The prosecution team should ensure that the case is fully prepared and ready for trial, having regard to each topic identified in the prescribed case progression forms, guidance notes and directions. What follows is not intended to be an exhaustive list. The prosecution should, in particular, ensure that:

- (a) All directions are complied with[12]
- (b) The case is prepared so as to present the evidence, having regard to the real issues, in the shortest and clearest way
- (c) There is timely disclosure (bearing in mind that only unused material which meets the criteria for disclosure should be disclosed and that the same criteria apply to CCTV recordings as to any other unused material)
- (d) Timely pre-trial applications are made (and, where necessary, determined) in relation to: special measures, bad character and hearsay
- (e) There is compliance with Crim PR Part 33 in relation to expert evidence
- (f) There is timely service, and any necessary pre-trial editing, of transcripts of interviews (whether with witnesses or defendants)
- (g) Witnesses and exhibits will be present at court when needed
- (h) The possibility of a witness failing to attend is anticipated and a timely application made for the issue of a summons
- (i) Arrangements have been made, if appropriate, for staggering the attendance of witnesses
- (j) Interpreters/signers have been arranged
- (k) There is timely service of skeleton arguments and copies/lists of authorities
- (l) If any sound/vision recordings are to be played, the quality is acceptable, a check is made to ensure there is compatible equipment at court and the recordings are provided to the court administration in time to be checked on that equipment
- (m) To consider, before the hearing and as a matter of urgency, the acceptability of a change of plea and/or basis of plea proposed by the defence
- (n) To notify the court immediately of anything which could significantly affect the progress of the case (including intended discontinuance)[13]
- (o) To apply for a direction as soon as it becomes apparent that a problem cannot be resolved without one and, in any event, in time to ensure that the hearing is effective[14]
- (p) A certificate of readiness is served if required by the court[15]

(q)   Any matters relevant to sentence can be put before the court,[16] there and then, if the defendant is convicted or enters a late plea of guilty

(r)   The prosecution file complies with the Manual of Guidance and the prosecution advocate is fully briefed so that he has the material and authority to deal with everything which may arise at the hearing

(s)   Should the defence serve s.9 statements upon the prosecution, seeking agreement to avoid the attendance of a witness, ensure careful consideration is given as to whether the witness should be required to attend so that only those witnesses who are needed in relation to the real issue(s) attend court. The defence and court should immediately be informed of any change

Witness Care Unit

4.6   The Witness Care Unit should:

(a)   Notify witnesses of hearing date immediately, tell the CPS of the notification and maintain contact with witnesses

(b)   Use the needs assessment to identify needs and inform the court

(c)   Use the Contact Directory to provide tailored interventions to secure attendance at court

(d)   At once inform the CPS if a witness appears to be unwilling to attend court so that timely application may be made for a witness summons

(e)   Provide the Witness Service with information on witnesses attending court, any special measures and details of any changes in circumstances

(f)   Keep victims/witnesses informed of special measures and the progress of the case

(g)   Share relevant information about victims and witnesses (e.g. reluctance of witness to attend court, changes in availability, difficulties caused by disability or childcare commitments) with the prosecution team

Defence Case Progression Function

4.7   The defence should ensure that the case is fully prepared and ready for trial, having regard to each topic identified in the prescribed case progression forms, guidance notes, and directions. What follows is not intended to be an exhaustive list. The defence should, in particular, ensure that:

(a)   All directions are complied with[17]

(b)   To prepare the case so as to present the evidence, having regard to the real issue(s), in the shortest and clearest way

(c)   There is timely application for further disclosure[18] (bearing in mind the precondition of the service of a defence statement and that only unused material which meets the criteria for disclosure should be disclosed and that the same criteria apply to CCTV recordings as to any other unused material)

(d)   Timely pre-trial applications are made (and, where necessary, determined) in relation to: special measures, bad character and hearsay

(e)   There is compliance with Crim PR Part 33 and a timely application for public funding in relation to expert evidence

(f)   There is timely service, and any necessary pre-trial editing, of transcripts of interviews (whether with witnesses or defendants)

(g)   Witnesses and exhibits will be present at court when needed

(h)   The possibility of a defence witness failing to attend is anticipated and a timely application made for the issue of a summons

(i)   Arrangements have been made, if appropriate, for staggering the attendance of defence witnesses

(j)   Interpreters/signers have been arranged

(k)   There is timely service of skeleton arguments and copies/lists of authorities

(l)   If any sound/vision recordings are to be played, the quality is acceptable, a check is made to ensure there is compatible equipment at court and the recordings are provided to the court administration in time to be checked on that equipment

(m)   The court is informed of any special arrangements which should be made for the defendant, having regard to his needs

(n)   The acceptability of a proposed change of plea and/or basis of plea is discussed with the prosecution, before the hearing and as a matter of urgency

(o)   The witness requirements are proactively reconsidered so that only those witnesses who are needed in relation to the real issue(s) attend court. The prosecution and court should immediately be informed of any change

(p)   The court is notified immediately of anything which could significantly affect the progress of the case (including an intention to plead guilty on an acceptable basis)[19]

(q)   Application is made for a direction as soon as it becomes apparent that a problem cannot be resolved without one and, in any event, in time to ensure that the hearing is effective[20]

(r)   The defendant is notified of the time, date and place of the hearing

(s)   The court and CPS are notified if the defendant is in custody to another court (providing sufficient details for a Home Office Production Order to be obtained)

(t)   A certificate of readiness is served if required by the court[21]

(u)   Any matters relevant to sentence can be put before the court,[22] there and then, if the defendant is convicted or enters a late plea of guilty

(v)   The defence advocate is fully briefed so that he has the material to deal with everything which may arise at the hearing

Court Case Progression Officer (CPO)

4.8   The Court Case Progression Officer should:

(a)   Monitor directions[23] made by the court and, in the event of non-compliance, refer to the court, if appropriate

(b)   Ensure that any communication received from the parties is dealt with promptly

(c)   Check readiness and take appropriate action. Any application to vacate a trial to be referred to a DJ(MC), Bench Chairman, Justices' Clerk or Deputy Justices' Clerk in accordance with local arrangements

(d)   Refer the matter to the court for a decision on whether the matter should be listed for further directions

(e)   Remind the defendant of the hearing time, date and venue, where agreed locally

(f)   If any sound/vision recordings are to be played, check there is compatible equipment at court. The parties should be responsible for checking the quality of their recordings and providing them to the court administration in a timely manner so they can be checked by the court administration on that equipment before the hearing

(g)   Ensure that interpreters/signers[24] for defence witnesses are warned to attend if appropriate

(h)   If certificates of readiness are required by the court, provide blank forms to the parties

Witness Service

4.9   The Witness Service should:

(a)   Provide pre-court visits for witnesses when referred and where resources allow[25]

(b)   Share relevant information about victims and witnesses (e.g. reluctance of witness to attend court, changes in availability, difficulties caused by disability or childcare commitments) with the prosecution/defence team

NOTES

1 Crim PR 3.8(1); 3.9(1)-(2)
2 Crim PR 1.2
3 That criminal cases be dealt with justly in accordance with Crim PR Part 1
4 Crim PR 3.3(b)
5 Crim PR 3.9(3)
6 Crim PR 3.9(2)(a)
7 Crim PR 3.4(4)(e)
8 Crim PR 3.2(2)(f)
9 Crim PR 3.5(2)(b)-(d), (e)
10 Crim PR 3.9(2)(a)-(c)
11 Crim PR 3.9(2)(d); 3.9(3)
12 Crim PR 3.9(2)(a)
13 Crim PR 3.9(2)(d)
14 Crim PR 3.6(2)
15 Crim PR 3.9(3)
16 Crim PR 1.1(2)(f)
17 Crim PR 3.9(2)(a)
18 S.8 CPIA
19 Crim PR 3.9(2)(d)
20 Crim PR 3.6(2)
21 Crim PR 3.9(3)
22 Crim PR 1.1(2)(f)
23 The Court CPO can monitor compliance by the prosecution/defence with directions by use of the PROGRESS case management tool, following rollout
24 Guidance on the selection and treatment of interpreters within the criminal justice system can be found at the following site: http://tinyurl.com/34le2u
25 HMCS has piloted the use of a DVD, Going to Court – witnesses, as a method of informing defence and prosecution witnesses on what to expect when attending court

Chapter 5   Trial, Newton hearing and sentence[1]

OBJECTIVES

(a) To achieve the overriding objective of dealing with the case justly[2]
(b) To ensure that the hearing is effective and proceeds without delay on the day when it is listed
(c) To ensure that the case is dealt with efficiently, expeditiously and proportionately[3] with the live evidence being confined to the real, disputed issue(s)[4]

ACTIONS

5.1 Case management on the day of the hearing

(a)   The parties should, before the hearing begins, actively assist the court to manage the case. The parties should not wait to be required to do so.[5] This means that, having reconsidered the case and any developments since earlier directions were given, the parties should be able to:

■   Explicitly identify the real issue(s); and
■   Provide the court with:

(i)   A list of the witnesses who will be called "live" to give evidence, in the order in which they will be called

- (ii) A list of any other material which will be made available to the court in the presentation of the case
- (iii) Agreement in relation to the way in which undisputed evidence is to be adduced (e.g. by admission or, if by reading a witness statement, reading only those parts which are relevant)
- (iv) Notice of any point of law which could affect the conduct of the hearing
- (v) Details of any special arrangements for the giving of evidence by a witness[6] or the participation of any person, including the defendant[7]
- (vi) A timetable[8] for the hearing (broken down by each witness – examination in chief and cross-examination – and each submission)

- (b) During the hearing, the parties should confine their submissions and questions to the real issue(s) and should be prepared to object if another party starts to explore matters which are irrelevant
- (c) If a witness is required to attend and either is not called or is asked no relevant questions by the party who required his attendance, that party may be required by the court to provide a full explanation
- (d) If the defendant fails to attend, the court will decide whether to proceed in his absence[9]
- (e) If a witness fails to attend court, the party intending to call that witness should determine with the other parties whether the evidence can be agreed or whether he can proceed regardless. If not, the party calling the witness must decide whether to apply to the court for an adjournment and/or a witness summons. He should expect to be required to provide detailed reasons for the witness's non-attendance, whether difficulties were foreseen and the prospects of a witness attending, should the case be adjourned
- (f) If a hearing is ineffective, the parties must be prepared to provide to the court a full explanation and identify the person responsible[10]

5.2 Sentence and committal for sentence

- (a) Where the defendant wishes other offences to be taken into consideration, the offences should be set out in writing, signed and put before the court. The police should be notified about what TICs have been accepted. If a defendant rejects previously admitted TICs, the CPS file should be clearly marked and consideration given to prosecuting the now denied offences
- (b) The parties must expect the court to proceed to sentence as soon as possible. If a pre-sentence report is required, the Probation Service should consider preparation of a fast delivery report where appropriate. Where a PSR has been prepared for a previous case involving the defendant, sufficient information may be available for sentencing purposes. Where a PSR is required a PSR pack should be given to the Probation Service officer at court on the same day to enable preparation of reports where practicable
- (c) Where the court's sentencing powers are insufficient, the court will consider committing the defendant for sentence

  - (i) Cases requiring pre-sentence report(s) or other reports should be identified and the reports prepared in readiness for the hearing in the Crown Court
  - (ii) The court administration should ensure an accurate memorandum of conviction is submitted to the Crown Court

RESPONSIBILITIES

Prosecution Advocate

5.3   In addition to preparing and conducting the case in compliance with the Rules and the guidance in the "actions" above, the prosecution advocate should:

(a)   Consider making an application to proceed in absence if the defendant does not attend

(b)   Check that prosecution witnesses are present when required and meet them[11] to answer any questions they may have about court procedures and to give an indication, where possible, of how long they will have to wait before giving evidence

(c)   Where a witness has not attended, consider making an application for the issue of a summons. The advocate must be in a position to inform the court of the history of contact with the witness

(d)   Endorse the prosecution file with details of the outcome, any directions made and record the next date of hearing or sentence

(e)   Ensure that any requests or actions are brought to the attention of the prosecution team for action

(f)   Where a pre-sentence report is requested, in the event of conviction, ensure the PSR pack is given to the Probation Service officer at court on the same day to enable preparation of reports where practicable

(g)   If the hearing is cracked or ineffective, complete the Cracked and Ineffective Trial Monitoring Form recording the reason for this and place the form before the court for consideration before leaving the court

(h)   Keep the witnesses informed of the progress of the case[12] and apply to the court for their release as soon as practicable if the trial is "cracked" or ineffective. If the trial "cracks", the witnesses should remain at the court if there might be a Newton hearing. If the trial is ineffective, the witnesses should be asked to remain at court while a new date is fixed

Police/enforcement officers

5.4   The Police/enforcement officers should:

Use every effort to serve witness summonses and execute warrants promptly

Witness Care Unit

5.5   The Witness Care Unit should:

(a)   Ensure that the tailored interventions are available to secure victims and witnesses attendance at court and provide the support required

(b)   Ensure victims and witnesses are notified of any future hearing date and are informed of the outcome of the hearing[13]

(c)   Thank victims and witnesses for their participation

Defence Advocate

5.6   In addition to preparing and conducting the case in compliance with the Rules and the guidance in the "actions" above the defence advocate should:

(a)   If the defendant fails to attend, consider whether his professional duty is to remain and to represent the defendant during the course of any trial in absence

(b)   Check that defence witnesses are present when required and meet them[14]

(c)   Where a witness has not attended, consider making an application for the issue of a summons. The advocate must be in a position to inform the court of the history of contact with the witness

(d)   Be ready to present plea in mitigation if the defendant is convicted or enters a late plea of guilty

(e)   Endorse the defence file with details of the outcome, any directions made and record the next date of hearing or sentence

(f)   Ensure that any requests or actions are brought to the attention of the defence team for action

(g)   If the hearing is cracked or ineffective, complete the form recording the reason for this and place the form before the court for consideration before leaving the court

(h)   Be prepared to make a quantified and supported application for a defendant's costs order in a specific sum if the defendant is acquitted

Magistrates' Courts Administration

5.7   Court Managers should:

Ensure that audio/video/DVD playback facilities are available for all courts centres where trials take place

5.8   The Court administration should:

(a)   Deal promptly with the preparation and issue of warrants within local and/or national targets

(b)   If the hearing is cracked/ineffective, ensure that the "Cracked and Ineffective Trial Monitoring Form" is completed by the advocates, recording the reasons for the crack/ineffectiveness. The form should be placed before the court for approval before the advocates leave the court

Witness Service

5.9   The Witness Service should:

(a)   Provide support to witnesses during the day and if necessary accompany witnesses to the court room where resources allow

(b)   Where appropriate, share information about victims and witnesses (e.g. reluctance of witness to attend court, changes in availability, difficulties caused by disability or childcare commitments) with the prosecution/defence team

(c)   Bring to the attention of the relevant advocate victim and witness needs not identified elsewhere

(d)   Ensure witness safety and security is considered by the court and that the "Witness security at court" guidance is followed

National Offender Management Service – Productions from Prison Custody

5.10 PECS (or the Prison Service, in the case of Category A prisoners) should:

(a)   Ensure that all persons in custody are produced at the court when required and taken to each court room promptly

(b)   Notify the court administration immediately of any problems anticipated or arising in respect of the production of persons in custody

National Offender Management Service – Probation Service

5.11 The Probation Service should:

(a)   Obtain a PSR pack from the prosecution and any appropriate information from the defence/defendant and report to the court on the same day if possible. An oral report may be appropriate

(b)   If a report (oral or written) really cannot be presented to the court on the same day, make an appointment with the defendant there and then (or make arrangements to see him in custody) so that the report is ready before the date fixed for sentence

NOTES

1 This refers to sentencing which cannot be done at the first hearing
2 Crim PR 1.1
3 Crim PR 1.1(2)(e), (g)
4 Crim PR 3.2(2)(a), (e); 3.3(a)
5 Crim PR 1.2(1); 3.3(a)
6 Crim PR 3.10(d); Consolidated Criminal Practice Direction III.29.1-3
7 Crim PR 3.10(e); Consolidated Criminal Practice Direction III.30.1-18
8 Crim PR 3.10(i); *R. v Jisl* [2004] EWCA Crim 696
9 9 Crim PR 3.8(2)(a); Consolidated Criminal Practice Direction I.13.3(c), 1.13.17-19
10 Crim PR 3.8(2)(e)
11 The prosecution should consider staggering the attendance time of witnesses, if this can be done without risking the progress of the case
12 Crim PR 1.1(2)(d)
13 6.7 Code of Practice for Victims of Crime
14 The defence should consider staggering the attendance time of witnesses, if this can be done without risking the progress of the case

Chapter 6   *Sending, committal, or transfer to the Crown Court for trial*

OBJECTIVE

To enable appropriate cases to be committed, sent or transferred to the Crown Court as soon as possible and to give directions so that they may be concluded there without undue delay

ACTIONS

6.1 Sending cases triable only on indictment[1]

(a)   The defence must expect to be required to give an indication of the likely plea[2] and prepare accordingly

(b)   If a guilty plea is indicated, the parties may apply for directions in relation to the service of papers and indictment, the preparation of a PSR and any other matters so that sentence may be passed at the first hearing in the Crown Court. If such a case requires management in the Crown Court (for example, to determine any issue arising out of a basis of plea or to decide whether a PSR is unnecessary) a party may apply for that matter to be decided, by hearing or otherwise, in accordance with local listing practice

(c)   Unless a preliminary hearing would automatically be held in accordance with the practice set by the Resident Judge, the parties should consider whether a preliminary hearing would further the overriding objective (having regard to the guidance notes accompanying the prescribed case management form). If it would, application should be made for a direction that a preliminary hearing be held on a date fixed in accordance with local listing practice

(d)   The parties should complete the prescribed case management forms[3] and actively consider, by particular reference to the real issue(s), whether the standard directions[4] should be varied or supplemented and, if they should, make application accordingly[5]

6.2 Committal to Crown Court for Trial

(a)   Where the court declines jurisdiction or the defendant elects Crown Court trial, unless the transfer provisions apply, the prosecution will be required to prepare the case for committal. If the committal cannot take place there and then, the prosecution will apply for an adjournment for the preparation of committal papers. In applying for an adjournment the prosecution should ensure that the application is for the shortest possible period

(b) After considering any representations by the parties, the court will decide whether to adjourn for committal and if so for how long
The procedure will then be as follows:

(i) There will normally be locally agreed timescales within which the police should provide the prosecution with the committal papers

(ii) In Full Code cases the key evidence should have been obtained before charge. In Threshold Test cases, the CPS will need to review the case upon receipt of the further evidence from the police. Tighter timescales will apply where the defendant is in custody

(iii) Obtaining the evidence (the police) and reviewing the evidence (the CPS) may need to be expedited

(iv) In all cases, the papers should be with the prosecution in good time to enable the prosecution to prepare the case for committal and to serve the papers on the defence sufficiently in advance of the hearing

(v) The defence must decide whether to concede there is a prima facie case and agree to committal without consideration of the evidence or to require the evidence to be considered by the court. If there is to be a contested committal hearing it is the responsibility of the defence to advise the court in advance so that either a new date can be fixed for the committal or in certain circumstances it may be possible for this to take place on the original hearing date

(vi) Timescales are subject to the length of any adjournment granted by the court

(c) If the court commits the case to the Crown Court for trial:

(i) The parties should complete the prescribed case management forms[6] and actively consider, by particular reference to the real issue(s), whether the standard directions[7] should be varied or supplemented and, if they should, make application accordingly[8]

(ii) the defence must expect to be required to give an indication of the likely plea[9] and prepare accordingly

6.3 Transfer of case

(a) The prosecution should serve a notice of transfer and draft indictment upon the court. The case is automatically transferred to the Crown Court and, subject to certain exceptions,[10] the jurisdiction of the magistrates' courts ceases

(b) The parties should complete the prescribed case management forms (which are the same as for committals for trial)[11] and actively consider, with particular reference to the real issue(s), whether the standard directions should be varied or supplemented and, if they should, make application accordingly[12]

RESPONSIBILITIES

Prosecution

6.4 The Prosecution Advocate should:

(a) Actively consider the needs of the case, having regard to the real issue(s), consider the standard directions and apply for such variation or additional directions as are needed to further the overriding objective

(b) Ensure that all directions (including those relating to listing) are communicated to the prosecution case progression officer

(c)   Actively consider whether any further investigation or other action is necessary (which may include responding to requests by the defence) and cause them to be pursued to a set timescale

(d)   Ensure that the defence has been served with the material to which they are entitled

Witness Care Unit

6.5 The Witness Care Unit should:

Ensure victims and witnesses have been notified of the outcome of the hearing and the next hearing date

Defence

6.6 The defence advocate should:

(a)   Actively consider the needs of the case, having regard to the real issue(s), consider the standard directions and apply for such variation or additional directions as are needed to further the overriding objective

(b)   Ensure that all directions (including those relating to listing) are communicated to the defence case progression officer

(c)   Actively consider whether any further investigation or other action is necessary and, if so, cause it to be pursued to a set timescale

Magistrates' Courts Administration

6.7 The Court administration should:

(a)   Deal promptly with the preparation of warrants within local and/or national targets

(b)   Deal promptly with the sending of cases to the Crown Court

(c)   Ensure that the notice of transfer is sent to the Crown Court

(d)   Send case progression forms to the Crown Court where necessary

Case Progression Officers

6.8 The case progression officers nominated[13] by each of the parties and by the court must monitor[14] all the directions (which means that they must find out what they are) and make sure that the court is kept informed of events that may affect the progress of the case[15]

National Offender Management Service – Productions from Prison Custody

6.9 PECS (or the Prison Service, in the case of Category A prisoners) should:

(a)   Ensure that all persons in custody are produced at the court when required and taken to each court room promptly

(b)   Notify the court administration immediately of any problems anticipated or arising in respect of the production of persons in custody

NOTES

1 s 51 Crime and Disorder Act 1998
2 Crim PR 3.8(2)(b)
3 Crim PR 3.11; Consolidated Criminal Practice Direction V.56.3
4 Consolidated Criminal Practice Direction V.56.6: "All those directions apply to a case unless the court otherwise orders"
5 Crim PR 3.3(b); 3.5(3): "Magistrates' courts may give directions that will apply in the Crown Court if the case is to continue there"

6 Crim PR 3.11; Consolidated Criminal Practice Direction V.56.3
7 Consolidated Criminal Practice Direction V.56.6: "All those directions apply to a case unless the court otherwise orders"
8 Crim PR 3.3(b); 3.5(3): "Magistrates' courts may give directions that will apply in the Crown Court if the case is to continue there"
9 Crim PR 3.8(2)(b)
10 Exceptions include bail and legal aid
11 Crim PR 3.11; Consolidated Criminal Practice Direction V.56.3
12 Crim PR 3.3(b); 3.5(3): "Magistrates' courts may give directions that will apply in the Crown Court if the case is to continue there"
13 Crim PR 3.4(1)(a)
14 The Court CPO can monitor compliance by the prosecution/defence with directions by use of the PROGRESS case management tool, following rollout
15 Crim PR 3.4(4)(a)-(b)

Appendix A   Listing of cases (Section 16 of the Crown Court Manual)

This section of the Crown Court Manual is issued under and with the authority of the Lord Chief Justice.

■ It sets out the principles applicable to listing in the Crown and magistrates' courts.
■ It supports the Criminal Procedure Rules 2005 which introduce new principles of case management to criminal cases. The changes made emphasise the fact:

  − that judges will be required to make firm arrangements for the listing of cases at the Plea and Case Management Hearing (or earlier)
  − that parties must comply with the directions and timetable then set so that cases are ready to be heard in accordance with that timetable
  − that cases commence promptly at the appointed hour in accordance with that timetable.

■ It sets out the new arrangements for the assignment of judges to cases.
■ It emphasises the importance, recently stressed by the Court of Appeal, of ensuring that no short hearings in other cases interrupt the prompt commencement or continuation of trials each day at the time appointed.

Contents

1. Introduction
2. Principles of listing
3. Setting the listing practice at each court centre

1.   INTRODUCTION

Listing is a judicial responsibility and function. The overall purpose is to ensure that, as far as possible, all cases are brought to a hearing or trial in accordance with the interests of justice, that the resources available for criminal justice are deployed as effectively as possible, and that, consistent with the needs of the victims, witnesses of the prosecution and the defence and defendants, cases are heard by an appropriate judge or bench with the minimum of delay.

The Concordat[1] states that judges are responsible for deciding on the assignment of cases to particular courts and the listing of those cases before particular judges, working with HMCS. Therefore:

(a) The Presiding Judges of the Circuit have the overall responsibility for listing on each Circuit/Region. As set out at paragraph 4(2) below, certain cases in the Crown Court must be referred to the Presiding Judges for directions; the Presiding Judges will be supported by a Regional Listing co-ordinator.

(b) In the Crown Court, subject to the supervision of the Presiding Judges, the Resident Judge at each Crown Court is responsible for listing at his/her Crown Court centre; the Resident Judge is responsible (following guidance or directions issued by the Lord Chief Justice and by the Senior Presiding Judge and Presiding Judges under paragraph IV 33 of the Consolidated Practice Direction) for determining the Listing Practice to be followed at that centre, for prioritising the needs of one case against another and deciding upon which date a case is listed and before which judge.

(c) The Listing Officer in the Crown Court is responsible for carrying out the day-to-day operation of Listing Practice under the direction of the Resident Judge. The Listing Officer at each Crown Court centre has one of the most important functions at that Crown Court and makes a vital contribution to the efficient running of that Crown Court and to the efficient operation of the administration of criminal justice.

(d) In the magistrates' court, the judicial members of the Justices Issues Group for each Area are responsible for determining the Listing Practice in that Area. The day-to-day operation of that Listing Practice is the responsibility of the Justices Clerk with the assistance of the Listing Officer.

(e) The Local Criminal Justice Board in each CJS Area is responsible for delivering the policies and aims of the National Criminal Justice Board by:

- Improving the performance of the local criminal justice agencies
- Improving provisions for victims, witnesses and others involved
- Improving public confidence

2.   PRINCIPLES OF LISTING

Lord Steyn summarised the guiding principle which must be followed:[2]

> "There must be fairness to all sides. In a criminal case this requires the court to consider a triangulation of interests. It involves taking into account the position of the accused, the victim and his or her family, and the public."

When setting the Listing Practice, the Resident Judge or the judicial members of the Justices Issues Group should, in addition to following any directions given by the Lord Chief Justice, the Head of Criminal Justice, the Senior Presiding Judge and the Presiding Judges, take into account the overall purpose of listing as set out above and, in addition, the following principles; these are not listed in order of priority or importance.

(a) Meeting the needs of victims and witnesses; each of whom may have differing needs – the young and the vulnerable require particular attention.

(b) Ensuring the timely trial of cases so that justice is not delayed.

- In general, each case should be tried within as short a time of its arrival in the court as is consistent with the interests of justice, the needs of victims and witnesses, and with the proper preparation by the prosecution and defence of their cases in accordance with the directions and timetable set before or at the Plea and Case Management Hearing.
- Priority should be accorded to the trial of young defendants, and cases where there are vulnerable or young witnesses.
- Custody time limits should be observed.
- Priority may also be accorded to other types of case.

(c) Providing for certainty, and/or as much advance notice as possible, as to the trial date.

(d) Seeing that a judge or bench with any necessary authorisation and of appropriate experience is available to try each case and, wherever desirable, there is judicial continuity.

(e) Taking into account the position of the defendant as to whether he/she is in custody or on bail.

(f) Striking a balance in the use of resources, by taking account of:

- The efficient deployment of the judiciary in the Crown Court, and in the magistrates' court the proper and efficient deployment of the judiciary as is consonant with the need for magistrates' competences to be maintained and the Venne criteria to be followed.
- The proper use of the court rooms available at the court.
- The provision in long cases for adequate reading time for the judiciary.
- The facilities in the available court rooms, including the security needs (such as a secure dock), size and equipment, such as video link facilities.
- The desirability of timing Plea and Case Management Hearings so that the trial advocates can attend.
- The proper use of those who attend the Crown Court as jurors.
- The need to return those sentenced to custody as soon as possible after the sentence is passed, and to facilitate the efficient operation of the prison escort contract.

(g) Providing:

- the defendant and the prosecution with the advocate of their choice where this does not result in undue delay to the trial of the case.[3]
- for the efficient deployment of advocates, lawyers and designated case workers of the Crown Prosecution Service, and other prosecuting authorities, and of the resources available to the independent legal profession, for example by trying to group certain cases together.

(h) Meeting the need for special security measures for category A and other high-risk defendants.

(i) Taking into account the impact of policies, targets and initiatives of:

- Her Majesty's Government and its agencies.
- Local Authorities, the Criminal Justice Board for the Area, the Chief Constable or Chief Crown Prosecutor for the Area and other local bodies.

Although the Listing Practice at each court centre will take into account these principles, the practice adopted will vary from court to court depending particularly on:

- The number of court rooms and the facilities available
- Location
- Workload – its volume and type
- The available number of advocates and lawyers
- The proximity of the prison, particularly for women, juveniles, and young offenders
- The surrounding geography and public transport facilities
- The effective trial rate, after allowing for cracked, ineffective and vacated trials

What is plain is that a Listing Practice that will operate successfully in a small two-court centre is unlikely to suit the needs of a metropolitan multi-court centre and vice versa. It may also mean that on occasions the Listing Practice set may result in the judge working in chambers on his judicial work.

3. SETTING THE LISTING PRACTICE AT EACH COURT CENTRE

(a) Determination

(i) The Resident Judge at each Crown Court and the judicial members of the Justices Issues Group in each Area will, in relation to the Crown Court and magistrates' courts respectively, set overall Listing Practice in a local area in accordance with the objectives and considerations set out above.

(ii) The Resident Judge, or the judicial members of the Justices Issues Group, as the case may be, will consider representations made by local criminal justice agencies and representatives of the defence and witnesses, in the setting of the Listing Practice and in the periodic reviews of that Listing Practice. Consultation with Local Criminal Justice Boards regarding local listing issues and the impact on cracked and ineffective trials should also take place.

(iii)   It will be for the Resident Judge, or the judicial members of the Justices Issues Group, to consider whether to do this by seeking comments in writing on the draft Listing Practice, or by convening a special meeting, or by discussing the issues at the court users' meetings referred to below, or otherwise conducting the consultation in the manner he or they consider best.

(b) **Monthly analysis of the performance**

(i)   The Court Manager, Listing Officer and/or Case Progression Officer should each month, or at such other period as may be specified by the Resident Judge or Bench Chairman and Justices Clerk:

■   Review the causes of ineffective, cracked and vacated trials and provide to the Resident Judge (or the Bench Chairman and Justices' Clerk and District Judge, as the case may be) an analysis of each case or specified categories of case and the lessons to be learnt.

■   In the Crown Court, provide to and discuss with the Resident Judge the list of any outstanding cases which are older than 20 weeks, or such other shorter period as is specified by the Resident Judge. This list can be provided by the Crest RAGE report.

(ii)   Monthly (or other periodic) meetings should be also arranged between the Court Manager, Listing Officer or Case Progression Officer and local court users (including the CPS, Witness Care Unit, the Witness Service, police and defence solicitors (where possible)) and representatives of the Local Criminal Justice Board to discuss:

■   The analysis of cracked, ineffective and vacated trials (based on enquiry into the matters disclosed by the form completed after the enquiry conducted by the judge or the chairman presiding over the court for that case).

■   The action that might be taken to address any similar problems in advance of the trial and to improve the provisions for witnesses.

The discussion of the analysis of the reasons for cracked, ineffective and vacated trials should be minuted, and copies of the minutes should be sent to all the parties to the cases discussed. The outcome of these discussions may provide information for the Resident Judge and judicial members of the Justices Issues Group respectively to contribute to his/her/their review of Listing Practice.

(c) **User Meetings**

(i)   The Resident Judge or the representatives of the Justices Issues Group respectively (such as the Justices' Clerk and/or legal advisers) will hold periodic court user meetings with representatives of local prosecutors or other criminal justice agencies and representatives of the defence.

(ii)   One of the agenda items will normally be the operation of the Listing Practice.

(d) **Resolution of difficulties**

(i)   Where difficulties arise, whether around listing generally or regarding specific cases, which cannot be resolved by the Listing Officer, the matter should be referred for consideration:

■   In the Crown Court, to the Resident Judge or the judge assigned to a specific case.

■   In the magistrates' courts, to the Justices' Clerk, if it relates to a specific case, or, if it relates to more general issues, to the judicial members of the Justices Issues Group and then, if necessary, to the Area Judicial Forum.

(ii)   Where resolution of disagreement, either in relation to the Crown Court or magistrates' courts cannot be reached locally, as set out in sub-paragraph (i), the issue should be referred without delay to the Presiding Judges or the Senior Presiding Judge.

NOTES

1 The agreement reached between the Lord Chief Justice and the Secretary of State for Constitutional Affairs and Lord Chancellor set out in statement to the House of Lords on 26 January 2004.

2 House of Lords – Attorney General's Reference No.3 of 1999 [2000] UKHL 63.

3 This does not in any way affect applications for changes in representation orders. For that, see the ruling of HH Judge Wakerley QC (as he then was) in *Asghar Ali* which has been circulated by the JSB.

Appendix B   Contents of expedited and evidential charging decision reports and case files (Manual of Guidance)

STRAIGHTFORWARD AND "GUILTY PLEA" CASES

Pre-charge Expedited Report For charging decision – to custody officer or Duty Prosecutor	Post-charge Expedited File For EFH court hearing
MG3/MG3A – Report/Further Report to Crown Prosecutor (for offences where CPS decide charge) MG11(s) – Key witness statement(s) or ROVI (if visually recorded). *If witnessed by police, use MG11 of one officer* MG15 – SDN or verbal summary of admissions (SDN can be written on officer's MG11) *PNC print suspect pre-cons, cautions, etc., including key prosecution witnesses* **Where applicable, include:** MG6 – relevant background information, e.g. Domestic Violence, racist incident, etc. MG13 – Application for Order on Conviction MG6A – Pre-Interview Briefing MG16 – Bad Character/Dangerous Offender MG17 – POCA Review Other compelling evidence, e.g. CCTV, photographs, etc.	MG1 – File front sheet MG4 – Charge sheet MG5 – Case file summary (unless the statements cover all elements of the case) MG6 – Case file information (if there is information for the investigator to record) MG10 – Witness non-availability (PYO only) MG11(s) – All Key witness statement(s) or ROVI (if visually recorded) SDN – may be written on MG15, MG5 or MG11 of officer) *PNC print suspect pre-cons, cautions, etc., including key prosecution witnesses* **Where applicable, include:** MG2 – Special Measures assessment MG3 – Report to Crown Prosecutor (for offences where CPS decide charge) MG3A – Further report to Crown Prosecutor MG4A/B/C – Bail Conditional/Vary/Security/Surety MG7 – Remand application MG8 – Breach of bail conditions MG11 – Other witness statements already taken MG13 – Application for order on conviction MG18 – Offences TIC MG19 – Compensation form (plus supporting documents) Copy of documentary exhibits/photos Crime Report – Hate Crime/Racist Incident, etc.
Once a charging decision has been made, the "Pre-charge Expedited Report" becomes the "Post-charge Expedited File" for court. →	

Pre-charge Expedited Report For charging decision – to custody officer or Duty Prosecutor		Post-charge Expedited File For EFH court hearing
Further Upgrading If a "not-guilty" plea is entered or the defendant is sent to the Crown Court, prepare a Full File.		

CROWN COURT AND NOT GUILTY CASES

Pre-charge Evidential Report For charging decision – to Custody Officer or Duty Prosecutor	Post-charge Evidential File For EAH court hearing	Upgrade to Full File For Crown Court or contested cases
MG3/MG3A – Report/Further Report to Crown Prosecutor (suggest charges) **MG5** – Case summary (unless the statements cover all elements of the case) **MG6** – Case file information disclosure schedules not required at this stage) **MG11(s)** – Key witness statement(s) or ROVI (if visually recorded). If witnessed by police, use MG11 of one officer, summarise evidence of others **MG15** – Interview record: (can be on MG5 or officer's MG11) *PNC print suspect pre-cons, cautions, etc., including key prosecution witnesses* **Where applicable, include:** **MG6A** – Pre-Interview Briefing **MG7** – Remand Application **MG13** – Application for order on conviction **MG16** – Bad Character/Dangerous Offender **MG17** – POCA Review Crime report & incident log Copies of Key documentary exhibits	**MG1** – File front sheet **MG4** – Charge sheet **MG5** – Case file summary (unless MG11(s) cover all elements of case) **MG6** – Case file information **MG10** – Witness non-availability **MG11(s)** – Key witness statement(s) or Index (if visually recorded) **MG12** – Exhibits list *Copies of Key exhibits/photos* **MG15** – Interview record – (can be on MG5, officer's MG11 or MG15) *PNC print suspect pre-cons, cautions, etc., including key prosecution witnesses* **Where applicable, include:** **MG2** – Special Measures assessment **MG3A** – Further report to Crown Prosecutor **MG4A/B/C** – Bail Conditional/Vary/Security/Surety **MG7** – Remand application **MG11** – Other witness statements **MG13** – Application for order on conviction **MG18** – Offences TIC **MG19** – Compensation form plus supporting documents **MG21/21A** – Forensic Crime Report – Hate Crime /Racist Incident, etc.	**MG6C** – Schedule of Non-sensitive unused materials **MG6D** – Schedule of sensitive material **MG6E** – Disclosure officer's report **MG9** – Witness list **MG11** – All other statements **Where applicable, include:** Custody record **MG2** – Special Measures assessment **MG6B** – police officer's disciplinary record **MG21/21A** – Forensic *PNC print suspect pre-cons, cautions, etc., including key prosecution witnesses*

Pre-charge Evidential Report	Post-charge Evidential File	Upgrade to Full File
For charging decision – to Custody Officer or Duty Prosecutor	For EAH court hearing	For Crown Court or contested cases
Once a charging decision has been made, the "Pre-charge Evidential Report" becomes the "Post-charge Evidential File" for court. →		
Further Upgrading? If a Crown Court case or a not guilty plea is likely, a Full File should be commenced.		

Part 2   The Crown Court

INTRODUCTION

What is the Criminal Case Management Framework?

It is a guide for participants involved in criminal case management to help them to prepare and conduct cases in compliance with the Criminal Procedure Rules[1] so that each case is brought to a fair conclusion as quickly as possible. It is not a substitute for the Criminal Procedure Rules or any part of them. The Rules (together with the provisions of the Consolidated Criminal Practice Direction[2]) must be complied with

This third edition of the adult Framework is issued in two parts:

(a) Part 1, the Magistrates' Courts was issued on 26 July 2007 and refers to adult cases in the magistrates' courts; and

(b) Part 2, the Crown Court (this document), covers adult cases in the Crown Court

This Framework does not cover cases involving offenders under the age of 18 years. A separate youth Framework will be issued

The Framework does not cover every possible activity needed for a case to achieve a just and effective outcome. It principally addresses case management. So, for example, it covers the case management role of advocates but not advocacy itself. It seeks to give effect to the Criminal Procedure Rules and the provisions of the Consolidated Criminal Practice Direction. References are made to guidance which is to be found elsewhere in, for example, codes and circulars. The Framework is consistent with s.35 (1) of the Interpretation Act 1976 where references to "he" imply "he or she"

What are the main changes?

- This edition is shorter than the 1st and 2nd editions (contested and uncontested cases are dealt with in one Part)
- It includes good practice recommendations from Resident Judges[3] e.g. reducing the number of unnecessary mention hearings
- It also includes recent changes such as the introduction of the Plea and Sentence document,[4] the introduction of Instructed Advocates[5] and revised guidance to list officers[6]
- There is a new "Useful Links" section
- It is loose-leaf to enable the inclusion of updates

How has the Framework been produced?

The Framework has been produced by CJS practitioners based in OCJR, in consultation with members of the judiciary, the Law Society, the Bar, the Witness Service, and CJS agencies including the CPS, the police, HMCS and NOMS

Who will use the Framework?

- Participants, as they consider how better to prepare and conduct cases in compliance with the Criminal Procedure Rules. The term "participants"[7] includes defendants and their legal advisers. Nothing in the Framework affects the rights of defendants or the professional obligations of legal advisers towards their clients
- Local Criminal Justice Boards
- Inspectorates

How can I access the Framework?

It is available in hard copy from homeoffice@prologuk.com or by calling 0870 241 4680 and online at www.cjsonline.gov.uk/framework as a printable pdf or interactive version

Comments on the Framework

If you have any comments or questions on the content of this Framework please email ccmf@cjs.gsi.gov.uk

NOTES

1 Crim PR Part 1: The Overriding Objective; Part 3: The Case Management Rules http://tinyurl.com/3cwal4
2 http://tinyurl.com/202jvs
3 Letter from the President of the Queen's Bench Division to Presiding Judges and Resident Judges "Suggestions for good practice following the Resident Judges' Conference", 4 June 2007
4 Attorney General's Guidelines on the acceptance of pleas and the prosecutor's role in the sentencing exercise, paragraph C6, as amended
5 Criminal Defence Service (Funding) Order 2007
6 Guidance for List Officers (following recommendations from Resident Judges Conference, November 2006 is available to Crown Court staff on the Ministry of Justice intranet (by selecting the "A – Z" button; clicking on "L" for Learning & Development; and selecting "Business Skills Team")
7 Crim PR 1.2(2)

USEFUL LINKS

We have made it easier for users to access electronic documents with lengthy web addresses by converting the web addresses to "Tiny URL" links. This does not in any way change the original web addresses; it just makes it easier to access information when typing it into your browser

Please enter the Tiny URL exactly as shown below

Attorney General's Guidelines on Disclosure	http://tinyurl.com/2wmgse
Addendum to paragraph C6 of the Attorney General's Guidelines on the Acceptance of pleas and the prosecutor's role in the Sentencing Exercise 2005	http://tinyurl.com/3appvj
Case Management Forms (HMCS website)	http://tinyurl.com/loob9
Code for Crown Prosecutors	http://tinyurl.com/26ogw2
Code of Practice for Victims of Crime, October 2005	http://tinyurl.com/2pdumm
Consolidated Criminal Practice Direction	http://tinyurl.com/2o2jvs
Control and Management of Heavy Fraud and other Complex Criminal Cases	http://tinyurl.com/22x67w
Criminal Procedure Rules	http://tinyurl.com/3cwal4
Crown Court Listing Officer CREST Guidance and Listing Officer Skills Workbook	The Crown Court Listing Officer CREST Guidance and Listing Officer Skills Workbook is available to Crown Court staff on the Ministry of Justice intranet (by selecting the "A–Z" button; clicking on "L" for Learning & Development; and selecting "Business Skills Team")
CJS Online	http://tinyurl.com/32r7zp
CPS/Bar Framework of Principles for Prosecution Advocates in the Crown Court, July 2007	http://tinyurl.com/2qocgl
CPS Homepage	http://tinyurl.com/29dhho
Disclosure: A Protocol for the Control and Management of unused material in the Crown Court	http://tinyurl.com/yutye6
Graduated Fee Payment Protocol, The General Council of the Bar of England and Wales, April 2007	http://tinyurl.com/3cdbbv
HMCS Homepage	http://tinyurl.com/ysbgph
Home Office Circulars	http://tinyurl.com/4lgme
Home Office Homepage	http://tinyurl.com/4pgyj
Joint Effective, Cracked, Ineffective and Vacated Trials in the Crown Court and the Magistrates' courts: Operation Guidance for Monitoring Scheme, Version 3, 1 October 2007	http://tinyurl.com/yntzvv
Ministry of Justice Homepage	http://tinyurl.com/2cl726

National Agreement on Arrangements for the use of Interpreters, Translators and Language Service Professionals in Investigations and Proceedings within the CJS, as revised 2007	http://tinyurl.com/2dusog
Office of Public Sector Information website – Legislation	http://tinyurl.com/zl734
Prosecution Team Guidance Offences to be taken into consideration	http://tinyurl.com/38t716
Prosecution Team Manual of Guidance 2004 Edition	http://tinyurl.com/337zkv
Protocol for Listing Cases where the Welsh Language is used (Wales and Cheshire Region), December 2005	http://tinyurl.com/32j2vo
See also Consolidated Criminal Practice Direction III.23 (Use of the Welsh language in courts in Wales)	
Sentencing Guidelines Council Homepage	http://tinyurl.com/2xahun
Victim Support – Going to Court leaflet for witnesses	http://tinyurl.com/ysf23y
Witness Charter	http://tinyurl.com/2bwl2l
Witness Security at Court guidance (Frontline Matters – an online resource for CJS practitioners)	http://tinyurl.com/yvvwom

The Route Map – (Anticipated) Not Guilty Plea Cases (non-traffic)

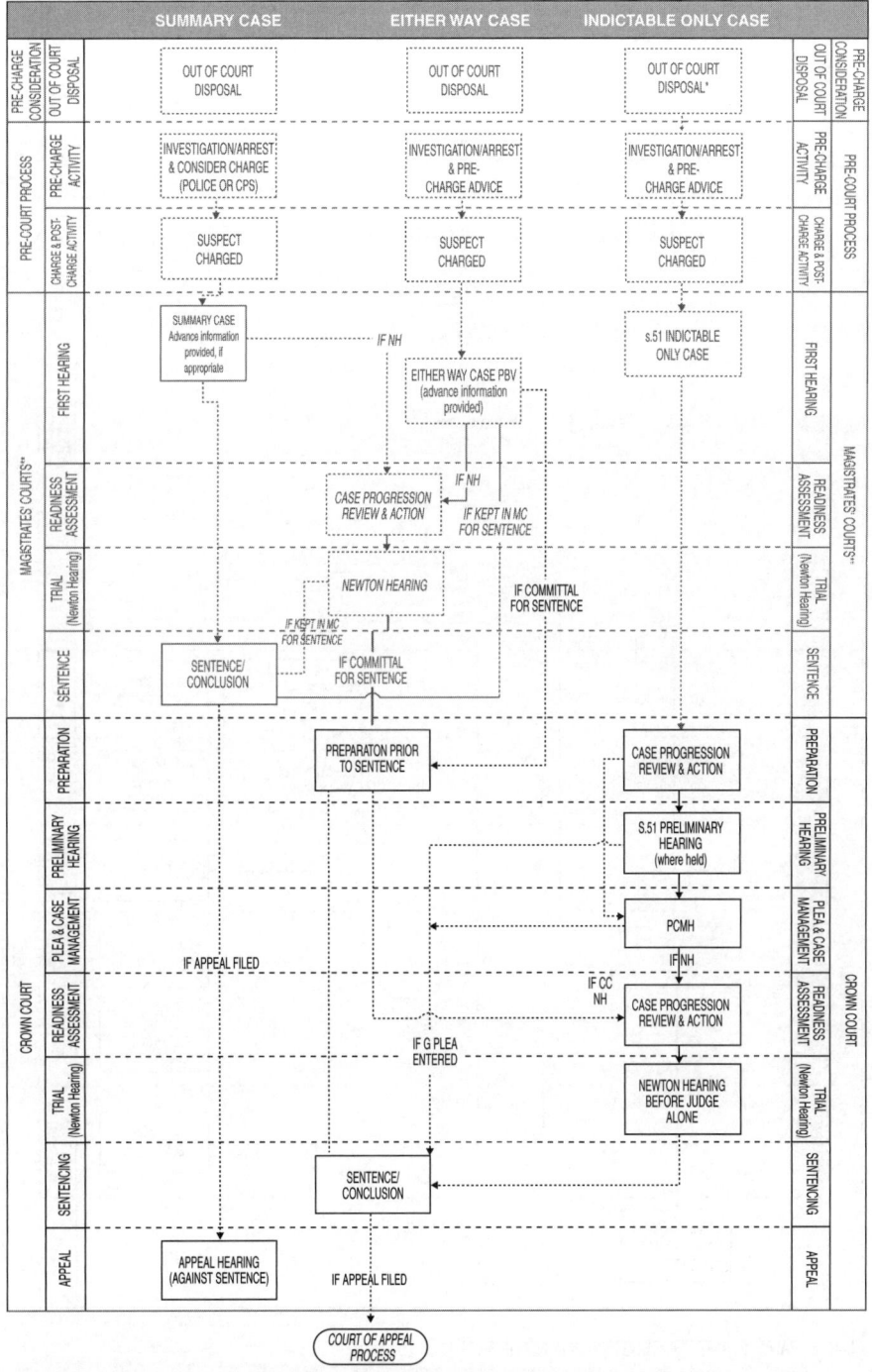

* A SIMPLE CAUTION IS THE ONLY OUT OF COURT DISPOSAL POSSIBLE IN INDICTABLE ONLY CASES AND MUST BE
  REFERRED TO THE CPS
** MAGISTRATES' COURT PROCESS IS CONTAINED IN PART 1

The Route Map – Not Guilty Plea Cases (non-traffic)

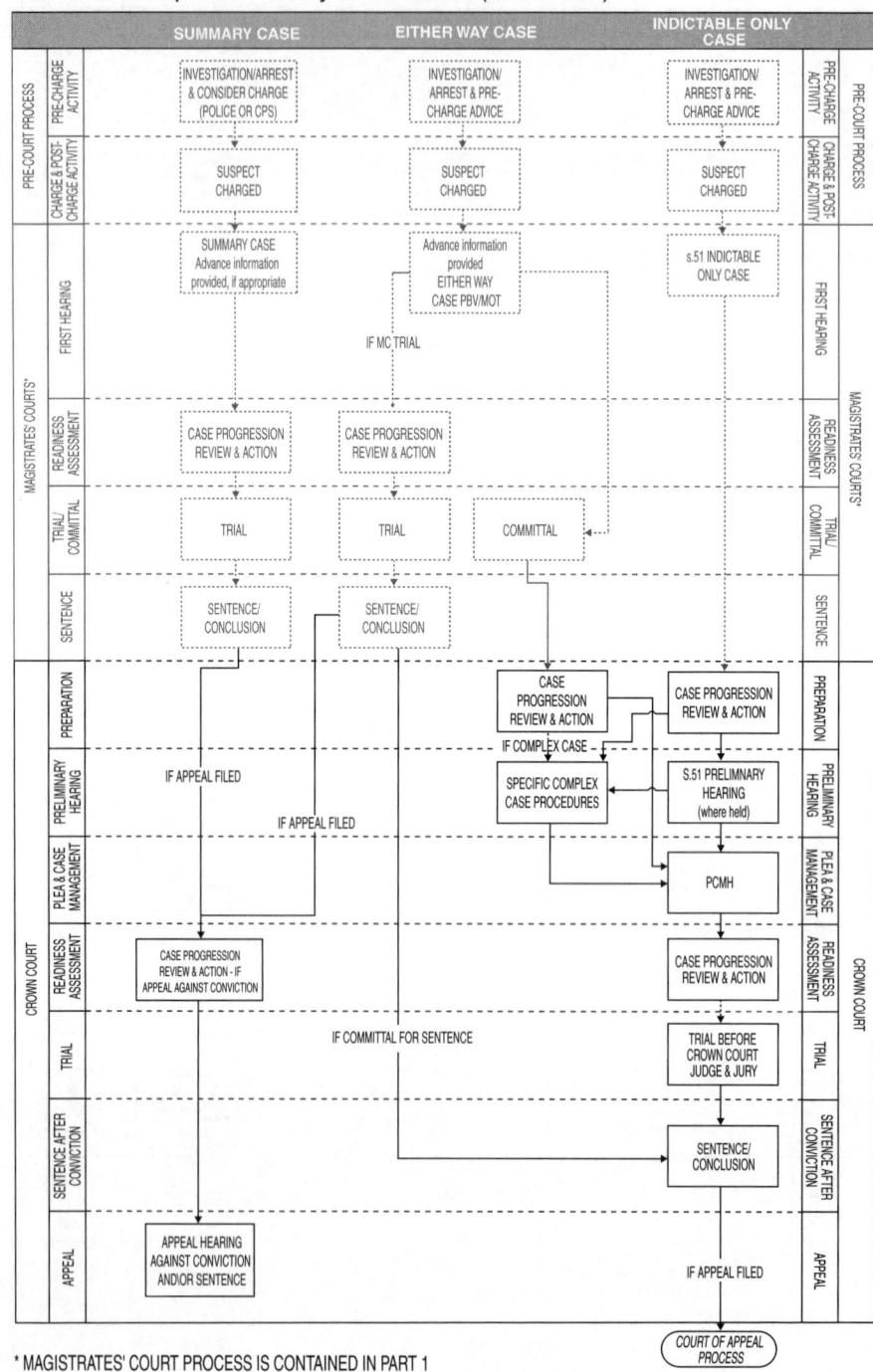

Chapter 1   Preparation before the first hearing in the Crown Court

OBJECTIVES

The case is managed in accordance with the overriding objective.[1] Cases can reach the Crown Court in a variety of ways but participants must always be prepared so that the first hearing is effective in compliance with the Crim PR and, in particular, to ensure that at the first hearing:

(i)   The plea can be taken (when this has not already happened) or, if this cannot occur, the defendant's[2] likely plea must be indicated

(ii) The real issue(s), the agreed evidence and the witnesses whose attendance is not required are identified[3]

(iii) The case (including sentence) can be completed there and then if there is to be a guilty plea or, if this is not achievable, directions[4] can be given to conclude it at the next hearing or as soon as possible thereafter.[5] If there is to be a not guilty plea, directions are given to progress the case expeditiously

ACTIONS

1.1   Compliance with directions made in the magistrates' courts

(a)   The parties must comply with the directions made in the magistrates' courts.[6] If directions are not complied with, the parties must expect the court to investigate the reason, identify who was responsible and take appropriate action[7]

(b)   The parties' and the court's CPOs must each monitor compliance with all of the directions (whether standard or not); ensure that the court is kept informed of events which may affect the progress of the case (including their own compliance or non-compliance[8] with directions); ensure that they can be contacted promptly about the case during ordinary business hours; act promptly and reasonably in response to communications about the case and, if unavailable, appoint a substitute[9]

(c)   The parties should ask for a hearing only if a problem cannot otherwise be resolved. Unnecessary hearings must be avoided.[10] If a matter cannot be resolved by agreement, a direction may be sought and/or made without a hearing (including by email, if approved by the court). "Mentions" should be listed only if there is a compelling reason[11]

(d)   Unless a preliminary hearing will automatically occur in accordance with the practice set by the Resident Judge, the parties must consider whether a preliminary hearing will further the overriding objective (having regard to any guidance notes accompanying the prescribed case progression form).[12] An application must be made for a direction that a preliminary hearing be held on a date fixed in accordance with directions of the Resident Judge or local listing practice

1.2   Representation[13]

Defence – Instructed Advocate

(a)   When appropriate, the defence must complete an application for a representation order as soon as practicable after being instructed

(b)   In furtherance of the overriding objective[14] and in order to achieve continuity of representation wherever possible, a single advocate must appear throughout the case for the defence. Where the defendant has the benefit of a representation order, the Instructed Advocate will be the person responsible for the defence case. Where a representation order provides for more than one advocate e.g. leading and junior, there will be an Instructed Advocate for each of these roles

(c)   The identity of the Instructed Advocate (or Advocates) must be notified to the court by the defence before the PCMH. Notification as to the identity of the Instructed Advocate must be in writing by email or by letter

(d)   Where no such prior notification of the Instructed Advocate has been given, this must be given at the PCMH using the prescribed case management form

(e)   The Instructed Advocate must not change unless:

  (i)   A date for trial is fixed at or before the PCMH and the Instructed Advocate is unable to conduct the trial due to his other pre-existing commitments

  (ii)   He is dismissed by the defendant or the defendant's solicitor and he has been granted permission by the court to withdraw from the case

  (iii)   He is required to withdraw because of his professional code of conduct (this may include other conflicting professional obligations)

(f)   Where an Instructed Advocate seeks to withdraw from the case he must:

  (i)   Apply to the court in writing for permission to withdraw or, where the request to withdraw takes place at the PCMH, he must make his application orally

  (ii)   Within seven days of the date of his withdrawal, notify the court in writing of the identity of the replacement Instructed Advocate, where known

(g)   It shall be the responsibility of the Instructed Advocate to claim the fees for the case and pay any substitute advocates who appear for the defence

Prosecution

(h)   The Prosecution must endeavour to identify those cases that are likely to be contested and should select the trial advocate as early as is practicable. In such cases, the trial advocate (whether external counsel or HCA) should be instructed as soon as possible after the case has been sent or committed to the Crown Court and, where possible, at least 14 days before the PCMH, so that any necessary advisory work and case preparation can be undertaken in good time to ensure that the PCMH is effective for the proper and efficient future management of the case.[15] The PCMH should be conducted by the trial advocate or an advocate who is able to make decisions and give the court the assistance which the trial advocate could be expected to give[16]

Court Administration

(i)   The court administration must determine any applications for legal representation which require administrative decisions within 48 hours of receipt[17]

(j)   In setting the listing policy, Resident Judges should ensure that list officers fix cases as far as possible to enable the trial advocate to conduct the PCMH and the trial,[18] as well as considering other issues, such as timeliness and the needs of the witnesses

RESPONSIBILITIES

Police

1.3   The Police must:

    (a)   Ensure that the witnesses' dates to avoid cover the "trial window" when one has been specified by the magistrates' court

    (b)   Keep the victims and witnesses informed of the progress of the case[19]

    (c)   Check whether a Victim Personal Statement has been made or requires updating and, if there is one, pass it to the prosecution team. If there is no Victim Personal Statement, check whether the victim would like the opportunity to make one

    (d)   In Wales, ascertain whether a witness will give evidence in Welsh or English and ensure this is brought to the attention of the court and prosecution team as soon as possible

Prosecution Team

1.4   The prosecution team must:

    (a)   Consider whether there is any unused prosecution material which might reasonably be considered capable of undermining the case for the prosecution or of assisting the case for the accused[20] and, if so, disclose it

    (b)   Review the evidence of all potential witnesses on an ongoing basis to determine the "real issues" and to agree evidence, where possible

    (c)   Prepare the case in compliance with the Crim PR so that the first hearing is effective.

    (d)   Prepare to open the case[21] so that the defendant can be sentenced after a guilty plea

    (e)   Prepare for the possibility that the defendant may be prepared to plead guilty to an alternative or lesser offence. The prosecution must be in a position to take a decision at court without recourse to an adjournment. If counsel has been instructed, he must have authority to make a decision or have access to a CPS lawyer who can instruct him

    (f)   Complete the prescribed case progression forms[22] in compliance with the Crim PR, Consolidated Criminal Practice Direction, and any guidance notes

    (g)   Identify the real issue(s)[23] and apply for any direction[24] needed to achieve the overriding objective[25] and comply with the detailed requirements of Part 3 of the Crim PR

    (h)   Prepare the case so that an early trial date can be fixed

    (i)   Ensure that all appropriate information, available to the prosecution, is before the court.[26] This will include recording any special needs[27] of any of the witnesses, e.g. children and vulnerable or intimidated witnesses, on the back of the MG11 and ensuring that any application for bail or to vary bail conditions can be dealt with without an adjournment. Where appropriate, the prosecution must be in a position to assist the court if reporting conditions are imposed or a surety needs to be taken, by providing details of the appropriate police station and its opening times. The prosecution should identify and prepare any bad character or hearsay applications

    (j)   Expect the court to follow the Protocol issued by the Lord Chief Justice[28] and prepare accordingly where the case is likely to last in excess of four weeks

Witness Care Unit or equivalent unit for other prosecuting agencies

1.5   The Witness Care/equivalent unit must:

    (a)   Obtain the witnesses' dates to avoid and the reasons for non-availability. Where dates to avoid have been obtained for hearing(s) in the magistrates' courts these must be updated prior to the first hearing in the Crown Court

(b)   Ensure that the victims and witnesses have been notified of the next pre-trial hearing date if they wish to attend[29]

(c)   Ensure that the special needs of the witnesses[30] (e.g. children and vulnerable or intimidated witnesses) and any intermediaries are brought to the attention of the prosecution team as soon as they are known. This may include a request to take or update a victim's personal statement. The court must also be notified if there is a vulnerable victim or witness involved in the case

(d)   Provide any victim who is to be called as a witness with a copy of the "Witness in Court" leaflet or current equivalent information leaflet[31]

(e)   In Wales, ascertain whether a witness will give evidence in Welsh or English and ensure that this is brought to the attention of the court and prosecution team as soon as possible

Defence Team

1.6   The defence team must:

(a)   Ensure that any application for a representation order is made as soon as possible and in time for the defendant to be advised and represented before the first hearing

(b)   Take instructions, give advice, and prepare the case in compliance with the Crim PR so that the first hearing is effective. This will include: considering the prosecution evidence, the defendant's antecedents, and any TICs; taking the defendant's instructions (including mitigation if there will or may be a guilty plea); and advising the defendant in relation to: the strength of the prosecution case, credit for a guilty plea, whether he should plead guilty to alternative or lesser offences and bail, where appropriate

(c)   Prepare to mitigate so that the defendant can be sentenced after a guilty plea

(d)   Complete the prescribed case progression forms[32] in compliance with the Crim PR, Consolidated Criminal Practice Direction and any guidance notes

(e)   Serve the defence statement within the statutory time period[33]

(f)   Identify the real issue(s),[34] apply for any direction[35] needed to achieve the overriding objective[36] and comply with the detailed requirements of Part 3 of the Crim PR. There is an ongoing duty to review the evidence of all potential witnesses to determine which can be agreed and which relate to "real issues"

(g)   Prepare so that an early trial date can be fixed

(h)   Ensure that appropriate information is available to the court[37] including any application for bail or to vary bail conditions, so that this can be dealt with without adjournment, and any special needs[38] of defence witnesses, e.g. children and vulnerable or intimidated witnesses. Also consider referral of the witnesses to the Witness Service

(i)   Identify the Instructed Advocate,[39] whereupon the Instructed Advocate must notify his details to the court by email or letter, taking into account any protocol or guidance as to procedure

(j)   Expect the court to follow the Protocol issued by the Lord Chief Justice[40] and prepare accordingly where the case is likely to last in excess of four weeks

(k)   In Wales, ascertain whether a witness will give evidence in Welsh or English and ensure that this is brought to the attention of the court and prosecution team as soon as possible

Crown Court Administration

1.7   The court administration must:

(a)   Determine all applications for legal representation which require administrative decisions within 48 hours of receipt[41]

(b)   Where the court has been notified that a vulnerable or intimidated victim is involved, ensure that the WCU is informed of the pre-trial hearing date. This must be no later than one working day after the date is set for vulnerable or intimidated victims and no later than three working days after the date is set for cases involving other victims

(c)   (In Wales) on receiving notice that Welsh is to be used by any party or witness, follow the "Protocol for listing cases where the Welsh language is used"[42] and, in particular, list the case for a PCMH before a Welsh-speaking judge

Court Case Progression Officer (CPO)

1.8 The Court Case progression officer must:

(a)   Review the paperwork to identify and monitor any directions made by the magistrates' court[43]

(b)   Ensure that confidential communications e.g. about possible pleas, are not passed to the court or other parties without agreement

National Offender Management Service – Probation Service

1.9 The Probation Service must:

Where the defendant has pleaded guilty and has been committed for sentence or where he has indicated that he is likely to plead guilty and the case has been listed for a plea and sentence hearing, obtain a PSR pack from the prosecution, including any victim's personal statement[44] obtained by the police, and any appropriate information from the defence/defendant and make an appointment to interview the defendant (whether on bail or in custody) so that the report is ready before the date fixed for sentence. The Probation Service should be in a position to provide an oral report or a FDR report, if appropriate

National Offender Management Service – Prison Service and prisoner escort services commissioned by PECS

1.10 With persons held in prison custody:

(a)   The Prison Service must ensure that the identities of all the persons in custody are notified to the appropriate escort contractor for production at court by the agreed process[45]

(b)   The escort contractor must ensure that all the prisoners notified to them for production at court are delivered to the courthouse and brought before the court by the agreed times

(c)   The escort contractor must notify the court administration immediately of any problems anticipated or arising in respect of the production of persons in custody

(d)   Where the defendant is appearing by way of a Prison Video Link, the Prison Service must ensure that he is available at the appropriate time

(e)   The escort contractor must ensure that there are arrangements in place for the remand forms, prepared by the prisons and attached to the Prison Escort Record forms, to be delivered to the court clerk's office before the hearing

NOTES

1 Crim PR 1.1
2 Crim PR 3.8(2)(b)
3 Crim PR 3.2(2)(a); 3.3(a)
4 Crim PR 3.2(3); 3.3(b); 3.5

5 Crim PR 3.8(1)
6 Crim PR 3.9(2)(a) and Crim PR 3.5(3)
7 Crim PR 3.8(2)(e)
8 Crim PR 3.8(2)(e)
9 Crim PR 3.4(4)
10 Crim PR 3.2(2)(f)
11 Guidance for List Officers (following recommendations from Resident Judges Conference November 2006)
12 Consolidated Criminal Practice Direction V.56.4
13 Graduated Fee Payment Protocol (General Council of the Bar of England and Wales) April 2007, http://tinyurl.com/3cdbbv
14 Crim PR 1.1
15 CPS/Bar Framework of Principles for Prosecution Advocates in the Crown Court, 5 July 2007, http://tinyurl.com/2qocgl
16 Consolidated Criminal Practice Direction IV.41.8
17 Some applications for legal representation require judicial determination e.g. applications for more than one counsel
18 Consolidated Criminal Practice Direction IV.41.8
19 Crim PR 1.1(2)(d)
20 Disclosure: A protocol for the control and management of unused material in the Crown Court, http://tinyurl.com/yutye6 and CPIA as amended by s.32 Criminal Justice Act 2003
21 Crim PC 1.1(2)(f); Consolidated Criminal Practice Direction III.26.1
22 Crim PR 3.11(1); Consolidated Criminal Practice Direction V.56
23 Crim PR 3.2(2)(a); 3.3(a)
24 Crim PR 3.3(b)
25 That criminal cases be dealt with justly in accordance with Crim PR Part 1
26 Crim PR 1.1(2)(f)
27 Youth Justice and Criminal Evidence Act 1999
28 Control and Management of Heavy Fraud and Other Complex Cases. Protocol issued by the Lord Chief Justice of England and Wales 22 March 2005 http://tinyurl.com/22x67w
29 Crim PR 1.1(2)(d)
30 Youth Justice and Criminal Evidence Act 1999
31 6.5 Code of Practice for Victims of Crime, October 2005 http://tinyurl.com/2pdumm
32 Crim PR 3.11(1); Consolidated Criminal Practice Direction V.56
33 Timescales for the service of defence statements are set out at 4.7(d)
34 Crim PR 3.2(2)(a); 3.3(a)
35 Crim PR 3.3(b)
36 That criminal cases be dealt with justly in accordance with Crim PR Part 1
37 Crim PR 1.1(2)(f)
38 Youth Justice and Criminal Evidence Act 1999
39 Paragraph 1.2 above and Advocate Graduated Fee Scheme April 2007
40 Control and Management of Heavy Fraud and Other Complex Cases http://tinyurl.com/22x67w. Protocol issued by the Lord Chief Justice of England and Wales 22 March 2005; South Eastern Circuit Presiding Judges Practice Direction for Heavy Fraud Trials Estimated to take 6 weeks or more, 10 May 2006 http://tinyurl.com/2unzog
41 Some applications for legal representation require judicial determination e.g. applications for more than one counsel
42 Protocol for listing cases where the Welsh language is used (Wales and Cheshire Region) December 2005 http://tinyurl.com/32j2vo
43 The Court CPO can monitor compliance by the prosecution/defence with directions by use of the PROGRESS case management tool, following rollout
44 Consolidated Criminal Practice Direction III.28, http://tinyurl.com/2o2jvs
45 Category A prisoners will be produced at court by the Prison Service

Chapter 2   Preliminary Hearing (indictable-only cases)[1]

OBJECTIVES

To make the preliminary hearing effective in compliance with the Crim PR and in particular to ensure that at the preliminary hearing:

(i) Consideration is given to furthering the overriding objective by taking the plea in appropriate cases

(ii) The real issue(s), the agreed evidence and the witnesses whose attendance is not required are identified[2]

(iii) The case (including sentence) can be concluded there and then if there is to be a guilty plea or, if this is not achievable, directions[3] can be given in order to complete it at the next hearing or as soon as possible thereafter.[4] If there is to be a not guilty plea, directions are given to progress the case expeditiously

(iv) The date for the PCMH or the trial or a trial window or the Newton hearing or sentence is fixed, if the case is not concluded at the Preliminary Hearing

(v) The case is managed in accordance with the overriding objective[5] and in compliance with the Crim PR

ACTIONS

2.1 Preliminary Hearing

(a) A preliminary hearing will take place where the defendant has been "sent" to the Crown Court but only when ordered by the magistrates' court, either because the Resident Judge has set the practice that a preliminary hearing is automatically held or because the parties have asked for one to further the overriding objective. If so ordered it will be listed in accordance with the directions of the Resident Judge at the Crown Court and must be held about fourteen days after "sending"[6]

(b) Where the magistrates' court has not ordered a preliminary hearing, the first hearing at the Crown Court will be as directed by the Resident Judge. The case may be fixed for a plea and sentence hearing, where the defendant has indicated in the magistrates' court that he is likely to plead guilty, or for a PCMH

(c) At the hearing, the prosecution will provide an outline of the offences for which the defendant has been sent to the Crown Court

2.2 Where the defendant does not attend

(a) Where the defendant does not attend court, the prosecution advocate shall consider the reasons for the defendant's non-attendance (where known) and, in the absence of a satisfactory reason, he will usually apply for a warrant not backed for bail. He will invite critical scrutiny of any material placed before the court on behalf of the defendant – in particular whether it appears to be reliable and relates specifically to the defendant's ability to attend court. A decision by the court not to issue a warrant will not prevent a later determination as to whether the defendant has committed an offence contrary to s.6 of the Bail Act

(b) The overriding objective[7] and the case management obligations prescribed by the Crim PR apply whether the defendant is present or not.[8] The parties' advocates must prepare for the hearing accordingly and, at the hearing, where possible and in accordance with the advocates' professional obligations to their clients, actively assist the court even if the defendant is absent

2.3 Where a guilty plea is entered

(a) The parties must be prepared for the court to pass sentence

(b) If the defendant pleads guilty on a basis which is materially different to the prosecution case, the difference(s) must be clearly identified in a written basis of plea and served on the court and on the prosecution advocate. The prosecution advocate must consider whether to accept, or to challenge, any of the facts asserted and must record his position on the written basis of plea before putting it to the court for approval. The parties' advocates must be prepared to make submissions to the court in relation to the necessity for a Newton hearing

(c) With the leave of the court, the parties must ensure that any TICs are put. The defence must confirm with the prosecution, which TICs are accepted and this information must be shared with the police. If a previously admitted offence is not accepted, the CPS file must be clearly marked and consideration given to prosecution

(d)   Careful consideration must be given as to whether to request a PSR. A PSR prepared for an earlier case involving the same defendant may provide sufficient information

(e)   If a PSR is ordered, the necessary information and assessment(s) must be provided to the court by the Probation Service in accordance with local practice, as agreed between the court and the Probation Service. The Probation Service should be in a position to provide an oral report or a FDR report, if appropriate

(f)   If sentence cannot be passed there and then, the parties must be able to provide the court with the appropriate information concerning bail including the details of the local police station (with suitable opening hours) should the court impose a reporting condition or if a surety needs to be taken

2.4 Where a not guilty plea is entered or a Newton hearing has been ordered

(a)   The parties must expect and be prepared for the court to give directions there and then to achieve the overriding objective

(b)   The parties must complete the prescribed case management forms[9] and consider whether standard directions[10] should be varied or supplemented and, if so, make applications accordingly[11]

(c)   The real issue(s) must be identified[12]

(d)   Only those witnesses who are relevant to a real issue are to be required to attend the trial.[13] Each party must expect to be required to justify the attendance of each and every witness by explicit reference to a real issue

(e)   The parties must provide the dates to avoid (and reasons, where available) of the witnesses who are to attend the trial

(f)   The parties must be able to provide a timetable of steps which need to be taken for the case to be ready for trial, so that the court may make directions accordingly[14]

(g)   The parties must be able to provide a timetable for the trial itself by reference to estimates of the length of: the evidence of each witness (in chief and in cross-examination), the presentation of agreed evidence and submissions on points of law

(h)   The trial will be fixed in accordance with the directions of the Resident Judge. Where possible, the trial/Newton Hearing advocates' availability must be provided to the court so it can be taken into consideration when any future hearings are fixed, along with other issues such as timeliness and the needs of the witnesses

(i)   The parties must be able to provide appropriate information when bail is considered[15] including details of the appropriate local police station (with suitable opening hours) should the court impose reporting conditions or if a surety needs to be taken

2.5 Where no plea is entered

(a)   The parties must expect and be prepared for the court to give directions there and then to achieve the overriding objective[16]

(b)   The parties must complete the prescribed case management forms[17] and consider whether the standard directions should be varied or supplemented and, if so, make an application accordingly

2.6 The defendant's preparation of his case and attendance at subsequent hearings

(a)   It is the defendant's responsibility to prepare his case and attend hearings when required so to do. Any other practices or provisions to which this Framework refers do not absolve him from those responsibilities

(b)   The court administration must if practicable provide the defendant with a written notice of the date of the next hearing before he leaves the court

(c)   Where agreed locally, the court administration may offer an additional reminder service, e.g. by text message

RESPONSIBILITIES

Prosecution Team

2.7 The Prosecution Advocate must:

(a)   Prepare and conduct the case to accomplish the actions set out above

(b)   In the event of a guilty plea, ensure that the Probation Service is given a PSR pack there and then or as provided by local arrangements

(c)   Ensure that the nominated CPO and any other member of the prosecution team who is responsible for the conduct of the case is aware of the directions that have been made

2.8 Prosecution Case Progression Officer

To comply with Crim PR 3.4(1), the prosecution must have nominated an individual responsible for progressing the case and must tell the other parties who he is and how to contact him

Police

2.9 The police

The police/court administration officer must use reasonable endeavours to execute warrants promptly and follow up any outstanding warrants

Witness Care Unit or equivalent unit for other prosecuting agencies

2.10 The Witness Care/equivalent unit must:

(a)   Notify the victims and prosecution witnesses of the outcome of the hearing and of the date of the next hearing[18]

(b)   Share information about the victims and prosecution witnesses (e.g. reluctance on the part of a witness to attend court or changes in availability) with the prosecution team

Defence Advocate

2.11 The Defence Advocate must:

(a)   Prepare and conduct the case to accomplish the actions set out above

(b)   Ensure that the nominated CPO and any other member of the defence team who is responsible for the conduct of the case is aware of the directions that have been made

Crown Court Administration

2.12 The Crown Court Administration must:

(a)   Deal promptly with the preparation and issue of warrants within local and/or national timescales and take all steps necessary to expedite the execution of bench warrants

(b)   Ensure that appropriate facilities, including video links, are available for any witness when special measures are ordered by the court

(c)   Where the court has been notified that a vulnerable or intimidated victim is involved, ensure that the WCU is informed of the pre-trial hearing dates. This must be no later than one working day after the date is set for vulnerable or intimidated victims and no later than three working days after the date is set for cases involving other victims

(d)   Record the directions made, record the next date of hearing[19] and provide a copy of the directions to the prosecution and the defence[20]

Court Case Progression Officer

2.13 Following the preliminary hearing, for matters proceeding to trial/ trial of issue, the court CPO must:

(a)   Notify the parties of his name and contact details

(b)   Check that the magistrates' courts CPO has recorded the details of the prosecution and defence CPOs and, if not, record the details and notify each party

(c)   Record the directions made and record the next date of hearing[21] and provide a copy of the directions to the prosecution and defence[22]

(d)   Ensure that appropriate facilities, including video links, are available for any witness when special measures have been ordered by the court

(e)   In accordance with the Witness Charter, and in conjunction with court listing officers, ensure, as far as possible, that cases involving a vulnerable or child witness are given priority when listing

National Offender Management Service – Probation Service

2.14 The Probation Service must:

(a)   In the event of a guilty plea, obtain a PSR pack from the prosecution and any appropriate information from the defence/defendant and report to the court in accordance with local practice, as agreed between the court and the Probation Service. An oral report may be appropriate

(b)   If a report (oral or written) cannot be presented to the court on the same day, obtain a PSR pack from the prosecution and make an appointment with the defendant if possible there and then or make arrangements to see him at a later stage, whether he is on bail or in custody, so that the report is ready before the date fixed for sentence

National Offender Management Service – Prison Service and prisoner escort services commissioned by PECS

2.15 With persons held in prison custody:

(a)   The Prison Service must ensure that the identities of all the persons in custody are notified to the appropriate escort contractor for production at court by the agreed process[23]

(b)   The escort contractor must ensure that all the prisoners notified to them for production at court are delivered to the courthouse and brought before the court by the agreed times

(c)   The escort contractor must notify the court administration immediately of any problems anticipated or arising in respect of the production of persons in custody

(d)   Where the defendant is appearing by way of a prison video link, the Prison Service must ensure that he is available at the appropriate time

(e)   The escort contractor must ensure that there are arrangements in place for the remand forms, prepared by the prisons and attached to the Prison Escort Record forms, to be delivered to the court clerk's office before the hearing

NOTES

1 s.51 Crime and Disorder Act 1998, Crim PR 12.2
2 Crim PR 3.2(2)(a); 3.3(a)

3 Crim PR 3.2 (3); 3.3(b); 3.5
4 Crim PR 3.8(1)
5 Crim PR 1.1
6 Consolidated Criminal Practice Direction IV.41.3
7 That criminal cases be dealt with justly in accordance with Crim PR Part 1
8 Crim PR 3.8(2)(a)
9 Crim PR 3.11; Consolidated Criminal Practice Direction IV41.10: "The PCMH form as set out in annex E must be used in accordance with the guidance notes"
10 Consolidated Criminal Practice Direction V56.6: "All those directions apply to a case unless the court otherwise orders"
11 Crim PR 3.3(b); 3.5
12 Crim PR 3.2(2)(a); 3.3(a)
13 Crim PR 1.1(2)(d), (e); 3.2(2)(a), (e); 3.3
14 Crim PR 3.8(2)(c)
15 Crim PR 1.1(2)(f)
16 That criminal cases be dealt with justly in accordance with Crim PR Part 1
17 Crim PR 3.11; Consolidated Criminal Practice Direction V56.2: "The form, read with the notes, constitutes a case progression timetable for the effective preparation of a case"
18 Crim PR 1.1(2)(d); The Code of Practice for Victims of Crime, October 2005 http://tinyurl.com/2pdumm
19 The Court CPO can monitor compliance by the prosecution/defence with directions by use of the PROGRESS case management tool, following rollout
20 Crim PR 3.11(2)
21 The Court CPO can monitor compliance by the prosecution/defence with directions by use of the PROGRESS case management tool, following rollout
22 Crim PR 3.11(2)
23 Category A prisoners will be produced at court by the Prison Service

Chapter 3   Plea and Case Management Hearing

OBJECTIVES

To make the PCMH effective in compliance with the Crim PR and in particular to ensure that at the hearing:

(i)   The plea can be taken[1]
(ii) The real issue(s), the agreed evidence and the witnesses whose attendance is not required are identified[2]
(iii) The case (including sentence) can be concluded at the PCMH if there is to be a guilty plea or, if this is not achievable, directions can be given in order to secure the most effective listing of the case. If there is to be a not guilty plea, directions are given to progress the case expeditiously
(iv) The date for the trial or trial window or the Newton hearing or sentence can be fixed when the case is not concluded
(v)   The case is managed in accordance with the overriding objective[3] and in compliance with the Crim PR

ACTIONS

3.1 Plea and Case Management Hearing

(a)   Where there is no preliminary hearing in "sent" cases, this will be the first hearing in the Crown Court, subject to applications for bail or mention hearings to deal with necessary preliminary issues

(b)   In "either-way" cases committed to the Crown Court, the first hearing will be the PCMH, subject to any applications for bail or mention hearings to deal with preliminary issues

(c)   The court will decide the process for PCMHs and will ensure that each case is listed for a PCMH

(d)   The PCMH will be conducted orally in each case

(e)   The Resident Judge may direct that wherever possible the parties and the court should communicate by email

3.2 Where the defendant does not attend

(a)   Where the defendant does not attend court, the prosecution advocate shall consider the reason for the defendant's non-attendance (where known) and, in the absence of a satisfactory reason, will usually apply for a warrant not backed for bail. He will invite critical scrutiny of any material placed before the court on behalf of the defendant and in particular whether it appears to be reliable and relates specifically to the defendant's ability to attend court. A decision by the court not to issue a warrant will not prevent the later determination of whether the defendant has committed an offence contrary to s.6 of the Bail Act

(b)   The overriding objective[4] and the case management obligations prescribed by the Crim PR apply whether the defendant is present or not. The parties' advocates must prepare for the hearing accordingly and at the hearing, where possible and in accordance with the advocates' professional obligations to their respective clients, actively assist the court even if the defendant is absent

3.3 Where a guilty plea is entered

(a)   The parties must be prepared for the court to pass sentence

(b)   If the defendant pleads guilty on a basis which is materially different to the prosecution case, the difference(s) must be clearly identified in a written basis of plea and served on the court and the prosecuting advocate. The prosecution advocate must consider whether to accept, or to challenge, any of the facts asserted and must record his position on the written basis of plea before putting it to the court for approval. The parties' advocates must be prepared to make submissions to the court in relation to the necessity for a Newton hearing

(c)   The parties must ensure that any TICs are put with leave of the court. The defence must confirm with the prosecution, which TICs are admitted and this information must be shared with the police. If a previously admitted offence is not accepted, the CPS file must be clearly marked and consideration given to prosecution

(d)   Careful consideration must be given as to whether to request a PSR. A PSR prepared for an earlier case involving the same defendant may provide sufficient information

(e)   If a PSR is ordered, the necessary information and assessments must be provided to the court by the Probation Service in accordance with local practice, as agreed between the court and the Probation Service. An oral report may be appropriate

(f)   If sentence cannot be passed there and then, the parties must be able to provide the court with the appropriate information concerning any application for bail[5] including the details of the local police station (with suitable opening hours) should the court impose a reporting condition or if a surety needs to be taken

3.4 Where a not guilty plea is entered or a Newton hearing has been ordered

(a)   The parties must expect and be prepared for the court to give directions there and then to achieve the overriding objective[6]

(b)   The parties must complete the prescribed case management forms and consider whether standard directions should be varied or supplemented and, if so, make applications accordingly

(c)   The real issue(s) must be identified.[7] Each question on the PCMH form must be addressed and, if relevant to the case, answered

(d)   Only those witnesses who are relevant to a real issue are to be required to attend the trial.[8] Each party must expect to be required to justify the attendance of each and every witness by explicit reference to a real issue

(e)   The parties must provide the dates to avoid (and reasons, where available) of the witnesses who are to attend the trial

(f)   The parties must be able to provide a timetable of those steps which need to be taken for the case to be ready for trial so that the court may make directions accordingly

(g)   The parties must be able to provide a timetable for the trial itself by reference to estimates of the length of: the evidence of each witness (in chief and in cross-examination), the presentation of agreed evidence and submissions on points of law[9]

(h)   The parties must be prepared to make necessary applications for special measures

(i)   The trial will be fixed in accordance with the directions of the Resident Judge. Where possible, the trial/Newton Hearing advocates' availability must be provided to the court so it can be taken into consideration when any future hearings are fixed along with other issues, such as timeliness and the needs of the witnesses

(j)   The parties must be able to provide appropriate information to the court when bail is considered,[10] including details of the appropriate local police station (with suitable opening hours) should the court impose reporting conditions or if a surety needs to be taken

RESPONSIBILITIES

Prosecution Team

3.5 The Prosecution must:

(a)   Produce, in accordance with the Attorney General's Guidelines, a Plea and Sentence document outlining the basis on which the case is to be opened and any relevant sentencing information[11]

(b)   Lodge the Plea and Sentence document with the court and serve it on the defence no later than seven days before the PCMH

(c)   Comply with the initial duty of disclosure; serve any application for special measures; and serve notice of any intention to introduce hearsay evidence or the defendant's bad character

3.6 The Prosecution Advocate must:

(a)   Prepare and conduct the case to accomplish the actions set out above

(b)   In the event of a guilty plea, ensure that the Probation Service is given a PSR pack there and then or as directed by local arrangements

(c)   Ensure that the nominated CPO and any other member of the prosecution team who is responsible for the conduct of the case is aware of the directions that have been made

3.7 Prosecution Case Progression Officer

To comply with Crim PR 3.4(1), the prosecution must have nominated an individual responsible for progressing the case and must tell the other parties who he is and how to contact him

Police

3.8 The police

The police/court administration officer must use reasonable endeavours to execute warrants promptly and follow up any outstanding warrants

Witness Care Unit or equivalent unit for other prosecuting agencies

3.9   The Witness Care/equivalent unit must:

(a)   Notify the victims and prosecution witnesses of the outcome of the hearing and of the date of the next hearing[12]

(b)   Share information about the victims and prosecution witnesses (e.g. reluctance on the part of a witness to attend court or changes in availability) and any intermediaries with the prosecution team

Defence Team

3.10 The Defence must:

(a)   In the event of a guilty plea, consider the Plea and Sentence Document upon receipt from the prosecution. The defence must be in a position to move immediately to sentencing by indicating which matters are in dispute

(b)   In the event of a not guilty plea, the defence must identify the real issues

Defence Advocate

3.11 The Defence Advocate must:

(a)   Prepare and conduct the case to accomplish the actions set out above

(b)   Ensure that the nominated CPO, and any other member of the defence team who is responsible for the conduct of the case, is familiar with the court's directions

Crown Court Administration

3.12 The Crown Court Administration must:

(a)   Deal promptly with the preparation, issue and execution of warrants within local and/or national timescales and take all steps necessary to expedite the execution of bench warrants

(b)   Ensure that appropriate facilities, including video links, are available for any witness when special measures are ordered by the court

(c)   Where the court has been notified that a vulnerable or intimidated victim is involved, ensure that the WCU is informed of the pre-trial hearing dates. This must be no later than one working day after the date is set for vulnerable or intimidated victims, and no later than three working days after the date is set for cases involving other victims

(d)   Where the court has been notified that a vulnerable or intimidated victim is involved, ensure that the WCU is informed of the decisions made at the PCMH. This must be within one working day of the decision being made for vulnerable or intimidated victims, and within three days for cases involving other victims

Court Case Progression Officer

3.13 Following the PCMH, for matters proceeding to trial/trial of issue, the court's CPO must:

(a)   Notify the parties of his name and contact details

(b)   Check that the magistrates' court CPO has recorded details of the prosecution and defence CPOs and, if not, record the details and notify the parties

(c)   Record the directions made, record the next date of hearing[13] and provide a copy of the directions to the prosecution and defence[14]

(d)   Ensure that appropriate facilities, including video links, are available for any witness when special measures have been ordered by the court

(e)   In accordance with the Witness Charter, and in conjunction with court listing officers ensure, as far as possible, that cases involving a vulnerable or child witness are given priority when listing

National Offender Management Service – Probation Service

3.14 The Probation Service must:

(a)   In the event of a guilty plea, obtain a PSR pack from the prosecution and any appropriate information from the defence/defendant and report to the court in accordance with local practice, as agreed between the court and the Probation Service. An oral report may be appropriate

(b)   If a report (oral or written) cannot be presented to the court on the same day, obtain a PSR pack from the prosecution and make an appointment with the defendant if possible there and then or make arrangements to see him at a later stage, whether he is on bail or in custody, so that the report is ready before the date fixed for sentence

National Offender Management Service – Prison Service and prisoner escort services commissioned by PECS

3.15 With persons held in prison custody:

(a)   The Prison Service must ensure that the identities of all the persons in custody are notified to the appropriate escort contractor for production at court by the agreed process[15]

(b)   The escort contractor must ensure that all the prisoners notified to them for production at court are delivered to the courthouse and brought before the court by the agreed times

(c)   The escort contractor must notify the court administration immediately of any problems anticipated or arising in respect of the production of persons in custody

(d)   Where the defendant is appearing by way of a prison video link, the Prison Service must ensure that he is available at the appropriate time

(e)   The escort contractor must ensure that there are arrangements in place for the remand forms, prepared by the prisons and attached to the Prison Escort Record forms, to be delivered to the court clerk's office before the hearing

NOTES

1 Crim PR 3.8(2)(b)
2 Crim PR 3.2(2)(a); 3.3(a)
3 Crim PR 1.1
4 That criminal cases be dealt with justly in accordance with Crim PR Part 1
5 Crim PR 1.1(2)(f)
6 That criminal cases be dealt with justly in accordance with Crim PR Part 1
7 Crim PR 3.2(2)(a); 3.3(a)
8 Crim PR 1.1(2)(d), (e); 3.2(2)(a), (e); 3.3
9 Crim PR 3.8(2)(c)
10 Crim PR 1.1(2)(f)
11 Addendum to paragraph C6 of the Attorney General's Guidelines on the Acceptance of pleas and the prosecutor's role in the Sentencing Exercise 2005, http://tinyurl.com/3appvj
12 Crim PR 1.1(2)(d); The Code of Practice for Victims of Crime, October 2005 http://tinyurl.com/2pdumm
13 The Court CPO can monitor compliance by the prosecution/defence with directions by use of the PROGRESS case management tool, following rollout
14 Crim PR 3.11(2)
15 Category A prisoners will be produced at court by the Prison Service

Chapter 4   Preparation for hearings (trials, Newton hearings and sentence) in the Crown Court

READINESS ASSESSMENT

OBJECTIVES

(a)   To ensure that everything is done to conclude the case at the next hearing or as soon possible thereafter[1]

(b)   To prepare the case according to the Crim PR and the directions made by the court[2]

(c)   To inform the court and other parties of anything which might adversely affect the progress of the case and achievement of the overriding objective[3] and to apply promptly for any necessary directions[4]

(d)   To certify readiness, if required by the court[5]

ACTIONS

4.1   Compliance with directions

(a)   The parties must comply with directions.[6] If directions are not complied with, the parties must expect the court to investigate the reason, identify who was responsible and take appropriate action[7]

(b)   The parties' and the court's CPOs must each monitor compliance with all the directions (whether standard or not), ensure that the court is kept informed of events which may affect the progress of the case (including their own compliance or non-compliance[8] with directions), ensure that they can be contacted promptly about the case during ordinary business hours, act promptly and reasonably in response to communications about the case and, if unavailable, appoint a substitute[9]

(c)   The parties should ask for a hearing only if a problem cannot otherwise be resolved. Unnecessary hearings must be avoided.[10] If a matter cannot be resolved by agreement, a direction may be sought and/or made without a hearing[11] by communication between the parties and the court, including by email. "Mentions" should be listed only if there is a compelling reason[12]

(d)   Where the case is likely to last in excess of four weeks the parties must expect the court to follow the Protocol issued by the Lord Chief Justice[13]

4.2   Pre-sentence readiness check

(a)   Each party must review the statutory provisions relevant to the court's sentencing powers and any relevant Sentencing Guidelines Council guidance and guideline cases and, where appropriate, bring them to the attention of the court

(b)   Prosecutors must undertake a review of the statutory provisions relating to any ancillary orders (such as anti-social behaviour orders, POCA orders, compensation orders) that may be relevant and consider, where appropriate, making applications to the court for such orders and providing drafts of the proposed orders. Prosecutors should be in a position to produce, in accordance with the Attorney General's Guidelines, a Plea and Sentence document outlining the basis on which the case is to be opened and any relevant sentencing information[14]

(c)   Material submitted by the prosecution or the defence relating to any technical preconditions for a particular sentence and/or ancillary order, must be available to the court as early as possible and in any event prior to the sentence hearing

4.3   Pre-trial readiness check

Each party must:[15]

(a)   Check that all of the court's directions (standard and case specific) have been complied with. In the event of any non-compliance[16] with directions, the court will take any action it considers necessary, or as agreed by the Resident Judge

(b)   Check that every reasonable step (including, where appropriate, seeking the issue of a witness summons) has been taken to make sure that the witnesses will attend when they are needed

(c)   Check that appropriate arrangements have been made for the presentation of evidence (e.g. admissions, interview summaries, video links and sound/ vision recordings)

(d)   Promptly inform the court and the other parties of anything that may affect the date or duration of the trial or significantly affect the progress of the case in any other way[17]

(e)   Give a certificate of readiness if required by the court[18]

RESPONSIBILITIES

Police

4.4   The Police must:

(a)   Ensure that the prosecution file is completed and submitted to the prosecutor in accordance with the Manual of Guidance

(b)   Ensure any actions or requests for information from within the prosecution team are acknowledged, responses are promptly given and any problems identified to the prosecution immediately

(c)   Respond promptly to correspondence from prosecution

4.5   Prosecution Team

The Prosecution team must ensure that the case is fully prepared and ready for trial having regard to each topic identified in the prescribed case progression forms, guidance notes and directions. What follows is not intended to be an exhaustive list. The prosecution must, in particular, ensure that:

(a)   All directions are complied with[19]

(b)   Matters raised by the defence in correspondence are responded to in a timely fashion, using email, where possible

(c)   The case is prepared so as to present the evidence, having regard to the real issues, in the shortest and clearest way (including by way of admissions)

(d)   There is timely disclosure (bearing in mind that only unused material which meets the criteria for disclosure must be disclosed and that the same criteria apply to CCTV recordings as to any other unused material). The requirements for disclosure must be reviewed in light of any change in the defence or new issues that arise[20]

(e)   Timely pre-trial applications are made (and, where necessary, determined) in relation to: special measures, bad character and hearsay evidence

(f)   There is compliance with Crim PR Part 33 in relation to expert evidence

(g)   There is timely service, and any necessary pre-trial editing, of transcripts of interviews (whether with witnesses or defendants) and video recordings. Similarly, there has been timely service of all the evidence on which the prosecution intend to rely

(h)   Witnesses and exhibits are at court when needed

(i)   The possibility that a witness may fail to attend is considered and a timely application made for the issue of a summons

(j)   Arrangements have been made, if appropriate, for staggering the attendance of witnesses

(k)   Interpreters/signers[21] have been arranged. In Wales, where the court has been notified that a defendant or witness will use Welsh, the court is responsible for ensuring that interpreters' simultaneous translation equipment has been arranged

(l)   There is timely service of skeleton arguments and copies/lists of authorities

(m)   If any sound/vision recordings are to be played, a check is made that the quality is acceptable, that there is compatible equipment at court and the recordings are provided to the court administration in time to be checked on that equipment

(n)   Consideration is given, before the hearing and as a matter of priority, to the acceptability of a change of plea and/or basis of plea proposed by the defence

(o)   The court is notified immediately of anything which could significantly affect the progress of the case (including intended discontinuance)[22]

(p)   Contact is made with the defence when it becomes apparent that a direction is needed to further the overriding objective and, if possible, the parties should agree the terms of the proposed order. The prosecution must draft any proposed order and lodge it with the court either in writing or electronically for approval, as appropriate

(q)   An application is made for a direction as soon as the need for one becomes apparent, for instance when agreement cannot be reached, and in any event in time to ensure that the hearing is effective.[23] The prosecution may be required by the court to apply in writing or electronically and must anticipate that the court may endeavour to deal with the application without the need for a hearing

(r)   A certificate of readiness is served if required by the court[24]

(s)   Any matters relevant to sentence can be put before the court,[25] there and then, if the defendant is convicted or enters a late plea of guilty

(t)   The prosecution file complies with the Manual of Guidance and the prosecution advocate is fully briefed so that he has the material and authority to deal with everything which may arise at the hearing

(u)   Witnesses must only be called where there is a real issue relating to their evidence. When the defence serves a s.9 statement on the prosecution seeking the agreement of the witness's evidence, the prosecution must give careful consideration to whether the witness's attendance is required. The defence and the court must immediately be informed of any change

Witness Care Unit or equivalent unit for other prosecuting agencies

4.6   The Witness Care/equivalent unit must:

(a)   Notify the witnesses of the hearing date immediately, inform the prosecuting agency of the notification and maintain contact with the witnesses

(b)   Conduct the needs assessment and inform the court and the prosecuting agency of the witness's ability to attend court or give evidence. This may inform any application for special measures or any other issue considered by the court, for example disability access or the position of any intermediaries

(c)   Ensure support needs are met, using the contact directory to provide tailored interventions where appropriate, in order to secure attendance at court

(d)   Immediately inform the prosecuting agency if a witness appears to be unwilling to attend court so that a timely application can be made for a witness summons

(e)   Provide the Witness Service with information on witnesses attending court, any special measures, details of any changes in circumstances and any referrals for pre-trial familiarisation visits

(f)   Keep the victims and the witnesses informed of special measures and the progress of the case

(g)   Share relevant information about the victims and witnesses (e.g. the reluctance of a witness to attend court, changes in availability, the need to make any reasonable adjustments to accommodate needs under the Disability Discrimination Act 1995, childcare commitments and the possible need for special measures) with the prosecution team

(h)   In Wales, confirm with witnesses their choice of language (Welsh or English) and notify the court immediately of any change

Defence Team

4.7   The defence must ensure that the case is fully prepared and ready for trial, having regard to each topic identified in the prescribed case progression forms, guidance notes, and directions. What follows is not intended to be an exhaustive list. The defence must, in particular, ensure that:

(a)   All directions are complied with[26]

(b)   Matters raised by the prosecution in correspondence are responded to in a timely fashion, using email, where possible

(c)   The case is prepared so as to present the evidence, having regard to the real issues, in the shortest and clearest way (including by way of admissions)

(d)   The defence statement is filed and complies with statutory requirements, both in terms of contents and in timing of the service of it on the prosecution and the court.[27] There is timely application for further disclosure[28] (bearing in mind the precondition of the service of a defence statement and that only unused material which meets the criteria for disclosure must be disclosed and that the same criteria apply to CCTV recordings as to any other unused material)

(e)   Timely pre-trial applications are made (and, where necessary, determined) in relation to: special measures, bad character and hearsay evidence and other pre-trial applications, including those made under s.41 Youth Justice and Criminal Evidence Act 1999 (cross examination of complainant in sexual offences cases)

(f)   There is compliance with Crim PR Part 33 and a timely application for public funding in relation to expert evidence

(g)   There is timely service, and any necessary pre-trial editing, of transcripts of interviews (whether with witnesses or defendants) and video recordings

(h)   Witnesses and exhibits are at court when needed

(i)   The possibility that a defence witness may fail to attend is considered and a timely application made for the issue of a summons

(j)   Arrangements have been made, if appropriate, for staggering the attendance of defence witnesses

(k)   Interpreters/signers[29] have been arranged for defence witnesses. In Wales, where the court has been notified that a defendant or witness will use Welsh, the court is responsible for ensuring that interpreters' simultaneous translation equipment has been arranged

(l)   There is timely service of skeleton arguments and copies/lists of authorities

(m)   If any sound/vision recordings are to be played, a check is made that the quality is acceptable, there is compatible equipment at court and the recordings are provided to the court administration in time to be checked on that equipment

(n)   The court is informed of any special arrangements which are to be made for the defendant having regard to his needs

(o)   The acceptability of a proposed change of plea and/or basis of plea is discussed with the prosecution, before the hearing and as a priority

(p)   The witness requirements are continually kept under review so that only those witnesses whose attendance is required in relation to the real issues attend court. The prosecution and court must immediately be informed of any change

(q)   The court is notified immediately of anything which could significantly affect the progress of the case (including if an acceptable guilty plea is proposed)[30]

(r)   Contact is made with the prosecution when it becomes apparent that a direction is needed to further the overriding objective and, if possible, the parties should agree the terms of the proposed order. The defence must draft any proposed order and lodge it with the court either in writing or electronically for approval, as appropriate

(s) An application is made for a direction as soon as the need for one becomes apparent, for instance when agreement cannot be reached, and in any event in time to ensure that the hearing is effective. The defence may be required by the court to apply in writing or electronically and must anticipate that the court may endeavour to deal with the application without the need for a hearing

(t) The defendant is notified of the time, date, and place of the hearing

(u) The court and prosecution are notified if the defendant is in custody by order of another court (providing sufficient details for a Home Office Production Order to be obtained)

(v) A certificate of readiness is served if required by the court[31]

(w) Any matters relevant to sentence can be put before the court,[32] there and then, if the defendant is convicted or enters a late plea of guilty

(x) The defence advocate is fully briefed so that he has the material to deal with all issues which may arise at the hearing

(y) Witnesses must only be called when there is a real issue relating to their evidence. When the prosecution serves a s.9 statement upon the defence seeking the agreement of the witness's evidence, the defence must give careful consideration to whether the witness's attendance is required. The prosecution and court must immediately be informed of any change

Crown Court Administration

4.8 The Court administration must:

Ensure that out-of-court decisions affecting vulnerable or intimidated victims, in relation to adjournments and postponements of scheduled hearings, reach the WCU no longer than one working day after the day on which the decision is made; and, in cases involving other victims, ensure that decisions reach the WCU no later than three working days after the day on which the decision is made

Court Case Progression Officer (CPO)

4.9 The Court Case Progression Officer must:

(a) Monitor directions[33] made by the court and, in the event of non-compliance,[34] refer to the court, if appropriate

(b) Ensure that any communication received from the parties is dealt with promptly

(c) Check readiness and take appropriate action. Any application to vacate a trial must be referred to the Resident or trial judge in accordance with local arrangements

(d) Remind the defendant of the hearing time, date and venue, in accordance with any local arrangements

(e) Ensure that appropriate facilities, including video links, are available for any witness with special needs[35] e.g. children and vulnerable or intimidated witnesses, when notified by the parties

(f) If any sound/vision recordings are to be played, check there is compatible equipment at court. The parties must be responsible for checking the quality of their recordings and providing them to the court administration in a timely manner so they can be checked by the court administration on that equipment before the hearing

(g) Ensure that interpreters/signers[36] for defendants are warned to attend if appropriate

(h)   If certificates of readiness are required by the court, provide blank forms to the parties

National Offender Management Service – Probation Service

4.10 The Probation Service must:

(a)   In the event of a guilty plea, obtain a PSR pack from the prosecution and any appropriate information from the defence/defendant and report to the court in accordance with local practice, as agreed between the court and the Probation Service. An oral report may be appropriate

(b)   If a report (oral or written) cannot be provided to the court on the same day, obtain a PSR pack from the prosecution and make an appointment with the defendant if possible there and then or make arrangements to see him at a later stage, whether he is on bail or in custody, so that the report is ready before the date fixed for sentence

Breach of Community Order/Suspended Sentence

(c)   Where breach proceedings are initiated, the Probation Service must:

(i)   Notify the court immediately of any intention to withdraw those proceedings

(ii)   Prepare the case according to rules of evidence

Witness Service

4.11 The Witness Service must:

(a)   Provide pre-court visits for witnesses when referred and when resources allow[37]

(b)   Share relevant information about the victims, witnesses and any intermediaries (e.g. reluctance of witness to attend court, changes in availability, the need to make any reasonable adjustments to accommodate needs under the Disability Discrimination Act 1995, childcare commitments and possible need for special measures) with the prosecution/defence team

NOTES

1 Crim PR 3.8(1); 3.9(1)-(2)
2 Crim PR 1.2
3 That criminal cases be dealt with justly in accordance with Crim PR Part 1
4 Crim PR 3.3(b)
5 Crim PR 3.9(3)
6 Crim PR 3.9(2)(a)
7 Crim PR 3.8(2)(e)
8 Crim PR 3.8(2)(e)
9 Crim PR 3.4(4)(e)
10 Crim PR 3.2(2)(f)
11 Crim PR 3.5(2)(b)-(e)
12 Guidance for List Officers (following recommendations from Resident Judges Conference November 2006) is available to Crown Court staff on the Ministry of Justice intranet (by selecting the "A – Z" button; clicking on "L" for Learning & Development; and selecting "Business Skills Team")
13 Control and Management of Heavy Fraud and Other Complex Cases. Protocol issued by the Lord Chief Justice of England and Wales, 22 March 2005 http://tinyurl.com/22x67w
14 Addendum to paragraph C6 of the Attorney General's Guidelines on the Acceptance of pleas and the prosecutor's role in the Sentencing Exercise 2005, http://tinyurl.com/3appvj
15 Crim PR 3.9(2)(a)-(c)
16 Crim PR 3.8(2)(e)
17 Crim PR 3.9(2)(d)
18 Crim PR 3.9(3)

19 Crim PR 3.9(2)(a)
20 Unless and until section 6B of the CPIA (introduced by CJA 2003, s.33(3)) is implemented, a defence statement cannot be updated or amended. However, should there be any change to the nature of the accused's defence, the matters of fact on which he takes issue with the prosecution or any alibi he intends to rely on, this should be set out in writing and served on the court and the prosecution immediately, not least to enable the prosecution to comply with its continuing duty under s.7A CPIA
21 National Agreement of Arrangements for the use of Interpreters, Translators and Language Service Professionals in Investigations and Proceedings within the Criminal Justice System, as revised 2007, http://tinyurl.com/2dusog
22 Crim PR 3.9(2)(d)
23 Crim PR 3.6(2)
24 Crim PR 3.9(3)
25 Crim PR 1.1(2)(f)
26 Crim PR 3.9(2)(a)
27 This is 14 days after receipt of initial disclosure or longer if it is extended by the court before the expiration of the 14 days
28 s.8 CPIA
29 National Agreement of Arrangements for the use of Interpreters, Translators and Language Service Professionals in Investigations and Proceedings within the Criminal Justice System, as revised 2007, http://tinyurl.com/2dusog
30 Crim PR 3.9(2)(d)
31 Crim PR 3.9(3)
32 Crim PR 1.1(2)(f)
33 The Court CPO can monitor compliance by the prosecution/defence with directions by use of the PROGRESS case management tool, following rollout
34 Crim PR 3.8(2)(e)
35 Youth Justice and Criminal Evidence Act 1999
36 National Agreement of Arrangements for the use of Interpreters, Translators and Language Service Professionals in Investigations and Proceedings within the Criminal Justice System, as revised 2007, http://tinyurl.com/2dusog
37 HMCS has launched a new DVD: Going to Court – A step by step guide to being a witness to Witness Care Units, defence lawyers and court-based Witness Service throughout England and Wales. The DVD is an interactive, multilingual and animated DVD to help witnesses and victims understand their role in the court process. New information leaflets for both prosecution and defence witnesses attending any criminal court across England and Wales have also been produced

Chapter 5   *Trial, Newton hearing and sentence*

OBJECTIVES

(a) To achieve the overriding objective[1] of dealing with the case justly
(b) To ensure that the hearing is effective and proceeds without delay on the day when it is listed
(c) To ensure that the case is dealt with efficiently, expeditiously and proportionately with the live evidence being confined to the real issue(s)[2]

ACTIONS

5.1 Case management on the day of the hearing

  (a)   The parties must, before the hearing begins, actively assist the court to manage the case. The parties must not wait to be required to do so.[3] This means that, having reconsidered the case and any developments since earlier directions were given, the parties must be able to:

  ■   Explicitly identify the real issues; and
  ■   Provide the court with:

    (i)   A list of the witnesses who are to be called "live" to give evidence, in the order in which it is proposed they will be called

(ii) A list of any other material to be introduced

(iii) *Any* agreement in relation to the way in which evidence is to be adduced (e.g. by admission or by reading the relevant parts of witness statements)

(iv) Notice of any point of law which could affect the conduct of the hearing

(v) Any special arrangements for a witness's evidence[4] or the participation of any person, including the defendant[5]

(vi) A timetable[6] for the hearing (broken down by each witness – examination in chief and cross-examination – and each submission)

(b) During the hearing, the parties must confine their submissions and questions to the real issues and must be prepared to object if another party starts to explore matters which are irrelevant

(c) The parties must expect the court actively to manage the case and, having identified the real issues, it may set time limits, for instance to curtail excessive questioning and submissions[7]

(d) If a witness is required to attend but either is not called or is not asked relevant questions by the party who required his attendance, that party may be required by the court to provide a full explanation

(e) If the defendant fails to attend, the court will decide whether to proceed in his absence[8]

(f) If a witness fails to attend court, the party intending to call that witness must determine with the other party or parties whether the evidence can be agreed or whether he can proceed nonetheless. If not, the party calling the witness must decide whether to apply to the court for an adjournment and/or a witness summons. He must expect to be required to provide detailed reasons for the witness's non-attendance, whether difficulties were foreseen and the prospects of a witness attending, if the case is adjourned

(g) Where a defendant has chosen to use Welsh in the proceedings and pleaded guilty or been convicted, the court must notify the Probation Service that he must be interviewed and the pre-sentence report prepared in Welsh

(h) If a hearing is ineffective, the parties must be prepared to provide the court with a full explanation

5.2 Sentence

(a) Where the defendant wishes other offences to be taken into consideration, the offences must be set out in writing, signed, and put before the court. The police must be notified as to which TICs have been accepted. If a defendant rejects previously admitted TICs, the prosecution file must be clearly marked and consideration given to prosecuting the now denied offences

(b) The parties must expect the court to proceed to sentence as soon as possible. If a pre-sentence report is required, the Probation Service must consider preparation of a FDR, where appropriate. Where a PSR has been prepared for a previous case involving the defendant, sufficient information may be available for sentencing purposes. Where a PSR is required, a PSR pack must be given to the Probation Service officer at court on the same day to enable preparation of reports where practicable. The Probation Service should be in a position to provide an oral report or a FDR report, if appropriate

(c) Where the defendant maintains, prior to final disposal, that the statutory criteria justifying an application to change a plea of guilty to a plea of not guilty are met, he must apply in writing (unless the court otherwise directs) setting out the reasons, by reference to the criteria, and he must serve the application on the court officer and the prosecutor[9]

RESPONSIBILITIES

Prosecution Advocate

5.3 In addition to preparing and conducting the case in compliance with the Crim PR and the relevant matters set out above, the prosecution advocate must:

  (a)   Consider making an application to proceed in his absence if the defendant does not attend

  (b)   Ensure that the prosecution witnesses are present and meet with them[10] in order to answer any questions they may have about court procedures, and to indicate, where possible, how long they will have to wait before giving evidence

  (c)   Where a witness does not attend, consider making an application for a summons. The advocate must be in a position to inform the court of the history of contact with the witness. The advocate must consider whether the case can proceed without the witness or whether all, or at least part of, the evidence can be agreed

  (d)   Endorse the brief or prosecution file with the details of the outcome, any directions made and the date and purpose of the next hearing

  (e)   Ensure that any preparatory work is brought to the attention of the prosecution team for action

  (f)   Where a pre-sentence report is requested in the event of conviction, ensure where practicable, the PSR pack is given to the Probation Service officer at court on the same day to enable preparation of reports

  (g)   If the hearing is cracked or ineffective, complete the Cracked and Ineffective Trial Monitoring Form recording the reason for this and place the form before the court for consideration before leaving the court[11]

  (h)   Keep the witnesses informed of the progress of the case[12] and apply to the court for their release as soon as practicable if the trial is "cracked" or ineffective. If the trial "cracks", the witnesses must remain at the court if a Newton hearing may be held. If the trial is ineffective, the witnesses must be asked to remain at court while a new date is fixed

  (i)   In the event of a conviction, review the Plea and Sentence Document prior to sentence to reflect any changes on which the case was presented to the court and ensure that the relevant statutory provisions, sentencing guidelines and guideline cases are up-to-date[13]

Police/enforcement officers

5.4 The Police/enforcement officers must:

Use every effort to serve witness summonses and use reasonable endeavours to execute warrants promptly and follow up any outstanding warrants

Witness Care Unit or equivalent unit for other prosecuting agencies

5.5 The Witness Care/equivalent unit must:

  (a)   Ensure that the tailored interventions are available to secure the victims and witnesses attendance at court and provide the support required

  (b)   Ensure the victims and the witnesses are notified of any future hearing date and are informed of the outcome of the hearing[14]

  (c)   Thank the victims and the witnesses for their participation

Defence Advocate

5.6 In addition to preparing and conducting the case in compliance with the Crim PR and the relevant matters set out above the defence advocate must:

(a)   If the defendant fails to attend, consider whether his professional duty is to remain and to represent the defendant during the course of any trial in absence

(b)   Check that defence witnesses are present when required and meet them[15]

(c)   Where a witness has not attended, consider making an application for a summons. The advocate must be in a position to inform the court of the history of contact with the witness. The advocate must consider whether the case can proceed without the witness or whether all, or at least part of, the evidence can be agreed

(d)   Be ready to present a plea in mitigation if the defendant is convicted or enters a late plea of guilty

(e)   Endorse the brief or defence file with the details of the outcome, any directions made and the date and purpose of the next hearing or sentence

(f)   Ensure that any preparatory work is brought to the attention of the defence team for action

(g)   If the hearing is cracked or ineffective, complete the form recording the reason for this and place the form before the court for consideration before leaving the court[16]

(h)   Be prepared to make a quantified and supported application for a defendant's costs order in a specific sum if the defendant is acquitted

Crown Court Administration

5.7   Court Managers must:

(a)   Ensure that audio/video/DVD playback facilities are available for all Crown Court centres where trials take place (and, in Wales, simultaneous translation facilities)

(b)   Ensure that facilities for special measures for use during the trial are available and, in respect of video links, are in full working order

5.8   The court administration must:

(a)   Deal promptly with the preparation, issue and execution of warrants within local and/or national targets

(b)   If the hearing is cracked/ineffective, ensure that the Cracked and Ineffective Trial Monitoring Form is completed by the advocates, recording the reasons. The form must be placed before the court for approval before the advocates leave the court[17]

(c)   Where court staff have been notified that there are vulnerable or intimidated victims and where adjournments and postponements of scheduled hearings are agreed without a court hearing, ensure that decisions reach the WCU no longer than one working day after the day on which the decision is made and, in cases involving other victims, decisions reach the WCU no later than three working days after the day on which the decision is made

(d)   Where the court has been notified that a vulnerable or intimidated victim is involved, ensure that the WCU is informed of the outcome of the trial in all cases within one working day of the decision being made and within three days for cases involving other victims

(e)   Ensure that where possible, the victims and the witnesses are directed to a separate waiting area and a seat in the courtroom away from the other parties, their witnesses and supporters

(f)   Ensure that witnesses are only asked to attend court on the day they are required to give evidence

(g)   Ensure that witnesses do not have to wait more than two hours and keep them informed about any delay

(h)   Ensure that appropriate facilities, including video links, are available for any witnesses with special needs,[18] e.g. children and vulnerable or intimidated witnesses, where notified by the parties

National Offender Management Service – Probation Service

5.9 The Probation Service must:

(a)   Obtain a PSR pack from the prosecution and any appropriate information from the defence/defendant and report to the court in accordance with local practice, as agreed between the court and the Probation Service. An oral report may be appropriate

(b)   If a report (oral or written) cannot be presented to the court on the same day, make an appointment with the defendant if possible there and then, or make arrangements to see him at a later stage, whether he is on bail or in custody, so that the report is ready before the date fixed for sentence

National Offender Management Service – Prison Service and prisoner escort services commissioned by PECS

5.10 Productions from Prison Custody:

(a)   The Prison Service must ensure that the identities of all persons in custody are notified to the appropriate escort contractor for production at court by the agreed process

(b)   The escort contractor must ensure that all the prisoners notified to them for production at court are delivered to the courthouse and brought before the court by the agreed times

(c)   Category A prisoners will be produced at court by the Prison Service

(d)   The escort contractor will notify the court administration immediately of any problems anticipated or arising in respect of the production of persons in custody

(e)   The escort contractor must ensure that there are arrangements in place for the remand forms, prepared by the prisons and attached to the Prison Escort Record forms, to be delivered to the court clerk's office before the hearing

Witness Service

5.11 The Witness Service must:

(a)   Provide support to witnesses and if necessary accompany witnesses to the courtroom when resources allow

(b)   Where appropriate, share information about the victims and witnesses (e.g. reluctance of the witness to attend court, changes in availability, the need to make reasonable adjustments to accommodate needs under the Disability Discrimination Act 1995, disability, childcare commitments and possible need for special measures) with the prosecution/defence team

(c)   Bring to the attention of the relevant advocate, victim and witness needs not already identified elsewhere

(d)   Ensure witness safety and security is considered by the court and that the "Witness Security at Court" guidance is followed

NOTES

1 Crim PR 1.1
2 R. v Jisl [2004] EWCA Crim 696
3 Crim PR 1.2(1); 3.3(a)
4 Crim PR 3.10(d); Consolidated Criminal Practice Direction III.29.1-3
5 Crim PR 3.10(e); Consolidated Criminal Practice Direction III.30.1-18

6 Crim PR 3.10(i); R. v Jisl [2004] EWCA Crim 696
7 R. v Jisl [2004] EWCA Crim 696
8 Crim PR 3.8(2)(a); Consolidated Criminal Practice Direction I.13.3(c), 1.13.17-19
9 Crim PR 39.3 as inserted by Criminal Procedure (Amendment No 2) Rules 2007 R10
10 The prosecution should consider staggering the attendance time of witnesses, if this can be done without risking the progress of the case
11 Joint Effective, Cracked, Ineffective and Vacated Trials in the Crown Court and the Magistrates' Courts: Operational Guidance for Monitoring Scheme, version 3, 1 October 2007 http://tinyurl.com/yntzvv
12 Crim PR 1.1(2)(d)
13 Addendum to paragraph C6 of the Attorney General's Guidelines on the Acceptance of pleas and the prosecutor's role in the Sentencing Exercise 2005, http://tinyurl.com/3appvj
14 6.7 Code of Practice for Victims of Crime, October 2005 http://tinyurl.com/kmxku
15 The defence should consider staggering the attendance time of witnesses, if this can be done without risking the progress of the case
16 Joint Effective, Cracked, Ineffective and Vacated Trials in the Crown Court and the Magistrates' Courts: Operational Guidance for Monitoring Scheme, version 3, 1 October 2007 http://tinyurl.com/yntzvv
17 Joint Effective, Cracked, Ineffective and Vacated Trials in the Crown Court and the Magistrates' Courts: Operational Guidance for Monitoring Scheme, version 3, 1 October 2007 http://tinyurl.com/yntzvv
18 Youth Justice and Criminal Evidence Act 1999

Chapter 6   Appeals from the magistrates' courts

OBJECTIVES

(a)   To achieve the overriding objective of dealing with the case justly

(b)   To ensure that the hearing is effective and proceeds without delay on the day when it is listed

(c)   To ensure that the case is dealt with efficiently, expeditiously and proportionately with the live evidence being confined to the real issue(s)

ACTIONS

6.1 Compliance with directions

(a)   The parties must comply with directions.[1] If directions are not complied with, the parties must expect the court to investigate the reason, identify who was responsible and take appropriate action[2]

(b)   The parties' and the court's CPOs must each monitor compliance with all the directions (whether standard or not), ensure that the court is kept informed of events which may affect the progress of the case (including their own compliance or non-compliance with directions[3]), ensure that they can be contacted promptly about the case during ordinary business hours, act promptly and reasonably in response to communications about the case and, if unavailable, appoint a substitute[4]

(c)   The parties must ask for a hearing only if a problem cannot otherwise be resolved. Unnecessary hearings must be avoided.[5] Even if a matter cannot be resolved by agreement, a direction may be sought and/or made without a hearing[6] by communication between the parties and the court, including by email. "Mentions" should be listed only if there is a compelling reason[7]

6.2 Readiness check (appeals against sentence)

(a)   Each party must review the statutory provisions relevant to the court's sentencing powers and any relevant Sentencing Guidelines Council guidance and guideline cases and bring them, where appropriate, to the attention of the court

(b)   The respondent must undertake a review of the statutory provisions relating to any ancillary orders (such as anti-social behaviour orders, POCA orders, compensation orders) that might be relevant

(c)   If there are technical preconditions to the passing of a particular sentence and/or ancillary order, which will be submitted by a party to be an appropriate sentence and/or ancillary order, that party must ensure that the material to satisfy those preconditions will be available to the court on the day of the appeal against sentence

(d)   The police/respondent must make all the victims aware of the Witness Service and explain that they will refer their details to the Witness Service unless they ask the police not to do so[8]

6.3   Readiness check (appeals against conviction)

Each party must:[9]

(a)   Ensure that all the court's directions (standard and case specific) have been complied with

(b)   Ensure that every reasonable step (including, where appropriate, seeking the issue of a witness summons) has been taken to make sure that the witnesses will attend when they are needed

(c)   Check that appropriate arrangements have been made for the presentation of written or other material

(d)   Promptly inform the court and the other parties of anything that may affect the date or duration of the appeal or significantly affect the progress of the case in any other way[10]

(e)   Give a certificate of readiness if required by the court[11]

(f)   The police/respondent must make all the victims aware of the Witness Service and explain that they will refer their details to the Witness Service unless they ask the police not to do so[12]

RESPONSIBILITIES

Police

6.4   The Police must:

(a)   Ensure any actions or requests for information from the respondent are acknowledged, responses are promptly given and any problems identified to the respondent team immediately

(b)   Respond promptly to correspondence from the respondent

6.5   Respondent Team

The Respondent team must ensure that the case is fully prepared and ready for appeal, having regard to each topic identified in the prescribed case progression forms, guidance notes and directions. What follows is not intended to be an exhaustive list. The respondent must, in particular, ensure that:

(a)   All directions are complied with.[13] If directions are not complied with, the respondent must expect the court to investigate the reason, identify who was responsible and take appropriate action[14]

(b)   Correspondence from the appellant is answered in a timely manner, using email where possible

(c)   The case is prepared so as to present the evidence, having regard to the real issues, in the shortest and clearest way (including by way of admissions)

(d)   Timely pre-appeal applications are made (and, where necessary, determined), for instance in relation to special measures, bad character and hearsay evidence

(e)   There is compliance with Crim PR Part 33 in relation to expert evidence

(f)   Witnesses and exhibits are at court when needed

(g)   The possibility that a witness may fail to attend is considered and a timely application is made for the issue of a summons

(h)   Arrangements have been made, if appropriate, for staggering the attendance of witnesses

(i)   Interpreters/signers have been arranged. In Wales, where the court has been notified that the appellant or witness will use Welsh, the court is responsible for ensuring that interpreters' simultaneous translation equipment has been arranged

(j)   There is timely service of skeleton arguments and copies/lists of authorities

(k)   If any sound/vision recordings are to be played, a check is made that the quality is acceptable, there is compatible equipment at court and the recordings are provided to the court administration in time to be checked on that equipment

(l)   The court is notified immediately of anything which could significantly affect the progress of the case

(m)   An application is made for a direction as soon as it becomes apparent that a problem cannot be resolved and, in any event, in time to ensure that the hearing is effective[15]

(n)   A certificate of readiness is served if required by the court[16]

(o)   The respondent's file complies with the Manual of Guidance and the respondent advocate is fully briefed so that he has the material and authority to deal with everything which may arise at the hearing

(p)   Should the appellant serve s.9 statements upon the respondent, careful consideration is given as to whether the witness is required to attend so that only those witnesses who are needed in relation to the real issues attend court. The appellant and court must immediately be informed of any change

Witness Care Unit or equivalent unit for other respondent

6.6   The Witness Care/equivalent unit should:

(a)   Notify the witnesses of the hearing date immediately, inform the respondent of the notification and maintain contact with the witnesses

(b)   Conduct a needs assessment and inform the court and the respondent of any issues that may impact on the attendance at court by a witness or his evidence so as to inform any application for special measures or other issues e.g. disability access

(c)   Ensure support needs are met, using the contact directory to provide tailored interventions, where appropriate, in order to secure the attendance of witnesses at court

(d)   Immediately inform the respondent if a witness appears to be unwilling to attend court so that a timely application can be made for a witness summons

(e)   Provide the Witness Service with information on the witnesses attending court, any special measures, details of any changes in circumstances and any referrals for pre-trial familiarisation visits

(f)   Keep the victims and the witnesses informed of special measures and of the progress of the case

(g)   Share relevant information about the victims and witnesses (e.g. the reluctance of a witness to attend court, changes in availability, the need to make any reasonable adjustments to accommodate needs under the Disability Discrimination Act 1995, childcare commitments and the possible need for special measures) with the respondent team

APPELLANT CASE PROGRESSION FUNCTION

6.7   The appellant should ensure that the case is fully prepared and ready for appeal, having regard to each topic identified in the prescribed case progression forms, guidance notes and directions. What follows is not intended to be an exhaustive list. The appellant should, in particular, ensure that:

(a)   All directions are complied with.[17] If directions are not complied with, they must expect the court to investigate the reason, identify who was responsible and take appropriate action[18]

(b)   Matters raised by the respondent in correspondence are responded to in a timely fashion, using email where possible

(c)   The case is prepared so as to present the evidence, having regard to the real issues, in the shortest and clearest way (including by way of admissions)

(d)   Timely pre-trial applications are made (and, where necessary, determined) in relation to: special measures, bad character and hearsay

(e)   There is compliance with Crim PR Part 33 and a timely application for public funding in relation to expert evidence

(f)   Witnesses and exhibits are at court when needed

(g)   The possibility that a witness may fail to attend is considered and a timely application is made for the issue of a summons

(h)   Arrangements have been made, if appropriate, for staggering the attendance of witnesses

(i)   Interpreters/signers have been arranged. In Wales, where the court has been notified that the appellant or witness will use Welsh, the court is responsible for ensuring that interpreters' simultaneous translation equipment has been arranged

(j)   There is timely service of skeleton arguments and copies/lists of authorities

(k)   If any sound/vision recordings are to be played, a check is made that the quality is acceptable, there is compatible equipment at court and the recordings are provided to the court administration in time to be checked on that equipment

(l)   The court is informed of any special arrangements which should be made for the appellant, having regard to his needs

(m)   If the appellant is to abandon the appeal, the respondent and the court should be advised in good time so as to avoid the unnecessary attendance of the witnesses

(n)   The witness requirements are proactively reconsidered so that only those witnesses who are needed in relation to the real issues attend court. The respondent and court should immediately be informed of any change

(o)   An application is made for a direction as soon as it becomes apparent that a problem cannot be resolved and, in any event, in time to ensure that the hearing is effective[19]

(p)   The appellant is notified of the time, date, and place of the hearing

(q)   The court and respondent team are notified if the appellant is in custody by order of another court (providing sufficient details for a Home Office Production Order to be obtained)

(r)   A certificate of readiness is served if required by the court[20]

(s)   The appellant advocate is fully briefed so that he has the material to deal with everything which may arise at the hearing

(t)   Should the respondent serve s.9 statements upon the appellant, careful consideration is given as to whether the witness is required to attend so that only those witnesses who are needed in relation to the real issues attend court. The respondent and court should immediately be informed of any change

Crown Court Administration

6.8   The Crown Court administration should:

(a)   Where court staff have been notified that there are vulnerable or intimidated victims and where adjournments and postponements of scheduled hearings are agreed without a court hearing, ensure that decisions reach the WCU no longer than one working day after the day on which the decision is made and, in cases involving other victims, decisions reach the WCU no later than three working days after the day on which the decision is made

(b)   Where the court has been notified that a vulnerable or intimidated victim is involved, ensure that the WCU is informed of decisions in all cases within one working day of the decision being made and within three days for cases involving other victims

(c)   In accordance with the Witness Charter, and in conjunction with court listing officers ensure, as far as possible, that cases involving a vulnerable or child witness are given priority when listing

Court Case Progression Officer (CPO)

6.9 The Court Case Progression Officer should:

(a)   Monitor directions[21] made by the court and, in the event of non-compliance,[22] refer to the court, if appropriate

(b)   Ensure that any communication received from the parties is dealt with promptly

(c)   Check readiness and take appropriate action. Any application to vacate an appeal is to be referred to the Resident or other nominated judge in accordance with local arrangements

(d)   Refer the matter to the court for a decision on whether the matter should be listed for further directions if a problem cannot otherwise be resolved

(e)   Remind the appellant of the hearing time, date and venue, where agreed locally

(f)   If any sound/vision recordings are to be played, check there is compatible equipment at court. The parties should be responsible for checking the quality of their recordings and providing them to the court administration in a timely manner so they can be checked by the court administration on that equipment before the hearing

(g)   Ensure that interpreters/signers[23] for appellant witnesses are warned to attend if appropriate. In Wales, where the court has been notified that the appellant or witness will use Welsh, the court is responsible for ensuring that interpreters' simultaneous translation equipment has been arranged

(h)   If certificates of readiness are required by the court, provide blank forms to the parties

National Offender Management Service – Probation Service

6.10 The Probation Service must:

(a)   Obtain a PSR pack from the respondent and any appropriate information from the appellant and report to the court in accordance with local practice, as agreed between the court and the Probation Service. The Probation Service should be in a position to provide an oral report or a FDR report, if appropriate

(b)   If a report (oral or written) cannot be presented to the court on the same day, make an appointment with the appellant if possible there and then, or make arrangements to see him at a later stage, whether he is on bail or in custody, so that the report is ready before the date fixed for sentence

Witness Service

6.11 The Witness Service must:

(a)   Provide pre-court visits for witnesses when referred and where resources allow[24]

(b)   Share relevant information about the victims and the witnesses (e.g. the reluctance of a witness to attend court, changes in availability, the need to make any reasonable adjustments to accommodate needs under the Disability Discrimination Act 1995, childcare commitments and possible need for special measures) with the respondent/appellant team

National Offender Management Service – Prison Service and prisoner escort services commissioned by PECS

6.12 With persons held in prison custody:

(a)   The Prison Service must ensure that the identities of all the persons in custody are notified to the appropriate escort contractor for production at court by the agreed process[25]

(b)   The escort contractor must ensure that all the prisoners notified to them for production at court are delivered to the courthouse and brought before the court by the agreed times

(c)   The escort contractor must notify the court administration immediately of any problems anticipated or arising in respect of the production of persons in custody

(d)   Where the defendant is appearing by way of a prison video link, the Prison Service must ensure that he is available at the appropriate time

(e)   The escort contractor must ensure that there are arrangements in place for the remand forms, prepared by the prisons and attached to the Prison Escort Record forms, to be delivered to the court clerk's office before the hearing

NOTES

1 Crim PR 3.9(2)(a)
2 Crim PR 3.8(2)(e)
3 Crim PR 3.8(2)(e)
4 Crim PR 3.4(4)(e)
5 Crim PR 3.2(2)(f)
6 Crim PR 3.5(2)(b)-(d), (e)
7 Guidance for List Officers (following recommendations from Resident Judges Conference November 2006) is available to Crown Court staff on the Ministry of Justice intranet (by selecting the "A – Z" button; clicking on "L" for Learning & Development; and selecting "Business Skills Team")
8 6.12 Code of Practice for Victims of Crime, October 2005 http://tinyurl.com/kmxku
9 Crim PR 3.9(2)(a)-(c)
10 Crim PR 3.9(2)(d)
11 Crim PR 3.9(3)
12 6.12 Code of Practice for Victims of Crime, October 2005 http://tinyurl.com/kmxku
13 Crim PR 3.9(2)(a)
14 Crim PR 3.8(2)(e)
15 Crim PR 3.6(2)
16 Crim PR 3.9(3)
17 Crim PR 3.9(2)(a)
18 Crim PR 3.8(2)(e)
19 Crim PR 3.6(2)
20 Crim PR 3.9(3)
21 The Court CPO can monitor compliance by the prosecution/defence with directions by use of the PROGRESS case management tool, following rollout
22 Crim PR 3.8(2)(e)
23 National Agreement of Arrangements for the use of Interpreters, Translators and Language Service Professionals in Investigations and Proceedings within the Criminal Justice System, as revised 2007, http://tinyurl.com/2dusog
24 HMCS has launched a new DVD: Going to Court – A step by step guide to being a witness to Witness Care Units, defence lawyers and court-based Witness Service throughout England and Wales. The DVD is an interactive, multilingual and animated DVD to help witnesses and victims understand their role in the court process. New information leaflets for both prosecution and defence witnesses attending any criminal court across England and Wales have also been produced
25 Category A prisoners will be produced at court by the Prison Service

Appendix A Listing of cases (Section 16 of the Crown Court Manual)

- This section of the Crown Court Manual is issued under and with the authority of the Lord Chief Justice. It sets out the principles applicable to listing in the Crown and magistrates' courts.
- It supports the Criminal Procedure Rules 2005 which introduce new principles of case management to criminal cases. The changes made emphasise the fact:
    - that judges will be required to make firm arrangements for the listing of cases at the Plea and Case Management Hearing (or earlier)
    - that parties must comply with the directions and timetable then set so that cases are ready to be heard in accordance with that timetable
    - that cases commence promptly at the appointed hour in accordance with that timetable.
- It sets out the new arrangements for the assignment of judges to cases.
- It emphasises the importance, recently stressed by the Court of Appeal, of ensuring that no short hearings in other cases interrupt the prompt commencement or continuation of trials each day at the time appointed

Contents

1. Introduction
2. Principles of listing
3. Setting the Listing Practice at each Court Centre

1. INTRODUCTION

Listing is a judicial responsibility and function. The overall purpose is to ensure that, as far as possible, all cases are brought to a hearing or trial in accordance with the interests of justice, that the resources available for criminal justice are deployed as effectively as possible, and that, consistent with the needs of the victims, witnesses of the prosecution and the defence and defendants, cases are heard by an appropriate judge or bench with the minimum of delay.

The Concordat[1] states that judges are responsible for deciding on the assignment of cases to particular courts and the listing of those cases before particular judges, working with HMCS. Therefore:

(a) The Presiding Judges of the Circuit have the overall responsibility for listing on each Circuit/Region. As set out at paragraph 4(2) below, certain cases in the Crown Court must be referred to the Presiding Judges for directions; the Presiding Judges will be supported by a Regional Listing co-ordinator.

(b) In the Crown Court, subject to the supervision of the Presiding Judges, the Resident Judge at each Crown Court is responsible for listing at his/her Crown Court centre; the Resident Judge is responsible (following guidance or directions issued by the Lord Chief Justice and by the Senior Presiding Judge and Presiding Judges under paragraph IV 33 of the Consolidated Practice Direction) for determining the Listing Practice to be followed at that centre, for prioritising the needs of one case against another and deciding upon which date a case is listed and before which judge.

(c) The Listing Officer in the Crown Court is responsible for carrying out the day-to-day operation of Listing Practice under the direction of the Resident Judge. The Listing Officer at each Crown Court centre has one of the most important functions at that Crown Court and makes a vital contribution to the efficient running of that Crown Court and to the efficient operation of the administration of criminal justice.

(d) In the magistrates' court, the judicial members of the Justices Issues Group for each Area are responsible for determining the Listing Practice in that Area. The day-to-day operation of that Listing Practice is the responsibility of the Justices Clerk with the assistance of the Listing Officer.

(e) The Local Criminal Justice Board in each CJS Area is responsible for delivering the policies and aims of the National Criminal Justice Board by:

- Improving the performance of the local criminal justice agencies
- Improving provisions for victims, witnesses and others involved
- Improving public confidence

2.   PRINCIPLES OF LISTING

Lord Steyn summarised the guiding principle which must be followed:[2]

"There must be fairness to all sides. In a criminal case this requires the court to consider a triangulation of interests. It involves taking into account the position of the accused, the victim and his or her family, and the public."

When setting the Listing Practice, the Resident Judge or the judicial members of the Justices Issues Group should, in addition to following any directions given by the Lord Chief Justice, the Head of Criminal Justice, the Senior Presiding Judge and the Presiding Judges, take into account the overall purpose of listing as set out above and, in addition, the following principles; these are not listed in order of priority or importance.

(a) Meeting the needs of victims and witnesses; each of whom may have differing needs – the young and the vulnerable require particular attention.

(b) Ensuring the timely trial of cases so that justice is not delayed.

- In general, each case should be tried within as short a time of its arrival in the court as is consistent with the interests of justice, the needs of victims and witnesses, and with the proper preparation by the prosecution and defence of their cases in accordance with the directions and timetable set before or at the Plea and Case Management Hearing.
- Priority should be accorded to the trial of young defendants, and cases where there are vulnerable or young witnesses.
- Custody time limits should be observed.
- Priority may also be accorded to other types of case.

(c) Providing for certainty, and/or as much advance notice as possible, as to the trial date.

(d) Seeing that a judge or bench with any necessary authorisation and of appropriate experience is available to try each case and, wherever desirable, there is judicial continuity.

(e) Taking into account the position of the defendant as to whether he/she is in custody or on bail.

(f) Striking a balance in the use of resources, by taking account of:

- The efficient deployment of the judiciary in the Crown Court, and in the magistrates' court the proper and efficient deployment of the judiciary as is consonant with the need for magistrates' competences to be maintained and the Venne criteria to be followed.
- The proper use of the courtrooms available at the court.
- The provision in long cases for adequate reading time for the judiciary.
- The facilities in the available courtrooms, including the security needs (such as a secure dock), size and equipment, such as video link facilities.
- The desirability of timing Plea and Case Management Hearings so that the trial advocates can attend.
- The proper use of those who attend the Crown Court as jurors.

- The need to return those sentenced to custody as soon as possible after the sentence is passed, and to facilitate the efficient operation of the prison escort contract.

(g) Providing:

- the defendant and the prosecution with the advocate of their choice where this does not result in undue delay to the trial of the case.[3]
- for the efficient deployment of advocates, lawyers and designated case workers of the Crown Prosecution Service, and other prosecuting authorities, and of the resources available to the independent legal profession, for example by trying to group certain cases together.

(h) Meeting the need for special security measures for category A and other high-risk defendants.

(i) Taking into account the impact of policies, targets and initiatives of:

- Her Majesty's Government and its agencies.
- Local Authorities, the Criminal Justice Board for the Area, the Chief Constable or Chief Crown Prosecutor for the Area and other local bodies.

Although the Listing Practice at each court centre will take into account these principles, the practice adopted will vary from court to court depending particularly on:

- The number of court rooms and the facilities available
- Location
- Workload – its volume and type
- The available number of advocates and lawyers
- The proximity of the prison, particularly for women, juveniles, and young offenders
- The surrounding geography and public transport facilities
- The effective trial rate, after allowing for cracked, ineffective and vacated trials

What is plain is that a Listing Practice that will operate successfully in a small two-court centre is unlikely to suit the needs of a metropolitan multi-court centre and vice versa. It may also mean that on occasions the Listing Practice set may result in the judge working in chambers on his judicial work.

3.   SETTING THE LISTING PRACTICE AT EACH COURT CENTRE

(a) **Determination**

(i)   The Resident Judge at each Crown Court and the judicial members of the Justices Issues Group in each Area will, in relation to the Crown Court and magistrates' courts respectively, set overall Listing Practice in a local area in accordance with the objectives and considerations set out above.

(ii)   The Resident Judge, or the judicial members of the Justices Issues Group, as the case may be, will consider representations made by local criminal justice agencies and representatives of the defence and witnesses, in the setting of the Listing Practice and in the periodic reviews of that Listing Practice. Consultation with Local Criminal Justice Boards regarding local listing issues and the impact on cracked and ineffective trials should also take place.

(iii)   It will be for the Resident Judge, or the judicial members of the Justices Issues Group, to consider whether to do this by seeking comments in writing on the draft Listing Practice, or by convening a special meeting, or by discussing the issues at the court users' meetings referred to below, or otherwise conducting the consultation in the manner he or they consider best.

(b) **Monthly analysis of the performance**

(i)   The Court Manager, Listing Officer and/or Case Progression Officer should each month, or at such other period as may be specified by the Resident Judge or Bench Chairman and Justices Clerk:

- Review the causes of ineffective, cracked and vacated trials and provide to the Resident Judge (or the Bench Chairman and Justices' Clerk and District Judge, as the case may be) an analysis of each case or specified categories of case and the lessons to be learnt.
- In the Crown Court, provide to and discuss with the Resident Judge the list of any outstanding cases which are older than 20 weeks, or such other shorter period as is specified by the Resident Judge. This list can be provided by the Crest RAGE report.

(ii)   Monthly (or other periodic) meetings should be also arranged between the Court Manager, Listing Officer or Case Progression Officer and local court users (including the CPS, Witness Care Unit, the Witness Service, police and defence solicitors (where possible)) and representatives of the Local Criminal Justice Board to discuss:

- The analysis of cracked, ineffective and vacated trials (based on enquiry into the matters disclosed by the form completed after the enquiry conducted by the judge or the chairman presiding over the court for that case).
- The action that might be taken to address any similar problems in advance of the trial and to improve the provisions for witnesses.

The discussion of the analysis of the reasons for cracked, ineffective and vacated trials should be minuted, and copies of the minutes should be sent to all the parties to the cases discussed. The outcome of these discussions may provide information for the Resident Judge and judicial members of the Justices Issues Group respectively to contribute to his/her/their review of Listing Practice.

(c) **User Meetings**

(i)   The Resident Judge or the representatives of the Justices Issues Group respectively (such as the Justices' Clerk and/or legal advisers) will hold periodic court user meetings with representatives of local prosecutors or other criminal justice agencies and representatives of the defence.

(ii)   One of the agenda items will normally be the operation of the Listing Practice.

(d) **Resolution of difficulties**

(i)   Where difficulties arise, whether around listing generally or regarding specific cases, which cannot be resolved by the Listing Officer, the matter should be referred for consideration:

- In the Crown Court, to the Resident Judge or the judge assigned to a specific case.
- In the magistrates' courts, to the Justices' Clerk, if it relates to a specific case, or, if it relates to more general issues, to the judicial members of the Justices Issues Group and then, if necessary, to the Area Judicial Forum.

(ii)   Where resolution of disagreement, either in relation to the Crown Court or magistrates' courts cannot be reached locally, as set out in sub-paragraph (i), the issue should be referred without delay to the Presiding Judges or the Senior Presiding Judge.

NOTES

1 The agreement reached between the Lord Chief Justice and the Secretary of State for Constitutional Affairs and Lord Chancellor set out in statement to the House of Lords on 26 January 2004.
2 House of Lords – Attorney General's Reference No.3 of 1999 [2000] UKHL 63.

3 This does not in any way affect applications for changes in representation orders. For that, see the ruling of HH Judge Wakerley QC (as he then was) in Asghar Ali which has been circulated by the JSB.

Abbreviations and glossary

ACPO	Association of Chief Police Officers
Advance Information (for anticipated Not Guilty Plea case)/PSR pack	A defendant charged with an either-way offence is entitled to receive Advance Information (evidence on which the prosecution intend to rely or a summary of the facts) before deciding whether to elect trial at the Crown Court or to consent to summary trial, or, if he is under 18, before entering a plea This obligation on the prosecution is set out in the Criminal Procedure Rules Part 21 The principle has been extended to cover summary-only cases in CJSSS areas in association with the Attorney General's Guidelines
Appeals against conviction	A defendant can appeal his conviction to the Crown Court, when there is a rehearing. The alternative route of appeal is to the Divisional court of the High Court by way of case stated or judicial review on the grounds that the magistrates erred in law
Appeals against sentence	A hearing where the appellant accepts his guilt but appeals to the Crown Court on the basis that the sentence imposed was excessive or legally incorrect. The appeal proceeds by way of a rehearing
Bail	The release of a suspect (pre-charge) pending the completion of an investigation or defendant (post-charge) prior to the completion of criminal proceedings. The grant of bail in all criminal proceedings is governed by the Bail Act 1976 as amended. There is a statutory right to bail, subject to exceptions
CC	Crown Court
Contact Directory	A directory compiled by the Witness Care Unit that contains details of local or national organisations, offering support. This enables a full range of options to be considered by Witness Care Officers, when conducting a full needs assessment with a victim or witness
CJS	**Criminal Justice System** The CJS consists of the police, CPS, RCPO, SFO, Prison and Probation Services (NOMS), and the courts' administration (Her Majesty's Courts Service). The CJS does not include the judiciary (judges and magistrates) and the defence
CPIA	Criminal Procedure and Investigations Act 1996
CPO	Case progression officer
CPS	Crown Prosecution Service

Crim PR	Criminal Procedure Rules
Crown Prosecutor	Crown Prosecutors are lawyers responsible for reviewing and, where appropriate, prosecuting criminal cases following investigation by the police. They also advise the police on the gathering of evidence and the charges to be laid in certain cases. The prosecutor will consider whether there is sufficient evidence and, if so, whether the public interest requires a prosecution. Although crown prosecutors work closely with the police or other investigator, they are responsible to the Crown Prosecution Service, an independent governmental organisation or other National Prosecution agencies
Disclosure (Defence)	Sources relating to disclosure by the defence are: (i) Part 1 CPIA and, for investigations begun on or after 4 April 2005, the 1996 Act as amended by the relevant provisions of Part 5, Criminal Justice Act 2003 and CPIA (Defence Disclosure Time Limits) Regulations 1997 (SI 1997 No 684) (ii) Attorney General's Guidelines on Disclosure 2005 (iii) Protocol for the control and management of unused material in the Crown Court 20 February 2006
Disclosure (Prosecution)	Sources relating to disclosure by the prosecution are: (i) Part 1, CPIA and, for investigations begun on or after 4 April 2005, the 1996 Act as amended by the relevant provisions in Part 5 of Criminal Justice Act 2003 (ii) Attorney General's Guidelines on Disclosure 2005 (iii) ACPO-CPS Disclosure Manual (iv) Protocol for the control and management of unused material in the Crown Court, 20 February 2006
DNA Guidance	Advice to the police and CPS in relation to DNA evidence, available locally and on the ACPO and CPS intranets
Either-Way cases	Offences that can be tried either in the magistrates' courts or the Crown Court
FDR	Fast Delivery Report
FTA	Failure to appear at court or at a police station
GP	Guilty plea
HCA	**Higher Court Advocate** A solicitor authorised to conduct advocacy on behalf of the prosecution or the defence in the Crown Court and other higher tribunals. In the CPS, HCAs also include in-house advocates (both solicitors and barristers)
Indictable-only cases	Offences which can be tried only in the Crown Court
Instructed Advocate	Where the defendant has the benefit of a representation order, the advocate (who may be a barrister or an HCA) who has primary responsibility for the defence case and who claims and will receive advocacy fees applied for and authorised under the representation order
MC	Magistrates' court

Mentions	Additional pre-trial hearings listed at the request of one or more party or by the court
NG	Not guilty plea
NH	**Newton hearing** A Newton hearing is held when a defendant admits his guilt but disputes the prosecution's version of events and the court needs to determine the basis on which he is to be sentenced
OCJR	**Office for Criminal Justice Reform** OCJR is a cross-departmental organisation; it supports all criminal justice agencies in working together to provide an improved service to the public. The OCJR is responsible for supporting the National Criminal Justice Board and relationships with the Local Criminal Justice Boards, and it reports to the Lord Chancellor and Secretary of State for Justice, the Home Secretary and the Attorney General
PCMH	**Plea and Case Management Hearing** A procedure in the Crown Court at which a defendant is required to enter his plea and the judge may make directions as to the progress of the case
Plea and Sentence Document	A document prepared by prosecution team identifying the aggravating and mitigating features of the offence and addressing the issues relating to sentence in accordance with the Addendum (to paragraph C6) of the Attorney General's Guidelines on the Acceptance of Pleas and the Prosecutor's Role in the Sentencing Exercise 2005
POCA	Proceeds of Crime Act 2002
Preliminary Hearing	Where the court so determines, this may be the first hearing of an indictable-only case prior to the PCMH at the Crown Court
PSR	Pre-Sentence Report
RCPO	Revenue and Customs Prosecutions Office
SDR	Standard Delivery Report
Sent cases	Indictable-only cases sent from the magistrates' courts directly to the Crown Court under s.51 of the Crime and Disorder Act 1998
SFO	Serious Fraud Office
Special measures	Measures which can be ordered by the court to improve the quality of the evidence given by a vulnerable witness
TICs	**Offences to be taken into consideration** A defendant may ask a court to consider taking other offences into consideration when passing sentence
Transfer	s.53 Criminal Justice Act 1991 (relating to some offences against children) and s.4 Criminal Justice Act 1987 (serious fraud) provide for transfer of these cases to the Crown Court without committal proceedings

Victim	Any person who has made an allegation to the police, or has had an allegation made on his behalf, that he has been directly subjected to criminal conduct (Para 3.1 The Code of Practice for Victims of Crime, October 2005). Therefore the use of this term does not imply that a suspect or defendant is in fact guilty, nor does it imply that his case has been prejudged
Victim Support and the Witness Service	Victim Support runs the Witness Service in every criminal court in England and Wales and gives information and support to witnesses, victims, their families and friends when they go to court. The Witness Service helps: ■ witnesses who are called to give evidence, including defence witnesses ■ victims of crime, their families and friends attending court for any reason ■ children as well as adults Like the rest of Victim Support, the Witness Service is free and independent of the police or courts
VIW	Vulnerable or Intimidated Witness
Warrants	The court may consider issuing a warrant for the arrest of: (i) a defendant who fails to answer to his bail or: (ii) a non-attending witness who has been served with a witness summons. The OCJR has produced guidance on "Getting defendants to court" which gives advice to prosecutors, in relation to applications for warrants, and to the police, in relation to the expeditious execution of warrants Copies are available upon request from FTAWarrants@cjs.gsi.gov.uk
WCU	**Witness Care Units** The role of witness care units is to provide a single point of contact to victims and prosecution witnesses and to provide them with regular updates in relation to the proceedings. In addition, they assess and meet the needs of the victims and witnesses in order to support them in their attendance at court
Witness Charter	The Witness Charter[1] sets out the level of service that all non-expert witnesses can expect to receive at every stage of the criminal justice process, from the moment they report a crime or incident through to court and post-trial support. It applies to all providers of services to witnesses in criminal proceedings, including police forces, WCUs, the CPS, HMCS, the Witness Service and the Bar and or defence solicitors. The charter is non-statutory and builds on the foundations laid by the introduction of the Code of Practice for Victims of Crime[2] and the roll-out of WCUs under the No Witness No Justice[3] (NWNJ) project

NOTES

1 http://tinyurl.com/2bwl2l 2
2 http://tinyurl.com/2pdumm
3 http://tinyurl.com/2uw2my

PRACTICE DIRECTION – DISCLOSURE: A PROTOCOL FOR THE CONTROL AND MANAGEMENT OF UNUSED MATERIAL IN THE CROWN COURT

20 February 2006

INTRODUCTION

(1) Disclosure is one of the most important – as well as one of the most abused – of the procedures relating to criminal trials. There needs to be a sea-change in the approach of both judges and the parties to all aspects of the handling of the material which the prosecution do not intend to use in support of their case. For too long, a wide range of serious misunderstandings has existed, both as to the exact ambit of the unused material to which the defence is entitled, and the role to be played by the judge in ensuring that the law is properly applied. All too frequently applications by the parties and decisions by the judges in this area have been made based either on misconceptions as to the true nature of the law or a general laxity of approach (however well-intentioned). This failure properly to apply the binding provisions as regards disclosure has proved extremely and unnecessarily costly and has obstructed justice. It is, therefore, essential that disclosure obligations are properly discharged – by both the prosecution and the defence – in all criminal proceedings, and the court's careful oversight of this process is an important safeguard against the possibility of miscarriages of justice.

(2) The House of Lords stated in *R v H and C* [2004] 2 AC 134, at 147:

> Fairness ordinarily requires that any material held by the prosecution which weakens its case or strengthens that of the defendant, if not relied on as part of its formal case against the defendant, should be disclosed to the defence. Bitter experience has shown that miscarriages of justice may occur where such material is withheld from disclosure. The golden rule is that full disclosure of such material should be made.

(3) However, it is also essential that the trial process is not overburdened or diverted by erroneous and inappropriate disclosure of unused prosecution material, or by misconceived applications in relation to such material.

(4) The overarching principle is therefore that unused prosecution material will fall to be disclosed if, and only if, it satisfies the test for disclosure applicable to the proceedings in question, subject to any overriding public interest considerations. The relevant test for disclosure will depend on the date the criminal investigation in question commenced (see the section on Sources below), as this will determine whether the common law disclosure regime applies, or either of the two disclosure regimes under the Criminal Procedure and Investigations Act 1996 (CPIA).

(5) There is very clear evidence that, without active judicial oversight and management, the handling of disclosure issues in general, and the disclosure of unused prosecution material in particular, can cause delays and adjournments.

(6) The failure to comply fully with disclosure obligations, whether by the prosecution or the defence, may disrupt and in some cases even frustrate the course of justice.

(7) Consideration of irrelevant unused material may consume wholly unjustifiable and disproportionate amounts of time and public resources, undermining the overall performance and efficiency of the criminal justice system. The aim of this Protocol is therefore to assist and encourage judges when dealing with all disclosure issues, in the light of the overarching principle set out in paragraph 4 above. This guidance is intended to cover all Crown Court cases (including cases where relevant case management directions are made at the Magistrates' Court). It is not, therefore, confined to a very few high profile and high cost cases.

(8) Unused material which has been gathered during the course of a criminal investigation and disclosed by the prosecution pursuant to their duties (as set out elsewhere in this Protocol) is received by the defence subject to a prohibition not to use or disclose the material for any purpose which is not connected with the proceedings for whose purposes they were given it (s. 17 CPIA). The common law, which applies to all disclosure not made under the CPIA, achieves the same result by the creation of an implied undertaking not to use the material for any purposes other than the proper conduct of the particular case (see *Taylor v Director of the Serious Fraud Office* HL [1999] 2 A.C. 177). A breach of that undertaking would constitute a contempt of court. These provisions are designed to ensure that the privacy and confidentiality of those who provided the material to the investigation (as well as those who are mentioned in the material) is protected and is not invaded any more than is absolutely necessary. However, neither statute nor the common law prevents any one from using or disclosing such material if it has been displayed or communicated to the public in open court (unless the evidence is subject to continuing reporting restriction), and moreover, an application can be made to the court for permission to use or disclose the object or information.

SOURCES

(9) It is not the purpose of this Protocol to rehearse the law in detail; however, some of the principal sources are set out here.

(10) The correct test for disclosure will depend upon the date the relevant criminal investigation commenced:

(a) In relation to offences in respect of which the criminal investigation began prior to 1 April 1997, the common law will apply, and the test for disclosure is that set out in *R v Keane* [1994] 1 W.L.R. 746; (1994) 99 Cr. App. R. 1.

(b) If the criminal investigation commenced on or after 1 April 1997, but before 4 April 2005, then the CPIA in its original form will apply, with separate tests for disclosure of unused prosecution material at the primary and secondary disclosure stages (the latter following service of a defence statement by the accused). The disclosure provisions of the Act are supported by the 1997 edition of the Code of Practice issued under section 23(1) of the CPIA (Statutory Instrument 1997 No. 1033).

(c) Where the criminal investigation has commenced on or after 4 April 2005, the law is set out in the CPIA as amended by Part V of the Criminal Justice Act 2003. There is then a single test for disclosure of unused prosecution material and the April 2005 edition of the Code of Practice under section 23(1) of the CPIA will apply (see SI 2005 No. 985).

The CPIA also identifies the stage(s) at which the prosecution is required to disclose material, and the formalities relating to defence statements. The default time limit for prosecution disclosure is set out in section 13 of the Act (see further at paragraph 13 below). The time limits applicable to defence disclosure are set out in the Criminal Procedure and Investigations Act 1996 (Defence Disclosure Regulations) 1997 (S.I. 1997 No. 684).

(10) Regard must be had to the Attorney General's Guidelines on Disclosure (April 2005). Although these do not have the force of law (*R v Winston Brown* [1995] 1 Cr. App. R. 191; [1994] 1 WLR 1599) they should be given due weight.

(11) Part 25 of the Criminal Procedure Rules 2005 (see SI 2005 No. 384) sets out the procedures to be followed for applications to the court concerning both sensitive and non-sensitive unused material. Part 3 of the Rules is also relevant in respect of the court's general case management powers, and parties should also have regard to the Consolidated Criminal Practice Direction.

(12) Parts 22 and 23 of the Criminal Procedure Rules are set aside to make provision for other rules concerning disclosure by the prosecution and the defence, although at the date of this Protocol there are no rules under those Parts.

THE DUTY TO GATHER AND RECORD UNUSED MATERIAL

(13) For the statutory scheme to work properly, investigators and disclosure officers responsible for the gathering, inspection, retention and recording of relevant unused prosecution material must perform their tasks thoroughly, scrupulously and fairly. In this, they must adhere to the appropriate provisions of the CPIA Code of Practice.

(14) It is crucial that the police (and indeed all investigative bodies) implement appropriate training regimes and appoint competent disclosure officers, who have sufficient knowledge of the issues in the case. This will enable them to make a proper assessment of the unused prosecution material in the light of the test for relevance under paragraph 2.1 of the CPIA Code of Practice, with a view to preparing full and accurate schedules of the retained material. In any criminal investigation, the disclosure officer must retain material that may be relevant to an investigation. This material must be listed on a schedule. Each item listed on the schedule should contain sufficient detail to enable the prosecutor to decide whether or not the material falls to be disclosed. The schedules must be sent to the prosecutor. Wherever possible this should be at the same time as the file containing the material for the prosecution case but the duty to disclose does not end at this point and must continue while relevant material is received even after conviction.

(15) Furthermore, the scheduling of the relevant material must be completed expeditiously, so as to enable the prosecution to comply promptly with the duty to provide primary (or, when the amended CPIA regime applies) initial disclosure as soon as practicable after:

- the case has been committed for trial under section 6(1) or 6(2) of the Magistrates' Courts Act 1980; or
- the case has been transferred to the Crown Court under section 4 of the Criminal Justice Act 1987, or section 53 of the Criminal Justice Act 1991; or
- copies of documents containing the evidence are served on the accused in according with the Crime and Disorder Act 1998 (Service of Prosecution Evidence) Regulations 2005 (S.I. 2005 No. 902), where the matter has been sent to the Crown Court pursuant to section 51 or 51A of the Crime and Disorder Act 1998; or
- a matter has been added to an indictment in accordance with section 40 of the Criminal Justice Act 1988; or
- a bill of indictment has been preferred under section 2(2)(b) of the Administration of Justice (Miscellaneous Provisions) Act 1933 or section 22B(3)(a) of the Prosecution of Offences Act 1985.

(16) Investigators, disclosure officers and prosecutors must promptly and properly discharge their responsibilities under the Act and statutory Code, in order to ensure that justice is not delayed, denied or frustrated. In this context, under paragraph 3.5 of the Code of Practice, it is provided "an investigator should pursue all reasonable lines of inquiry, whether these point towards or away from the suspect".

(17) CPS lawyers advising the police pre-charge at police stations should consider conducting a preliminary review of the unused material generated by the investigation, where

this is practicable, so as to give early advice on disclosure issues. Otherwise, prosecutors should conduct a preliminary review of disclosure at the same time as the initial review of the evidence. It is critical that the important distinction between the evidence in the case, on the one hand, and any unused material, on the other, is not blurred. Items such as exhibits should be treated as such and the obligation to serve them is not affected by the disclosure regime.

(18) Where the single test for disclosure applies under the amended CPIA disclosure regime, the prosecutor is under a duty to consider, at an early stage of proceedings, whether there is any unused prosecution material which is reasonably capable of assisting the case for the accused. What a defendant has said by way of defence or explanation either in interview or by way of a prepared statement can be a useful guide to making an objective assessment of the material which would satisfy this test.

(19) There may be some occasions when the prosecution, pursuant to surviving common law rules of disclosure, ought to disclose an item or items of unused prosecution material, even in advance of primary or initial disclosure under section 3 of the CPIA. This may apply, for instance, where there is information which might affect a decision as to bail; where an abuse of process is alleged; where there is material which might assist the defence to make submissions as to the particular charge or charges, if any, the defendant should face at the Crown Court; and when it is necessary to enable particular preparation to be undertaken at an early stage by the defence. Guidance as to occasions where such disclosure may be appropriate is provided in *R v DPP ex parte Lee* (1999) 2 Cr App R 304. However, once the CPIA is triggered (for instance, by committal, or service of case papers following a section 51 sending) it is the CPIA which determines what material should be disclosed.

THE JUDGE'S DUTY TO ENFORCE THE STATUTORY SCHEME

(20) When cases are sent to the Crown Court under section 51 of the Crime and Disorder Act 1998, the Crime and Disorder Act 1998 (Service of Prosecution Evidence) Regulations 2005 allow the prosecution 70 days from the date the matter was sent (50 days, where the accused is in custody) within which to serve on the defence and the court copies of the documents containing the evidence upon which the charge or charges are based (in effect, sufficient evidence to amount to a prima facie case). These time limits may be extended and varied at the court's direction. Directions for service of these case papers may be given at the Magistrates' Court.

(21) While it is important to note that this time limit applies to the service of evidence, rather than unused prosecution material, the court will need to consider at the Magistrates' Court or preliminary hearing whether it is practicable for the prosecution to comply with primary or initial disclosure at the same time as service of such papers, or whether disclosure ought to take place after a certain interval, but before the matter is listed for a PCMH.

(22) If the nature of the case does not allow service of the evidence and initial or primary disclosure within the 70, or if applicable 50, days (or such other period as directed by the Magistrates' Court), the investigator should ensure that the prosecution advocate at the Magistrates' Court, preliminary Crown Court hearing, or further hearing prior to the PCMH, is aware of the problems, knows why and how the position has arisen and can assist the court as to what revised time limits are realistic.

(23) It would be helpful if the prosecution advocate could make any foreseeable difficulties clear as soon as possible, whether this is at the Magistrates' Court or in the Crown Court at the preliminary hearing (where there is one).

(24) Failing this, where such difficulties arise or have come to light after directions for service of case papers and disclosure have been made, the prosecution should notify the court and the defence promptly. This should be done in advance of the PCMH date, and prior to the date set by the court for the service of this material.

(25) It is important that this is done in order that the listing for the PCMH is an effective one,

as the defence must have a proper opportunity to read the case papers and to consider the initial or primary disclosure, with a view to timely drafting of a defence case statement (where the matter is to be contested), prior to the PCMH.

(26) In order to ensure that the listing of the PCMH is appropriate, Judges should not impose time limits for service of case papers or initial/primary disclosure unless and until they are confident that the prosecution advocate has taken the requisite instructions from those who are actually going to do the work specified. It is better to impose a realistic timetable from the outset than to set unachievable limits. Reference should be made to Part 3 of the Criminal Procedure Rules and the Consolidated Practice Direction in this respect.

(27) This is likewise appropriate where directions, or further directions, are made in relation to prosecution or defence disclosure at the PCMH. Failure to consider whether the timetable is practicable may dislocate the court timetable and can even imperil trial dates. At the PCMH, therefore, all the advocates – prosecution and defence – must be fully instructed about any difficulties the parties may have in complying with their respective disclosure obligations, and must be in a position to put forward a reasonable timetable for resolution of them.

(28) Where directions are given by the court in the light of such inquiry, extensions of time should not be given lightly or as a matter of course. If extensions are sought, then an appropriately detailed explanation must be given. For the avoidance of doubt, it is not sufficient merely for the CPS (or other prosecutor) to say that the papers have been delivered late by the police (or other investigator): the court will need to know why they have been delivered late. Likewise, where the accused has been dilatory in serving a defence statement (where the prosecution has complied with the duty to make primary or initial disclosure of unused material, or has purported to do so), it is not sufficient for the defence to say that insufficient instructions have been taken for service of this within the 14-day time limit: the court will need to know why sufficient instructions have not been taken, and what arrangements have been made for the taking of such instructions.

(29) Delays and failures by the defence are as damaging to the timely, fair and efficient hearing of the case as delays and failures by the prosecution, and judges should identify and deal with all such failures firmly and fairly.

(30) Judges should not allow the prosecution to abdicate their statutory responsibility for reviewing the unused material by the expedient of allowing the defence to inspect (or providing the defence with copies of) everything on the schedules of non-sensitive unused prosecution material, irrespective of whether that material, or all of that material, satisfies the relevant test for disclosure. Where that test is satisfied it is for the prosecutor to decide the form in which disclosure is made. Disclosure need not be in the same form as that in which the information was recorded. Guidance on case management issues relating to this point was given by Rose LJ in *R v CPS (Interlocutory Application under sections 35/36 CPIA)* [2005] EWCA Crim 2342.

(31) Indeed, the larger and more complex the case, the more important it is for the prosecution to adhere to the overarching principle in paragraph 4 and ensure that sufficient prosecution resources are allocated to the task. Handing the defence the "keys to the warehouse" has been the cause of many gross abuses in the past, resulting in huge sums being run up by the defence without any proportionate benefit to the course of justice. These abuses must end.

THE DEFENCE CASE STATEMENT

(32) Reference has been made above to defence disclosure obligations. After the provision of primary or initial disclosure by the prosecution, the next really critical step in the preparation for trial is the service of the defence statement. It is a mandatory requirement for a defence statement to be served, where section 5(5) of the CPIA applies to the proceedings. This is due within 14 days of the date upon which the prosecution has complied with, or purported to comply with, the duty of primary or initial disclosure.

Service of the defence statement is a critical stage in the disclosure process, and timely service of the statement will allow for the proper consideration of disclosure issues well in advance of the trial date.

(33) There may be some cases where it is simply not possible to serve a proper defence case statement within the 14-day time limit; well founded defence applications for an extension of time under paragraph (2) of regulation 3 of the Criminal Procedure and Investigations Act 1996 (Defence Disclosure Time Limits) Regulations 1997 may therefore be granted. In a proper case, it may be appropriate to put the PCMH back by a week or so, to enable a sufficient defence case statement to be filed and considered by the prosecution.

(34) In the past, the prosecution and the court have too often been faced with a defence case statement that is little more than an assertion that the Defendant is not guilty. As was stated by the Court of Appeal in *R v Patrick Bryant* [2005] EWCA Crim 2079 (per Judge LJ, paragraph 12), such a reiteration of the defendant's plea is not the purpose of a defence statement. Defence statements must comply with the requisite formalities set out in section 5(6) and (7), or section 6A, of the CPIA, as applicable.

(35) Where the enhanced requirements for defence disclosure apply under section 6A of the CPIA (namely, where the case involves a criminal investigation commencing on or after 4 April 2005) the defence statement must spell out, in detail, the nature of the defence, and particular defences relied upon; it must identify the matters of fact upon which the accused takes issue with the prosecution, and the reason why, in relation to each disputed matter of fact. It must further identify any point of law (including points as to the admissibility of evidence, or abuse of process) which the accused proposes to take, and identify authorities relied on in relation to each point of law. Where an alibi defence is relied upon, the particulars given must comply with section 6(2)(a) and (b) of the CPIA. Judges will expect to see defence case statements that contain a clear and detailed exposition of the issues of fact and law in the case.

(36) Where the pre-4 April 2005 CPIA disclosure regime applies, the accused must, in the defence statement, set out the nature of the defence in general terms, indicate the matters upon which the defendant takes issue with the prosecution and set out (in relation to each such matter) why issue is taken. Any alibi defence relied upon should comply with the formalities in section 5(7)(a) and (b) of the Act.

(37) There must be a complete change in the culture. The defence must serve the defence case statement by the due date. Judges should then examine the defence case statement with care to ensure that it complies with the formalities required by the CPIA. As was stated in paragraph 35 of *R v H and C* [2004]:

If material does not weaken the prosecution case or strengthen that of the defendant, there is no requirement to disclose it. For this purpose the parties' respective cases should not be restrictively analysed. But they must be carefully analysed, to ascertain the specific facts the prosecution seek to establish and the specific grounds on which the charges are resisted. The trial process is not well served if the defence are permitted to make general and unspecified allegations and then seek far-reaching disclosure in the hope that material may turn up to make them good. Neutral material or material damaging to the defendant need not be disclosed and should not be brought to the attention of the court.

(38) If no defence case statement – or no sufficient case statement – has been served by the PCMH, the judge should make a full investigation of the reasons for this failure to comply with the mandatory obligation of the accused, under section 5(5) of the CPIA.

(39) If there is no – or no sufficient – defence statement by the date of PCMH, or any pre-trial hearing where the matter falls to be considered, the judge must consider whether the defence should be warned, pursuant to section 6E(2) of the CPIA, that an adverse inference may be drawn at the trial. In the usual case, where section 6E(2) applies and there is no justification for the deficiency, such a warning should be given.

(40) Judges must, of course, be alert to ensure that defendants do not suffer because of the

faults and failings of their lawyers, but there must be a clear indication to the professions that if justice is to be done, and if disclosure to be dealt with fairly in accordance with the law, a full and careful defence case statement is essential.

(41) Where there are failings by either the defence or the prosecution, judges should, in exercising appropriate oversight of disclosure, pose searching questions to the parties and, having done this and explored the reasons for default, give clear directions to ensure that such failings are addressed and remedied well in advance of the trial date.

(42) The ultimate sanction for a failure in disclosure by the accused is the drawing of an inference under section 11 of the CPIA. Where the amended CPIA regime applies, the strict legal position allows the prosecution to comment upon any failure of defence disclosure, with a view to seeking such an inference (except where the failure relates to identifying a point of law), without leave of the court, but often it will be helpful to canvass the matter with the judge beforehand. In suitable cases, the prosecution should consider commenting upon failures in defence disclosure, with a view to such an inference, more readily than has been the practice under the old CPIA regime, subject to any views expressed by the judge.

(43) It is vital to a fair trial that the prosecution are mindful of their continuing duty of disclosure, and they must particularly review disclosure in the light of the issues identified in the defence case statement. As part of the timetabling exercise, the judge should set a date by which any application under section 8 (if there is to be one) should be made. While the defence may indicate, in advance of the cut-off date, what items of unused material they are interested in and why, such requests must relate to matters raised in the accused's defence statement. The prosecution should only disclose material in response to such requests if the material meets the appropriate test for disclosure, and the matter must proceed to a formal section 8 hearing in the event that the prosecution declines to make disclosure of the items in question. Paragraphs 4(iv) – (vi)(a) of the Lord Chief Justice's March 2005 Protocol for the Control and Management of Heavy Fraud and Other Complex Criminal Cases should be construed accordingly.

(44) If, after the prosecution have complied with, or purported to comply with, primary or initial disclosure, and after the service of the defence case statement and any further prosecution disclosure flowing there from, the defence have a reasonable basis to claim disclosure has been inadequate, they must make an application to the court under section 8 of the CPIA. The procedure for the making of such an application is set out in the Criminal Procedure Rules, Part 25, r 25.6. This requires written notice to the prosecution in the form prescribed by r 25.6(2). The prosecution is then entitled (r 25.6(5)) to 14 days within which to agree to provide the specific disclosure requested or to request a hearing in order to make representations in relation to the defence application. As part of the timetabling exercise, the judge should set a date by which any applications under section 8 are to be made and should require the defence to indicate in advance of the cut-off date for specific disclosure applications what documents they are interested in and from what source; in appropriate cases, the judge should require justification of such requests.

(45) The consideration of detailed defence requests for specific disclosure (so-called "shopping lists") otherwise than in accordance with r 25.6, is wholly improper. Likewise, defence requests for specific disclosure of unused prosecution material in purported pursuance of section 8 of the CPIA and r 25.6, which are not referable to any issue in the case identified by the defence case statement, should be rejected. Judges should require an application to be made under section 8 and in compliance with r 25.6 before considering any order for further disclosure.

(46) It follows that the practice of making blanket orders for disclosure in all cases should cease, since such orders are inconsistent with the statutory framework of disclosure laid down by the CPIA, and which was endorsed by the House of Lords in *R v H and C* (supra).

LISTING

(47) It will be clear that the conscientious discharge of a judge's duty at the PCMH requires a good deal more time than under the old PDH regime; furthermore a good deal more work is required of the advocate. The listing of PCMHs must take this into account. Unless the court can sit at 10am and finish the PCMH by 10.30am, it will not therefore usually be desirable for a judge who is part-heard on a trial to do a PCMH.

(48) It follows that any case which raises difficult issues of disclosure should be referred to the Resident Judge for directions. Cases of real complexity should, if possible, be allocated to a specific trial judge at a very early stage, and usually before the PCMH.

(49) Although this Protocol is addressed to the issues of disclosure, it cannot be seen in isolation; it must be seen in the context of general case management.

PUBLIC INTEREST IMMUNITY

(50) Recent authoritative guidance as to the proper approach to PII is provided by the House of Lords in *R v H and C* (supra). It is clearly appropriate for PII applications to be considered by the trial judge. No judge should embark upon a PII application without considering that case and addressing the questions set out in paragraph 36, which for ease of reference we reproduce here:

"36. When any issue of derogation from the golden rule of full disclosure comes before it, the court must address a series of questions:

(1) What is the material which the prosecution seek to withhold? This must be considered by the court in detail.

(2) Is the material such as may weaken the prosecution case or strengthen that of the defence? If No, disclosure should not be ordered. If Yes, full disclosure should (subject to (3), (4) and (5) below be ordered.

(3) Is there a real risk of serious prejudice to an important public interest (and, if so, what) if full disclosure of the material is ordered? If No, full disclosure should be ordered

(4) If the answer to (2) and (3) is Yes, can the defendant's interest be protected without disclosure or disclosure be ordered to an extent or in a way which will give adequate protection to the public interest in question and also afford adequate protection to the interests of the defence?
This question requires the court to consider, with specific reference to the material which the prosecution seek to withhold and the facts of the case and the defence as disclosed, whether the prosecution should formally admit what the defence seek to establish or whether disclosure short of full disclosure may be ordered. This may be done in appropriate cases by the preparation of summaries or extracts of evidence, or the provision of documents in an edited or anonymised form, provided the documents supplied are in each instance approved by the judge. In appropriate cases the appointment of special counsel may be a necessary step to ensure that the contentions of the prosecution are tested and the interests of the defendant protected (see paragraph 22 above). In cases of exceptional difficulty the court may require the appointment of special counsel to ensure a correct answer to questions (2) and (3) as well as (4).

(5) Do the measures proposed in answer to (4) represent the minimum derogation necessary to protect the public interest in question? If No, the court should order such greater disclosure as will represent the minimum derogation from the golden rule of full disclosure.

(6) If limited disclosure is ordered pursuant to (4) or (5), may the effect be to render the trial process, viewed as a whole, unfair to the defendant? If Yes, then fuller disclosure should be ordered even if this leads or may lead the prosecution to discontinue the proceedings so as to avoid having to make disclosure.

(7)   If the answer to (6) when first given is No, does that remain the correct answer as the trial unfolds, evidence is adduced and the defence advanced?

It is important that the answer to (6) should not be treated as a final, once-and-for-all, answer but as a provisional answer which the court must keep under review."

(51) In this context, the following matter are emphasised:

(a)   The procedure for making applications to the Court is as set out in the Criminal Procedure Rules 2005, Part 25 (r 25.1 – r 25.5);

(b)   Where the PII application is a Type 1 or Type 2 application, proper notice to the defence is necessary to allow them to make focused submissions to the court before hearing an application to withhold material; the notice should be as specific as the nature of the material allows. It is appreciated that in some cases only the generic nature of the material can properly be identified. In some wholly exceptional cases (Type 3 cases) it may even be justified to give no notice at all. The judge should always ask the prosecution to justify the form of notice given (or the decision to give no notice at all).

(c)   The prosecution should be alert to the possibility of disclosing a statement in redacted form by, for example simply removing personal details. This may obviate the need for a PII application, unless the redacted material in itself would also satisfy the test for disclosure.

(d)   Except where the material is very short (say a few sheets only), or where the material is of such sensitivity that do so would be inappropriate, the prosecution should have supplied securely sealed copies to the judge beforehand, together with a short statement of the reasons why each document is said to be relevant and fulfils the disclosure test and why it is said that its disclosure would cause a real risk of serious prejudice to an important public interest; in undertaking this task, the use of merely formulaic expressions is to be discouraged. In any case of complexity a schedule of the material should be provided showing the specific objection to disclosure in relation to each item, leaving a space for the decision.

(e)   The application, even if held in private or in secret, should be recorded. The judge should give some short statement of reasons; this is often best done document by document as the hearing proceeds.

(f)   The tape, copies of the judge's orders (and any copies of the material retained by the court) should be clearly identified, securely sealed and kept in the court building in a safe or stout lockable cabinet consistent with its security classification, and there should be a proper register of all such material kept. Some arrangement should be made between the court and the prosecution authority for the periodic removal of such material once the case is concluded and the time for an appeal has passed.

THIRD PARTY DISCLOSURE

(52) The disclosure of unused material that has been gathered or generated by a third party is an area of the law that has caused some difficulties: indeed, a Home Office Working Party has been asked to report on it. This is because there is no specific procedure for the disclosure of material held by third parties in criminal proceedings, although the procedure under section 2 of the Criminal Procedure (Attendance of Witnesses) Act 1965 or section 97 of the Magistrates' Courts Act 1980 is often used in order to effect such disclosure. It should, however, be noted that the test applied under both Acts is not the test to be applied under the CPIA, whether in the amended or unamended form. These two provisions require that the material in question is material evidence, ie, immediately admissible in evidence in the proceedings (see in this respect *R v Reading Justices ex parte: Berkshire County Council* [1996] 1 Cr. App. R. 239, *R v Derby*

Magistrates' Court ex parte B [1996] AC 487; [1996] 1 Cr App R 385 and *R v Alibhai and others* [2004] EWCA Crim 681).

(53) Material held by other government departments or other Crown agencies will not be prosecution material for the purposes of section 3(2) or section 8(4) of the CPIA, if it has not been inspected, recorded and retained during the course of the relevant criminal investigation. The Attorney General's Guidelines on Disclosure, however, impose a duty upon the investigators and the prosecution to consider whether such departments or bodies have material which may satisfy the test for disclosure under the Act. Where this is the case, they must seek appropriate disclosure from such bodies, who should themselves have an identified point for such enquiries (see paragraphs 47 to 51, Attorney General's Guidelines on Disclosure).

(54) Where material is held by a third party such as a local authority, a social services department, hospital or business, the investigators and the prosecution may seek to make arrangements to inspect the material with a view to applying the relevant test for disclosure to it and determining whether any or all of the material should be retained, recorded and, in due course, disclosed to the accused. In considering the latter, the investigators and the prosecution will establish whether the holder of the material wishes to raise PII issues, as a result of which the material may have to be placed before the court. Section 16 of the CPIA gives such a party a right to make representations to the court.

(55) Where the third party in question declines to allow inspection of the material, or requires the prosecution to obtain an order before handing over copies of the material, the prosecutor will need to consider whether it is appropriate to obtain a witness summons under either section 2 of the Criminal Procedure (Attendance of Witnesses) Act 1965 or section 97 of the Magistrates' Court Act 1980. However, as stated above, this is only appropriate where the statutory requirements are satisfied, and where the prosecutor considers that the material may satisfy the test for disclosure. *R v Alibhai and others* supra makes it clear that the prosecutor has a "margin of consideration" in this regard.

(56) It should be understood that the third party may have a duty to assert confidentiality, or the right to privacy under article 8 of the ECHR, where requests for disclosure are made by the prosecution, or anyone else. Where issues are raised in relation to allegedly relevant third party material, the judge must ascertain whether inquiries with the third party are likely to be appropriate, and, if so, identify who is going to make the request, what material is to be sought, from whom is the material to be sought and within what time scale must the matter be resolved.

(57) The judge should consider what action would be appropriate in the light of the third party failing or refusing to comply with a request, including inviting the defence to make the request on its own behalf and, if necessary, to make an application for a witness summons. Any directions made (for instance, the date by which an application for a witness summons with supporting affidavit under section 2 of the 1965 should be served) should be put into writing at the time. Any failure to comply with the timetable must immediately be referred back to the court for further directions, although a hearing will not always be necessary.

(58) Where the prosecution do not consider it appropriate to seek such a summons, the defence should consider doing so, where they are of the view (notwithstanding the prosecution assessment) that the third party may hold material which might undermine the prosecution case or assist that for the defendant, and the material would be likely to be "material evidence" for the purposes of the 1965 Act. The defence must not sit back and expect the prosecution to make the running. The judge at the PCMH should specifically enquire whether any such application is to be made by the defence and set out a clear timetable. The objectionable practice of defence applications being made in the few days before trial must end.

(59) It should be made clear, though, that "fishing" expeditions in relation to third party material – whether by the prosecution or the defence – must be discouraged, and that, in

appropriate cases, the court will consider making an order for wasted costs where the application is clearly unmeritorious and ill-conceived.

(60) Judges should recognise that a summons can only be issued where the document(s) sought would be admissible in evidence. While it may be that the material in question may be admissible in evidence as a result of the hearsay provisions of the CJA (sections 114 to 120), it is this that determines whether an order for production of the material is appropriate, rather than the wider considerations applicable to disclosure in criminal proceedings: see R v Reading Justices (supra), upheld by the House of Lords in R v Derby Magistrates' Court (supra).

(61) A number of Crown Court centres have developed local protocols, usually in respect of sexual offences and material held by social services and health and education authorities. Where these protocols exist they often provide an excellent and sensible way to identify relevant material that might assist the defence or undermine the prosecution.

(62) Any application for third party disclosure must identify what documents are sought and why they are said to be material evidence. This is particularly relevant where attempts are made to access the medical reports of those who allege that they are victims of crime. Victims do not waive the confidentiality of their medical records, or their right to privacy under article 8 of the ECHR, by the mere fact of making a complaint against the accused. Judges should be alert to balance the rights of victims against the real and proven needs of the defence. The court, as a public authority, must ensure that any interference with the article 8 rights of those entitled to privacy is in accordance with the law and necessary in pursuit of a legitimate public interest. General and unspecified requests to trawl through such records should be refused. If material is held by any person in relation to family proceedings (eg, where there have been care proceedings in relation to a child, who has also complained to the police of sexual or other abuse) then an application has to be made by that person to the family court for leave to disclose that material to a third party, unless the third party, and the purpose for which disclosure is made, is approved by Rule 10.20A(3) of the Family Proceedings Rules 1991 (SI 1991 No. 1247). This would permit, for instance, a local authority, in receipt of such material, to disclose it to the police for the purpose of a criminal investigation, or to the CPS, in order for the latter to discharge any obligations under the CPIA.

CONCLUSION

(63) The public rightly expects that the delays and failures which have been present in some cases in the past where there has been scant adherence to sound disclosure principles will be eradicated by observation of this Protocol. The new regime under the Criminal Justice Act and the Criminal Procedure Rules gives judges the power to change the culture in which such cases are tried. It is now the duty of every judge actively to manage disclosure issues in every case. The judge must seize the initiative and drive the case along towards an efficient, effective and timely resolution, having regard to the overriding objective of the Criminal Procedure Rules (Part 1). In this way the interests of justice will be better served and public confidence in the criminal justice system will be increased.

LAW SOCIETY PRACTICE NOTE – CRIMINAL PROCEDURE RULES: IMPACT ON SOLICITORS' DUTIES TO THE CLIENT

31 March 2008

STATUS OF THIS PRACTICE NOTE

Practice notes are issued by the Law Society as a professional body for the use and benefit of its members. They represent the view of the Society on what a standard of good practice in a particular area is. Solicitors are not required to follow them. Nor are they intended to represent the only standard of good practice which solicitors can follow.

Practice notes are not legal advice. While care has been taken to ensure that they are accurate, up to date and useful, the Law Society can accept no legal liability, other than liability for death or personal injury arising from negligence, for any loss or damage suffered by any person who acts in reliance on their contents or in reliance on any statement or representation made in them.

INTRODUCTION

The Court of Appeal in *R v K* has recently underlined the importance of the Criminal Procedure Rules 2005, making it clear that the rules:

> "impose duties and burdens on all the participants in a criminal trial, including the judge, and the preparation and conduct of criminal trials is dependent on, and subject to, these rules…"[1]

The purpose of this practice note is to provide assistance to the profession in seeking to define the extent of these duties and burdens, and to identify and address the ethical problems that are likely to arise from their imposition. It will examine the following:

1.   The solicitor's duty to the court.
2.   The solicitor, the client and the court – "a divided loyalty".
3.   The Criminal Procedure Rules ("CPR").
4.   The approach of the court towards solicitors under CPR.

1.   THE SOLICITOR'S DUTY TO THE COURT

Solicitors are officers of the court and have therefore always owed duties to the court. The introduction of the CPR has "effected a sea change in the way in which cases should be conducted"[2] by imposing extra duties and burdens upon the criminal practitioner. The rules define with precision the full extent, not only of the duties already owed to the court by solicitors involved in the preparation and conduct of criminal trials, but also those now imposed by the CPR.

The nature of those obligations was described by the House of Lords in *Arthur J.S. Hall and Co. v Simons* (AP).[3] Lord Hope's comments, whilst specifically referring to advocates, are of wider application:

> "..it is necessary to appreciate the extent of that duty and the extent to which the efficiency of our systems of criminal justice depends on it. The advocate's duty to the court is not just that he must not mislead the court, that he must ensure that the facts are presented fairly and that he must draw the attention of the court to the relevant authorities even if they are against him. *It extends to the whole way in which the client's case is presented, so that time is not wasted and the court is able to focus on the issues as efficiently and economically as possible.*"[4] (emphasis added)

The Solicitors' Code of Conduct

The recently issued Solicitor's Code of Conduct effectively mirrors the earlier professional rules governing the solicitor's duty to the court.[5] Of particular relevance is the following rule:

> **Rule 11 – Litigation and advocacy**
>
> **11.02 Obeying court orders:**
>
> You must comply with any court order requiring you or your firm to take, or refrain from taking, a particular course of action.

The relevant guidance, entitled "Obeying Court Orders 11.02", states:

> 19. You have a responsibility to ensure that you comply with any court order made against you. Similarly, you must advise your clients to comply with court orders made against them. If you are the recipient of a court order which you believe to be defective you must comply with it unless it is revoked by the court. If your client is the recipient of an order you believe to be defective you must discuss with the client the possibility of challenging it and explain to the client the client's obligation to comply if the order is not overturned.

The general guidance to Rule 11 also indicates, in paragraph 5:

> If you are a solicitor you are an officer of the court and you should take all reasonable steps to assist in the smooth running of the court but only insofar as this is consistent with your duties to your client.

2.   THE SOLICITOR, THE CLIENT AND THE COURT: "A DIVIDED LOYALTY"[6]

Dual duties

The role of the solicitor when acting on behalf of a client who is actually or potentially the subject of criminal proceedings can be a complex one. As a lawyer the solicitor owes professional duties to his or her client, as well as – as one of its officers – to the court. On occasions these various duties may conflict with each other.

Whilst the court is entitled to expect the solicitor to act towards it with integrity, neither misleading nor deceiving it, the court should not demand that the solicitor in so acting should breach professional duties owed by the solicitor towards his or her client(s). Indeed, as explained below, the solicitor's proper discharge of the duty to their client should not cause him or her to be accused of being in breach of their duty to the court.[7]

The solicitor's core duties

The core duties of a solicitor set the standards that will meet the needs of both clients and society. In balancing their allegiance to the rule of law and the proper administration of justice on the one hand, and working in partnership with a client on the other, criminal solicitors must have in mind the core duties which are set out in Rule 1 of the Solicitors' Code of Conduct:

Rule 1 – Core duties

1.01 Justice and the rule of law

You must uphold the rule of law and the proper administration of justice.

1.02 Integrity

You must act with integrity.

1.03 Independence

You must not allow your independence to be compromised.

1.04 Best interests of clients

You must act in the best interests of each client.

1.05 Standard of service

You must provide a good standard of service to your clients.

1.06 Public confidence

You must not behave in a way that is likely to diminish the trust the public places in you or the profession.

Two specific professional obligations require comment. They are the duty to maintain client confidentiality, and the need to avoid a conflict of interest between clients.

Confidentiality

A solicitor is under a professional and legal obligation to keep the affairs of clients confidential and to ensure that all members of his or her staff do likewise.[8] This duty of confidence is fundamental to the fiduciary relationship that exists between solicitor and client. It extends to all matters divulged to a solicitor by a client, or on his or her behalf, from whatever source. The provisions for dealing with the protection of clients' confidential information are set out in Rule 4 of the new Solicitor's Code of Conduct.

Confidentiality and legal professional privilege

Certain confidential communications, however, can never be revealed without the consent of the client; they are privileged against disclosure. This protection is called legal professional privilege ("LPP").

What communications are privileged?

Not everything that lawyers have a duty to keep confidential is privileged. Only those confidential communications falling under either of the two heads of privilege – "advice privilege" or "litigation privilege" – are protected by LPP.

Advice privilege

Communications between a lawyer (acting in his or her capacity as a lawyer) and a client are privileged if they are *confidential* and *for the purpose of seeking legal advice from a lawyer or providing legal advice to a client.*

Merely because a client is speaking or writing to his or her solicitor does not make that communication privileged – it is only those communications between the solicitor and the client relating to the matter in which the solicitor has been instructed for the purpose of obtaining legal advice that will be privileged. Such communications do not need to "contain advice on matters of law and construction, provided that they are directly related to the performance by the solicitor of his professional duty as legal adviser of his client."[9]

Litigation privilege

Under this head the following are privileged:

Confidential communications made, *after litigation has started, or is "reasonably in prospect"*, between:

- a lawyer and a client
- a lawyer and an agent (whether or not that agent is a lawyer), or
- a lawyer, or his or her client, and a third party

for the *sole or dominant purpose* of litigation, whether:

- for seeking or giving advice in relation to it, or
- for obtaining evidence to be used in it, or
- for obtaining information leading to obtaining such evidence

The importance of the solicitor's role in the criminal justice system was emphasised by the House of Lords when considering the nature and extent of LPP. In *R v Derby Magistrates' Court ex parte B* Lord Taylor of Gosforth CJ said:

> "The principle which runs through all these ... is that a man must be able to consult his lawyer in confidence, since otherwise he might hold back half the truth. The client must be sure that what he tells his lawyer will never be revealed without his consent. Legal professional privilege is thus much more than an ordinary rule of evidence, limited in its application to the facts of a particular case. It is a fundamental condition on which the administration of justice as a whole rests."[10]

In *R (Morgan Grenfell & Co Ltd) v Special Commissioner of Income Tax* Lord Hoffmann describes LPP as:

> "...a fundamental human right long established in the common law. It is a necessary corollary of the right of any person to obtain skilled advice about the law. Such advice cannot be effectively obtained unless the client is able to put all the facts before the adviser without fear that they may be afterwards disclosed and used to his prejudice."[11]

Conflict of interest

Rule 3 of the new Conduct Rules sets out clearly the provisions for dealing with conflicts of interest. Detailed guidance with specific regard to criminal practitioners is included in the Guidance to Rule 3, which was drafted by the Law Society after close consultation with the Department for Constitutional Affairs and the Legal Services Commission.[12] This guidance recognises the need to balance the solicitor's duty to the proper administration of justice carefully with his or her duty towards the client, and sets out how to avoid conflicts from arising.

How can a solicitor's professional duties to his client conflict with his duty to the court?

A few examples may serve to illustrate the point:

1. If a conflict of interest arises during criminal proceedings between two or more clients represented by the same solicitor, the solicitor must withdraw from one or more clients. This is bound to cause inconvenience to the court and to other parties with consequent financial loss (normally to the legal aid fund).

2. A solicitor may hold factual information (for instance the name and address of a possible witness) which is of crucial importance to a party to the proceedings. When requested, or served with a witness summons, to produce this information the solicitor declines to do so.[13]

3. Professionally proper advice may be given by a solicitor at a police interview which may later be viewed by a court, in changed circumstances, as "unhelpful", "obstructive" or "ill advised".[14]

Whilst, understandably, the court when confronted with one of these problems, may consider itself entitled to an explanation, and frustrated by its absence, in the majority of cases, the court should understand that the solicitor's duty of confidentiality to his or her client absolutely forbids the provision of reasons, because the information sought by the court will be privileged. At most, the solicitor can only inform the court that his or her professional duties prevent their continuing to act and/or providing the information sought. As was recently underlined by Lord Justice Rose in *R v G & B*:

> "We think it right, both in principle and pragmatically, that whether a solicitor or barrister can properly continue to act is a matter for him or her, not the court, although of course the court can properly make observations on the matter. ... Absent exceptional circumstances, such as an obvious attempt by a defendant to abuse the system by repeated applications, we think it is unlikely that, if leading counsel tells a judge that he is embarrassed to continue acting, the judge will not permit a change of representation".[15]

3.   THE CRIMINAL PROCEDURE RULES

In the *Chorley Justices* case Lord Justice Thomas said:

> "In April 2005 the Criminal Procedure Rules came into effect. By 15th April they were in force. They have effected a sea change in the way in which cases should be conducted ... The rules make clear that the overriding objective is that criminal cases be dealt with justly; that includes acquitting the innocent and convicting the guilty, dealing with the prosecution and defence fairly, respecting the interests of witnesses, dealing with the case efficiently and expeditiously, and also, of great importance, dealing with the case in a way that takes into account the gravity of the offence, the complexity of what is in issue, the severity of the consequences to the defendant and others affected and the needs of other cases. Rule 1.2 imposes upon the duty of participants in a criminal case to prepare and conduct the case in accordance with the overriding objective, to comply with the rules and, importantly, to inform the court and all parties of any significant failure, whether or not the participant is responsible for that failure, to take any procedural step required by the rules.

> "Rule 3.2 imposes upon the court a duty to further that overriding objective by actively managing the case."[16]

What do the CPR say?

    1.1   The overriding objective:

        (1)   The overriding objective of this new code is that criminal cases be dealt with justly.

        (2)   Dealing with a criminal case justly includes –

            (a)   acquitting the innocent and convicting the guilty;

(b)   dealing with the prosecution and the defence fairly;

(c)   recognising the rights of a defendant, particularly those under Article 6 of the European Convention on Human Rights;

(d)   respecting the interests of witnesses, victims and jurors and keeping them informed of the progress of the case;

(e)   dealing with the case efficiently and expeditiously;

(f)   ensuring that appropriate information is available to the court when bail and sentence are considered; and

(g)   dealing with the case in ways that take into account –

(i)   the gravity of the offence alleged,

(ii)   the complexity of what is in issue,

(iii) the severity of the consequences for the defendant and others affected, and

(iv)   the needs of other cases.

1.2   The duty of the participants in a criminal case:

(1)   Each participant, in the conduct of each case, must –

(a)   prepare and conduct the case in accordance with the overriding objectives;

(b)   comply with these Rules, practice directions and directions made by the court; and

(c)   at once inform the court and all parties of any significant failure (whether or not that participant is responsible for that failure) to take any procedural step required by these Rules, any practice direction or any direction of the court. A failure is significant if it might hinder the court in furthering the overriding objective.

Keeping the court informed whilst protecting the client's rights

It is essential to appreciate that the purpose of Rule 1.2 (1) (c) is to enable the court to control the preparation process and avoid ineffective and wasted hearings. When something goes wrong because of a failure of a defendant to co-operate with his or her solicitors the court should be aware of this and if the solicitor fails to keep the court informed, he or she risks breaching their duty to the court under the provisions of the Rules.

> "Lawyers conducting litigation owe a divided loyalty. They have a duty to their clients, but they may not win by every means. They also owe a duty to the court and the administration of justice ... Sometimes the performance of these duties to the court may annoy the client."[17]

The concept of the solicitor apparently putting the court's interests above those of the client has caused many solicitors to question where their duty lies. The answer is to be found in Rule 1.1(2)(c) which indicates that one of the requirements of the overriding objective is "to recognise the rights of a defendant, particularly those under Article 6 of the ECHR European Convention on Human Rights".

The relevant rights of a defendant in this context are:

■   the presumption of innocence
■   the right to silence and privilege against self-incrimination
■   the "fundamental human right"[18] to legal professional privilege

This is explicitly explained in the note of the Lord Chief Justice to the Rules where it is stated:

> "The presumption of innocence and a robust adversarial process are essential features of the English legal tradition and of the defendant's right to a fair trial. The overriding

objective acknowledges those rights. It must not be read as detracting from a defendant's right to silence or from the confidentiality properly attaching to what passes between a lawyer and his client."

The last of these rights means that a court cannot ask a solicitor to reveal what a defendant has told him or her if it is privileged, unless the defendant consents. Rather, he or she has a duty to the client not to reveal it.

However solicitors *can* clearly be required by the CPR, or by a direction of the court made under its case management duties arising from the CPR, to provide information that will enable the court process to proceed efficiently and expeditiously, but only if in so doing none of the defendant's rights listed above, is encroached upon.

Informing the client

R v K[19] makes it clear that the CPR impose duties and burdens upon solicitors in a criminal trial and that their preparation for and conduct of criminal trials is dependent upon and subject to the CPR.

It is important that clients should be made aware of these duties and the Law Society would advise solicitors to explain to their clients at the outset, and also in the terms of business/retainer letter, that whilst privileged communications can never be divulged to the court without the client's authority, solicitors are under a duty to provide information to the court which is not privileged and which enables the court to further the overriding objective by actively managing the case.

Informing the court

Therefore, if a solicitor is aware of any significant failure (whether or not the defendant is responsible for that failure) to take any procedural step required by the CPR or any practice direction or any direction of the court, it is neither a breach of the defendant's right to silence, nor legal professional privilege, for the solicitor to reveal that he or she has been unable to comply with the court's order.

It would not involve a breach of legal professional privilege for the court to ask the defendant or his or her lawyer to reveal whether instructions have been given, for the purpose of allowing the court to ensure that the case is ready to proceed.[20] It would be a breach, of course, for the court to ask what has been said between them. Courts should be aware that there are difficulties in asking a solicitor to confirm any more than this, for example, whether or not the solicitor has prepared a proof of evidence.

Particular difficulties will arise if a client changes his or her instructions in circumstances where it is proper for the solicitor to continue acting.[21] If the change in instructions will cause delay, whilst the solicitor must inform the court of the likelihood of delay, privilege will prevent disclosure of the reason for it.[22]

Identifying the issues in a case

Both before the coming into force of the CPR, in *R v Gleeson*[23] and since, in the *Chorley Justices* case,[24] the Court of Appeal and the Divisional Court have emphasised the duty upon practitioners to identify the real issues in a case early. It has been held that to do so does not offend the right of silence nor the privilege against self-incrimination (*Gleeson*); if a defendant refuses to do so, he can derive no advantage from this, nor "attempt an ambush at trial":

> "The duty of the court is to see that justice is done. That does not involve allowing people to escape on technical points or by attempting, as happened here, an ambush. It involves the courts in looking at the real justice of the case and seeing whether the rules have been complied with by 'cards being put on the table' at the outset and the issues being clearly identified."[25]

Defence witnesses

Can a court order the defence solicitor or the defendant to disclose of the identity and other details of non-alibi defence witnesses?

Sections 6C and 11 of the Criminal Procedure and Investigations Act 1996 (as amended by s.35 Criminal Justice Act 2003) which specifically require disclosure by the accused to the court and prosecution of defence witness details, at the risk of adverse comment and inference, have yet to be brought into force.

In *R (on the application of Kelly) v Warley Magistrates Court (the Law Society intervening*[26] Lord Justice Laws stated:

> "… it is clear that litigation privilege attaches to the identity and other details of witnesses intended to be called in adversarial litigation, civil or criminal, whether or not their identity is the fruit of legal advice."[27]

The Court emphasised the need for a litigant to be able protect the confidentiality of the material he or she, or his or her lawyer, prepares for the presentation of a case, and this need for protection is the rationale for advice and litigation privilege.

> "If there were no confidentiality such as both rights protect, and every litigant were liable to disclose the building blocks of his case stage by stage as they were developed, the scope for witnesses being discouraged, false points being taken, and the truth being distorted would surely be very greatly increased."[28]

The Court held the CPR had no authority to allow a court to override LPP unless the main legislation containing the CPR's *vires* conferred such authority expressly or by necessary implication. The relevant provision, s.69 of the Courts Act 2003, contained nothing of the kind and therefore a court had no power to make an order for a defendant to reveal the identity and/or other details of witnesses he or she intends to call.

Sanctions for non-compliance

In reaching its decision in *Kelly*, the Court was influenced by the nature of the original direction for disclosure of defence witness details and the open ended form of the relevant CP Rule. The absence of any sanction for failure to comply with the case management order for disclosure rendered the original order to disclose an *unconditional* order which, as such, infringed LPP.

If the Rules had contained provisions which set conditions upon the right to call live evidence, the privilege attaching to the material would be unaffected. The Court by making such an order would merely be making it a condition of a party's ability to call live evidence at trial, that prior notice of such evidence be provided. It would not mean that the party could be compelled to disclose LPP material – only if he or she wanted to use such material as falls within the order as evidence would the party be required as a precondition to disclose it in advance.

As a consequence of the decision in Kelly, the CPR have been amended.[29] As the Explanatory Note to the new Rule explains:

> "7.3   Part 3 of the Criminal Procedure Rules 2005 sets out the general duties and powers of the court, and the duties of the parties, relevant to the pre-trial preparation of a criminal case; and the rules in that Part set out the specific powers that the court may exercise for that purpose. However, the rules in that Part of the Criminal Procedure Rules 2005 contained no sanctions for a party's failure to comply with a procedure rule or with a case management direction made by the court. The court's powers to make a costs order in consequence of such a failure, to adjourn the case or, in some circumstances, to exclude evidence or to draw adverse inferences from the late introduction of an issue or

evidence, are powers that are conferred by other legislation and under some other procedure rules.

7.4   In the case of *R (Kelly) v Warley Magistrates' Court* [2007] EWHC 1836 (Admin), the Administrative Court considered rules 3.5 and 3.10 of the Criminal Procedure Rules and held that the absence of any appropriate sanction within Part 3 rendered ineffectual the case management direction that was in issue in that case. Having considered that judgment, the Rule Committee has decided to amend rules 3.5 and 3.10, and the note to rule 3.5, to make the court's powers to impose sanctions explicit.... "

The substituted Rule 3.10 provides:

"3.10   In order to manage a trial or (in the Crown Court) an appeal:

(a)   the court must establish, with the active assistance of the parties, what disputed issues they intend to explore; and

(b)   the court may require a party to identify:

(i)   which witnesses that party wants to give oral evidence,

(ii)   the order in which that party wants those witnesses to give their evidence,

(iii)   whether that party requires an order compelling the attendance of a witness,

(iv)   what arrangements are desirable to facilitate the giving of evidence by a witness,

(v)   what arrangements are desirable to facilitate the participation of any other person, including the defendant,

(vi)   what written evidence that party intends to introduce,

(vii)   what other material, if any, that person intends to make available to the court in the presentation of the case,

(viii)   whether that party intends to raise any point of law that could affect the conduct of the trial or appeal, and

(ix)   what timetable that party proposes and expects to follow."

A new case management power has been added as Rule 3.5(6):

"(6)   If a party fails to comply with a rule or a direction, the court may:

(a)   fix, postpone, bring forward, extend, cancel or adjourn a hearing;

(b)   exercise its powers to make a costs order; and

(c)   impose such other sanction as may be appropriate."

The note to the new Rule 3.5 has also been expanded as follows:

"At the end of the note after rule 3.5 (The court's case management powers), insert:

'See also rule 3.10. The court may make a costs order under:

(a)   section 19 of the Prosecution of Offences Act 1985, where the court decides that one party to criminal proceedings has incurred costs as a result of an unnecessary or improper act or omission by, or on behalf of, another party;

(b)   section 19A of that Act, where the court decides that a party has incurred costs as a result of an improper, unreasonable or negligent act or omission on the part of a legal representative;

(c)   section 19B of that Act, where the court decides that there has been serious misconduct by a person who is not a party.

Under some other legislation, including Parts 24, 34 and 35 of these Rules, if a party fails to comply with a rule or a direction then in some circumstances:

(a)   the court may refuse to allow that party to introduce evidence;

(b)   evidence that that party wants to introduce may not be admissible;

(c)   the court may draw adverse inferences from the late introduction of an issue or evidence.

See also:

section 81(1) of the Police and Criminal Evidence Act 1984 and section 20(3) of the Criminal Procedure and Investigations Act 1996 (advance disclosure of expert evidence);

section 11(5) of the Criminal Procedure and Investigations Act 1996 (faults in disclosure by accused); section 132(5) of the Criminal Justice Act 2003 (failure to give notice of hearsay evidence).'."

The new Rules apply in cases in which the defendant is charged on or after 7 April 2008.

What is the effect of the new rules? By virtue of the sanctions now available to it in the new Rule 3.5(6), a court which makes an order for disclosure under the substituted Rule 3.10, does not in so doing infringe LPP. Such an order merely sets conditions on the right to call live evidence.

Practitioners should therefore be aware that if an order has been made for prior disclosure relating to any of the categories set out in Rule 3.10, in the event that they wish to call live evidence, they *must give serious consideration to the consequences of a failure to comply with the order before calling that evidence*. Such failure could result in the court exercising its power to make a costs order,[30] for instance, if an adjournment is necessary for the prosecution to run criminal record checks on the witness. Other sanctions are also available, including the power to draw adverse inferences.

Whilst the court also has the power to exclude evidence, the Administrative Court in Kelly emphasised the need for sanctions to be "proportionate" and "no more than might reasonably be required for the proper working of such a regulation." Mitting J stated "I am inclined to think that the imposition of an effective sanction, such as a prohibition on relying on the evidence of a witness not previously identified, would require primary legislation".[31]

Certificates of Readiness

Certificates of Readiness can and do cause problems. Questions such as "have all necessary steps been taken to have the case ready for trial?", "what remains to be done?", or "is anything preventing the case being ready on time?" may bring to light the fact that the solicitor will not be ready for trial because of the defendant's fault; the fact of this state of unreadiness offends none of the defendant's rights, as set out above. It is suggested that any embarrassment to the solicitor's relationship with the client can be avoided by explicitly explaining to the client the duty of the solicitor to the court in such circumstances. This can be done in the initial terms of business, which should be clearly set out in writing and accepted by the client at the start of the retainer.

However, solicitors must carefully consider questions such as "Is the defendant in contact with his solicitors and confirmed that he will attend his trial?" Whilst the first part of the question is not objectionable, the second part could involve the disclosure of a privileged communication.

Non-attendance at trial

If a client tells the solicitor that he or she is not going to attend the trial, the solicitor is placed in an invidious position as far as the solicitor's duty to the court is concerned, for such information, in all likelihood, will be privileged; in which event the solicitor cannot waive the client's privilege, and nor can the court order him or her to do so.

The general guidance to Rule 11 indicates, in paragraph 5:

If you are a solicitor you are an officer of the court and you should take all reasonable steps to assist in the smooth running of the court but only insofar as this is consistent with your duties to your client. Difficulties are likely to arise, for example, where the defendant client absconds in a criminal case. If the client does fail to attend:

(a)   in relation to your duty of confidentiality you may properly state that you are without instructions, but may not disclose information about the client's whereabouts; and

(b)   in relation to your duty to act in the client's best interests, you may consider it appropriate to withdraw from the hearing where, having regard to the client's best interests, you believe you cannot properly represent the client. There may be cases where you would be able to proceed in the absence of your client, for example, where you may infer that the defendant expects you to continue to represent them or where a legal point can be taken which would defeat the prosecution case.

A solicitor should therefore be careful to ensure that he or she advises the client in writing in the initial terms of business/retainer letter (and repeats such advice should it become apparent that the client is, or may be, contemplating non-attendance) that not only is the client under a legal duty to attend the trial, but in the event that without good reason he or she does not attend:

■   he or she will commit an offence, and
■   can be tried in their absence, and
■   if convicted, the Court of Appeal may be slow to allow an appeal

4.   THE APPROACH OF THE COURT TOWARDS SOLICITORS UNDER THE CPR

In managing the case in accordance with the overriding objective, the court has a duty to deal with the defence *"fairly"*.[32] Fairness in this context is to be viewed by reference to the reasoning of Lord Hobhouse in *Medcalf v Mardell*:

"It is fundamental to a just and fair judicial system that there be available to a litigant (criminal or civil), in substantial cases, competent and independent legal representation. The duty of the advocate is with proper competence to represent his lay client and promote and protect fearlessly and by all proper and lawful means his lay client's best interests. This is a duty which the advocate owes to his client but it is also in the public interest that the duty should be performed. The judicial system exists to administer justice and it is integral to such a system that it provide within a society a means by which rights, obligations and liabilities can be recognised and given effect to in accordance with the law and disputes be justly (and efficiently) resolved. The role of the independent professional advocate is central to achieving this outcome, particularly where the judicial system uses adversarial procedures.

"It follows that the willingness of professional advocates to represent litigants should not be undermined either by creating conflicts of interest or by exposing the advocates to pressures which will tend to deter them from representing certain clients of from doing so effectively. ... Unpopular and seemingly unmeritorious litigants must be capable of being represented without the advocate being penalised or harassed whether by the executive, the judiciary or anyone else. Similarly, situations must be avoided where the advocate's conduct of a case is influenced not by his duty to his client but by concerns about his own self-interest."[33]

Whilst these comments refer specifically to advocates in the criminal process, they were considered to have equal application to the "instructing solicitor" by the Court of Appeal when Lord Hobhouse's reasoning was recently adopted by the Court in relation to solicitors in the context of the court's wasted costs jurisdiction:

> "The role of the independent professional advocate in the administration of justice must be borne in mind and also the need not to undermine it by illegitimate pressures."[34]

Withdrawing from a case

If a solicitor has to withdraw from a case, the court should be cautious in pressing the solicitor to explain the reasons for this, for to give such an explanation would require him or her to disclose privileged communications with their client. In *R v G & B* Lord Justice Rose said:

> "...it is for counsel and solicitors, not the court, to make that decision in the light of all the circumstances known to them, some of which may not, for reasons of legal privilege or otherwise, be known to the court".[35]

Requiring a solicitor to attend court

Similarly the court should be slow to order a solicitor to attend court to answer its questions, particularly if these can be adequately answered by letter. The Law Society is concerned at the practice apparently adopted by some courts which, after notification by a defence solicitor of a failure to take a procedural step required by the CPR, have "ordered" the solicitor or a partner of the firm to attend court in person (expressly unpaid) to explain the reason for the failure. The Law Society considers such an approach to be unfair; not only is it extremely doubtful that the court actually has power to make such an "order", the financial cost of complying for instance, by cancelling other appointments, could far exceed that of a wasted costs order, for which the Court of Appeal has set strict guidelines to ensure fairness to the solicitor.[36] The preferred approach should be for the solicitor to explain to the court in writing, as fully as his or her duty of confidentiality permits, the reason for the failure, and in the event that the court is not satisfied, it should then consider invoking its wasted costs powers.

In *R (on the application of Howe) v South Durham Magistrates' Court*[37] a witness summons was issued against a solicitor with a view to proving through him the identity of a defendant, charged with driving disqualified, for whom he acted, and for whom he had previously acted in the proceedings in which the defendant had been disqualified. Whilst in the specific circumstances the Court indicated that the justices were right to issue the witness summonses, Lord Justice Rose expressed the Court's concern that witness summonses should only be served on solicitors as a "last resort". Having referred to the speech of Lord Taylor of Gosforth in *R v Derby Magistrates' Court ex parte B* (quoted above) on the fundamental importance of legal professional privilege to the administration of justice, Lord Justice Rose stated:

> "More widely, outside the scope of legal professional privilege, *the maintenance of confidence between lawyer and client is of central importance in our administration of justice*. It is therefore important for prosecuting authorities and Justices[38] to note that applications for a summons to serve on a lawyer, with a view to proving the identity of a defendant for whom he or she previously acted, should not become a matter of routine in relation to offences of driving while disqualified, or indeed any other offence.

> On the contrary, such a course should, in my judgment, be the route of last resort to be followed only when no other reasonably practicable means of proving identity exists."[39] (Emphasis added.)

Whilst these comments specifically refer to the service of a witness summons with a view to proving identity, they are, in the view of the Law Society, of wider application; for a solicitor to be served with a witness summons to explain a perceived failure to comply with the CPR is highly likely to strike at the "maintenance of confidence between lawyer and client" which Rose LJ considered to be of such central importance in the administration of justice.

Questioning a solicitor

On the rare occasions that it is considered appropriate for the court to put questions to a solicitor in court, adopting the comments of Lord Justice Rose that the "maintenance of confidence between lawyer and client is of central importance in our administration of justice",
the Law Society would hope that when questioning a solicitor, courts should decide
at an early stage whether a wasted costs order is contemplated. If it is contemplated, then the wasted costs procedures set out below should be adopted from thereon.

In summary:

■   It is ultimately a matter for the solicitor, not the court, to decide whether he or she can properly continue to act.
■   A solicitor cannot be ordered by the court to divulge privileged communications with a client.
■   If the court wishes a solicitor to attend before it in the course of a trial, the issue of a witness summons should be the route of last resort, and only in circumstances in which he or she is required to provide material evidence and the court is of the opinion that he or she will not voluntarily attend as a witness.
■   If the court is considering making criticism of a solicitor, that solicitor should be invited to attend court and the wasted costs procedures adopted.

Wasted Costs Orders (WCO)

When a court is considering making a WCO it should follow the guidance set out in the provisions of the *Practice Direction (Costs: Criminal Proceedings)*.[40] Practitioners should familiarise themselves with these provisions. Of particular importance are the following requirements:

■   The court must formulate carefully and concisely the complaint and grounds upon which a WCO may be sought.
■   The court should allow the solicitor to make representations. The solicitor should formally be told clearly what he or she is said to have done wrong and invited to comment.
■   The solicitor alleged to be at fault should be given sufficient notice of a complaint made against him or her, and given a proper opportunity to respond to it.
■   The court should make full allowance for the possible difficulty caused by client confidentiality/legal professional privilege for a legal representative in answering criticism.
■   Where a legal representative is precluded by legal professional privilege from giving a full answer to any criticism, a court should not make such criticism unless, proceeding with extreme care, it is satisfied that there was nothing that the representative could say, if permitted, to answer the criticism and that it was in all of the circumstances fair to make such criticism.
■   The court must be satisfied that there has been an improper, unreasonable or negligent act or omission *and* that, as a result, costs have been incurred by a party. A mere mistake is not sufficient to justify an order – there must be a more serious error. The primary object is not to punish but to compensate.
■   The principles of the court's WCO jurisdiction (especially in relation to the solicitor's duties when a client fails to attend trial) have recently been reviewed by the Court of Appeal (Criminal Division) in *Re: Mr Harry Boodhoo, Solicitor*,[41] and practitioners are encouraged to read the Court's judgment.

Keeping the Law Society informed

The Law Society is aware of the difficulties that are being faced by practitioners whilst the CPR "bed down". Different practices are apparently being adopted at different courts. If solicitors encounter problems they are encouraged to bring these to the attention of the Law Society (phone 0207 242 1222) in the hope that a consistent approach can be achieved for all those on whom the burdens and duties imposed by the CPR fall.

NOTES

1 [2006] EWCA Crim 724 at paragraph 6, [2006] 2 All ER (Note) 552
2 Per Thomas LJ in *R (on the application of the DPP) v Chorley Justices & Anor* [2006] EWHC 1795 at paragraph 24
3 [2000] UKHL 38, [2002] 1 AC 615
4 Per Lord Hope at page 715
5 The new Solicitor's Code of Conduct entered force on 1 July 2007.
6 See Lord Hoffmann in *Arthur J.S. Hall and Co. v Simons* (AP) [2000] UKHL 38, [2002] 1 AC 615 at page 686
7 See *Medcalf v Mardell* [2002] UKHL 27 and [2003] 1 AC 120 per Lord Hobhouse at paragraph 55.
8 At the time of writing, Practice Rule 16E of the Solicitors' Practice (Confidentiality and Disclosure) Amendment Rule 2004, in effect since April 2006, applies. From 1 July 2007, when the new Solicitors' Code of Conduct comes into effect, this will become Rule 4.01.
9 Per Lord Carswell in *Three Rivers District Council v Governor of the Bank of England (No 6)* [2004] UKHL 48, at paragraph 111, and [2005] 1AC 610 at page 680.
10 [1996] AC 487 at page 507
11 [2002] UKHL 21 at paragraph 7, and [2003] 1 AC 563 at page 606
12 See Guidance to Rule 3 – Conflict, Co-defendants, paragraph 24 – 36. This was also published by the Law Society in the Criminal Practitioners' Newsletter, no 61, July 2005.
13 In *R v Derby Magistrates' ex parte B* (1996) AC 487 Lord Nicholls of Birkenhead said, at page 510, "subject to recognised exceptions, communications seeking professional legal advice, whether or not in connection with pending court proceedings, are absolutely and permanently privileged from disclosure even though, in consequence, the communications will not be available in court proceedings in which they might be important evidence".
14 See PACE Code C paragraph 6D.
15 [2004] EWCA Crim 1368, and [2004] 2 Cr App R 37
16 *R (on the application of the DPP) v Chorley Justices & Anor* [2006] EWHC 1795 at paragraph 24
17 *Arthur J S Hall & Co. v Simons* [2000] UKHL 38, and [2002] 1 AC 615 per Lord Hoffmann at page 686
18 As per Lord Hoffmann in *Morgan Grenfell*, above
19 [2006] EWCA Crim 724 at paragraph 6, [2006] 2 All ER (Note) 552
20 See *R v Cowan* [1996] 1 Cr App R 1 at page 9. The Court of Appeal ruled that for counsel to be asked by the trial judge (in accordance with paragraph 3 of the *Practice Direction (Crown Court: Defendant's Evidence)* [1995] 2 Cr App R 192) if he had advised the defendant concerning adverse inferences in the event of him not giving evidence, did not breach privilege as it did not concern anything confidential.
21 Of course if the change of instructions is such that the solicitor has to withdraw, privilege will prevent him or her disclosing the reasons.
22 If the change of instructions identifies fresh issues in the case, then of course the solicitor has an obligation under the CPR to identify *these* to the court – see below.
23 [2003] EWCA Crim 3357 at paragraph 36, (2004) Cr App R 29
24 *R (on the application of the DPP) v Chorley Justices & Anor* [2006] EWHC 1795. See also *Malcolm v DPP* [2007] EWHC 363 (Admin)
25 Per Thomas LJ in *Chorley Justices* at paragraph 27
26 [2007] EWHC 1836
27 paragraph 20
28 paragraph 22
29 The Criminal Procedure (Amendment No 3) Rules 2007, SI 2007/3662
30 See part 4 of this Practice Note for the principles to be applied
31 paragraph 37
32 See CPR 1.1(2)(b)
33 [2002] UKHL 27 paragraphs 51 and 52, [2003] 1 AC 120 at page 141
34 Per Pill LJ in *Re: Mr Harry Boodhoo, Solicitor* [2007] EWCA Crim 14 at paragraph 49
35 see paragraph 19 of *R v G & B* [2004] 2 Cr App R 37, [2004] EWCA Crim 1368
36 See below

37 [2004] EWHC 362 (Admin), [2005] RTR 4
38 The Law Society is aware of no reason why this should not also apply to judges in the Crown Court.
39 at paragraphs 41 and 42
40 [2004] 2 All ER 1070, Part VIII.1: Costs against Legal Representatives
41 41 [2007] EWCA Crim 14